Nessus Network Auditing, Second Edition

Russ Rogers Technical Editor

Mark Carey
Paul Criscuolo
Mike Petruzzi

KEY	SERIAL NUMBER
001	HJIRTCV764
002	PO9873D5FG
003	829KM8NJH2
004	BAL923457U
005	CVPLQ6WQ23
006	VBP965T5T5
007	HJJJ863WD3E
008	2987GVTWMK
009	629MP5SDJT
010	IMWQ295T6T

PUBLISHED BY
Syngress Publishing, Inc.
Elsevier, Inc.
30 Corporate Drive
Burlington, MA 01803

Nessus Network Auditing, Second Edition

Printed and bound in the United Kingdom

Transferred to Digital Print 2011

ISBN 13: 978-1-59749-208-9

Publisher: Andrew Williams
Technical Editor: Russ Rogers
Page Layout and Art: SPi Publishing Services

For information on rights, translations, and bulk sales, contact Matt Pedersen, Commercial Sales Director and Rights, at Syngress Publishing; email m.pedersen@elsevier.com.

Technical Editor

Russ Rogers (CISSP, CISM, IAM, IEM, HonScD), author of the popular *Hacking a Terror Network* (Syngress Publishing, ISBN 1-928994-98-9), co-author on multiple other books including the best selling *Stealing the Network: How to Own a Continent* (Syngress, ISBN 1-931836-05-1), *Network Security Evaluation Using the NSA IEM* (Syngress, 1-597490-35-0) and Editor in Chief of *The Security Journal*; is currently a penetration tester for a Federal agency and formerly the Co-Founder and Chief Executive Officer of Security Horizon; a veteran-owned small business based in Colorado Springs, CO. Russ has been involved in information technology since 1980 and has spent the last 18 years working professionally as both an IT and INFOSEC consultant. Russ has worked with the United States Air Force (USAF), National Security Agency (NSA), and the Defense Information Systems Agency (DISA). He is a globally renowned security expert, speaker, and author who has presented at conferences around the world including Amsterdam, Tokyo, Singapore, Sao Paulo, and cities all over the United States.

Russ has an Honorary Doctorate of Science in Information Technology from the University of Advancing Technology, a Masters Degree in Computer Systems Management from the University of Maryland, a Bachelor of Science in Computer Information Systems from the University of Maryland, and an Associate Degree in Applied Communications Technology from the Community College of the Air Force. Russ is currently pursuing a Bachelor of Science in Electrical Engineering from the University of Colorado at Colorado Springs. He is a member of ISSA and ISC2 (CISSP) and co-founded the Security Tribe (securitytribe.com). He also teaches at and fills the role of Professor of Network Security for the University of Advancing Technology (uat.edu).

Russ would like to thank his kids and father for being so supportive over all these years. Thanks and shout outs go out to Chris Hurley, Jeff Thomas, Brian Baker, Mark Carey, Mike Petruzzi, Paul Criscuolo, Dan Connelly, Ping Look, Greg Miles, Johnny Long, Joe Grand, Ryan Clarke, Luke McOmie, and Eddie Mize.

Contributing Authors

Mark Carey (CISSP, IAM) has been involved with the Computer Security Industry for over twenty years. He has pioneered techniques and written a number of exploits. Mark has presented on Information Security topics for The United States Army, The United States Air Force, NASA, and several Corporations in the United States and UK. He has worked for several major Midwestern banks, insurance companies, and credit unions, as well as a brief engagement writing video games. He is currently employed as a technology and technique developer and penetration tester for a Federal agency, and as a freelance consultant upon occasion.

Mark was educated at Ohio Northern and The Ohio State University, and has a CISSP and IAM certification.

Mark would like to thank: my beloved wife Karen and daughter Katie, for being wonderful and tolerant of my (over)-working habits and generally wonderful, my sister, Robin (and all my nieces and nephews), the team: Chris Hurley, Jeff Thomas, Brian Baker, Mike Petruzzi, Paul Criscuolo, Dan Connelly, Kevin Kerr, and George Armstrong, all my friends (you know who you are), my fans, and everyone who believed in me and made me who I am. A special thank you to Charles Smith (Spike) for all the help in learning to write, right. A special tip of the hat to Andy Riffle, Mike Cappelli, William Knowles, just for being great friends.

Paul Criscuolo (CISSP) has been involved in the Computer Security Industry for over 15 years, with the rare distinction of having export experience in both the defensive and offensive aspects of INFOSEC. For the last 4 years, Paul has worked as a penetration tester for a Federal agency. He was involved with the Computer Incident Advisory Capability (CIAC) working incidents for the Department of Energy (DOE). Paul was the Incident Response and Intrusion Detection Team lead at Los Alamos National Laboratory, writing a number of intrusion detection tools that have resulted in technologies licenses from the DOE, and created technology startups with those licenses. He has also consulted with Fortune 500 companies, assisting in incident response and recovery. Paul has presented at a number of conferences, written papers, and instructed training seminars about network security and incident response.

Paul would like to thank: my wife Pamela and kids, Sarah and Nicholas, for being at my side every step of the way and putting up with my crazy hours over the years. Everything I do is for you guys. My parents, A.L. and Celia, for putting up with my "wasted potential" and rebel attitude all those years and yet still believing in me and molding me to the man I am today. To my brother and sister for all the love and scripts over the years … keep them both coming. Special thanks go to the team: George Armstrong, Brian Baker, Mark Carey, Dan Connelly, Chris Hurley, Mike Petruzzi, Russ Rogers, and Jeff Thomas for their patience and teaching continue to improve my skills every day. And to the group in LA: Mike Fisk, Chris Kemper, Alex Kent, Ben Uphoff, Ron Wilkins, and Phil Wood for the sharing of ideas, humor, and tough times in the trenches.

Mike Petruzzi is a senior penetration tester in the Washington, D.C. area. Mike has performed a variety of tasks and assumed multiple responsibilities in the information systems arena. He has been responsible for performing the role of Program Manager and InfoSec Engineer, System Administrator and Help Desk Technician and Technical Lead for companies such as IKON and SAIC. Mike also has extensive experience performing risk assessments, vulnerability assessments and certification and accreditation. Mike's background includes positions as a brewery representative, liquor salesman, and cook at a greasy spoon diner.

I would like to thank my Dad and brothers for their constant inspiration and support. I would also like to thank Chris Hurley, Dan Connelly and Brian Baker for making me look forward to going to work each day (It's still a dream job!). I'd like to thank Mark Wolfgang, Jeff Thomas, Paul Criscuolo and Mark Carey and everyone else I work with (too many to list) for making the trips more fun. I would like to thank HighWiz and Stitch for giving me endless grief for just about everything (No, I will not play for your team). Finally, I would like to thank everyone that I have worked with in the past for making me work harder everyday.

Contents

## Chapter 1

Vulnerability Assessment

Solutions in this chapter:

- **What Is a Vulnerability Assessment?**
- **Automated Assessments**
- **Two Approaches**
- **Realistic Expectations**

☑ **Summary**

☑ **Solutions Fast Track**

☑ **Frequently Asked Questions**

Introduction

In the war zone that is the modern Internet, manually reviewing each networked system for security flaws is no longer feasible. Operating systems, applications, and network protocols have grown so complex over the last decade that it takes a dedicated security administrator to keep even a relatively small network shielded from attack.

Each technical advance brings new security holes. A new protocol might result in dozens of actual implementations, each of which could contain exploitable programming errors. Logic errors, vendor-installed backdoors, and default configurations plague everything from modern operating systems to the simplest print server. Yesterday's viruses seem positively tame compared to the highly optimized Internet worms that continuously assault every system attached to the global Internet.

To combat these attacks, a network administrator needs the appropriate tools and knowledge to identify vulnerable systems and resolve their security problems before they can be exploited. One of the most powerful tools available today is the vulnerability assessment, and this chapter describes what it is, what it can provide you, and why you should be performing them as often as possible. Following this is an analysis of the different types of solutions available, the advantages of each, and the actual steps used by most tools during the assessment process. The next section describes two distinct approaches used by the current set of assessment tools and how choosing the right tool can make a significant impact on the security of your network. Finally, the chapter closes with the issues and limitations that you can expect when using any of the available assessment tools.

What Is a Vulnerability Assessment?

To explain vulnerability assessments, we first need to define a vulnerability. For the purposes of this book, a *vulnerability* refers to any programming error or misconfiguration that could allow an intruder to gain unauthorized access. This includes anything from a weak password on a router to an unpatched programming flaw in an exposed network service. Vulnerabilities are no longer the realm of just system crackers and security consultants; they have become the enabling factor behind most network worms, spyware applications, and e-mail viruses.

Spammers are increasingly relying on software vulnerabilities to hide their tracks; the open mail relays of the 1990s have been replaced by compromised "zombie" proxies of today, called botnets, created through the mass exploitation of common vulnerabilities. A question often asked is, "Why would someone target my system?" The answer is that most exploited systems were not targeted; they were simply one more address in a network range being scanned by an attacker. Spammers do not care whether a system belongs to an international bank or your grandmother Edna; as long as they can install their relay software, it makes no difference to them.

Vulnerability assessments are simply the process of locating and reporting vulnerabilities. They provide you with a way to detect and resolve security problems before someone or something can exploit them. One of the most common uses for vulnerability assessments is their capability to validate security measures. If you recently installed a new firewall or intrusion detection system (IDS), a vulnerability assessment allows you to determine how well that solution works. If your assessment completes and the IDS didn't fire off a single alert, it might be time to have a chat with the vendor.

The actual process for vulnerability identification varies widely between solutions; however, they all focus on a single output—the report. This report provides a snapshot of all the identified vulnerabilities on the network at a given time. Components of this report usually include a list of each identified vulnerability, where it was found, what the potential risk is, and how it can be resolved. Figure 1.1 shows a sample Nessus Security Scanner report for a large network with multiple vulnerabilites on multiple hosts.

Figure 1.1 Sample Nessus Report, Nessus Client

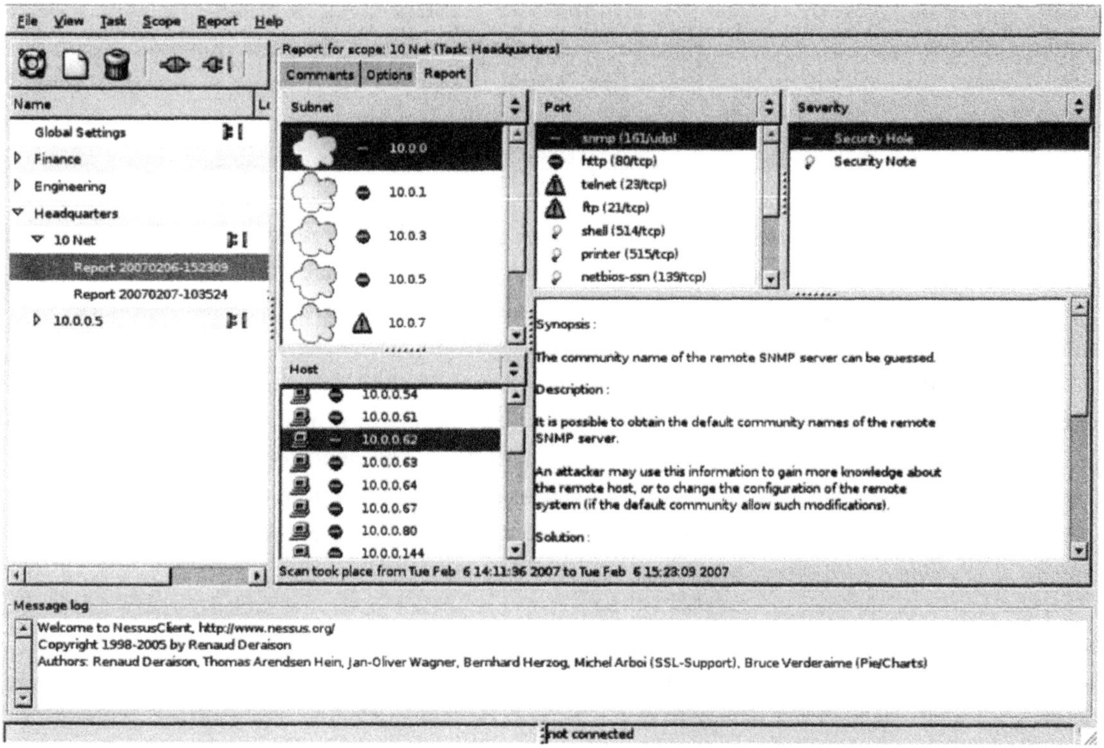

Why a Vulnerability Assessment?

Vulnerability assessments have become a critical component of many organizations' security infrastructures; the ability to perform a networkwide security snapshot supports a number of security and administrative processes. When a new vulnerability is discovered, the network administrator can perform an assessment, discover which systems are vulnerable, and start the patch installation process. After the fixes are in place, another assessment can be run to verify that the vulnerabilities were actually resolved.

This cycle of assess, patch, and verify has become the standard method for many organizations to manage their security issues. In fact, many are required, by an outside oversight group, to perform regular assessments of the network. Organizations must be able to show that the ongoing requirements of information security are being addressed in a timely manner. An organization can perform vulnerability assessments at regular intervals and have trend reports showing that exposed services are continually being addressed via patches until the vulnerability is no longer a threat.

Quite a few organizations have integrated vulnerability assessments into their system rollout process. Before a new server is installed, it first must go through a vulnerability assessment and pass with flying colors. This process is especially important for organizations that use a standard build image for each system; all too often, a new server can be imaged, configured, and installed without the administrator remembering to install the latest system patches. Additionally, many vulnerabilities can only be resolved through manual configuration changes; even an automated patch installation might not be enough to secure a newly imaged system.

Unlike many other security solutions, vulnerability assessments can actually assist with day-to-day system administration tasks. Although the primary purpose of an assessment is to detect vulnerabilities, the assessment report can also be used as an inventory of the systems on the network and the services they expose. Assessment reports are often used to generate task lists for the system administration staff, allowing them to prevent a worm outbreak before it reaches critical mass.

Asset classification is one of the most common non-security uses for vulnerability assessment tools. Knowing how many and what types of printers are in use will help resource planning. Determining how many Windows 2000 systems still need to be patched can be as easy as looking at your latest report. The ability to quickly glance at a document and determine what network resources might be overtaxed and those that are not being used efficiently can be invaluable to topology planning.

Assessment tools are also capable of detecting corporate policy violations; many tools will report peer-to-peer services, shared directories of copyright protected materials, and unauthorized remote access tools. If a long-time system administrator leaves the company, an assessment tool can be used to verify that a backdoor was not left in the firewall. If bandwidth use suddenly spikes, a vulnerability assessment can be used to locate workstations that have installed file-sharing software.

One of the most important uses for vulnerability assessment data is event correlation; if an intrusion does occur, a recent assessment report allows the security administrator to determine how it occurred and what other assets might have been compromised. If the intruder gained access to a network consisting of unpatched Web servers, it is safe to assume that he gained access to those systems as well.

Notes from the Underground...

Intrusion Detection Systems

One of the most common questions asked by people first learning about vulnerability assessments is how they differ from an IDS. To understand the differences between these complimentary security systems, you will also need to understand how an IDS works. When people speak of IDSs, they are often referring to what is more specifically known as a network intrusion detection system (NIDS). A NIDS' role is to monitor all network traffic, pick out malicious attacks from the normal data, and send out alerts when an attack is detected. This type of defense is known as a *reactive security measure*; it can only provide you with information after an attack has occurred. In contrast, a vulnerability assessment provides you with the data you need before the attack happens, allowing you to fix the problem and prevent the intrusion. For this reason, vulnerability assessments are considered a proactive security measure.

Assessment Types

The term *vulnerability assessment* is used to refer to many different types and levels of service. A host assessment normally refers to a security analysis against a single system, from that system, often using specialized tools and an administrative user account. In contrast, a network assessment is used to test an entire network of systems at once. Network assessments are by far the most common and the most complex.

Host Assessments

Host assessment tools were one of the first proactive security measures available to system administrators and are still in use today. These tools require that the assessment software be installed on each system you want to assess. This software either can run stand-alone or be linked to a central system on the network. A host assessment looks for system-level vulnerabilities such as insecure file permissions, missing software patches, noncompliant security policies, and outright backdoors and Trojan horse installations.

The depth of the testing performed by host assessment tools makes it the preferred method of monitoring the security of critical systems. The downside of host assessments is that they require a set of specialized tools for the operating system and software packages being used, in addition to administrative access to each system that should be tested. Combined with the substantial time investment required to perform the testing and the limited scalability, host assessments are often reserved for a few critical systems.

The number of available and up-to-date host assessment solutions has been decreasing over the last few years. The tools that were used religiously by system administrators just a few years ago have now fallen so far behind as to be nearly useless. Many of the stand-alone tools have been replaced by agent-based systems that use a centralized reporting and management system. This transition has been fueled by a demand for scalable systems that can be deployed across larger server farms with a minimum of administrative effort. The only stand-alone host assessment tools used with any frequency are those targeting nontechnical home users and part-time administrators for small business systems.

Although stand-alone tools have started to decline, the number of "enterprise security management" systems that include a host assessment component is still increasing dramatically. The dual requirements of scalability and ease of deployment have resulted in host assessments becoming a component of larger management systems. A number of established software companies offer commercial products in this space, including, but not limited to, Internet Security System's System Scanner, Computer Associates eTrust Access Control product line, and BindView's bvControl software.

Network Assessments

Network assessments have been around almost as long as host assessments, starting with the Security Administrator Tool for Analyzing Networks (SATAN), released by Dan Farmer and Wietse Venema in 1995. SATAN provided a new perspective to administrators who were used to host assessment and hardening tools; instead of analyzing the local system for problems, it allowed you to look for common problems on any system connected to the network. This opened the gates for a still-expanding market of both open-source and commercial network-based assessment systems.

A network vulnerability assessment involves locating all live systems on a network, determining what network services are in use, and then analyzing those services for potential vulnerabilities. Unlike the host assessment solutions, this process does not require any configuration changes on the systems being assessed. Network assessments can be both scalable and efficient in terms of administrative requirements and are the only feasible method of gauging the security of large, complex networks of heterogeneous systems.

Although network assessments are very effective for identifying vulnerabilities, they do suffer from some severe limitations, including not being able to detect certain types of backdoors, complications with firewalls, and the inability to test for certain vulnerabilities due to the testing process itself being dangerous. Network assessments can disrupt normal operations, interfere with many devices (especially printers), use large amounts of bandwidth, and create large amounts of log files on the systems being assessed. Additionally, many vulnerabilities are exploitable by an authorized but unprivileged user account and cannot be identified through a network assessment.

Automated Assessments

The first experience that many people have with vulnerability assessments is using a security consulting firm to provide a network audit. This type of audit is normally comprised of both manual and automated components; the auditors will use automated tools for much of the initial legwork and follow it up with manual system inspection. While this process can provide thorough results, it is often much more expensive than simply using an automated assessment tool to perform the process in-house.

The need for automated assessment tools has resulted in a number of advanced solutions being developed. These solutions range from simple graphical user interface (GUI) software products to stand-alone appliances that are capable of being linked into massive distributed assessment architectures. Due to the overwhelming number of vulnerability tests needed to build even a simple tool, the commercial market is easily divided between a few well-funded independent products and literally hundreds of solutions built on the once open-source Nessus Security Scanner, by Tenable Network Security. These automated assessment tools can be further broken into two types of products: those that are actually obtained, through either purchase or download, and those that are provided through a subscription service.

Stand-Alone vs. Subscription

The first category of products includes most open-source projects and about half of the serious commercial contenders. Some examples include the Nessus Security Scanner, IBM Internet Security Systems' Internet Scanner Software, and SAINT Corporation's Network Vulnerability Scanner. These products are either provided as a software package that is installed on a workstation, or a hardware appliance that you simply plug in and access over the network.

The subscription service solutions take a slightly different approach; instead of requiring the user to perform the actual installation and deployment, the vendor handles the basic configuration and simply provides a Web interface to the client. This is primarily used to offer assessments for Internet-facing assets (external assessments), but can also be combined with an appliance to provide assessments for an organization's internal network. Examples of products that are provided as a subscription service include Qualys' QualysGuard, Beyond Security's Automated Scan, Foundstone's Foundscan, and Digital Defense's Frontline product.

The advantages of using a stand-alone product are obvious: all of your data stays in-house, and you decide exactly when, where, and how the product is used. One disadvantage, however, is that these products require the user to perform an update before every use; otherwise, the vulnerability checks might be outdated and missing recent vulnerabilities. The advantages of a subscription service model are twofold: the updates are handled for you, and since the external assessment originates from the vendor's network, you are provided with a real-world view of how your network looks from the Internet.

The disadvantages to a subscription solution are the lack of control you have over the configuration of the device and the potential storage of vulnerability data on the vendor's systems. Some hybrid subscription service solutions have emerged that resolve both of these issues through leased appliances in conjunction with user-provided storage media for the assessment data. One product implementing this approach is nCircles' IP360 system, which uses multiple dedicated appliances that store all sensitive data on a removable flash storage device.

The Assessment Process

Regardless of what automated assessment solution is used, it will more than likely follow the same general process. Each assessment begins with the user specifying what address, or address ranges, should be tested. This is often implemented as either a drop-down list of predefined ranges or a simple text widget where the network address and mask can be entered. Once the addresses are specified, the interface will often present the user with a set of configuration options for the assessment; this could include the port ranges to scan, the bandwidth settings to use, or any product-specific features. Most importantly, a list of available checks needs to be selected to ensure that a thorough test is made of the targets. After all of this information is entered, the actual assessment phase can begin. Figure 1.2 shows the assessment configuration screen for the Nessus Security Scanner.

Figure 1.2 Nessus Plugin Selection

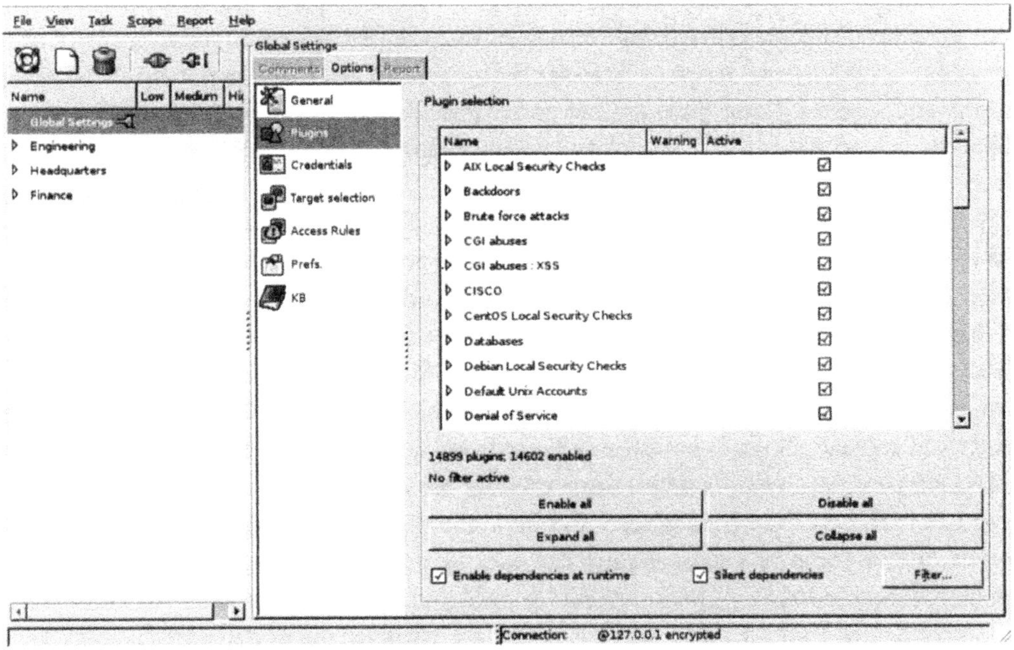

Detecting Live Systems

The first stage of a network vulnerability assessment is to determine which Internet Protocol (IP) addresses specified in the target range actually map to online systems. For each address specified by the user, one or more probes are sent to elicit a response. If a response is received, the system will place that address in a list of valid hosts. In the case of heavily firewalled networks, most products have an option to force scan all addresses, regardless of whether a response is received during this stage.

The types of probes sent during this stage differ wildly between assessment tools; although almost all of them use Internet Control Message Protocol (ICMP) "ping" requests, the techniques beyond this are rarely similar between two products. The Nessus Security Scanner has the capability to use a series of TCP connection requests to a set of common ports to identify systems that might be blocking ICMP messages, which allows the scanner to identify systems behind firewalls or those specifically configured to ignore ICMP traffic. After a connection request is sent, any response received from that system will cause it to be added to the list of tested hosts. Many commercial tools include the capability to probe specific User Datagram Protocol (UDP) services in addition to the standard ICMP and TCP tests. This technique is useful for detecting systems that only allow specific UDP application requests through, as is commonly the case with external DNS and RADIUS servers.

Identifying Live Systems

After the initial host detection phase is complete, many products will use a variety of fingerprinting techniques to determine what type of system was found at each address in the live system list. These fingerprinting techniques range from Simple Network Management Protocol (SNMP) queries to complex TCP/IP stack-based operating system identification.

This stage can be crucial in preventing the assessment from interfering with the normal operation of the network; quite a few print servers, older UNIX systems, and network-enabled applications will crash when a vulnerability assessment is performed on them. Indeed, the biggest problem that most administrators encounter with automated assessment tools is that they can disrupt network operations. Often, the administrator will have to spend time rebooting devices, retrieving garbage printouts from network-attached print servers, and debugging user problems with network applications. This identification stage can often be used to detect and avoid problematic systems before the following stages cause problems.

Enumerating Services

Once the host detection and identification steps are complete, the next stage is normally a port scan. A port scan is the process of determining what TCP and UDP services are open on a given system. TCP port scans are conducted by sending connection requests to a configured list of port numbers on each system. If the system responds with a message indicating that the port is open, the port number is logged and stored for later use. UDP port scanning can often provide inconsistent results, since the nature of the protocol makes obtaining consistent results difficult on most networks.

There are 65,536 available TCP ports; however, most assessment tools will only perform a port scan against a limited set of these. Limiting the scan to a subset of the available ports reduces the amount of time it takes to perform the assessment and substantially decreases the bandwidth required by the assessment (in terms of packets per second, not the total number of bytes). The downside of not scanning all available ports is that services that are bound to nonstandard, high port numbers are often completely ignored by the assessment. The Nessus Security Scanner provides an option that allows the user to define how these ports are treated. The default is to consider all nonscanned TCP ports as open, which can take quite a bit of time during the assessment, especially in cases where heavy packet filters or firewalls are in place. Figure 1.3 shows the Nessus Security Scanner options for performing the service enumeration phase of the assessment.

Figure 1.3 Nessus Enumerating Services, open source client

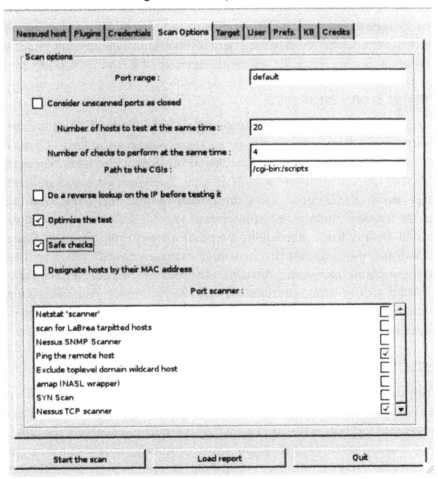

Identifying Services

After the port scan phase, many assessment tools will try to perform service identification on each open port. This process starts with sending some common application requests and analyzing the responses against a set of signatures. When a signature matches a known application, this information is stored for the later use and the next service is tested. Although not all assessment tools use this stage, the ones that do can provide much more accurate results, simply by knowing which vulnerabilities to check for on what ports.

The Nessus Security Scanner includes a robust service identification engine, capable of detecting more than 90 different application protocols. This engine uses a set of application probes to elicit responses from each service. After each probe is sent, the result is matched against a list of known application signatures. When a matching signature is found, the port number and protocol are stored for future use and the engine continues with the next service. If the Secure Sockets Layer (SSL) transport protocol is detected, the engine will automatically negotiate SSL on the service before sending the application probes. This combination of transport-level and service-level identification allows the system to accurately detect vulnerabilities, even when the affected service is on a nonstandard port.

The HyperText Transfer Protocol (HTTP) is a great example of a service that is often found on a port other than the default. Although almost all standard Web servers will use TCP port 80, literally thousands of applications install an HTTP service on a port other than 80. Web configuration interfaces for many Web application servers, hardware devices, and security tools will use nonstandard ports. E-mail protocols such as Simple Mail Transfer Protocol (SMTP), Post Office Protocol 3 (POP3), and Internet Message Access Protocol (IMAP) are often configured with the SSL transport protocol and installed on nonstandard ports as well. A common misconfiguration is to block SPAM relaying on the primary SMTP service, but trust all messages accepted through the SSL-wrapped SMTP service on a different port. Additionally, this phase prevents an application running on a port normally reserved for another protocol from either being ignored completely by the scan, or resulting in numerous false positives.

Identifying Applications

Once the service detection phase is complete, the next step is to determine the actual application in use for each detected service. The goal of this stage is to identify the vendor, type, and version of every service detected in the previous stage. This information is critical for quite a few reasons, the least of which being that the vulnerability tests for one application can actually cause another application to crash. An example of this is if a Web server is vulnerable to a long pathname overflow; if any other vulnerability test sends a request longer than what is expected by this system, the application will crash. To accurately detect this vulnerability on this Web server without crashing it, the system needs to first identify that specific application and then prevent any of the problematic vulnerability tests from running against it.

One of the biggest problems with most assessment tools is *false positives*, or simply reporting vulnerabilities that do not actually exist on the tested systems. The most common cause for false positives is either missing or incomplete application identification before a vulnerability test is run. When the developers of these assessment tools are writing the vulnerability tests, they often assume that the system they are interacting with is always going to be the product in which the vulnerability was discovered. Different applications that offer the same service will often respond to a probe in such a way that it convinces the vulnerability test that a flaw was found. For this reason, application identification has become one of the most critical components of modern assessment tools.

Identifying Vulnerabilities

After every online host has been identified, each open port has been mapped to a known service, and the known services have been mapped to specific applications, the system is finally ready to begin testing for vulnerabilities. This process often starts with basic information-gathering techniques, followed by active configuration probes, and finally a set of custom attacks that can identify whether a given vulnerability exists on a given system.

The vulnerability identification process can vary from simple banner matching and version tests, to complete exploitation of the tested flaw. When version detection and banner matching are used to identify a vulnerability, false positives often result due to application vendors providing updated software that still displays the banner of the vulnerable version. For this reason, version numbers are often consulted only when there is no other way to safely verify whether the vulnerability exists.

The only way to identify a large percentage of common vulnerabilities is to try to exploit the flaw. This often means using the vulnerability to execute a command, display a system file, or otherwise verify that the system is indeed vulnerable to an attack by a remote intruder. Many buffer overflow and input manipulation vulnerabilities can be detected by triggering just enough of the flaw to indicate that the system has not been patched, but not enough to actually take down the service. The assessment tool has to walk a fine line between reliable vulnerability identification and destructive side effects.

Vulnerability tests that use banner checks will encounter problems when the tested service has been patched, either by the vendor or system administrator, but the version number displayed to the network has been updated. This is a relatively common practice with open-source UNIX-based platforms and certain Linux distributions.

Reporting Vulnerabilities

After the analysis is finished, the final stage of the assessment process is reporting. Each product has a unique perspective on how reports should be generated, what they should include, and in what formats to provide them. Regardless of the product, the assessment report will list the systems discovered during the assessment and any vulnerabilities that were identified on them. Many products offer different levels of reporting depending on the audience; it is useful to provide a high-level summary to management while at the same time being able to give a system administrator a report that tells him or her what systems need to be fixed and how to do so. One of the popular features in many assessment tools is the capability to show trend reports of how a given network fared over time. Figure 1.4 shows the Nessus Security Scanner's HTML graph report summary section with the most vulnerable services on the network.

Figure 1.4 Nessus Report Summary, HTML Graph Format

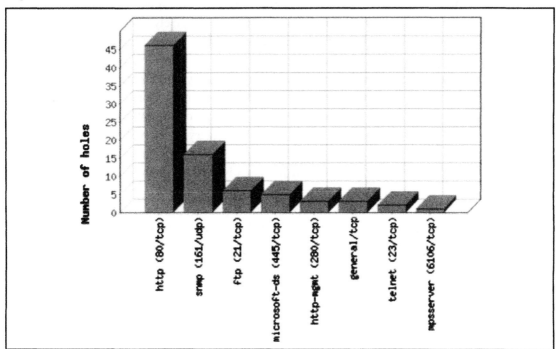

Two Approaches

When performing an automated vulnerability assessment, the actual perspective of the test can have a huge impact on the depth and quality of the results. Essentially, there are two different approaches to vulnerability testing: administrative and outsider. Each has distinct advantages and disadvantages, and many of the better assessment tools have migrated to a hybrid model that combines the best features of both approaches. Understanding these different approaches can provide insight into why two different assessment tools can provide such completely different results when used to test the same network.

Administrative Approach

The administrative approach performs the assessment from the perspective of a normal, authenticated system administrator. The assessment tool might require that it be launched by an authenticated administrative user or provided with a user account and password. These credentials can be used to detect missing patches, insecure configuration settings, and potentially vulnerable client-side software (such as e-mail clients and Web browsers).

This is a powerful approach for networks that consist of mostly Windows-based systems that all authenticate against the same domain. It combines the deep analysis of a host assessment with the network assessment's scalability advantages. Since almost all of the vulnerability tests are performed using either remote Registry or remote file system access, there is little chance that an assessment tool using this method can adversely affect the tested systems. This allows assessments to be conducted during the day, while the systems are actively being used, without fear of disrupting a business activity.

The administrative approach is especially useful when trying to detect and resolve client-side vulnerabilities on a network of workstations. Many worms, Trojans, and viruses propagate by exploiting vulnerabilities in e-mail clients and Web browser software. An assessment tool using this approach can access the Registry of each system and determine whether the latest patches have been installed, whether the proper security settings have been applied, and often whether the system has already been successfully attacked. Client-side security is one of the most overlooked entry points on most corporate networks; there have been numerous cases of a network with a well-secured perimeter being overtaken by a network simply because a user visited the wrong Web site with an outdated Web browser.

Unfortunately, these products often have some severe limitations as well. Since the testing process uses the standard Windows administrative channels—namely, the NetBIOS services and an administrative user account—anything preventing this channel from being accessed will result in inaccurate scan results. Any system on the network that is configured with a different authentication source (running in stand-alone mode, on a different domain, or authenticating to a Novell server) will not be correctly assessed. Network and host-based firewalls can also interfere with the assessment.

This interference is a common occurrence when performing assessments against a system hosted on a different network segment, such as a demilitarized zone (DMZ) or external segment behind a dedicated firewall. Additionally, network devices, UNIX-based servers, and IP-enabled phone systems might also be either completely missed or have only minimal results returned. Additionally, since these products often only check for the existence of a patch, they will often report vulnerabilities in services that are not enabled. An example of this is a certain Windows-based commercial assessment tool that will report missing Internet Information Server (IIS) patches even when the Web server has not been enabled or configured.

This type of testing shines when used to verify a networkwide patch deployment, but should not be relied upon as the only method of security testing. Microsoft's Security Baseline Scanner is the best example of an assessment tool that uses this approach alone. Many of the commercial assessment tool offerings were originally based on this approach and have only recently started to integrate different techniques into their vulnerability tests. The differences between administrative and hybrid solutions is discussed at length in the section *The Hybrid Approach*.

The Outsider Approach

The outsider approach takes the perspective of the unauthenticated malicious intruder who is trying to break into the network. The assessment process is able to make decisions about the security of a system only through a combination of application fingerprinting, version identification, and actual exploitation attempts. Assessment tools built on this approach are often capable of detecting vulnerabilities across a much wider range of operating systems and devices than their administrative approach counterparts can.

When conducting a large-scale assessment against a network consisting of many different operating systems and network devices, the outsider approach is the only technique that has a chance of returning accurate, consistent results about each discovered system. If a system is behind a firewall, only the exposed services will be tested, providing you with the same information that an intruder would see in a real-life attack. The reports provided by tools using this approach are geared to prevent common attacks; this is in contrast to those tools using the administrative approach that often focus on missing patches and insecure configuration settings. In essence, the outsider approach presents a much more targeted list of problems for remediation, allowing the administrator to focus on the issues that would be the first choices for a potential intruder.

Although this approach is the only plausible method of conducting a vulnerability assessment on a homogeneous network, it also suffers from a significant set of drawbacks. Many vulnerabilities simply can not be tested without crashing the application, device, or operating system. The result is that any assessment tools that test for these types of vulnerabilities either provide an option for "intrusive" testing, or always trigger a warning when a potentially vulnerable service is discovered. Since the outsider approach can only detect what is visible from the point in the network where the assessment was launched, it might not report a vulnerable service bound to a different interface on the same system. This is an issue with reporting more than anything else, as someone reviewing the assessment report might not consider the network perspective when creating a list of remediation tasks for that system.

The Hybrid Approach

Over the last few years, more and more tools have switched to a hybrid approach for network assessments. They use administrative credentials when possible, but fall back to remote fingerprinting techniques if an account is either not available or not accepted on the tested system. The quality of these hybrid solutions varies greatly; the products that started with the administrative approach have a difficult time when administrative credentials are not available, whereas the products based on the outsider approach often contain glitches when using an administrative account for tests. Overall, though, these products provide results that are often superior to those using a single approach. The Nessus Security Scanner and eEye's Retina product are examples of tools that use this approach.

One of the greatest advantages of tools using the outsider approach is that they are often able to determine whether a given vulnerability exists, regardless of whether a patch was applied. As many Windows network administrators know, installing an operating system patch does not actually guarantee that the vulnerability has been closed. A recent vulnerability in the Microsoft Windows Network Messenger service allowed a remote attacker to execute arbitrary code on a vulnerable system. Public exploits for the vulnerability started circulating, and companies were frantically trying to install the patch on all their internal workstations. Something that was overlooked was that for the patch to take, the system had to be rebooted after it was applied. Many sites used automated patch installation tools to update all their vulnerable systems, but completely forgot about the reboot requirement.

The result was that when an assessment was run using a tool that took the administrative approach, it reported the systems as patched. However, when an assessment was run using the Nessus Security Scanner, it reported these systems as vulnerable. The tool using the administrative approach simply checked the Registry of each system to determine whether the patch had been applied, whereas the Nessus scan actually probed the vulnerability to determine if it was still vulnerable. Without this second assessment, the organization would have left hundreds of workstations exposed, even though the patches had been applied. The Registry analysis used by many tools that take the administrative approach can miss vulnerabilities for a number of other reasons as well. The most common occurrence is when a hotfix has been applied to resolve a vulnerability, and then an older service pack is reapplied over the entire system. The changes installed by the hotfix were overwritten, but the Registry entry stating that the patch was applied still exists. This problem primarily affects Windows operating systems; however, a number of commercial UNIX vendors have had similar issues with tracking installed patches and determining which ones still need to be applied.

Recently, many of the administrative and hybrid tools have developed new techniques for verifying that an installed patch actually exists. Shavlik Technology's HFNetChk Pro will actually check the last reboot time and compare it to the hotfix install date. The Nessus Security Scanner actually accesses the affected executables across the network and verifies the embedded version numbers.

The drawbacks to the hybrid approach are normally not apparent until the results of a few large scans are observed; because the administrative approach is used opportunistically, vulnerabilities that are reported on a system that accepts the provided user account might not be reported on a similar system that uses a different authentication realm. If the administrator does not realize that the other system might be vulnerable as well, it could lead to a false sense of security. These missed vulnerabilities can be difficult to track down and often fall under the radar of administrative tasks. Because there is a higher chance of these systems not being patched, the hybrid approach can actually result in more damage during an intrusion or worm outbreak simply because it might not be apparent that they were not patched. Although the administrative approach suffers from the same issue, tools using the administrative approach take it for granted that systems outside of the authentication realm will not be tested.

Realistic Expectations

When the first commercial vulnerability assessment tools started becoming popular, they were advertised as being able to magically identify every security hole on your network. A few years ago, this might have held true, simply because tracking vulnerability information was considered an obscure hobby at best and the number of publicly documented vulnerabilities was still relatively small. These days, the scenario is much different, where there were a few hundred well-documented vulnerabilities before, there are literally thousands of them now, and they don't even begin to scratch the surface when it comes to the number of flaws that can be used to penetrate a corporate network. Figure 1.5 show the increase in reported vulnerabilities by year.

Figure 1.5 Reported Vulnerabilities

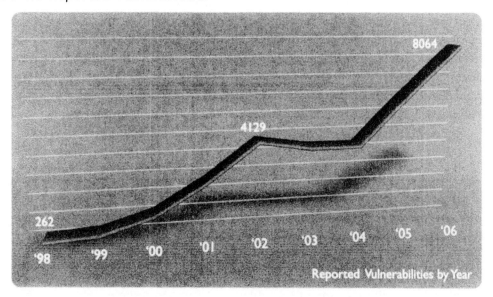

In addition to the avalanche of vulnerabilities, the number and type of devices found on your average corporate network has exploded. Some of these devices will crash, misbehave, or slow to crawl during a network vulnerability assessment. A vulnerability test designed for one system might cause another application or device to stop functioning altogether, annoying the users of those systems and potentially interrupting the work flow. Assessment tools have a tough job; they have to identify as many vulnerabilities as possible on systems that must be analyzed and categorized on the fly, without reporting false positives, and at the same time avoid crashing devices and applications that simply weren't designed with security in mind. Some tools fare better than others; however, all current assessment tools exhibit this problem in one form or another.

When someone first starts to use a vulnerability assessment system, he or she often notices that the results between subsequent scans can differ significantly. This issue is encountered more frequently on larger networks that are connected through slower links. There are quite a few different reasons for this, but the core issue is that unlike most software processes, remote vulnerability testing is more of an art form than a science. Many assessment tools define a hard timeout for establishing connections to a service or receiving the result of a query; if an extra second or two of latency occurs on the network, the test could miss a valid response. These types of timing issues are common among assessment tools; however, many other factors can play into the consistency of scan results.

Many network devices provide a Telnet console that allows an administrator to reconfigure the system remotely. These devices will often set a hard limit on the number of concurrent network connections allowed to this service. When a vulnerability assessment is launched, it might perform multiple tests on a given port at the same time; this can cause one check to receive a valid response, while another gets an error message indicating that all available connections are being used. If that second check was responsible for testing for a default password on this particular device, it might completely miss the vulnerability. If the same scan was run later, but the default password test ran before one of the others, it would accurately detect the vulnerability at the expense of the other tests. This type of timing problem is much more common on network devices and older UNIX systems than on most modern workstations and servers, but can ultimately lead to inconsistent assessment results.

Tools & Traps...

Assessing Print Servers

Almost all vulnerability assessment tools have one thing in common; they are capable of eating a print server alive. The problem stems from the fact that many print servers offer a variety of network services that can be used to spool documents directly to the attached printer. The most common issue is that a print server supports the Direct Print

Protocol, essentially a TCP service that accepts connections and prints out any data it receives. This can cause problems with automated assessment tools, as the service identification phase can often cause reams of paper to printed out, covered in what appears to be garbage.

Issues related to the custom FTP service that many print servers run. This server will allow authentications using any username and password combination and simply prints out any files that are uploaded. If the assessment tool is looking for insecure FTP configurations, it might end up printing out a test file when running against a print server. To compound matters, quite a few print servers have such shoddy TCP/IP implementations that a simple port scan can take them offline, and a full power cycle is required to return them to service.

Embedded operating systems are another major issue today in tracking false positives. All-in-One copy machines, manufactured by Canon or Xerox for example, are becoming more common place in corporate networks. They allow for increased productivity by networking this new type of system, allowing for all employees to print, copy, and staple all from their office. These new systems appear to be a standard computer from the assessment tools perspective because they often are equipped with a version of the Windows operating system, a TCP/IP stack, and shared hard drives. Over time, they will start to show more vulnerabilities because updating the embedded OS requires a service call from the manufacturer or is simply impossible, increasing the number of false positives in the report.

Dynamic systems are the bane of the vulnerability assessment tools. If an assessment is in full swing and a user decides to reboot his workstation for one reason or another, the assessment tool will start receiving connection timeouts for the vulnerability tests. Once the system comes back online, any subsequent tests will run normally; however, all tests launched during the period of downtime will result in missing vulnerability results for that system. This type of problem is incredibly difficult to detect when wading through a massive assessment report, and at this time only a handful of commercial systems offer the capability to detect and rescan systems that restart during the assessment process.

Although most assessment tools have undergone an extraordinary amount of refinement and testing, false positives continue to be the main source of annoyance for network administrators and security consultants alike. A false positive is simply a vulnerability that is reported, but does not actually exist on the tested system. Nonstandard Web servers, backported software packages, and permissive match strings inside vulnerability test scripts are the top causes for false positives.

The Web server software that provides a configuration console for many network devices is notorious for causing false positives; instead of returning a standard "404" error response for nonexistent files, these systems will often return a success message for any file that is requested from the system. In response, almost all of the popular assessment tools have developed some form of Web server fingerprinting that allows their system to work around these strange Web servers. These solutions range from incredibly robust, such as the one found in the recent versions of the Nessus Security Scanner, to almost not worth the bother, like certain commercial products.

Vulnerability assessment tools are still no replacement for a manual security audit by a team of trained security experts. Although many assessment tools will do their best to find common vulnerabilities in all exposed services, relatively simple vulnerabilities are often missed. Custom Web applications are by far the most common example of this; often, they were written under a tight deadline and for a very small user base, resulting in code that might not perform adequate security checks on all input. Although the chances of an auto-mated assessment tool being able to find a vulnerability in this software are slim, a security analyst, experienced with Web application testing, could easily pinpoint a number of security issues in a short period of time. Just because an automated assessment does not find any vulnerabilities does not mean that none exists.

Summary

As the number of discovered vulnerabilities increases every day, networks are becoming increasingly difficult to keep secure. Vulnerability assessments have become the preferred method of managing security flaws for many organizations. The ability to quickly identify misconfigured and unpatched systems, combined with the ease of use and accuracy of many assessment tools, has changed the way many administrators manage their systems. Network vulnerability assessments provide the wide view of security weaknesses on a given network, supplemented by host assessment solutions that provide granular hardening steps for critical systems.

The traditional process of system hardening and patch application has been left in the dust; the sheer quantity of vulnerabilities is more than any administrator can keep track of, especially for diverse networks. Automated assessment solutions have come to the rescue, with both stand-alone and subscription-based options. The average administrator no longer needs to become a security savant simply to keep his or her systems secure. The same repeatable process allows administrators to track, resolve, and verify vulnerabilities.

Although almost all assessment tools advertise their capability to detect and report all critical vulnerabilities, the way these systems are designed and the techniques they use for vulnerability tests vary widely. Not all assessment solutions are created equally; tools using the administrative approach are almost useful when it comes to identifying vulnerabilities in network devices and across large networks. At the same time, tools using the outsider approach are restricted by the technical limitations of the vulnerabilities themselves, often ignoring vulnerabilities that they simply are unable to test. Fortunately, many of the more popular solutions have solidified around a hybrid approach for vulnerability testing, allowing for unprecedented levels of accuracy and depth.

Vulnerability assessments are not a security panacea; although they excel at detecting vulnerabilities in widely deployed products, even relatively simply flaws can be missed. The current market of assessment tools can often cause problems with network devices, slow internetwork links, and custom applications. No matter what tool you use, false positives will always be a significant problem; although many solutions have made huge steps in reducing these, backported patches and vague version identifiers will guarantee that these never entirely disappear. The depth and flexibility of a manual vulnerability assessment will always be better than any automated solution; there is no replacement for a skilled analyst manually reviewing your systems, network architecture, and in-house applications.

Solutions Fast Track

What Is a Vulnerability Assessment?

- ☑ A vulnerability is any flaw that an attacker can use to gain access to a system or network.

- ☑ Vulnerability assessments provide a snapshot of the security posture of your network.

- ☑ Host assessments provide detailed information about the weaknesses on a system.

- ☑ Network assessments pinpoint flaws that a remote attacker can use to gain access.

Automated Assessments

- ☑ Manual assessments are no longer feasible due to the sheer number of vulnerabilities that exist.

- ☑ Stand–alone and subscription assessment models each have distinct advantages.

- ☑ Automated assessments tend to follow the same process regardless of the tool.

- ☑ The assessment process is essentially staged information gathering.

Two Approaches

- ☑ Two assessment tools can provide very different results depending on the approach.

- ☑ The administrative approach is often safest, but might not be reliable.

- ☑ The outsider approach provides the same information an attacker would have.

- ☑ Robust assessment tools use a hybrid approach for maximum vulnerability coverage.

Realistic Expectations

- ☑ Assessments can cause a myriad of side effects on your average corporate network.

- ☑ Consistency between assessments is often less than ideal.

- ☑ False positives will always be an issue, but recent tools are making progress.

- ☑ Manual security audits still provide better results than any assessment tool can.

Frequently Asked Questions

Q: I am planning to use a vulnerability assessment tool at my organization. Is there any reason to assess the internal networks as well as the external?

A: While systems exposed to the Internet should always be incorporated into a vulnerability assessment plan, internal assessments can actually reduce the risk to the organization even more. When a new worm appears that exploits one or more known vulnerabilities, the first step an organization should take is to secure all external and internal systems. An internal assessment can be used to verify that internal assets are not at risk to an automated attack. Internal networks are vulnerable to infection through users who are compromised through their e-mail clients and Web browsers; a worm infection on an internal network segment can result in the inability for the business to function. Additionally, unethical consultants, disgruntled employees, and visitors using the network can leverage insecure systems to gain access to sensitive information.

Q: What is the difference between a vulnerability assessment and a penetration test?

A: One of the biggest problems with the security industry is consistent naming of services. A strong contributing fact is that many security firms are selling "penetration tests" that are nothing more than a vulnerability assessment using automated tools. A vulnerability assessment is the process of identifying vulnerabilities on a network, whereas a penetration test is focused on actually gaining unauthorized access to the tested systems. A penetration test is a great way to determine how well your security measures respond to a real-life attack, but might not result in a detailed analysis of every system on your network.

Q: Can a vulnerability assessment find users with weak passwords?

A: Although manual vulnerability assessments can include password auditing, automated vulnerability assessment tools are rarely able to detect common or weak passwords. The reason behind this is not that the tool is not technically able to perform the check, but that the process of testing each user could result in an account lockout. This is primarily the case with Windows domains; however, it can also apply to many commercial UNIX systems. While some automated assessment tools will test for accounts with a default or blank password, they would still not be able to detect an account with a simple one-character password.

Q: My organization uses an intrusion prevention system (IPS). What complications will this cause with a vulnerability assessment?

A: The goal of an IPS is to block hostile traffic before it reaches a potentially vulnerable system. Many automated assessment solutions depend on being able to send a specially crafted attack probe and to determine whether the system is vulnerable by analyzing the response. If the IPS blocks the initial probe, the vulnerability assessment will not be able to accurately detect that vulnerability. The solution to this is either to configure the IPS to specifically ignore traffic originating from the vulnerability assessment tool, or only run the tool from the protected side of the IPS. Most assessment tools are not designed to bypass these systems; however, an advanced intruder could easily detect the IPS and find a way to exploit a vulnerability while avoiding the IPS's block. Evading IDSs could easily be a book of its own; however, suffice it to say that what the IPS is looking for might not be what the intruder sends, yet might still be able to successfully exploit the vulnerability.

## Chapter 2

Introducing Nessus

Solutions in this chapter:

- **What Is It?**
- **The *De Facto* Standard**
- **History**
- **Basic Components**

☑ **Summary**

☑ **Solutions Fast Track**

☑ **Frequently Asked Questions**

Introduction

"At first, hapless one, he prayed with serene soul, rejoicing in his comely garb. But when the blood-fed flame began to blaze from the holy offerings and from the resinous pine, a sweat broke forth upon his flesh, and the tunic clung to his sides, at every joint, close-glued, as if by a craftsman's hand; there came a biting pain that racked his bones; and then the venom, as of some deadly, cruel viper, began to devour him."

—Sophocles (440-430 BCE)

Nessus was a centaur in Sophocles' ancient manuscript, "The Death of Heracles." This beastly creature dupes the wife of Heracles into giving her husband a garment that has been poisoned, thus bringing an end to the mighty Heracles. One could speculate for quite a while on how this ancient and mythological tale might have inspired the name of the most widespread open-source vulnerability scanner in use today. However, speculation is all that it would be, as according to Renaud Deraison, he has "no special reason" for dubbing his project Nessus.

Renaud does, however, have a special reason to be proud. The Nessus Vulnerability Scanner has been one of the many successful security-centric open-source projects. It found its place as a tool of the unfunded security researcher, and of the highly funded security consultant. It also has the distinction of being one of a handful of tools to successfully migrate from an open source project to a commercially available software package. Nessus enjoys accolades from many years of competitive product reviews and was recently picked as one WindowsSecurity.com's "best products of 2007." Nessus' best accolade comes from a security survey released every three years from SecTools.org. This survey allows the security professionals to list their favorite tools, both commercial and open source. In the 3 years the survey was released, 2000, 2003, and 2006, Nessus has taken first place. These surveys bring in huge amounts of participation from experts in the security arena and Nessus is consistently best of class.

In this chapter, we explore the myriad reasons why so many people use Nessus. We discuss the history of the Nessus project and detail its basic components. We also spend some time looking at the effect it has had on the best practices of today.

What Is It?

Nessus was not the world's first free open-source vulnerability scanner. However, it is the most ubiquitous open source scanner ever developed The Nessus Vulnerability Scanner was conceived early in 1998. At the time, open-source vulnerability scanners had fallen behind the well-funded commercial products of the same ilk. It was then that Renaud Deraison decided to start a project that would become known as Nessus.

Nessus is a robust vulnerability scanner that is well suited for large enterprise networks. The fact that it remains free makes it well suited for the security budget, too. Its extensibility allows its users to leverage their own expertise in developing vulnerability checks. This same feature allows for quick updates of current vulnerabilities from the large community of users who keep the vulnerability checks one of the most comprehensive and up to date.

Renaud co-founded Tenable Network Security in 2002 and started providing paid support for the Nessus Vulnerability Scanner. This answered the only criticism against using an open source product. Organizations could now pay for reliable assistance or a fully supported appliance to operate their Nessus scanner. Starting with version 3 of scanning engine, Nessus was no long offered under the General Public License (GPL). It has remained free however on every platform. The ability to create plugins remains under the new scanning engine and, that is where the real power of the scanner comes from; its community of users contributing plugins. In addition, the knowledge base built into each plugin continues to make Nessus one of the most valued tools to secure networks.

The *De Facto* Standard

The fact that Nessus now finds itself as a high-ranking contender in traditional product testing is a testament to its rapid adoption and continued use, as well as its ability to compete with the best the commercial world has to offer. In 2001, Greg Shipley performed a product review of vulnerability scanners for *Network Computing Magazine*. Although this review discovered that at the time, no scanner detected all of the 17 vulnerabilities tested, it did show Nessus as the leader, detecting 15 of the 17 vulnerabilities in the review.

A couple of years later, in 2003, *Information Security Magazine* of TechTarget performed a review of the top-five vulnerability scanners. In their review, they tested for 10 known vulnerabilities. Of the products tested, Nessus came in second place, detecting 6 of the 10, with the first-place winner detecting 9.

What do these reviews tell us about Nessus? There is more data here than meets the eye. First, the very placement of a completely open-source product in reviews with the industry leaders of commercial vulnerability scanners tells us that Nessus is a contender in this realm. Next, the fact that Nessus came in first place in the first review explains one reason why so many security service providers use Nessus. A free product that outperforms commercial products in competitive reviews is always a good thing to have. Combined with in-house code improvements or signature checks often added by service providers, Nessus often becomes an amazingly strong tool.

The second-place showing in the second review could have been caused by many factors typically solved by the advocacy of the product's company during the review process. It is common for reviewers to have product representatives assist them during initial configuration of the software being reviewed. Nessus, however, relies on the user base to be the advocates, and thus does not share the same product review advantages that commercial scanners do.

Nessus is a must-have in the security consultant's cadre of tools. The fact that it is free (and we really can't stress this enough) is cause enough to use it. However, its flexible architecture provides yet another reason. The client/server architecture of Nessus makes scans more scaleable, manageable, and even more precise. Many users set up a nessusd server, which performs scans at the request of a client running on another machine. Employing this configuration provides the consultant many ways to build a business model around Nessus, as we'll explore throughout the book.

Many commercial providers of security services use Nessus, and a few of them provide periodic internal scans on a subscription basis by taking advantage of the Nessus client/ server architecture. Quite often, they will ship a Nessus appliance, loaded with the current Nessus plugins as well as their very own custom checks, to a client site where it performs the scanning. This allows the service provider to scan from any point within the client's network without sending consultants on-site. Some businesses even go so far as to write all of the plugins they use from scratch, using none of the Nessus community's checks. Regardless of how commercial security providers apply Nessus to their business model, the vast majority of security services firms use Nessus to some extent.

The security consultant for hire is not the only beneficiary of the free and flexible nature of Nessus. In-house security teams throughout the IT industry employ Nessus internally. They use the client/server model to a different end, however. The in-house security team will often deploy nessusd servers throughout their network, allowing the remote execution of timely scans without the bandwidth spikes caused by using a traditional scanner to scan the entire network from a single point. This also allows the practitioner to scan each machine from an optimal point, so that internal firewalling rules don't interfere with the test. Additionally, this added ability to write custom plugins for Nessus allows the in-house security engineer to mold Nessus to the unique environmental factors of her enterprise network, from custom or otherwise rare third-party applications to particular filtering mechanisms in place.

The commercial software product space is also leveraging Nessus. Many software suites available today that focus on general security workflow and management, such as the Security Information Management (SIM) space, provide tight "low-level" integration to Nessus. Sometimes, these products will simply consume the XML output of a Nessus scan; other times, they might scan a host whenever a specific network event occurs. Whether used alone or in conjunction with other software, due to its free, flexible, and extensible foundations, Nessus remains the *de facto* standard for many different security experts with many different security needs.

Notes from the Underground...

The Dark Side of Security Consultants

The myriad reasons that make Nessus such a great tool for security consultants also enable a dark phenomenon in the world of network security. All too often, consulting firms claim to have expertise in network security yet add minimal value to the output of their tools. For example, "Alice" performs vulnerability assessments for her firm, Yet Another Security Group (YASG). Her routine for performing vulnerability assessments begins by executing a free Nessus scan, and exporting the resultant report to the portable document format (PDF). Alice then prints out the report and places it in a $5.00 binder with her company logo on it. Alice finishes the process by delivering her report to the customer and referring them to the Nessus reference links for any further assistance they might need with remediation. She then receives her check for $20,000 as her customer reluctantly hands over the payment.

The issue here is not that Alice has used Nessus; in fact, this same issue haunts customers of consulting groups who use commercial scanners. Nay, the dark side of Alice's process lies in the fact that Alice provided zero value-add to what the customer could have easily done for free. Alice should have used Nessus as a starting point, and further examined each of the vulnerable hosts, not only to verify the vulnerability detections to be true, but to determine what level of risk these vulnerabilities posed for the customer. Is that CHARGEN-ECHO denial-of-service (DoS) vulnerability on the printer, or is it on the "old-but-still-in-use" VMS financials system? Is there a matching vulnerable host that can complete the requisite pair for the attack? What's the risk of such an attack occurring, and what effect could it have on the organization? This level of contextualization and vulnerability prioritization is not just a "nice-to-have" differentiator of an assessment; it should be a requirement for any customer who falls under regulatory compliance.

Further more, Alice should have been using other tools as well, both commercial and open source. If you are responsible for in-house security and decide to have a third party provide a different perspective of your network security posture, request a sample report as part of the proposal process. In the case that they have no sanitized reports to provide, ask them to describe their method. If they won't provide either, find another security firm to provide the assessment.

History

It was 1998, and the network security industry was just getting into full swing as it rode on the tails of the dot-com era. Bugtraq, a mailing list that tracks security flaws, had yet to evolve into a full database and was a strictly underground effort run on a shoestring budget. Vulnerability scanners were being sold commercially for large sums of money to corporate IT departments with the cost rising in direct proportion to the number of devices being examined. The last remaining open-source scanner, the Security Administrator Tool for Analyzing Networks (SATAN), had been surpassed by commercial scanners, which proved to be more comprehensive. Network security was quickly rising in cost as the Internet moved out of the hands of the National Science Foundation and into the hands of private industry. Soon, the growth of the Internet skyrocketed as dot-com financial trends brought increasingly more "eyeballs" to the Internet, leading to a subsequent increase in cyber interlopers testing the limits of this growing frontier.

It was in this environment that Renaud Deraison created the project known as Nessus. It was an answer to the ever-increasing prices of commercial vulnerability scanners, and the relative stagnation of the SATAN project. Nessus was a framework, but it would require a community of knowledgeable security researchers working for free to bring Nessus up to the level of a full-fledged product.

Ever since Nessus first came on the scene in 1998, the community has grown by leaps and bounds. At the time of this book's first publication, the general Nessus mailing list had over 1357 participants with around 50 active posters. The Nessus Development mailing list consisted of 149 participants with approximately 15 active posters, and the Plugins Writers mailing list had 114 active users with 15 active posters.

On October 5, 2005, Tenable Network Security announced that the next version of Nessus, version 3, would no longer be open-source and become a proprietary license. The Nessus 3 engine is still free and allows for the community to release plugin updates, but charges for support and the latest vulnerability audits, including PCI, SCADA, and OS specific configurations. The Nessus 2 engine and a minority of the plugins are still GPL. Some developers have forked independent open source projects based on Nessus as a consequence. Examples are OpenVAS and Porz-Wahn. Tenable Network Security has still maintained the Nessus 2 engine and has updated it several times since the release of Nessus 3.

The activity on the two main Nessus mailing lists speaks volumes about the past and the future of Nessus. Each month, more people are introduced to Nessus, and each month the community grows even stronger. Security researchers learn of the existence, popularity, and strength of Nessus in many ways. Some of them stumble across it after using their favorite search engine to find "Free Security Scanner." Others find out by word of mouth. Still others learn about Nessus in security training such as that found at the Sysadmin, Audit, Network, Security Institute (SANS Institute). SANS offers a weeklong class detailing the tools of the security trade, and spends a good deal of time introducing students to Nessus and conducting a workshop on its installation and use.

Regardless of how people become aware of Nessus, the obvious trend is that the community surrounding the Nessus Project will continue to grow and continue to support the tradition of a free, up-to-date, vulnerability scanner.

Basic Components

What makes Nessus such a wonderful tool is the unique architecture on which it is built. The flexibility and resourcefulness of the Nessus architecture has taken every element of the security lifecycle into consideration. From the large-scale batch execution of vulnerability scans that capture the data, to the graphical and hyperlinked reports that represent the data, to the fix descriptions that are invaluable in patch remediation, all of these aspects create the foundation of a healthy security posture. We will touch on several of the components of this architecture, including:

- The Nessus Client and Server
- The Nessus Plugins
- The Nessus Knowledge Base

Client and Server

Originally, vulnerability scanners were all client based. A consultant would bring his or her laptop into a customer's site and plug in at the best possible location in the network to execute a scan. A scan on any network address space would take anywhere from an entire afternoon to a few days, depending on the breadth of the network and the depth of the scan parameters. This would render the laptop unusable for the amount of time the scan required.

The Nessus Project took this aspect of vulnerability assessments into strong consideration from its inception. To conquer this problem and many others, the Nessus Project adopted a client/server model for its foundation. This allows the security analyst to "detach" from the vulnerability scan and use his resources for other items while Nessus continues to do what it does best. This is just one benefit of leveraging the client/server model of Nessus. There are, in fact, many innovative ways to build a business model around this architecture, or to streamline the in-house vulnerability assessment process.

For example, let's say a security-consulting firm receives a contract to perform an on-site vulnerability assessment. Once the consultant arrives and obtains access to the customer network, he can fire up his Nessus client and securely connect to his firm's nessusd server. Once our sharp consultant initiates the external assessment, he can then detach his client from the server, knowing that the data will be ready for him later. Meanwhile, he can then begin his scan of the internal network using whatever equipment he brought along for the engagement.

Another more obvious benefit of this architecture is scalability. A machine with more memory and processing power can run more tests at once, decreasing the scanning time. This results in a scan that finishes more quickly and leaves the consultant's laptop free, allowing him to interact with the network, providing context for findings. He'll take this opportunity to identify the roles of machines found during the scan, interviewing the organization's personnel as necessary. He can also perform manual verification of any findings, which is critically important to a high-quality vulnerability assessment. Every vulnerability scanner generates "false positives," or inaccurate statements of vulnerability. It's the engineer's job to confirm each vulnerability manually, so the on-site staff isn't left with both inaccurate vulnerability reporting and increased risk of ulcer.

From the perspective of in-house security teams, this architecture can be leveraged in a much different way. One of the problems that plague the in-house vulnerability assessment team is the internal firewall. Internal firewalls often have address translation tables, and the rapid-fire connections caused by vulnerability scanners quickly fill these tables, causing some firewalls to drop older connections. This adverse phenomenon affects both the users of the network and the assessment team's own scan. This effect, underscored by the overall bandwidth use of network scanners in general, can cause enough impact on the network to discourage frequent vulnerability scans altogether. By distributing nessusd servers throughout the enterprise network, the in-house security assessment team can bypass the traditional network issues caused by vulnerability scanners and easily automate frequent and periodic scans, ensuring a stronger overall security posture (see Figure 2.1).

Figure 2.1 In-House Network with Nessus Servers

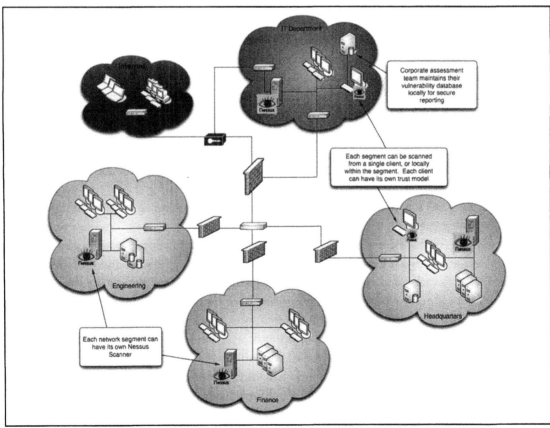

The Nessus client can connect to the nessusd server in many ways that employ both encryption and authentication. Which way would suit your network interests best? The first thing to consider is whether the nessusd server is located on the local loopback. If the nesssud server you want to connect to is in fact listening only on 127.0.0.1, then using the unencrypted scheme will be sufficient. This is the only case where you should ever use the "unencrypted" option. While there might be safe configurations where you can rely on unencrypted traffic with a certain amount of confidence, the only fully safe configuration is where no unencrypted traffic touches the physical network. This warning against unencrypted traffic, of course, becomes even more critical when the Nessus server is authenticating to various hosts or network components—the client must pass the relevant passwords to the server across its control connection. Use the encryption—it's much better than being embarrassed by your network administrator or an attacker on your network, each of whom can redirect and sniff traffic.

When using encryption, you can choose from Transmission Layer Security (TLS) or one of three versions of Secure Sockets Layer (SSL). SSL was created by Netscape as they created their first commercial browser, while TLS is an IETF standard based on SSL. These levels of encryption can be enforced by the nessusd server based on your encryption policy.

The next item you will want to consider when deciding which method of connection bests suits your network is related to the authentication scheme. At the time of this writing, Nessus supports both password-based and certificate-based authentication. This allows the security team to integrate Nessus with its current public key infrastructure (PKI) if desired. It also adds an additional layer of security in the defense of a set of data that could potentially allow any unauthorized viewer administrative control over network resources. This follows from the security principle of "Defense in Depth," the idea that multiple layers of defenses allow the defense to stand when an attacker is able to compromise one or more layers. Which authentication scheme and encryption method should you choose? This question should involve at least one meeting of the in-house security team before it is answered.

Damage & Defense...

Nessus and MySQL

The flexible Nessus architecture also has a feature that allows logging of the vulnerabilities found to a MySQL database. This database can be located on the same system as nessusd, or it can be located remotely in a much more centralized and protected

Continued

location within the security infrastructure. One post to the Nessus list in early 2001 from the creator of the MySQL addition for Nessus pointed out that this data could be used for cross-correlation with alerts from intrusion detection systems (IDSs) in an effort to escalate those issues when the system is indeed vulnerable to such an attack. In his scenario, he would allow certain IDS events to execute a Nessus scan on the host for that specific vulnerability and, if subsequently found vulnerable, automatically notify the appropriate personnel.

The MySQL component of the Nessus architecture provides many uses. Some shops have homebrew scripts that comb their Nessus vulnerability database for all of the actions required for the respective system administrator of each of these systems. They then provide weekly reports to the other work centers of matters that need attention. This also allows for the possibility of trending over time. Reporting on vulnerability trends over time can provide management with the requisite metrics for obtaining an increased security budget in either time or money. They can also be used to show proof of compliance for many regulatory compliance initiatives such as British Standard 7799 and Sarbanes-Oxley.

If your company's networks are not being reviewed with a tool like Nessus with any frequency, then maybe the company should start this process. You can be sure that someone is indeed scanning the network, whether authorized or not.

The Plugins

Traditional security scanners require updates from the vendor to test for latest vulnerabilities, and often the release of these updates are less than timely. Nessus provides an excellent framework that really sets it apart from other scanners with the introduction of the Nessus Attack Scripting Language (NASL, pronounced naz-ul). NASL allows security analysts to quickly create their own plugins for vulnerability checks. The result is that teams can easily add their security expertise to their Nessus scans by creating custom vulnerability tests. It also allows the in-house security team to create vulnerability checks for the protocols and services that are unique to their networks.

Many security auditors need to create custom tests for in house applications or configurations that are unique to their environment. This often leads to the writing of their scanner, reinventing the wheel by duplicating most of the technology that every security scanner utilizes; the mechanism to generate the payload and push packets across the wire. NASL allows for the quick generation of the unique test for the application.

NASL most closely resembles C. It is specifically designed with security in mind, as it will only communicate with the host it is passed as an argument, and it will not execute any local commands. With this sandbox snug around the NASL interface, it is unlikely that a plugin can perform unexpected operations. Tenable has provided an extensive framework to test new plugins and a language that allows for robust tests and detailed reports. NASL is also built to share information between security tests. This is achieved through use of the "Knowledge Base."

The Knowledge Base

The Knowledge Base allows today's plugins to leverage the data gleaned by earlier plugins. Consider a security check that tests for the existence of a web server, and, if one is found, attempts to discern which implementation of HTTP is actually running. The plugin has the capability to set the value of a variable in the Nessus Knowledge Base for that host. Let's say that in one specific instance, our NASL script executes and finds Apache running on the remote host. The plugin then sets the host-specific Knowledge Base variable of "www/banner/80" to "Apache/1.3.29 (Unix) PHP/4.3.4 mod_ssl/2.8.16 OpenSSL/0.9.7a."

This allows all subsequent plugins the capability to read the value of "www/banner/80." Now, let's assume our next plugin reads this value. If it finds the string "OpenSSL/0.9.7a" in the returned value, it reports that this host is vulnerable due to an outdated version of OpenSSL. In this way, every plugin uses information already derived by more primitive plugins. Renaud suggests that plugins writers use the Knowledge Base as much as possible. This will serve to extend the capabilities of Nessus and speed up the performance of future plugins, which can search the Knowledge Base for data instead of having to traverse the network for it.

Summary

Ever since its beginnings in early 1998, the Nessus Project has been attracting security researchers from all walks of life. It continues this growth today. It has been adopted as a *de facto* standard by the security industry, vendor, and practitioner alike, many of which rely on Nessus as the foundation to their security practices.

Nessus employs many security features that allow for an easy fit into any security infrastructure. The encryption and authentication mechanisms are robust. The sandbox-like feature of the NASL interface keeps the plugins focused and behaving as expected.

Because of its ease of deployment and its extensible scripting language, Nessus enjoys a full community of developers and users who continue to push the envelope of innovation, in spite of becoming a closed source project back in 2005.

Solutions Fast Track

What Is It?

☑ Nessus is a free and up-to-date vulnerability scanner.

☑ It is feature rich and has a flexible/extensible architecture.

☑ The Nessus Scanner has a large community of volunteers writing audit plugins.

The *De Facto* Standard

☑ Nessus is a high-ranking contender in traditional product testing.

☑ Many commercial providers of security services use Nessus.

☑ In-house security teams throughout the IT industry employ Nessus.

☑ Many software suites available today provide low-level integration to Nessus.

History

☑ The Nessus Project was started in 1998 by Renaud Deraison.

☑ Nessus was conceived amidst stagnation of other open-source scanners and the rise in cost of commercial scanners.

☑ The Nessus community continues to grow at an exponential rate.

☑ Tenable Network Security announced in October 2005 that starting with version 3 of the scanning engine, the code will be proprietary license only.

☑ Over 20,000 security checks are available as of February 2008.

Basic Components

☑ The Nessus Project adopted a client/server model for its foundation. This client/server model allows the security analyst to "detach" from the vulnerability scan and use his resources for other items while Nessus continues to do what it does best.

☑ The Nessus client can connect to the nessusd server in many ways that employ both encryption and authentication.

☑ The Nessus Attack Scripting Language (NASL) allows security analysts to quickly create their own plugins for vulnerability checks.

☑ The Knowledge Base allows Nessus to share data gleaned from one plugin with the processes of another plugin. In this way, each plugin builds upon previously executed plugins.

Frequently Asked Questions

Q: How can I subscribe to the Nessus mailing lists?

A: Point your browser to lists.nessus.org. All of the archives and instructions to subscribe can be found there.

Q: If I use a centralized MySQL server for a backend database, won't the MySQL authentication credentials be sent unencrypted? How can I leverage a centralized database in a safe and secure manner?

A: Yes, that is true! The best thing to do is to get smart on SSH port forwarding. Using this will allow you to point each nessusd server at 127.0.0.1 as the MySQL database's IP address. This port accepts data and forwards it across an encrypted tunnel to the real MySQL database, thus marshalling your database entries over an encrypted tunnel to the actual database.

Q: Management won't let us use open-source software of any kind unless we can purchase support. Do any companies provide support for Nessus?

A: Yes. In fact, Tenable Security, which is listed on the Nessus home page, has positioned much of its business model around offering commercial support and services for Nessus. Tenable was actually begun by Ron Gula, developer of the Dragon IDS, and Renaud Deraison, Nessus' creator. Tenable can be found via www.tenablesecurity.com.

Q: How do I install Nessus?

A: Read the next chapter!

## Chapter 3

Installing Nessus

Solutions in this chapter:

- Nessus Version Comparison
- Picking a Server
- Nessus 2.2.x Install Guide
- Nessus 3.x Install & Upgrade Guide
- Final Steps
- Installing a Client

☑ Summary

☑ Solutions Fast Track

☑ Frequently Asked Questions

Introduction

There are many options to the security professional on what tools can be used to accomplish an organization's goal of maintaining a secure computing environment. When it comes to the Nessus Security Scanner, the first question that needs to be answered is which version to install. We will discuss some of the differences between the two Nessus versions and go through the install process for both.

Nessus is quite possibly one of the easiest packages to install. The myriad ways available to security analysts to deploy Nessus in their environment makes it a perfect match for the security organization that wants to control every aspect of an application. For this reason, there are many issues to consider when provisioning Nessus for your environment:

- Will you use many servers or just one?

- Will users be authenticated by password or client-side certification?

- Will this installation update and maintain itself, or will you perform this maintenance manually?

This chapter examines these questions, as well as examining the different methods of installation and their requisite skill sets. You can then choose your installation method based on your operating system preference, deployment process, skill level, and desired level of configurability. The popularity of the Nessus scanner has made it available to many different operating systems and many different network environments.

Nessus Version Comparison

Nessus 3.0 is a big departure from previous versions and created a bit of an uproar. This latest version of the vulnerability scanner is no longer open source. The security community felt that closing the source code was the first step in charging for the security scanner. The fear is that it is risky to invest time, resources, and code into a project that could be changed at any point. Time has shown that these fears were unfounded. Tenable Network Security has released a number of versions of the security scanner since their announcement, while still keeping the product free of charge. Over time, enhancements utilized in the 3.x version of the source code have been ported to the 2.2 branch of the source code. As another example, one feature that is no longer in the version 3 tree is IDS-evasion.

With all that said, everyone should be using version 3.x branch of the security scanner. Version 3 made a number of advancements in the methods compared to version 2.x. In comparisons between the software branches, Nessus version 3 reduces system load by 12 times that of version 2 and uses as much as half as much memory. This translates into scan times twice as fast as the former code base. Almost all of these improvements are due to enhancements to the NASL Engine. NASL is the language used to describe all the vulnerability checks

Nessus uses, and the NASL engine is in charge of reading each script and executing it. (See Chapter 11 for much more on NASL.)

Figure 3.1 Nessus 3x Speed Improvements

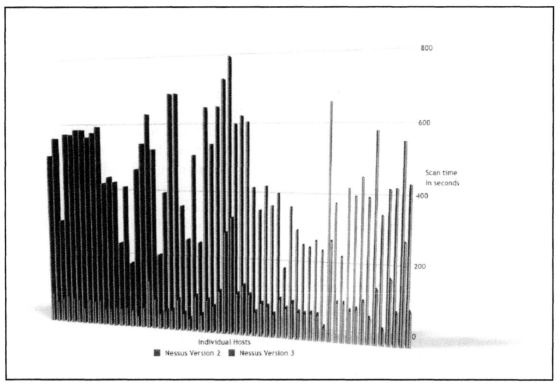

Performance is not the only reason to upgrade to version 3 of the code. The number of supported operating systems is greatly improved. Version 2 will only install on UNIX systems, while version 3.0 is also supported on Windows; an important addition to many organizations that only has Windows support staff. Nessus 3 can also conduct audits that ensure a system has been configured per a specific policy, such as the NSA's guide for hardening Windows severs (see Chapter 13 for more information on Nessus policy audits). The latest version of the Nessus Scanner introduced IPv6 support, improved control of network bandwidth usage during scanning, a unified cross-platform client, and a new, more robust reporting format.

Picking a Server

The first item of business when preparing for the installation of a nessusd server is provisioning the system that will be home to your Nessus installation. The factors that go into deciding what OS, platform, network location, and so forth will all vary depending on the purpose and duties of the server. First, ensure that your system will not be performing double duty. Many times, the security organization requests a server and the first thing IT wants to do is to install a network management system on it. Quite frequently, someone will ask to put yet another arbitrary application on the system, thinking that perhaps the security organization might just have some spare cycles to share with the rest of the organization. No matter what the reason, the security organization should never allow another application to invade the Nessus installation unless it is a process that runs directly in tandem with the security process.

The sensitivity of the data that Nessus will be collecting, mixed with the amount of resources required while running a scan, creates a justification for the security organization to be greedy with its resources in this case. It is also often tempting to allow other members of the security organization to have shell access to systems that sit deep in the organization as a jumping-off point to other resources. Many times, a security analyst might want to leverage a system in a specific location to sniff traffic on that segment, or perhaps test some other theory relative to the security posture. Ensure that a process is in place to allow these activities in a limited fashion if necessary, without detracting from the resources required to perform the scheduled and nonscheduled vulnerability scans.

Supported Operating Systems

After determining what the scope of the system will be in conjunction with the Nessus process, the next step is to determine which operating system best suits your organization's needs. When considering which operating system to use, the security organization has a wide variety of choices. Nessus will install on just about any Linux distribution or UNIX operating system, from the BSD UNIX family to Solaris and Mac OS X. Version 3 of the Nessus branch also introduced a Windows version of the server. The excuse of not having the expertise in house to support this product is gone with such a wide variety of supported operating systems.

Tenable Network Security has increased the supported versions greatly with the introduction of its version 3. Nessus has binary packages available for Windows, Mac OS X, Solaris, FreeBSD, Red Hat, SuSE, Debian, Ubuntu, and Fedora. If your operating system of choice is one of these, you have no worries about trusted binary packages or performance. Other Linux distributions, such as Gentoo, have used these binary packages and created their own way of installing on their OS. Besides creating a security issue (see this section's sidebar "Trusting Binary Packages"), the performance of the Nessus install can be slower than expected because of library linking and other issues. In addition, these unsupported operating system install packages are often not the latest version available. Keep these issues in mind when picking an operating system for your scanner.

Tools & Traps…

Trusting Binary Packages

The problem with using binary packages is that a third party is often introduced: The packager. Very often, this packager is completely unrelated to, and not vetted at all by, the developer. He's often just some guy who volunteered to create binary packages. The developers generally accept the offer so they won't have to learn how to create packages for the given packaging system. This introduces another variable where vulnerabilities can be leveraged. This leaves an untrustworthy party very capable of adding a crafty surprise to the source code before compiling or, often worse, to the installation scripts.

Remember, if an untrustworthy party creates the binaries from source, he can modify the installation contents or process to do anything he wants. Since your installer runs as root, the package creator has the ability to completely compromise your system! Most packaging solutions, including RPM, allow the package creator to include shell commands to be executed with root privilege before or after the file installation. If you don't know the person or organization creating them, or at least trust a party that's vetted the creator, you might want to compile the code yourself!

Minimal Hardware Specifications

The next step in provisioning a system for Nessus is specifying the required hardware. This is going to depend heavily on the environment Nessus will be scanning. If you will be scanning a class C address space (~255 hosts) and you expect to perform a scan like this very quickly, then you will want to ensure more than one processor (as Nessus is multithreaded) and between 1GB to 2GB of RAM. For a general scan that might take a few hours to perform, this is obviously overkill. However, for an internal scanning machine, time will be of the essence. There will be a limit to what your network can handle, but its capacity will grow over time, and thus it is better to ensure that the network continues as the bottleneck and not the system itself.

If your budget or choice of hardware is more limited, here are a few tips. First and foremost, memory is the greatest factor limiting how many hosts you can scan at once and how many tests you can run simultaneously. Increase processing power only after you've installed as much memory as is financially feasible. Second, make sure to scan multiple machines at the same time. This will ensure your scan isn't entirely halted by a single odd machine.

Third, make sure to run several tests/plugins at time, so that a single high-latency plugin doesn't slow your entire test. For example, if you have one plugin that takes 40 seconds while the next four take 10, with the delay solely due to latency, running two plugins at a time should take 40 seconds, while one at a time will take 80. To sum this up, here's a data point from Renaud Deraison, creator of Nessus and co-author of this book. With 128 megabytes of *free* memory, you can achieve the best speed scanning 10 targets at once with five tests at a time. On a system with 256 megabytes of free memory, you would scan 20 targets with 10 tests. Remember, these estimates are based on *free* memory. A Linux machine with 256 megabytes of RAM will probably only have 128 to 192 megabytes of free memory.

Network Location

Since we've been making sure that the network provides the bottleneck, the last item to consider during the provisioning of the Nessus server will be the location of this system on the network. Once again, size matters. If your network is small enough, say around 255–512 hosts, then one Nessus server might do the trick for you and thus network location becomes much simpler to determine. In the case of the small network, find the location that has the fewest number of routing devices between the Nessus server and the majority of the targets to be scanned. If possible, ensure that no firewall exists between the Nessus server and its target selection. This will reduce the computational and bandwidth-related load on the routing devices produced by the scans.

If you're deploying Nessus on a large network, a bit more thought is required. You can deploy multiple nessusd servers throughout the network, all waiting for the cue to scan their targets. Once triggered, these Nessus servers will then execute this scan simultaneously. Tenable has provided a good option for centralizing this type of activity through its Security Center product. The sweet spot you are trying to find here is the 24-hour window. If your entire network can be scanned inside one 24-hour window, then you are on the right path to having an extremely useful vulnerability assessment process. The process in this situation becomes divided into two phases. The first phase involves deploying multiple Nessus servers according to the same process and using the same concepts as when deploying only one. For example, ensure that there are a minimum number of network routing devices between the Nessus server and the targets of the scan. Figure 3.2 illustrates how the distributed placement of Nessus scanners can be leveraged.

The second phase involves attempting to scan and potentially shifting scanning machines based on your results. You might find that some areas of your network take longer to scan than others due to greater numbers of targets located in those areas or targets with more open ports or other sources of latency. In those situations, you can add another server, move an existing server from one position to another, or simply configure one server to scan hosts for which another was previously responsible. At this point, you can try again for that temporal sweet spot: the 24-hour scan.

Figure 3.2 Nessus Distributed Placement

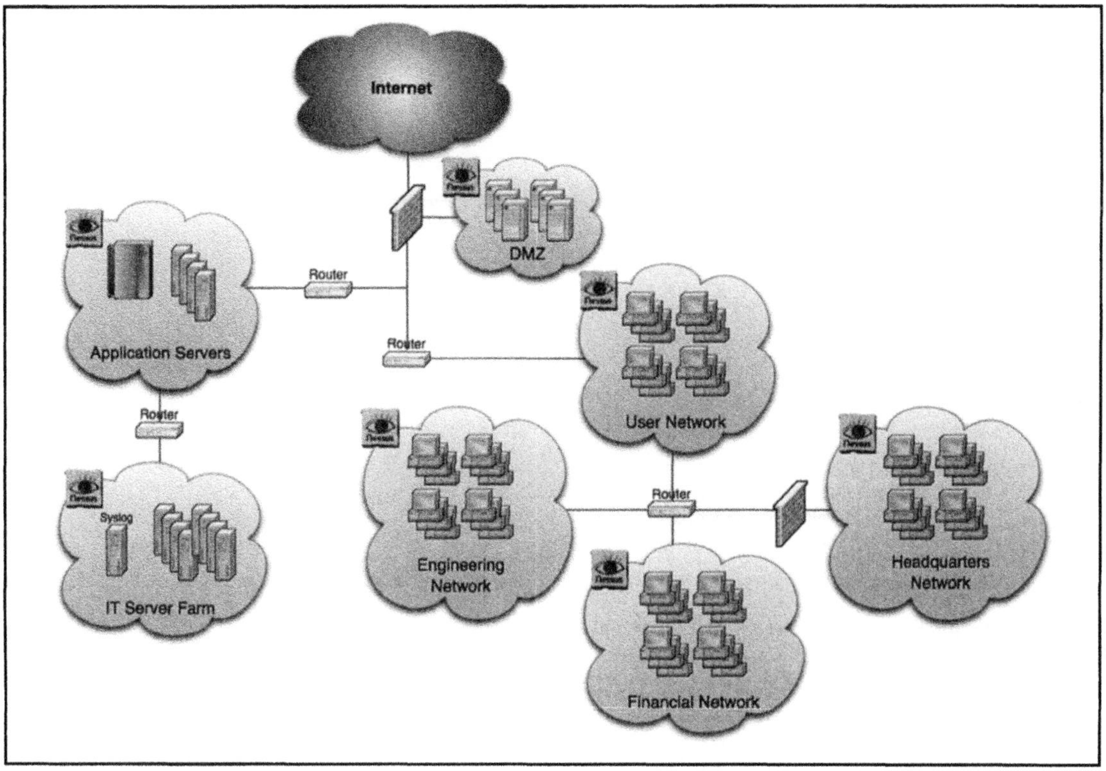

Nessus 2.2.x Install Guide

There are several methods for installing Nessus version 2.2.x. Compiling from source is always recommended due to security and performance concerns. The quickest installation method is to download the install script from Tenable and execute it. The third method is to use the operating systems method to install packages. RPM and apt-get are two popular methods to get third-party software into the Linux operating environment. We will cover the first two methods, nessus_installer script and compile from source in this chapter.

Nessus Install Script

The script can be found at http://www.nessus.org/download/. See Figure 3.3 for all the available versions. Select the latest version of the 2.2.x code branch labeled "installer (all UNIX systems)". Make sure you enter a valid email address in order to receive your activation code. This code will enable you to automatically update the plugins to get the most comprehensive audit possible.

Figure 3.3 Nessus.org Download Site

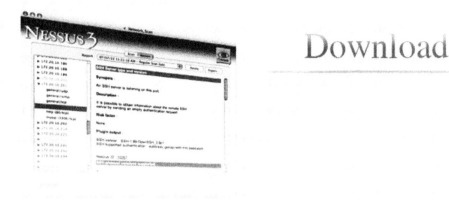

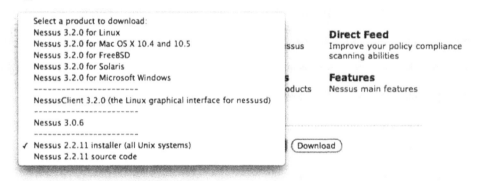

After downloading nessus-installer.sh from one of these mirror sites, read the script, and make sure you understand what each command does. Also, ensure that you have all the dependencies for the Nessus Security Scanner. Table 3.1 is a list of packages and minimum versions that are required:

Table 3.1 Required packages for Nessus 2.2.x

Command line only	Graphical Interface
sharutils 4.2.1	sharutils 4.2.1
openssl 0.9.6	openssl 0.9.6
	glib 1.2.10
	freetype 2.1.3
	fontconfig 2.1
	XFree86 4.3 or Xorg-x11 6.8
	gtk+ 1.2.10
	gdk-pixbuf 0.18.0

Finally, execute:

```
sh nessus-installer-2.2.x.sh
```

The install script contains all the necessary source code to successfully install this version of Nessus. There are a few things you should be prepared with before proceeding. The first is the MD5 hashes for the install package. This will help ensure that the install script is the approved version provided by Tenable. The second is the install location for the Nessus binaries. The default location is /usr/local, but this is often not in the default path. Finally, you will need the activation code in order to get the full set of plugins. This code was e-mailed to you after you completed the form to download the install script. While this is not required to complete the install process, it will allow the installer to download the latest plugins and save an extra step.

Notes from the Underground…

MD5 Weakness

When it comes to verifying the authenticity of a file, many people have historically relied on the MD5 one-way hashing algorithm developed in 1991 by Ron Rivest of RSA Data Security while at MIT. One-way hashes have many uses, only one of which is an attempt to verify file integrity.

Continued

The problem with relying on MD5 hashes as a method of ensuring file authenticity is the ease in which this method can be circumvented. For example, let's say Alice decides to maintain an RPM of Nessus on her Apache web site. Eventually, Alice's web site becomes very popular among users who rely on her up-to-date RPMs. Her users adapt an automatic process of installing these RPMs automatically via custom scripts, which also check the MD5 hash to be safe. One day, Bob discovers a new vulnerability in the Apache web server version that Alice uses to host her web site. Bob then replaces the RPM with a version laden with a Trojan that sends all scan data back to him. Bob notices that Alice's users are recommended to verify each package based on the MD5 hash that accompanies each RPM, so he simply runs his evil RPM through the MD5 hash algorithm and places the result on the site as well.

Now, all of Alice's users will verify the RPM based on the MD5 and find that it appears to be authentic. They will feel safe to install it and subsequently they will be sending all of their scan data back to Bob, who is an eager receiver. This form of a Man-In-The-Middle attack is a common occurrence, making the reliance on a private-public key combination imperative. Following the practice of verifying file authenticity based on digital signatures is part of defense-in-depth and removes the possibility of a web site compromise affecting the authenticity of the files located there.

See the sidebar titled "Asymmetric Encryption" later in this chapter for a detailed description of the strength of digital signatures.

The install script will prompt for the install directory, then compile the included source code, and finally remove any old versions of the scanner and replace it with the version just compiled. If any of the dependencies are not found, the script will error out before prompting the user for the install directory. The script will also look to compare the MD5 hashes with the file downloaded with the install script. If these hashes are not found, it will simply skip this step. Once the install is complete, Nessus will ask you to enter the activation code. The activation process is shown in Figure 3.4.

Figure 3.4 Activation Process for Nessus Version 2

```
-------------------------------------------------------------------
                 Nessus installation : Registration
-------------------------------------------------------------------

If you want to get a full plugin feed from http://www.nessus.org, you
need to register at http://www.nessus.org/plugins/.

If you already registered and received an activation code, please enter
it below if you want to activate it now :

Activation code : 174D-XXXX-D97A-YYYY-DF1D
Your activation code has been registered properly - thank you.
Now fetching the newest plugin set from plugins.nessus.org...
Your Nessus installation is now up-to-date.
```

Installation from Source

The same dependencies exist for the Nessus install script and installing from source. There are four main components for installing from source. They should be installed in the following order. Again, make sure you register with Tenable with a valid email address. This will ensure that the Nessus install will be with the latest plugin set after entering your activation code.

1. `nessus-libraries-x.x.tar.gz`

2. `libnasl-x.x.tar.gz`

3. `nessus-core.x.x.tar.gz`

4. `nessus-plugins.x.x.tar.gz`

After downloading these files from the Tenable web site, extract them (as seen in Figure 3.5). Each tar command creates a directory for each of the four components.

Figure 3.5 Executing tar zxf on Each File

```
# ls -l
total 17840
-rw-r--r--@ 1 paul   staff    367829 Mar 12 08:05 libnasl-2.2.11.tar.gz
-rw-r--r--@ 1 paul   staff    680220 Mar 12 08:06 nessus-core-2.2.11.tar.gz
-rw-r--r--@ 1 paul   staff    428265 Mar 12 08:09 nessus-libraries-2.2.11.tar.gz
-rw-r--r--@ 1 paul   staff   7647308 Mar 12 08:11 nessus-plugins-2.2.11.tar.gz
# tar zxf libnasl-2.2.11.tar.gz
# tar zxf nessus-core-2.2.11.tar.gz
# tar zxf nessus-libraries-2.2.11.tar.gz
# tar zxf nessus-plugins-2.2.11.tar.gz
# ls -lt
total 17840
-rw-r--r--@  1 paul   staff   7647308 Mar 12 08:11 nessus-plugins-2.2.11.tar.gz
-rw-r--r--@  1 paul   staff    428265 Mar 12 08:09 nessus-libraries-2.2.11.tar.gz
-rw-r--r--@  1 paul   staff    680220 Mar 12 08:06 nessus-core-2.2.11.tar.gz
-rw-r--r--@  1 paul   staff    367829 Mar 12 08:05 libnasl-2.2.11.tar.gz
drwxr-xr-x@ 27 paul   staff       918 Mar 12 02:28 nessus-libraries
drwxr-xr-x@ 21 paul   staff       714 Mar 12 02:28 nessus-plugins
drwxr-xr-x@ 19 paul   staff       646 Mar 12 02:28 libnasl
drwxr-xr-x@ 34 paul   staff      1156 Mar 12 02:28 nessus-core
#
```

./configure

After each of the tar files has been extracted into its respective directory, it's time to begin the configuration and compilation steps. The order in which this is done is extremely important. First, we will make sure that we are the root user, and then switch to the *nessus-libraries* directory and execute the following command:

```
# ./configure
```

This will check our system for the required libraries and tools and prepare the makefile used to set compilation options and installation paths for Nessus on our system. It also creates a script titled *uninstall-nessus* that we will use to uninstall our old version without losing our old configuration.

If we have an older version of Nessus installed that we're replacing, we must run the following command as root before continuing:

```
# ./uninstall-nessus
```

The script will prompt us as to whether we want to delete our older configuration files and keys. Unless we're simply removing Nessus from the system, we want to choose "n" for "no" here. Now, since we are simply upgrading the Nessus application and do not want to start from scratch, we choose "n." This will remove any files installed during our previous Nessus installations, leaving us ready to compile the Nessus-libraries.

The next step is to execute the *make* command. We simply type *make* on a line by itself and press the **Enter** key. The make program will begin compiling object files and linking them together, sending all sorts of output to the screen. This will take some time. Once this is done, we must switch user (su) to root, so that we can install the newly compiled files.

To install the compiled files, we first switch user to root with the `su` command:

```
# su -
```

We will be given a prompt at which to enter the root password, like so:

```
Password: <enter root password>
```

After typing the root password and getting our root prompt, we now run the following command:

```
# make install
```

This command installs all compiled files from the nessus-libraries tarball into their target directories, which are subdirectories of /usr/local by default. Now, this destination directory, or "prefix," can be changed by passing the command-line argument

```
-prefix=/some/other/directory
```

to the configure script.

Tools & Traps…

Do Not Run Configure or Make as Root

You may have noticed that the process shown for compiling Nessus doesn't run either *configure* or *make* as the root user. An important concept in security is the principle of Least Privilege, which dictates that you give any program (or user) only what privilege it actually requires to do its task. This decreases the damage that a hostile or compromised program (or user) can do.

As is the case when compiling most UNIX programs, these two compilation commands don't require root privilege to run—they simply compile the software. Only the *make install* step actually requires root privilege, as it needs to install software outside of the user's home directory. We use *su*, the UNIX switch-user command, to use root privilege only when necessary.

This might seem like an academic point, but it was vitally important when an attacker compromised a major distribution server for the massively popular tool tcpdump. The attacker didn't actually Trojan the tcpdump code; instead, he modified the configure script. The configure script installed a Trojan, which sent a shell back to the attacker whenever an administrator compiled the code on a system. Administrators who ran the *configure* script as root gave the attacker root access on their system, while every other administrator only gave the attacker access as a normal user. You can read more about this incident at: www.us-cert.gov/federal/archive/advisories/FA-2002-30.html

It's also worth noting that users who check PGP signatures of any software, source or otherwise that they download seldom are caught by Trojaned software.

Upon completion of the file installation from our *make install* command, the output will give you a few additional items to examine or modify. First, it states that /usr/local/bin should be in your path. To determine this, execute the following command:

```
echo $PATH
```

You should see something similar to the following output:

```
/usr/local/sbin:/usr/local/bin:/usr/sbin:/usr/bin:/sbin:/bin:/usr/bin/X11
```

In our scenario, we do in fact have /usr/local/bin in our path. If we did not, we can remedy the situation by adding it to our path. We also need to add /usr/local/sbin, so we might as well do that now as well. Execute the following command:

```
# export PATH=$PATH:/usr/local/bin:/usr/local/sbin
```

To place this directory in our path more permanently, along with every other user's path, we should add it to the command that sets the PATH in the global system files specific to the shell in use. For instance, the primary user shell on most Linux distributions is bash, which reads /etc/profile on a new user login. We can add the relevant line to the end of /etc/profile by executing this command as root:

```
# echo "export PATH=$PATH:/usr/local/bin" >>/etc/profile
```

The last file that the post-compilation notes exhort us to modify is the /etc/ld.so.conf file. It asks us to ensure that /usr/local/lib is in that file, and then to execute *ldconfig* after adding it. To verify that /usr/local/lib is found in this file on our Linux system, we simply execute the following command:

```
# grep /usr/local/lib /etc/ld.so.conf
```

If this returns a line that reads exactly "/usr/local/lib" then we have nothing to do. Otherwise, we'll need to add it to this file, running *ldconfig* afterward. We accomplish this via the command sequence:

```
# echo "/usr/local/lib" >>/etc/ld.so.conf
# ldconfig
```

On Solaris, we'd execute this command instead:

```
# export LD_LIBRARY_PATH=$LD_LIBRARY_PATH:/usr/local/lib
```

Now we are ready to change to the libnasl directory and perform the same *./configure* and *make* sequences. Remember to switch down to your regular user account until you need root for the final step. First, exit the root shell:

```
# exit
```

Now compile libnasl:

```
# cd ../libnasl
# ./configure
# make
# su -
Password: <enter root password>
# make install
```

Nessus-core is next on our compilation path. It is here that the option of removing the dependency on GTK is performed, if you desire. Our command sequence looks very similar to that of the last package, with the simple addition of our configuration option. Of course, we will omit this option if we want to use the GTK graphical user interface (GUI) for Nessus:

```
# exit
# cd ../nessus-core
# ./configure --disable-gtk
```

```
# make
# su
Password: <enter root password>
# make install
```

Our final compilation to perform is for the nessus-plugins. Much like the prior three packages we had to compile, we now execute the following commands:

```
# exit
# cd ../nessus-plugins
# ./configure
# make
# su -
Password: <enter root password>
# make install
```

After this last step, our installation is complete. All required software has been compiled and installed in the required directories on the system. While this might seem complicated versus the one-line binary package install, it truly is simple. This command sequence becomes second nature to you as you compile and install Nessus, or even other open-source software, a few times. Our next step will be to perform the initial configuration of the Nessus server.

Nessus 3 Install Guide

Tenable Network Security has greatly enhanced the install process for version 3 of the Nessus scanner. In this section, we will discuss how to install the binary packages for each of the supported operating systems. Each OS has its own installer package, like RPM for Red Hat or pkgadd for Solaris. Download the latest version of Nessus from http://www. nessus.org/downoad/, and then follow the instructions below for your operating system. Note, unless otherwise mentioned, all commands should be executed with root privileges. Nessus 3 is installed in */opt/nessus* for Linux distributions, */usr/local/nessus/* for FreeBSD, /Applications/Nessus for OS X, and finally *C:\Program Files\Tenable\Nessus* on Windows operating systems.

Mac OS X Install Process

Nessus is available for Mac OS X 10.4 and 10.5. To install Nessus on Mac OS X, you need to download the file *Nessus-3.x.x.dmg.gz*, and then double click on it to mount it on the desktop. Once the volume "Nessus 3" appears on the desktop, double click on the file *Nessus 3.mpkg*. During the install process you will be prompted for administrator's username and password. Both the client and the server can be installed at this time and is recommended. Follow the installer's instructions to successfully install on OS X.

The OS X installer installs a client for Nessus by default. It is recommended that both the server and client be installed together. This is unique to the Windows and OS X installers.

Figure 3.6 Mac OS X Installer

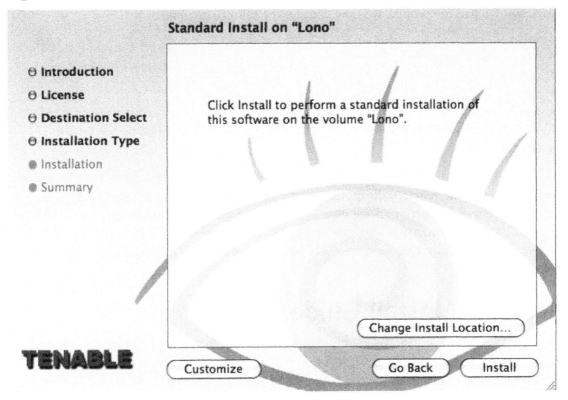

Once the installer has completed, we need to create a Nessus server certificate. The certificates are required for secure communication between the client and the server. Open a terminal window and execute the following commands on the server:

```
# sudo su -
# /Library/Nessus/run/sbin/nessus-mkcert
```

Executing this command will initiate a Curses-based interface that will query you for a few configuration items. (Curses is a kind of text-based GUI language.) These are items common to certificate identification such as shelf life of the certificates and location information to be associated with the certificate. Figure 3.7 shows what the interaction will look like. You will have to provide the correct information for your company.

Figure 3.7 Creation of the Nessus Server Certificate

```
nessusd (Nessus) 3.2.0. for Linux
(C) 1998 - 2008 Tenable Network Security, Inc.


-----------------------------------------------------------------------
                    Creation of the Nessus SSL Certificate
-----------------------------------------------------------------------

This script will now ask you the relevant information to create the SS
certificate of Nessus. Note that this information will *NOT* be sent to
anybody (everything stays local), but anyone with the ability to connect
to your Nessus daemon will be able to retrieve this information.


CA certificate life time in days [1460]:
Server certificate life time in days [365]:
Your country (two letter code) [FR]: US
Your state or province name [none]: MA
Your location (e.g. town) [Paris]: Boston
Your organization [Nessus Users United]:
-----------------------------------------------------------------------
                    Creation of the Nessus SSL Certificate
-----------------------------------------------------------------------

Congratulations. Your server certificate was properly created.

/Library/Nessus/run/etc/nessus/nessusd.conf updated

The following files were created :

. Certification authority :
   Certificate = /Library/Nessus/run/com/nessus/CA/cacert.pem
   Private key = /Library/Nessus/run/var/nessus/CA/cakey.pem

. Nessus Server :
    Certificate = /Library/Nessus/run/com/nessus/CA/servercert.pem
    Private key = /Library/Nessus/run/var/nessus/CA/serverkey.pem

Press [ENTER] to exit
```

The next step is to register the server with Tenable in order to receive plugin updates. Use the activation code sent to you by Tenable to the address you registered when downloading the install packages. Click on the **Nessus Server Manager** and enter an Administrator's password. Enter the code in the appropriate field and click "Register". Figure 3.8 shows the registration interface.

Figure 3.8 Mac OS X Activation interface

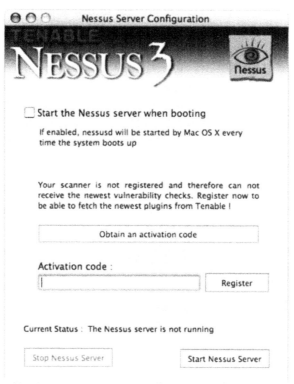

Once you have successfully registered with Tenable, users need to be added to maintain separation of duties and accountability. The Server Management interface will look like Figure 3.9. Click on the **Manage Users** button to see a list of users active on this server. Because this is a fresh install, the only user present is call *localuser*. This user can connect to the server installed only on this system. It cannot be modified or deleted. For the purpose of testing, this is sufficient, but to properly separate duties and have accountability, users will need to be added to the system. Click on the **+**, and to delete a user, click the **−**. If you wish to change the password of an existing user, select the username and click **edit**. Note: You cannot rename a user. To do this, you need to delete the old user and then create a new one with the appropriate credentials.

Figure 3.9 Mac OS X Server Manager Interface

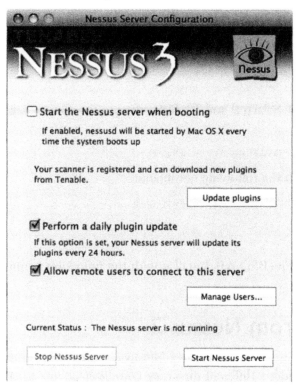

The final step to installing the Nessus server is to update the plugins supplied with the install binary. It is highly recommended that you do this before running you first scan. The set of plugins that comes with the installer is small and will provide an incomplete picture of the status of your network. Simply click on the **Update Plugins** button and the Server Manager will show a progress bar while downloading them from the Tenable server.

UNIX Install Process
Fresh Installation
Red Hat and SUSE

Nessus 3 is available for Red Hat ES 3, ES 4, ES 5, and ES 5 x86-64; Fedora Core 7 and 8; and SUSE 9.3 and 10.0. Install it with the following command depending on your version:

```
# rpm –ivh Nessus-3.2.0-es3.i386.rpm
```

Debian

Nessus 3 is available for Debian 4 and 4 x86-64. Install it with the following command:

```
# dpkg -i Nessus-3.2.0-debian4_i386.deb
```

Solaris

Nessus 3 is available for Solaris 9 and 10. First, uncompress the package with the following command:

```
# gunzip Nessus-3.2.0-solaris-sparc.pkg.gz
```

Then, install it with the following command:

```
# pkgadd -d ./Nessus-3.2.0-solaris-sparc.pkg
```

FreeBSD

Nessus is available for FreeBSD 6.0. Install it with the following command:

```
# pkg_add Nessus-3.2.0-fbsd6.tbz
```

Upgrading from Nessus 2

This section will explain how to upgrade a Nessus 2.x installation to Nessus 3.x. Since Nessus 3 is installed under a different directory, (*/usr/local/nessus/* for FreeBSD versions and */opt/nessus/* for all the other versions) required files from the old installation will need to be manually copied. Note that the instructions below assume that all files for Nessus 2 have been previously installed under the */usr/local/* directory structure. Make the appropriate adjustments if your installation is different.

It is possible to run both versions of Nessus on the same system. Each version is installed under different paths. All of the following commands need to be executed with root privileges. The fist step in upgrading is stopping the old Nessus service, *nessusd,* with the following command:

```
# killall nessusd
```

Note that this will terminate all active scans. Next, follow the install instructions for the appropriate operating system discussed earlier in this section. Finally, we need copy a number of configuration files from the version 2 install location to the new location for Nessus 3.

User management is directory based in Nessus, so moving user accounts is fairly straightforward. Copy the users with the command as follows:

```
# cp -r /usr/local/var/nessus/users/* /opt/nessus/var/nessus/users/
```

and for FreeBSD users

```
# cp -r /usr/local/var/nessus/users/* /usr/local/nessus/var/nessus/users/
```

Next, copy the file *nessus-fetch.rc* to the appropriate Nessus 3 directory to save your plugin activation code. If you do not, you will have to contact Tenable to get a new activation code and register your new install with that code. Here is the command to migrate your existing code:

```
# cp /usr/local/etc/nessus/nessus-fetch.rc /opt/nessus/etc/nessus/
```

and for FreeBSD users

```
# cp /usr/local/etc/nessus/nessus-fetch.rc /usr/local/nessus/etc/nessus/
```

Then, make sure the permissions are as follows:

```
-rw------ 1 root root 398 Mar 28 03:12 nessus-fetch.rc
```

The next step is to edit the file */opt/nessus/etc/nessus/nessusd.conf* to make sure that the *admin_user* is set properly. To do this, make sure that that the following options are correct:

```
plugin_upload = yes
admin_user = <ADMIN>
```

Where *<ADMIN>* is the name of the admin user defined in the Nessus 2 file */usr/local/etc/nessus/nessud.conf.*

Optionally, if you wish to remove the old installation of Nessus, issue the following command. It is a good idea to ensure that Nessus 3 is configured and running properly before following this step. It might be wise to revisit this command after following the instructions in the Configuring Nessus in the next section.

```
# /usr/local/sbin/uninstall-nessus
```

Configuring Nessus for UNIX

For a *nessusd* Nessus server to communicate properly with a Nessus client, the administrator must execute a few more steps before running the client. The first step is to ensure that the install directory is in the default path. For example, on Red Hat Enterprise, Nessus 3 is installed in */opt/nessus*. Follow these steps to ensure the install directory is included in the path.

```
# echo $PATH
```

If the path reported is lacking the required directories, run:

```
# export PATH=$PATH:/opt/nessus/sbin:/opt/nessus/bin
```

The next step is to register our installation of Nessus with Tenable. If you registered at the time you downloaded the install binary, you received an activation code to the e-mail you registered with. This registration code is good only one time and if you reinstall either the OS or the Nessus binaries, you will have to re-register with Tenable, unless you save a copy of the *nessus-fetch.rc* file, located in */opt/nessus/etc/nessus.*

Now, we need to ensure the communication between the server and the client is secure by creating the appropriate certificates. Execute the following command on the server to start the process:

```
# nessus-mkcert
```

If OpenSSL is installed, then executing this command will initiate a Curses-based interface that will query you for a few configuration items. These are items common to certificate identification such as shelf life of the certificates and location information to be associated with the certificate. Figure 3.10 shows what the interaction will look like. You will have to provide the correct information for your company.

Figure 3.10 Creation of the Nessus Server Certificate

```
nessusd (Nessus) 3.2.0. for Linux
(C) 1998 - 2008 Tenable Network Security, Inc.

-------------------------------------------------------------------
                    Creation of the Nessus SSL Certificate
-------------------------------------------------------------------

This script will now ask you the relevant information to create the SS
certificate of Nessus. Note that this information will *NOT* be sent to
anybody (everything stays local), but anyone with the ability to connect
to your Nessus daemon will be able to retrieve this information.


CA certificate life time in days [1460]:
Server certificate life time in days [365]:
Your country (two letter code) [FR]: US
Your state or province name [none]: MA
Your location (e.g. town) [Paris]: Boston
Your organization [Nessus Users United]:
-------------------------------------------------------------------
                    Creation of the Nessus SSL Certificate
-------------------------------------------------------------------

Congratulations. Your server certificate was properly created.

/opt/nessus/etc/nessus/nessusd.conf updated

The following files were created :

. Certification authority :
   Certificate = /opt/nessus//com/nessus/CA/cacert.pem
   Private key = /opt/nessus//var/nessus/CA/cakey.pem

. Nessus Server :
    Certificate = /opt/nessus//com/nessus/CA/servercert.pem
    Private key = /opt/nessus//var/nessus/CA/serverkey.pem

Press [ENTER] to exit
```

Tools & Traps...

Asymmetric Encryption

One of the fundamental elements of encryption is the requirement of a key. When a user encrypts a file, a key is used to provide a high enough degree of randomness in the resultant cipher text. The cipher text also requires a key to decrypt it back into the original plaintext. These key pairs come in two varieties. The first variety is termed *symmetric* and includes the use of two identical keys. Although this method has been used for many years, primarily where communication is limited to two parties, it is extremely vulnerable to crypto attacks. If any side of the communication is compromised, then any future communications are assumed compromised as well. Today, many protocols still use symmetric encryption in a limited fashion where keys are only valid for the length of one session. Even still, the key is stored in memory on either side of the connection.

Asymmetric encryption employs the use of two completely different keys. First, there is the public key associated with a person, or sometimes an organization, which is often used to encrypt any message anyone would want to send to this person in a secure fashion. The private key, kept safe from compromise by the intended recipient of the encrypted message, is then used to reveal the plaintext from the cipher text. In this fashion, anyone can encrypt a message to anyone else. However, only the recipient can decrypt the message. The public key is usually available from key servers, web servers, or other places accessible by users expected to send messages to the recipient. A common searchable repository of keys is located at pgp.mit.edu.

Another function of the asymmetric key pair applied in Public Key Cryptography is the *digital signature*. Whenever someone wants to send a document that is verifiably authentic, he can encrypt it with his secret private key. This document can then be decrypted with the user's public key located in the public domain. Sometimes, merely an MD5 or SHA-1 hash of the document is encrypted and then placed in the plaintext document in an attempt at brevity.

Creating a User Account

Once the server certificates have been created, the next step in setting up a nessusd server is the creation of users. To add a user, execute the following command:

```
# nessus-adduser
```

You will immediately be asked for a username—in this case, we used "centaur." The next order of business is to specify the type of authentication to use with this user. You can choose "pass" or "cert." If "cert" is selected, then nessus-adduser will ask you for follow-on certificate-related information. If you select "pass," you will be prompted twice for your password for verification.

Typically, it is best to be able to authenticate users based on what is known as *two-factor authentication.* This is where users are tested for something they know and something they have. In this case, these would be the password and the client certificate, respectively. Unfortunately, nessus-adduser does not leverage the defense-in-depth of two factor authentication at this time.

The nessus-adduser utility will ask for any rules that you might want to specify to limit the access of the user you're creating. This is a very robust feature of Nessus and should not be underutilized. Any number of rules can be specified per user, including none at all. Each rule consists of one line and follows this syntax:

```
accept|deny ip/mask
     and
default accept|deny
```

If, for example, you want to allow this user the ability to scan only hosts between 192.168.0.1 and 192.168.0.255, you would use the following rules:

```
accept 192.168.0.0/24
default deny
```

The first rule specifies which address space this user is allowed to scan. The second rule, or default rule, stipulates that this user is not allowed to scan any other address. Using these rules, a well-defined sandbox can be established for each user, ensuring that the users will only be able to leverage the power of Nessus over a well-defined subset of hosts that they have authorization to scan. Often, each administrator is only allowed to scan hosts for which she is responsible.

After detailing each of the desired rules for this user, you must hold down **Ctrl** and press the **D** key. You will then be presented with the information you have provided thus far, accompanied by a query for confirmation:

```
# nessus-adduser
Using /var/tmp as a temporary file holder

Add a new nessusd user
----------------------
Login : centaur
Authentication (pass/cert) [pass] : pass
Login password :
Login password (again) :

User rules
----------
```

```
nessusd has a rules system which allows you to restrict the hosts that centaur
has the right to test. For instance, you may want him to be able to scan his own
host only.

Please see the nessus-adduser(8) man page for the rules syntax

Enter the rules for this user, and hit ctrl-D once you are done :
(the user can have an empty rules set)
accept 192.168.0.0/24
default deny

Login            : centaur
Password         : **********
DN               :
Rules1           :
accept 192.168.0.0/24
default deny

Is that ok ? (y/n) [y]
```

Simply press **y** and **Enter** and the addition of our new user is complete.

Tools & Traps…

Individual Account-ability

Nessus can be configured to allow different users access to different areas of the network. This enables an entire litany of imaginative uses. For example, the security organization might set up the Nessus server in such a way that it becomes part of the system administration workflow. After granting scanning authorization to each area of the network only to those system administrators responsible for it, the frequency of scans can be monitored by the Nessus administrator. This allows the security organization to determine how proactive each department within the organization is in regard to risk mitigation. Followed up with some corporate security awareness training for the newly anointed system administrators allows for a more involved security process that can be monitored as it progresses.

Many times, the security team ends up in an adversarial relationship with other areas of the organization. The security team can have the difficult job of delivering bad news about current problems, which can end up making someone in the organization look bad. In other cases, the problem is one of uncertainty. System and network

Continued

administrators know the security team is looking at the environment, but don't know either the focus of the inspection or what results will be revealed. While this kind of problem can often be corrected socially within the organization by senior management, there are technical measures that the security team can take. One is to give each administrator the ability to view his own security vulnerability report. This takes the security organization out of the *messenger-to-be-shot* or *stick-wielding* role, and empowers the responsible administrators to take greater ownership of their vulnerabilities. The most motivated administrators will often fix many of the simpler vulnerabilities on their own this way, thus gaining the opportunity to reduce the problem list before they meet with the security team. This tends to mitigate whatever ill will might be felt by most administrators toward the security organization. For some reason, people tend to take criticism better from a machine than from a potentially aloof security analyst. It's important to still keep records of some periodic audits, to provide both good internal knowledge and external motivation, but site security definitely improves when administrators have vulnerability data before those audits.

Windows Install Process

Nessus 3 is available for Windows 2000, XP, Server 2003, Server 2008, and Vista. Nessus is distributed as an executable installation file. Download the file to the system that will become the nessus server. Nessus should only be installed using an administrative account and not by a user of less privilege. The install package will prompt the user for a few options, like install directory. One thing you should consider when installing Nessus 3 on a Windows platform is that you may be limited in functionality; not by Nessus, but by Microsoft. For example, the compliance audit functionality of Nessus 3 will not work under the Home versions of the Windows operating system because the OS lacks the appropriate built-in functionality to allow these scans.

The Windows installer also installs a client for Nessus by default. It is recommended that both the server and client be installed together, as shown if Figure 3.11.

Figure 3.11 Windows Installer

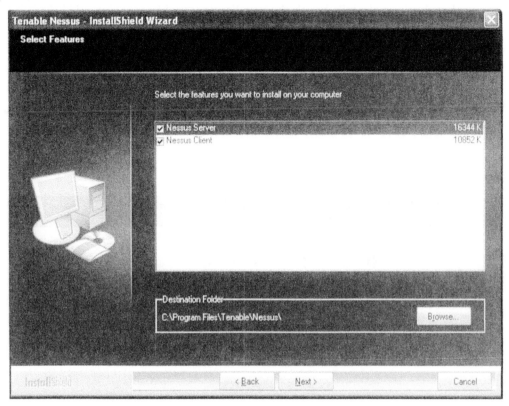

The Windows installer also takes you through a number of steps that traditionally are part of the configuration stage. The first step is the option to register your Nessus install with Tenable. This will allow you to receive the latest plugins. If this step is completed, Nessus will prompt the installer with the option to download the latest plugins from Tenable. It is recommended that both of these steps be followed at this time. Figure 3.12 illustrates the registration process.

Figure 3.12 Windows Registration Process

Once the registration process is complete, the installer will ask if you wish to upgrade the plugins that come pre-installed with the installer. It is highly recommended that you do this process before running you first scan. The set of plugins that come with the installer is small and will provide an incomplete picture of the status of your network. Figure 3.13 shows the update process. The entire process uses three steps. The first downloads the package from the Tenable server, the second extracts the archive, and the final step is to install all the plugins.

Figure 3.13 Windows Plugin Update Process

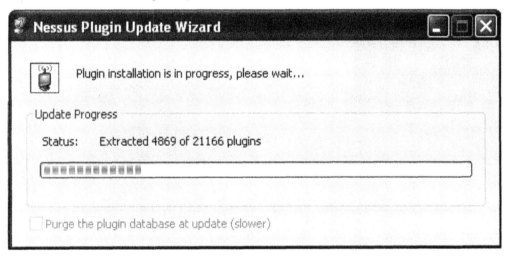

The final step in the windows install process is to create a user to access the server. The model that Nessus was created upon is separation of duties and accountability. See the Tools and Traps section in the configuring Nessus under the UNIX section for more details. Navigate to the Tenable folder under your Start menu and click on User Management to create a new user. Click on the "New User" icon on the top menu and enter the credentials are needed. Figure 3.14 illustrates this interface. In most cases, password is the type of authentication you will select. Proceed to enter a username and enter a password that meets you security needs. When ready, click "OK" to create the new user.

Figure 3.14 Windows New User Process

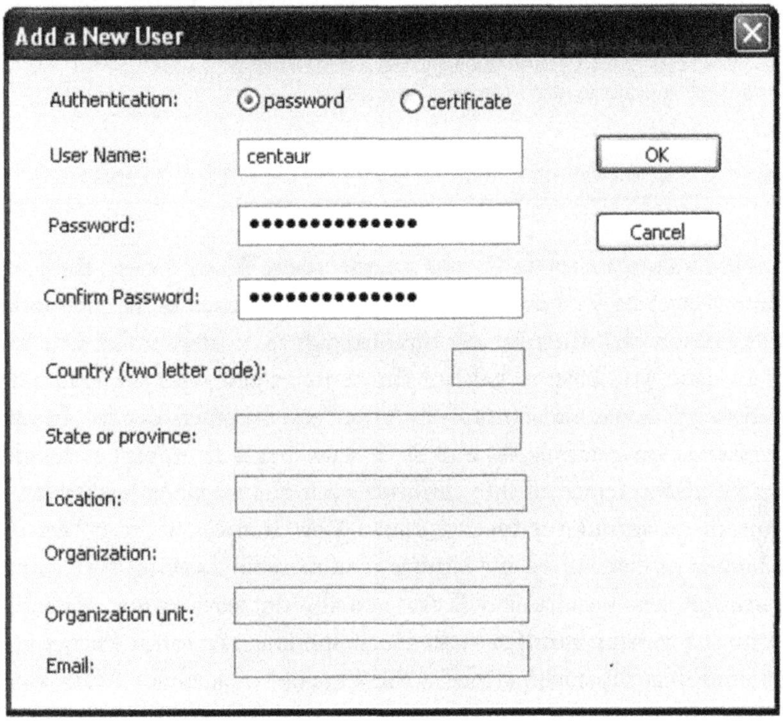

To delete a user from the "User Management" interface, click the "Delete" icon. If you wish to change the password of an existing user, or rename a user, you will need to delete the user first and then create a new one with the appropriate credentials.

Final Steps

The final step to configuring your Nessus server is to make any modifications required to the server configuration. In the UNIX environments, this file is located in */opt/nessus/etc/nessus/nessusd.conf*. Mac OS X has this file located in */Library/Nessus/<arch>/etc/nessus/nessusd.conf*. Windows has moved away from this model slightly and uses all options passed from the client to affect scan options. Note any options passed from the client at scan time will supersede the server configuration. To modify this file, view it using your favorite text editor. For example:

```
vi /opt/nessus/etc/nessus/nessud.conf
```

Several different items can be tweaked in this configuration file; however, we are only going to focus on a few. The first item specifies how much Nessus can impact the network during scans. This item is *max_hosts*, which controls how many total simultaneous hosts Nessus will run tests at once. The second item is *max_checks*, which limits the number of simultaneous checks are against each host.

```
# Maximum number of simultaneous hosts tested :
max_hosts = 40
# Maximum number of simultaneous checks against each host tested :
max_checks = 5
```

By default, these values are set to 40 and 5 respectively. When setting these, you will want to test it at different levels to see how it impacts the performance of the network. On one hand, you want to ensure that these are set high enough as to allow a full scan in a timely fashion. On the other hand, you have to balance this requirement with the load placed on the network. For a network that is not commonly busy, these numbers can be set rather high for the first couple of tests; for example, 40 and 10. If scans begin to impact network performance, or perhaps even the performance of the scan itself, scale this numbers back a bit.

The next option to consider is the *safe_checks*. This controls weather Nessus will rely simply on the banner to determine if a service is vulnerable. Leaving this option set to "yes" will speed the scan process because it will not actually test services for vulnerabilities. It will compare the returned version number with the vulnerable version it knows and report the results. Keep in mind that this speed comes at the expense of accuracy. Many operating systems will simply patch the vulnerabilities and not increment the version number. Setting this option to "no" will reduce the number of false positives the results will present, but increase the risk of crashing delicate servers. In this author's experience, if your network is running modern operating systems that are still supported by their vendors, it is OK to disable *safe_checks*. Legacy systems like VAX/VMS have a tendency to fall over when facing a stiff breeze, never mind an exhaustive vulnerability test.

```
# Safe checks rely on banner grabbing :
safe_checks = yes
```

Many of these items become default settings that can be modified later for each scan via the client. The following two items, for example, become default settings for the way Nessus conducts its port scans, whether with Nmap or the built-in Nessus scanner:

```
# Range of the ports the port scanners will scan :
# 'default' means that Nessus will scan ports found in its
# services file.
port_range = default
# Ping hosts before scanning them?
ping_hosts = yes
```

port_range sets the default range of ports that Nessus will scan. For the most comprehensive scans, we'll obviously want to set this to 0–65535, but again at the cost of speed. *ping_hosts* tells

Nessus whether it should scan only hosts that respond to pings. Again, for comprehensive scans, we'd want to set this to "no," as many hosts that are well-firewalled do not respond to pings even though their applications will interact with the network. Now, both of these settings can and probably should be set primarily through the client when you're using Nessus with only one user. When you have multiple users around the site using Nessus, you'll want to set extremely well thought-out defaults in this file, ensuring that less knowledgeable users get the best defaults possible.

Now, once all of the modifications are complete, save this file and exit your text editor. For a complete list of all of the directives used in *the nessusd.conf* file, please refer to the man page for nessusd.

Tools & Traps...

The man Page

The man page for nessusd lists all of the options used for configuring the nessusd server. Pay close attention to *checks_read_timeout*, which covers performing scans over slow links; *use_mac_addr* for scanning DHCP enabled networks; and *safe_checks*, which is used for disabling checks that might cause a denial of service (DoS) on important network resources. That said, if the network resource is important enough to turn off denial-of-service checks during normal frequent scans, then the resource is important enough to schedule an outage to ensure your systems are not vulnerable to these.

Table 3.2 Configure Options

Configure Options	Corresponding Functions
plugins_folder	Contains the location of the plugins older. The default locations for each operating system are listed below.
	Mac OS X: /Library/Nessus/run/lib/nessus/plugins
	UNIX: /opt/nessus/lib/nessus/plugins
	Windows: C:\Program Files\Tenable\Nessus\plugins

Continued

Table 3.2 Continued. Configure Options

Configure Options	Corresponding Functions
Logfile	Path to the logfile. You can enter syslog if you want the nessusd messages to be logged via syslogd. You can also enter stderr if you want the nessusd logs to be written on stderr. Because nessusd is a sensitive program, you should keep your logs. Therefore, entering syslog is usually not a good idea and should be done only for debugging purposes.
max_checks	The number of plugins that will run against each host being tested. Note that the total number of processes will be max_checks x max_hosts, so you need to find a balance between these two options. Note that launching too many plugins at the same time might disable the remote host, either temporarily (for example, inetd closes its ports) or definitely (the remote host crashes because it is asked to do too many things at the same time), so be careful.
be_nice	If this option is set to "yes," then each child forked by nessusd will nice(2) itself to a very low priority. This might speed up your scan, as the main nessusd process will be able to continue to spew processes, and this guarantees that nessusd does not deprive other important processes from their resources.
log_whole_attack	If this option is set to "yes," nessusd will store the name, pid, date, and target of each plugin launched. This is helpful for monitoring and debugging purposes; however, this option might make nessusd fill your disk rather quickly.
log_plugins_name_at_load	If this option is set to "yes," nessusd will store the name, pid, date, and target of each plugin launched. This is helpful for monitoring and debugging purposes; however, this option might make nessusd fill your disk rather quickly.
dumpfile	Some plugins might issue messages, most of the time to inform you that something went wrong. If you want to read these messages, set this value to a given filename. If you want to save space, set this option value to /dev/null.

Continued

Table 3.2 Continued. Configure Options

Configure Options	Corresponding Functions
cgi_path	By default, nessusd looks for default CGIs in /cgi-bin and /scripts. You can change these to something else to reflect the policy of your site. The syntax of this option is the same as the shell $PATH variable: path1:path2:…
port_range	The default range of ports that the scanner plugins will probe. The syntax of this option is flexible; it can be a single range ("1–1500"), several ports ("21, 23, 80"), or several ranges of ports ("1–1500, 32000–33000"). Note that you can specify UDP and TCP ports by prefixing each range by T or U. For instance, the following range will make nessusd scan UDP ports 1 to 1024 and TCP ports 1 to 65535 : "T:1-65535,U:1-1024".
optimize_test	By default, nessusd does not trust the remote host banners. This means that it will check a web server claiming to be IIS for Apache flaws, and so on. This behavior might generate false positives and will slow the scan somehow. If you are sure the banners of the remote host have not been tampered with, you can safely enable this option, which will force the plugins to perform their job only against the services they have been designed to check.
checks_read_timeout	Number of seconds that the security checks will wait when doing a recv(). You should increase this value if you are running nessusd across a slow network link (testing a host via a dial-up connection, for example).
non_simult_ports	Some services (in particular, SMB) do not appreciate multiple connections at the same time coming from the same host. This option allows you to prevent nessusd to make two connections on the same given ports at the same time. The syntax of this option is "port1[, port2….]". Note that you can use the KB notation of nessusd to designate a service formally. For example, "139, Services/www" will prevent nessusd from making two connections at the same time on port 139 and on every port that hosts a web server.

Continued

Table 3.2 Continued. Configure Options

Configure Options	Corresponding Functions
plugins_timeout	This is the maximum lifetime, in seconds of a plugin. It might happen that some plugins are slow because of the way they are written or the way the remote server behaves. This option allows you to make sure your scan is never caught in an endless loop because of a nonfinishing plugin.
safe_checks	Most of the time, nessusd attempts to reproduce an exceptional condition to determine if the remote services are vulnerable to certain flaws. This includes the reproduction of buffer overflows or format strings, which might make the remote server crash. If you set this option to "yes," nessusd will disable the plugins that have the potential to crash the remote services, and will at the same time make several checks rely on the banner of the service tested instead of its behavior toward a certain input. This reduces false positives and makes nessusd nicer toward your network; however, this might make you miss important vulnerabilities (as a vulnerability affecting a given service might also affect another one).
auto_enable_dependencies	Nessus plugins use the result of each other to execute their job. For example, a plugin that logs into the remote SMB registry will need the results of the plugin that finds the SMB name of the remote host and the results of the plugin that attempts to log in to the remote host. If you want to only select a subset of the plugins available, tracking the dependencies can quickly become tiresome. If you set this option to "yes," nessusd will automatically enable the plugins that are depended on.
use_mac_addr	Set this option to "yes" if you are testing your local network and each local host has a dynamic IP address (affected by DHCP or BOOTP), and all the tested hosts will be referred to by their MAC address.
Rules	Path to the rules database.

Now that we have configured our server to meet the specific needs of our organization, it is time to launch Nessusd into action. Mac OS X users need to launch the Nessus Server Configuration and click **Start Nessus Server**. Note, you will be prompted for the Administrator password. In the Windows environment, double click **Nessus Server Configuration** and ensure the Server IP is properly set. If you wish to only allow client connections from the localhost, leave the default configuration. Otherwise, enter the proper address and click **save**. See Figure 3.15. The interface will prompt you to restart the service and answer in the affirmative. The colored light on the top of the interface will indicate the status of the service: green for active and running normal, yellow for changing state and red for stopped. For UNIX environments execute the following command as root:

```
# nessusd -D
```

Figure 3.15 Windows Nessus Server Configuration

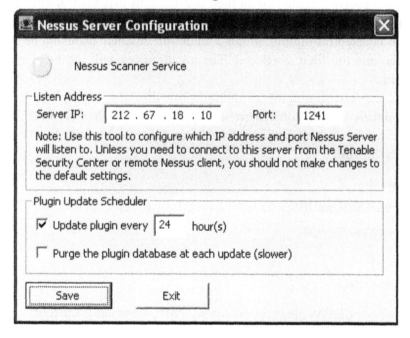

In any environment, it will take a few seconds for nessusd to return a from a status change. A progress bar will be shown as plugins and dependencies are loaded in Mac OS X and UNIX, while the yellow indicator will be shown in Windows. A quick *netstat* command will allow us to see if nessusd is indeed running on our system:

```
# netstat -an | grep 1241
tcp  0  0 0.0.0.0:1241  0.0.0.0:*  LISTEN
```

If the nessusd server is running on a multi-homed system or there is any other reason you want to force it to listen on a specific IP address, you can accomplish this via use of the *–a* switch. Additionally, you can specify on which port *nessusd* should listen. Since nessusd does not display a banner after a successful connection, it is quite easy to hide a Nessus server simply by modifying the listening port. An example of this type of configuration is as follows:

```
nessusd[0] -D -a 192.168.0.1 -p 41942
```

We've chosen port 41942 simply because attackers are less likely to scan that port unless they're doing a full 65,536 port scan. Most attackers use Nmap in its default mode, where it doesn't scan any TCP ports outside of the 1200 or so named in the accompanying nmap-services file.

Installing a Client

The power of the distributed Nessus architecture is found in accessing the Nessusd servers via clients. Nessus provides clients for all their distributions that share a unified feel. If the default options were used while installing on Mac OS X or Windows, the client was already installed. If you disabled this option, simply execute the installer again and de-select the server and make sure the client is selected. The install process will add the client to your operating system.

Linux operating systems require an additional install package, as well as the XWindows System (X11) installed. At this time, there is no Solaris NessusClient available, but other options will be explained later in this section. NessusClient is available for the following UNIX/Linux platforms:

- Debian 4
- Red Hat ES 4 and ES 5
- Fedora Core 7 and 8
- SuSE 10.3
- Ubuntu 7.10

The NessusClient RPM file is approximately 5MB in size and named in the format *NessusClient-X.X.X-OS.hardware.rpm*. The RPM can be downloaded from http://www.nessus. org/download/, as shown in Figure 3.3 earlier in this chapter. Install the appropriate RPM for your operating system. For example, to install in Ubuntu:

```
# rpm -ivh NessusClient-3.2.0-ubuntu710.i386.deb
```

This will install the client in /opt/nessus. To execute the client, execute the following command:

```
# NessusClient
```

One other option for a graphical client is to install Nessconnect. This is a client that only requires Java Runtime environment. It is similar to NessusClient in that it will execute scans and pass server options at run time. It also provides local session management, scan templates, and some extra reporting options including vulnerability trending.

The main drawback with this client is that it is much more memory intensive. The memory used for the client could go to improving scan performance. Additionally, the project is freshly out of its beta stage. This does not reflect on performance as much as documentation. At the time of this writing, its documentation was in its infancy. Figure 3.16 has a couple of snapshots of Nessconnect in action.

Figure 3.16 Nessconnect

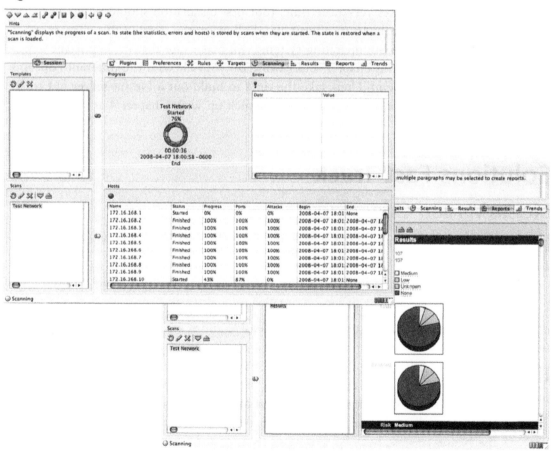

Summary

Nessus is a very powerful framework and comes equipped with many powerful methods of installation. Even still, some thought is required by the security analyst who will be managing the project to deploy Nessus into the enterprise. Before enterprise deployment, you need to consider questions involving which method to use for installation, what kind of hardware to deploy on, and how frequently updates should be done. This chapter serves to start you on the path, giving you reasoning and processes to enable you to make the best decisions in both design and implementation.

Nessus is best leveraged by a sound vulnerability assessment policy and process to back it up. The studious security analyst will spend some time researching the best way to leverage the flexible framework that makes Nessus perform so well.

Configuring Nessus takes very little time. Your first installation should be up and running within approximately 15 to 30 minutes. Following the steps in this chapter as highlighted for the appropriate operating systems will make sure that no important steps are missed. Read through this chapter, and familiarize yourself with the different concepts as well as the FAQs at the end. Then, take the time to build out a Nessus server just to see how easy it is. At that point, you will be ready to pick up with Chapter 4 as you venture into your first scan.

Solutions Fast Track

Nessus Version Comparison

☑ Nessus version 3 is as much as 16 times faster than version 2 and requires much less CPU and Memory to accomplish its scan.

☑ Nessus version 3 has introduced a number of protocol APIs to create a more comprehensive analysis of servers installed on a network.

☑ Nessus version 2 is still maintained by Tenable and is available for download.

Picking a Server

☑ A Nessus server should never be thought of as just another server from which arbitrary applications can be executed. Full system resources should be dedicated to the Nessus process, both for reasons of security and performance.

☑ Don't skimp on RAM or processors. When forced to decide, increase RAM.

☑ Place the Nessus server as close to the targets as possible with as few as possible network routing devices between the server and targets. Many firewalls and routers may be slowed or incapacitated due to the heavy bandwidth usage placed on them by a Nessus scan.

☑ Monitor scans closely when you first deploy Nessus, tuning Nessus to cause minimal strain on network resources.

Installation

☑ Software prerequisites are GTK for version 2.2.x. The additional requirements of X11 and OpenSSL for version 2.2.x and 3.x.

☑ Be sure to register with Tenable with an active email address when you download the install packages. You will receive an activation code to that email address.

☑ The Nessus server is available from Tenable for Mac OS X, Solaris, many Linux distributions and Windows.

Configuring Nessus

☑ Register your Nessus installation with Tenable to get the latest plugins.

☑ Create a server certificate for encrypted communications between the server and clients.

☑ User credentials are required for separation of duties and accountability.

☑ After starting the Nessus listener, check to make sure it is listening on port 1241 using *netstat -an*. The netstat command's arguments vary with platform.

Installing a Client

☑ Mac OS X and Windows will install a client with the server if the default options are used.

☑ Linux users can download NessusClient from http://www.nessus.org/download/ for a graphical client.

☑ Other operating systems with a window manager and a Java Runtime environment can use the third party client Nessconnect.

Frequently Asked Questions

Q: What should I be most concerned about when picking where a scan should originate?

A: There is much you should be concerned with and the answer is never an easy one. The first question you should ask yourself is what attack vector are you wishing to simulate? You might be interested in an internal view of your network, scan across VLAN segments, or even externally through a firewall to see what your exposure is to the outside world.

Q: How long will it take to scan a Class C address space?

A: There is no absolute answer to this. The factors impacting the answer in your case will be proximity of the targets to the Nessus server, host discovery methods, availability of the targets, general network load, and the applications running on the targets. Your mileage may vary.

Q: I have a unique installation question that wasn't answered previously; where can I go for help?

A: Read through the rest of this book. If your question still has not been answered, then visit www.nessus.org to read their FAQ or mailing lists.

## Chapter 4

Running Your First Scan

Solutions in this chapter:

- Preparing for Your First Scan
- Starting the Nessus Client
- Policy Configuration
- Target Selection
- Starting the Scan
- Nessus command line tool

☑ Summary

☑ Solutions Fast Track

☑ Frequently Asked Questions

Introduction

As you are probably already aware, the realm of security problems is large, varied, and rapidly changing. Nessus' success in this realm is a result of its extensively configurable design and its large, varied, and easily augmented library of scanning modules. It can provide a broad, bird's-eye view of a network, locate specific types of systems, investigate a particular service, or (if used without care) bludgeon the networked systems into complete collapse. The key to using the Nessus scanner safely and effectively is understanding not only your network, but the available options as well, and how they can impact your network.

This chapter walks you through the process of planning, configuring, and running your first Nessus scan. Even if you already have experience using the Nessus scanner, this chapter might still provide insight about the different configuration choices and how you can use them to improve your scan results.

Effective use of Nessus requires careful planning beforehand. The user should have a clear goal in mind and make use of all available information to refine the scanning approach (goal and approach to be refined at each step). In this chapter, we assume that you are scanning an isolated test network or a well-known subnet of your real network. Recommended settings for your first scan are provided in the *Solutions Fast Track* section at the end of this chapter. We will discuss the issues you need to address before you start any scan, and review each section of the Nessus client. Note that we will be using the client that is available from Tenable Network Security (www.tenablesecurity.com) for the purposes of this chapter because it interfaces best with the server. We will also explore what scan options are available from the command line.

Preparing for Your First Scan

Running Nessus requires planning and practice. In guiding you through your first practice scanning session with Nessus, this chapter will also take you through your first planning session for your scan. The issues addressed here: authorization, risk vs. benefit, providing authentication information, and plugin selection. All of these issues should be reviewed before *each and every* scan you perform.

Authorization

The most important thing to do before you launch a network scan is to obtain authorization, preferably in written form. Whom you should obtain this authorization from depends on the network you are testing. If you are planning to use Nessus on the internal network at your company, the CIO/CSO and senior administrative staff should be contacted. In the case of externally hosted systems, you might have to contact the hosting company or ISP and let them know about your intent to perform security scans against those systems. The tests that Nessus performs often look identical to a real attack by an unauthorized intruder, so make sure that the people monitoring system log files, intrusion detection systems (IDSs), and firewalls know when you are going to scan and from what address. There might be things you don't know about the network that could impact your scans. There might also be things about the network that could be impacted *by* your scans. If this first scan turns out to be an unannounced denial-of-service (DoS) attack, then there probably won't be a second scan.

Risk vs. Benefit

Information Technology and security can be viewed as an endless sequence of risk-benefit decisions. There is no such thing as complete security on an operational environment: some systems must be allowed to communicate with others, some services must be run, and some accounts must be allowed access. Broadly speaking, there are two kinds of risks associated with any Nessus scan: denial of service and missed information. Each type of risk must be balanced against certain benefits that might go with it (see Table 4.1).

Table 4.1 Risks vs. Benefits in a Nessus Scan

Risks	Benefits
Denial of Service	Decisions can be made to either upgrade the delicate system/service or better protect the services it provides with router ACLs or a firewall.
Missed information by failing to scan certain targets thoroughly	By narrowing your scan in terms of target and/or types of scan, you can run a much faster, safer scan that focuses on a specific goal.

Denial of Service

Nessus scans can be quite disruptive to certain targets. A poorly planned scan (or even a well-planned one) has the potential to shut down services, crash systems, confuse networks, and, in the case of some networked printers, generate large amounts of meaningless printout.

However, if your network contains such vulnerable targets, it is almost certainly preferable for you to discover them before someone outside the organization does. Remember that your decision to avoid activity that might disrupt your organization doesn't mean that others won't intentionally disrupt your organization. This is a very sensitive issue, obviously, and needs to be discussed with all parties that depend on the network. There are techniques to protect sensitive devices. One example is the many organizations that are forced to run legacy systems due to in-house developed software applications have made the choice to segment the service and the few users that require it off from the rest of the network.

Missing Information

As a rule, the more detailed a network scan is, the longer it takes to complete. Nessus has many options that allow you to scan more quickly by focusing your vulnerability scan on a particular target, service, or vulnerability. It also has a tremendously useful feature, the Knowledge Base, which can be leveraged to avoid scanning the same things repeatedly, among other things. Other Nessus options help ensure that your scans are unlikely to disrupt the normal functioning of their targets.

Each of these options allows you to improve the speed or the efficiency of your scan by accepting the risk of missing something because you weren't looking for it. When you focus a vulnerability scan on certain targets, services, or types of vulnerability, you are choosing *not* to look at other targets, services, or types of vulnerability. If you use the Knowledge Base to avoid repeating a test more than once a week, you are accepting the risk that no significant problems will appear during that week. If you choose to avoid scan strategies that might impact badly on operational systems, you won't know if those systems would be so impacted until someone else tries it.

If you could be completely certain about what was happening on your network, you wouldn't need to scan it. Most of your scans will be streamlined one way or another by narrowing the scope of discovery, but always be aware of what you have decided *not* to look for.

Even on a small network that you understand fully, the first scan should be a careful mapping expedition to build a picture of the network and its systems. For one thing, you might be wrong. You might not really know everything about the network. (Even if you do, think how much better you will feel when Nessus agrees with you.) Beyond that consideration, though, this first scan is your first live exercise with Nessus, so it's a good idea to keep it simple.

Providing Authentication Information

Certain types of protocols available for Nessus scans involve authentication of one sort or another and will be explored much more effectively if you provide Nessus with appropriate authentication information. In particular, many of the plugins used to scan for vulnerabilities in Windows systems assume that Nessus can access the Windows registries, and verify the versions of the installed DLLs. This can only happen if Nessus can provide authentication that will grant it registry access. If you want to examine network devices using the SNMP protocol, you will need to provide Nessus with the appropriate public and private community strings (which hopefully are not "public" and "private," respectively, but you and Nessus still need to know that).

When you are planning your scan, consider whether authentication could or should play a role, and have the appropriate information available. As we mentioned in the introduction, to get the most out of Nessus, careful planning is required. What type of scan are you hoping to accomplish? If you are looking for what vulnerabilities are on a system in total, authentication will enable a number of security tests to be run on the remote system. If you are looking for the perspective of a malicious user on the network, authentication will provide too detailed a view.

Plugin Selection

Plugin selection is addressed inside the Policy section, but it's important enough to be part of your initial planning. Tenable creates and maintains the vast majority of plugins available, but a few are contributed by third party authors and vary considerably in the way they are written and how they operate. Think about what you want to do, select plugins that might help you do it, and check the source code of the plugin to understand how it identifies vulnerabilities. If the plugin is designed to detect a known Trojan program, for example, it might simply test for an open port that the Trojan is known to use, or it might actually send data to the suspected Trojan and compare the response with known signatures. You need to know what the plugins are doing to interpret their findings correctly.

Notes from the Underground...

Security Officers

The current trend is to make the IT security function distinct from network (and system) support, IT security must exist in the framework developed by network (and system) administrators. Before you install Nessus, you should sit down with the rest of the IT support staff and get as accurate a picture of the network as possible. The network and system support staff might be able to save you a lot of time and trouble. If you know where firewalls are installed, you can make sure that you have a Nessus server *inside* the firewall to get a fast, accurate scan. If you know that a certain subnet has *only* Windows desktops on it, you can restrict your scan of that subnet to Windows vulnerabilities. (Of course, you will still want to check periodically to make sure that no one has installed something else without telling anyone—like the saying goes: *Trust, but verify!*)

Starting the Nessus Client

You need to start the client to tell the server what to do. The way Nessus was developed was to create a disturbed network of scanners, the servers, available to a few clients. The servers will do the actual scanning, while the clients will typically collect the logs and results for analysis.

To start the client, type **/opt/nessus/bin/NessusClient** on the Linux operating systems or click on the **Nessus Client** icon in the Linux window managers, Mac OS X, and Windows. You will get a display like the one in Figure 4.1.

Figure 4.1 Nessus Client

Tenable's Nessus Client is a commercial product that has moved to a unified view for all platforms. It is based on a clean source code branch and is optimized to interface with the Nessus 3 server without any extra features from legacy code. This new code base allows the server and clients to interact utilizing as few of the system resources as possible, but still provide the configurability and speed required. This allows users to easily navigate the interface and move from system to system without a learning curve. A couple of the features for this new client are an XML style results file format that can contain multiple scan results, including the policy and targets used to create the results, in a single file for easy exporting. The interface also is updated with scan results in real time, allowing the user to start investigating as quickly as possible, verses other clients waiting until the scan is complete before showing the actual results.

The top of the interface presents the user with a **Scan** and **Report** tab. The bottom of the GUI presents the user with a **Connect** button and a series of addition and subtraction buttons to add options to the Targets and Policy panes. To start, we need to connect to a server. By selecting the "Connect" button, we will be presented with the window shown in Figure 4.2. This interface allows us to select a server that contains the plugins and user accounts created during the install. Since this is a fresh install, the local host will be the only available server. The Mac and Windows version of the client already have the credentials configured to access the server locally. For the Linux environments, the configuration will need to be edited to match the login and password information entered by running the **/opt/nessus/sbin/nessus-adduser** command during the installation process outlined in the previous chapter.

Now select the server title and click **Connect**. During the server connection process, there will be a progress bar displayed while the plugins are downloaded to the client from the server. The delay time will vary, depending on the speed of the server and the number of plugins the authenticated user has access to. For the purposes of testing, this is adequate, but let's walk through the interface to see how a new server is added.

Figure 4.2 Nessus Connection Manager

Select the **+** to add a new server. Figure 4.3 illustrates the interface for the editing a server, whether it is new or existing. The hostname can be either an IP address or a qualified domain name. Leave the port filled as is, unless you altered the server configuration. Finally, enter the credentials to properly authenticate to that server. Make sure you enter the password correctly, but you will be notified during the connection process if the credentials do not match. When everything is set correctly, click the **Save** button. To remove a server, click the **−**. Unlike the localuser account, which the Nessus install process has created for us, the "localhost" server can be removed. The **Edit** button allows the changing to an existing server. To utilize this, click on the server name first, then select **Edit**.

Figure 4.3 Nessus Connection Editor

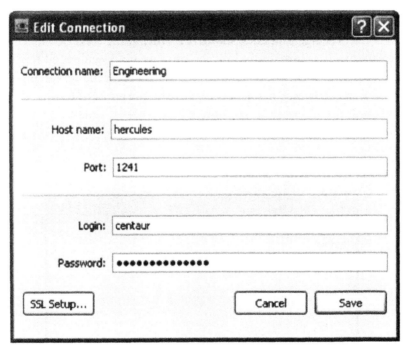

Policies

One of the most important improvements Tenable has brought to Version 3 of the scanner is the policy feature. This allows a client the ability to conduct a variety of scans, which are highly configurable, from a single interface with minimal impact to the user. Note that any options set by the policy used to conduct a scan will override the settings described in Chapter 3 during the server configuration. Older versions of Nessus had a cumbersome method to accomplish the same goals, but lack in one important feature, portability. Tenable's Version 3.2 introduced a new format for scan results called the .nessus format. It is an XML style file, which contains not only the results for the scan, but the policy that was used to conduct the scan as well. This allows users to create a policy, conduct a scan, and then transfer the results to another systems or user for analysis, keeping all the history in a single file. The next section will discuss how to create a scan policy in great detail, because this feature can be used for many compliance issues that face organizations today. Tenable has already created two policies available to those that purchase the Direct Feed that address compliance on Windows and UNIX servers.

The Nessus client comes with 2 policies, Default scan policy and Microsoft Patches. They are listed on the right hand panel of the client, under the heading "Select a scan Policy", which will be referred as the Policy panel. Use these policies as references when you start to develop your own. To edit an existing policy, select one from the Policy panel and click the **Edit** button under that same pane. To remove a policy, select a policy one and click the − button. To create a new policy, simply click the + button under the Policy pane. Figure 4.4 shows what the user should see when a new policy is started. Note, the two policies provided with the installation were created on an older version of a client and thus do not have all the options that a fresh policy will have.

The Policy editor has a number of tabs along the top of the interface, and each tab has a number of fields for the user to edit. The rest of this section will go into the details that will determine how the scan for this policy will be carried out. By creating a new policy and adjusting it to fit the needs of your network, you will have a template than can be easily adjusted for all your scanning needs. Note that no action can be done to any of the policies until successfully connected to a Nessus server, and any setting in the Policy will supersede the settings on the server.

Figure 4.4 Nessus Connection Editor

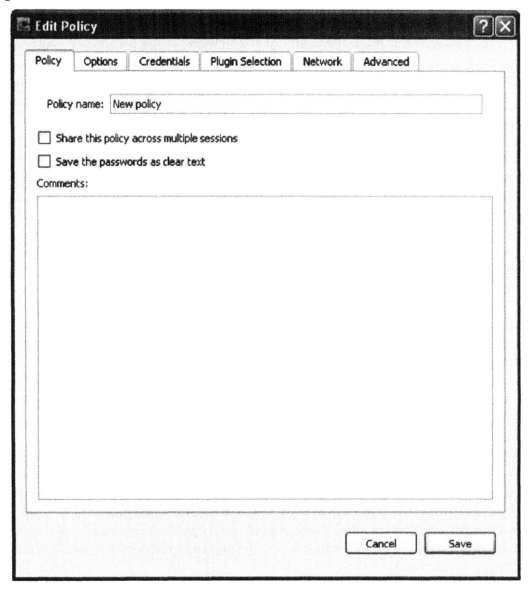

Policy Tab

This first tab will determine how the policy will be saved and how some of the results will be saved. The "Policy name" field is for naming the policy. This will be displayed in the Policy Panel when the Nessus Client starts, if the "Share this policy across multiple sessions" is selected. Note that policies can have the same name, so be careful to give each policy a descriptive, unique name.

The check box labeled **Share this policy across multiple sessions** will allow this policy to be used again, with a different target list. For example, let's use the network that was depicted in Figure 3.2 in the previous chapter. We could create a policy on a laptop, scan the Engineering segment, then move the laptop physically behind the firewall of the Headquarters network and use the same policy on this set of targets. This option only refers to sessions on the local workstation, for the user that creates the policy, and not across the network of scanners. Make sure the policy is saved via the main menu with "Save" or "Save As…" from the "File" menu. Otherwise, this policy will only be available for this scan session, and will be lost as soon as the client is closed.

The next option, called "Save passwords as clear text" is important if you plan on conducting a scan on one system and analyze the results on a second. The default behavior for the Nessus Client is to save passwords discovered during the scan process to be encrypted, and stored in the .nessus results file. The key to decrypt these passwords stays with the system that conducted the scan. Therefore, the second system analyzing the results will be able to see that there is a password issue, but not be able to decrypt the password. Enable "Save passwords as clear text" to have the password stored with the .nessus results, and not require a key to see them. Keep in mind the security implications of having this detailed login information in a single location. If the passwords are stored in clear text, and the results file is lost, anyone can find these passwords with a text editor.

The final field in this tab is a comment field. This can be any text you wish to help give context to the policy. For example, the Microsoft Patches policy states what the policy was created for and what is required to properly execute this policy on a network.

Options Tab

The Options tab allows global parameters to be set for modules being run by the scanner. Figure 4.5 shows the interface once the "Options" tab is selected.

Figure 4.5 Policy Editor, Options Tab

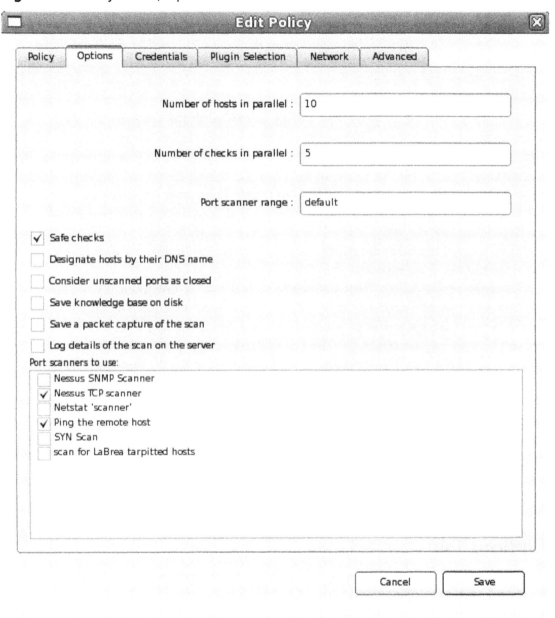

The first three options will have the most affect on the system performance and scan time. "Number of hosts in parallel" refers to the number of hosts that will be scanned at the same time. Once the scan starts, the first 10 live hosts will start to be interrogated. The 11th host will not start until one of the first 10 is completely scanned. The "Number of checks in parallel" tells the client how many plugins will be ran against a host at a time. Therefore, if the default settings are used, the Nessus client will be conducting about 50 checks at any one time. The final option to affect performance is the "Port scanner range". The default port list is 1–1024. For example, to scan just for netbios, use a range such as "137–139". To make the port scan for netbios a little more complete, we can include a couple more ports by using commas, "137–139,135,445". The order we enter the ports does not matter and make sure that the quotes are left out when entering the ranges into the Nessus client.

Notes from the Underground...

Scan Performance

Something to consider when tuning these three options is that while your scanner could be newer with lots of system resources, it might be able to handle say 200 checks at a time (10 hosts with 20 checks) without any problem. But if you are scanning a network with legacy systems, the 20 concurrent checks on an older system might cause performance issues on the target. It might be better to scan 40 hosts with 5 checks.

Port scanning will affect the scan time in that the default list of ports is a little under 9000 ports. If the port range is increased to include all ports, each port scan will take about 7 times as long. Couple this with the lag time generated by the large number of hosts be protected with personal firewalls, this is the one area that can greatly affect scan time.

"Safe Checks" is an option that improves the impact of a vulnerability scan on the target hosts. Over the years, Tenable has compiled a list of devices that can be adversely affected when scanned. "Safe Checks" will prevent these devices from being scanned. This option tells Nessus to use the banner version numbers from the discovery phase to determine if a host is vulnerable to an attack. This will leave a much smaller footprint on a target host, but will also result in many more false positives. Many venders, like Red Hat, do not always update version numbers when a security update is installed, thus, scan time will improve, but the amount of time to sift through the results, removing the false positives is much higher. By default, this option is enabled.

The Nessus results are typically sorted by IP address. To have the results display hostnames instead and sorted by their hostname, enable the option "Designate hosts by their DNS name". This will also affect scan performance if the target list is large, and the DNS tables are not updated properly. The delay in resolving an IP address can take as long as 12 seconds before timing out.

"Consider unscanned ports as closed" will tell the Nessus scanner that all other ports not included in the port range scan as closed. This prevents all plugins that are targeted against ports outside that range from running. For example, if the port range for the scan is left at the default (1–1024), any plugins that check the port range of 6000–6010 for open X11 displays will not launch due to Nessus believing that those ports are closed. Without this setting, the port scan will be conducted on ports 1–1024, and then Nessus will progress to executing the plugins selected in the policy. Those plugins will scan the target host on just the ports it is concerned with, and add that information to the knowledge base for future plugins. If the ports are open, the plugins will then run their tests. Use this option if you are scanning out of a proxy firewall and want to leave things to port 80/443 or if your target is behind a firewall and we want to target known open ports. Otherwise, it will spend time probing ports that are closed and go into a wait state for responses.

Nessus can remember what it learns from a scan, and reuse that information during subsequent scans. We showed an example with the port scanning in the previous paragraph. Nessus calls this the knowledge base. Selecting **Save knowledge base on disk** option tells the scanner to save the knowledge base to the server for later use. Chapter 9 goes into further details about this feature.

"Save a packet capture of the scan" option will save packet traces of the scan. These records can be useful in diagnosing the network you are scanning. These packet traces can be used to see if the results coming back from a host are true or being spoofed from an intrusion prevention system (IPS), determine which plugin interacts poorly with a sensitive system, and proving if a target was scanned or not. Keep in mind that the number of packets generated during a scan is huge. If you enable this option and rip off a full Nessus scan of a class B address space, make sure you have the disk space to handle the volume of packet data that will generated.

To save log results of the scan to the server, select the "Log details of the scan on the server" option. Otherwise, these log results are saved to the host conducting the scan.

The final option we will discuss is how to interact with the Nessus port scanner. Table 4.2 will describe these options.

Table 4.2 Port Scanner Options

Nessus SNMP Scanner	Scan targets looking for SNMP responses. If this setting is used, then plugins that search for known SNMP vulnerabilities will be used. For example many Cisco router checks use the SNMP version string to determine if a target is vulnerable. These plugins will not be run if this option is not enabled.

Continued

Table 4.2 Continued. Port Scanner Options

Nessus TCP Scanner	Utilize Nessus' built in TCP scanner to identify open ports. This scanner is optimized for the Nessus environment and has some self-tuning features. Further configuration for this scanner can be found under the advanced features tab. This is the default port scanner.
Netstat 'scanner'	Make use of the netstat program to find open ports. It relies on the netstat port being open or a SSH connection can be established to the target with credentials provided in the next tab. This is intended for UNIX-based systems.
Ping the remote host	If this option is enabled, then the port scanner will determine if the hosts is live before conducting a port scan. Further configuration as to which type of "pings" can be found under the Advanced tab. If this option is disabled, then all hosts will be treated as if they are firewalled. Scan times will increase if this option is turned off, but a more complete picture will be painted in the results.
SYN Scan	SYN packets are sent to the port and waits for a SYN/ACK in reply, or the first 2 parts of a three-way handshake. If the reply is not received in the defined time range, the port is considered close. This type of scan is good for interrogating systems behind a firewall, and is quicker than the TCP scanner. This also has the adverse affect of leaving resources tied up on the target because the connection is never terminated properly. In some cases, these open connections will tie resources for 255 seconds on the target host.
scan for LaBrea tarpitted hosts	LaBrea tarpits are a form of a honeypot. They are deployed to slow the discovery phase of an attack by representing fake hosts. Nessus will attempt to determine if every host it discovers is a real system or one of these systems designed to slow an attacker. Again, the more you know about your network, the better you can configure your policy. In most cases, this options should be disabled.

Long time users might remember when Nessus utilized the third party port scanning tool, Nmap to accomplish the OS fingerprinting and determining open ports of remote systems. Nmap is no longer part of the Nessus scanner and is not recommended for integration into the Nessus environment. The main reason is that the latest version of Nessus spawns a thread for each host it scans. So it is designed to conserve the systems recourses within each thread. Nmap is designed to scan large network blocks quickly, not really with system resources in mind.

Tenable has found other ways to adapt to the system resource friendly model. To get the most accurate determination for a remote host, Nessus users should use credentials inside the Nessus scan. We will go into more details in the next section about credentials, but basically, you are allowing Nessus to login to the remote host to run further tests. It is trivial to determine the operating system at this level, and the scan results will also benefit by verifying patch levels of applications by inspecting the DLLs.

If Nessus cannot login to the remote system, fingerprinting is accomplished with Xprobe, based on Ofir Arkin's ICMP fingerprinting research. Xprobe uses ICMP packets instead of Nmap's TCP packets to determine the remote hosts operating system, with as high a level of accuracy.

Credentials Tab

One of the features that Nessus was the first to pioneer was the ability to conduct local checks on a system during a remote vulnerability assessment, called the hybrid scan. The credentials tab is how Nessus enables this. Giving Nessus credentials to the target system will allow for a more thorough testing of each targets local system, like the Windows Registry.

The credentials tab is basically a drop down menu. By selecting one of the protocols, different options will be available in the area below the drop down menu. See Figure 4.6 for the Windows credentials. Windows, SSH, Kerberos, Oracle, and clear text are the protocols supported.

Figure 4.6 Policy Editor, Credentials Tab

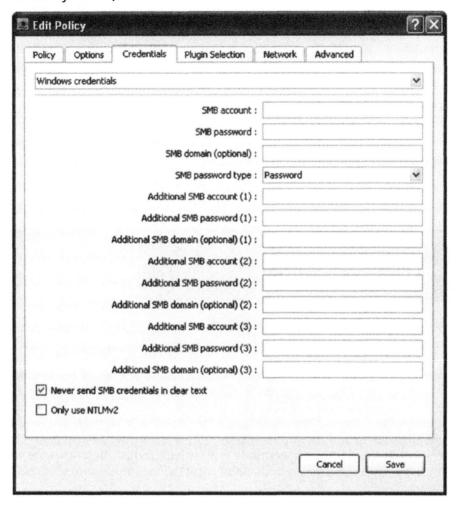

The Windows credentials allows for multiple domains to be tested at a single time. Simply enter the username, password, and optionally, the domain name that the target host is aware of. A total of 4 can be entered. The domain name is only needed if the account name is different on the domain from that on the Nessus server. Regardless of the credentials used in the policy, Nessus always attempts to log into a Windows server with the following combinations:

- Administrator account without a sufficient password
- Random username and password to test Guest accounts
- No username or password to test Null sessions

Two important options to consider are at the bottom of the interface. The first, "Never send SMB credentials in clear text", helps prevent the communication channel between the Nessus scanner and the target to be more secure. This prevents the communication session from being sniffed to gather login information. The second is "Only use NTLMv2". NTLMv2 is cryptographically more secure than NTLM or LANMAN. Nessus will always attempt to log into a Windows system with NTLMv2, and this option will prevent the other authentication methods from being utilized. When windows credentials are provided, a number of extra checks are enabled. The most impressive of which are DLL version checks to see if the proper patches have been installed. This basically eliminates false positives created by old versions of code running on a target system.

Security Best Practices...

Creating an Account for Auditing

By default, remote registry access is typically only available to Domain administrators. While it would be possible to create an account on a domain, and give it domain administrator privileges; it would not be the most secure method to enable local tests by your Nessus scanner. It is a poor security practice to have more administrator accounts than absolutely necessary, but just as poor to share credentials for any purpose. An interesting side affect of conducting a hybrid scan with administrator privileges is that results are often less accurate than when done with an account that has just the necessary privileges. For example, it is difficult to test file shares for incorrect file permissions because the domain administrator has much more access than a normal user.

On the other hand, it is a common mistake to create a local account for Nessus scans that don't have enough privileges to log on remotely and do anything of value. By default, Windows XP and Vista will assign new local accounts "Guest" privileges if they are logged in remotely.

Ty Gast, of the Security Assurance Group, wrote a terrific white paper on how to create a couple accounts for Nessus testing that have just the right level of privilege to give accurate scan results and not allow excess rights to the file system. It is called "Utilizing domain Credentials to Enhance Nessus Scans, and can be downloaded at: www.nessus.org/documentation/nessus_domain_whitepaper.pdf.

SSH can be utilized to obtain local information from remote UNIX systems for patch auditing and compliance checks. There are fields for username and password for the account that will perform the checks on the target system. A more secure method would be to create SSH public and private keys to properly authenticate to the system. Nessus allows for this as well. Much like the Windows section illustrated, this account should be dedicated to the Nessus scanner and have the appropriate privileges. Keep in mind that Nessus 3.2 has extended support for different encryption algorithms. The algorithms now supported are "blowfish-cbc", "aes128-cbc", "aes192-cbc", "aes256-cbc", and "3des-cbc". Some commercial variants of SSH do not have support for the blowfish algorithm, possibly for export reasons. It is also possible to configure an SSH server to only accept certain types of encryption. Check your SSH server to be certain the correct algorithm is supported.

The Nessus implementation of Kerberos authentication is for SSH only and supports the "des-cbc" encryption algorithm. Nessus also supports use of Kerberos authentication in a Windows domain. To configure this, the IP address of the Kerberos Domain Controller (actually, the IP address of the Windows 2003 Active Directory Server) must be provided. Reverse DNS lookups must be properly configured for this to work. The Kerberos interaction method must be *gssapi-with-mic*. An overview of how Nessus interacts with Kerberos is as follows:

- End-user gives the IP of the KDC

- *nessusd* asks *sshd* if it supports Kerberos authentication

- *sshd* says yes

- *nessusd* requests a Kerberos ticket granting ticket, along with login and password

- Kerberos sends a ticket back to *nessusd*

- *nessusd* gives the ticket to *sshd*

- *nessusd* is logged in

The Nessus client also supports Oracle and clear text protocols. The editing of these fields is similar to the Windows and SSH options. The clear text protocols supported are telnet, *rsh*, and *rexec*.

Plugin Selection Tab

Nessus has over 20,000 security checks, and all of them can be found in the Plugin Selections tab of the policy editor. Plugins can be found by "family" or individually by ID or name. Figure 4.7 shows the interface in the policy editor for the plugin selections. Almost all Nessus plugins are written in Nessus Attack Scripting Language (NASL). NASL was designed specifically for developing Nessus plugins and includes a function library that makes it very convenient for performing security tests. Refer to Chapter 11 for more information about the NASL language.

Figure 4.7 Policy Editor, Plugin Selection Tab

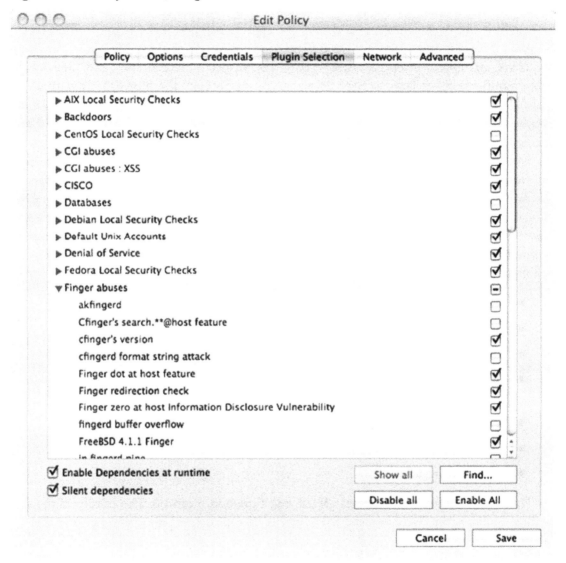

When opening the Plugin Selection tab, the user will see the full list of "families" that the each plugin belongs to. Figure 4.7 illustrates expanding a family and displaying a list of plugins that belong to a family. Selecting the **expand** icon to the left of the family name will show each of plugins that are in that family. The check boxes on the right of each plugin are for selecting a plugin for use in the policy. The check box to the right of a plugin family title will toggle all plugins in that family. Figure 4.7 also shows that when all plugins in a family are select, the family title check box will be checked, if all are off, the check box is blank, and if some of the plugins are selected, a – "will be displayed. Once the plugins are displayed, you can select and deselect each individual plugin as you wish.

Under the list of plugins, there are a series of buttons. The first button we will discuss is the "Find" button. Nessus has provided a method for searching all the plugins installed on the server. By clicking on **Find** the search interface similar to Figure 4.8 is displayed. The pull down menu will allow the user to search for plugin by ID, Name, or Family. The interface will return any plugins matching the search criteria. To return to the plugin family display, select the **Show all** button. The "Show all" button is normally unavailable until a search is conducted. Finally, to enable all plugins, select **Enable All**, and to disable all plugins, you guessed it, select **Disable all**.

Figure 4.8 Policy Editor, Plugin Selection Search Interface

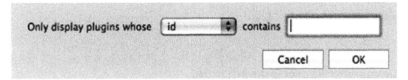

Damage and Defense...

Plugins and DoS

Plugins are considered dangerous if the testing process could cause the target application or operating system to crash. The plugins in the DoS category are designed to test for issues that would allow an unauthorized intruder to crash or disable network resources. Most of the plugins in the DoS category perform the test by actually launching a DoS attack on the target system and verifying that it no longer responds. Obviously, you don't want to do this in a production environment without careful prearrangement. It is not uncommon for a plugin that safely checks for a single vulnerability to inadvertently trigger a crash in another application or the operating system.

Many plugins depend on the data obtained from other plugins to perform their specific vulnerability tests. If plugin A depends on plugin B, and you enable A, but do not enable B, plugin A will not be launched. If you check the box labeled **Enable dependencies at runtime**, Nessus will make sure that all plugins that your selection requires are enabled automatically. "Silent dependencies" will limit the amount of plugin data included in the report. If this option is checked, the list of dependencies is not included in the report. Please note, as new plugins are received during the update process, they will be added to a plugin family automatically, but they will not be enabled until explicitly selected.

If you wish to learn more about a specific plugin, the group at Tenable has an expanded function search available on their website, as seen in Figure 4.9. It is available at www.nessus.org/plugins/index.php?view=search. The interface allows the searching for plugins by name, report, family, author, CVE ID, Bugtraq ID, Plugin ID, and other cross-references. When the results are returned, the user can click on either the ID or the plugin title to get detailed information. It will provide the description that will be provided in the .nessus report if found to be true, a link to the actual NASL source, as well as links to other resources on the internet that will further describe the issue or provide patch information. Figure 4.10 shows an example of the detailed search results from the Nessus.org web site.

Figure 4.9 Nessus.org Plugin Search Utility

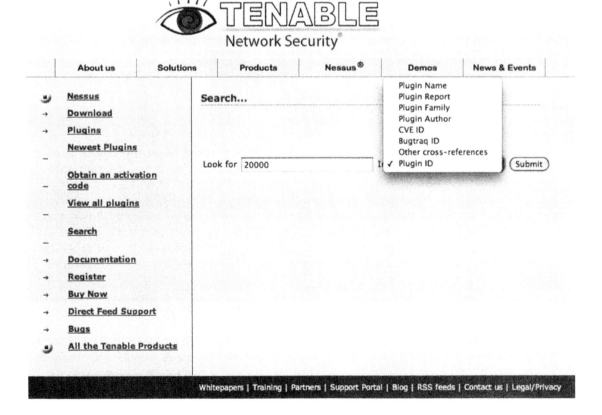

Figure 4.10 Nessus.org Plugin Search Utility Results

| About us | Solutions | Products | Nessus® | Demos | News & Events |

Nessus
→ **Download**
→ **Plugins**
Newest Plugins

Obtain an activation code
View all plugins

Search

→ **Documentation**
→ **Register**
→ **Buy Now**
→ **Direct Feed Support**
→ **Bugs**
All the Tenable Products

Vulnerability in Plug and Play Could Allow Remote Code Execution and Local Elevation of Privilege (905749)

This script is Copyright (C) 2005-2007 Tenable Network Security
View the source code of this plugin here

Family   Windows : Microsoft Bulletins
Nessus Plugin ID   20000
Bugtraq ID   15065
CVE ID   CVE-2005-2120

Description:

Synopsis :

A flaw in the Plug and Play service may allow an authenticated attacker to execute arbitrary code on the remote host and therefore elevate his privileges.

Description :

The remote host contain a version of the Plug and Play service which contains a vulnerability in the way it handles user-supplied data.

An authenticated attacker may exploit this flaw by sending a malformed RPC request to the remote service and execute code within the SYSTEM context.

Solution :

Microsoft has released a set of patches for Windows 2000 and XP :

http://www.microsoft.com/technet/security/bulletin/ms05-047.mspx

Risk factor :

Medium / CVSS Base Score : 6
(AV:R/AC:L/Au:R/C:C/A:C/I:C/B:N)

Whitepapers | Training | Partners | Support Portal | Blog | RSS feeds | Contact us | Legal/Privacy

Network Tab

The Network tab helps adjust how Nessus uses the network during the scan process. These settings can be adjusted to maximize results with minimal network impact. By default, Nessus will use whatever processing and networking power the hardware will allow.

Often, this will cause the system to become unresponsive and overloaded. These settings shown in Figure 4.11 will help fine-tune the scan process to the systems needs.

Figure 4.11 Policy Editor, Network Tab

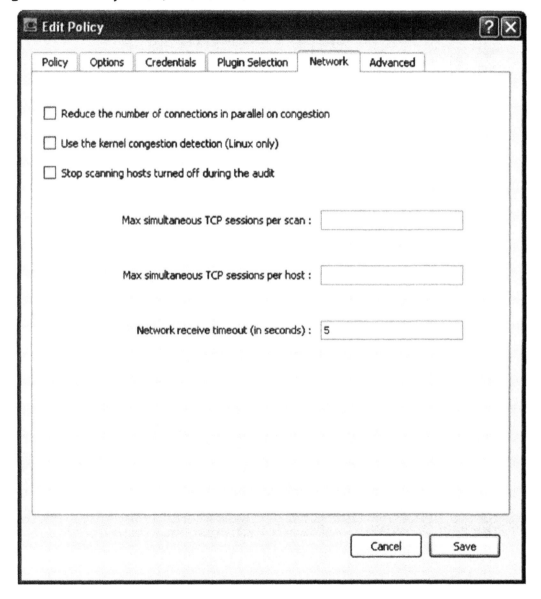

The Network tab has three check boxes and three form fields. The first check box, "Reduce the number of connections in parallel on congestion", tells the Nessus process to detect when the network pipe is approaching its capacity. If it detects this, it will throttle back the scan rate to accommodate and alleviate the congestion. Once the congestion has passed, Nessus will automatically throttle the scan rate back up to use the available space within the network pipe again. "Use the kernel congestion detection" allows Nessus to monitor the CPU and other internal timers for congestion, and then scale back accordingly. This is for Linux environments only. Like the previous check box, the scan process will ramp back up as available CPU time becomes available. Finally, "Stop scanning hosts turned off during the audit" is used to help make the scan more efficient. Often a host will be shut down in mid scan, or become unresponsive after a Denial of Service check. Continuing to scan these hosts will cause unnecessary traffic across the network and delay the next host from being started in the scan process. Enable this option to have Nessus detect when a host is unresponsive and discontinue the scan.

The first of the three form fields is "Max simultaneous TCP sessions per scan". It will limit the number of TCP packets that are sent from the scanner at the same time, for the entire scan. Setting this to a lower number will help prevent the number of threads from getting out of hand and will often improve results. This is an important field to adjust if rate limiting network equipment might be interfering with the scan. "Max simultaneous TCP sessions per host" is similar to the previous but TCP sessions are limited by host. This can improve results on legacy targets and can prevent the target from dropping packets due to limitations on the host and the speed of incoming packets. Finally, "Network receive timeout" is the default time Nessus will wait for a response from a target, unless the plugin specifically specifies otherwise. If you are scanning over a slow network, you might want to increase this number from the default value of 5 seconds.

Advanced Tab

The Advanced tab is unique in that it is the only interface that will change depending on a number of factors. The biggest being which type of plugin feed the server was registered with. A server with the Direct Plugin feed will have more available Advanced options than a scanner with the Registered Plugins feed. The list may also change depending on what plugins are added or modified in the future. Figure 4.12 shows the available option headers for Mac OS X, with the Registered Plugins feed, from the drop down menu. Fewer options are available on the Windows system, while more are available on the Linux client. This is due to the number of third party tools that are available for each operating system. Hydra and Nikto are easily configured in the Linux environments, thus creating more options.

Figure 4.12 Policy Editor, Advanced Tab

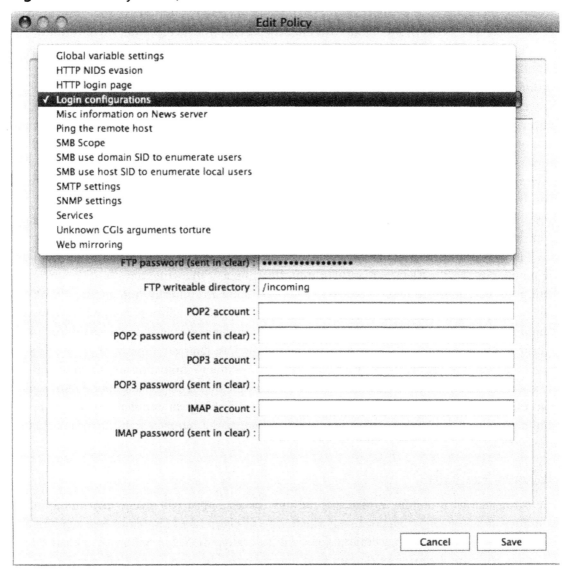

Table 4.4 shows a detailed list of options available with the version 3.2 of the client. The shaded rows in blue depict options only available on the Direct Plugin feed for Nessus. For more information on Hydra and Nikto, refer to their man pages or go to the web sites listed in Table 4.3 for more information. At the time of this writing, these third party tools can only interact with the Linux client, even though they can be installed on Mac OS X. Hydra is the defacto standard for brute force login attempts. It supports the most common protocols including POP3, IMAP, SMB, MS-SQL, MYSQL, and Cisco auth. Nikto is a web

server scanner that looks for over 3500 potentially dangerous files, 250 server specific problems, and over 900 fingerprints for determining server versions. Nikto A great addition if you are not conducting a hybrid scan with credentials.

Table 4.3 Third party tools project websites

Hydra	http://freeworld.thc.org/thc-hydra/
Nikto	http://www.cirt.net/nikto2

Notes from the Underground...

TCP/IP Basics

Making good decisions about port scanner options requires a basic understanding of the network protocols that underlie these scans. Communications protocols can be divided into *connection-oriented* and *connectionless* varieties. Connectionless protocols are the simpler of the two. Information is transmitted from the source without any particular measures to ensure that the information is received uncorrupted (or at all) by the destination. Connection-oriented protocols, by contrast, don't send information until the source of the transmission has contacted the destination and received confirmation that the destination is prepared to accept the transmission. Once the transmission of information begins, all packets (chunks of information) transmitted are either acknowledged by the destination or retransmitted from the source.

In TCP/IP, the connection-oriented protocol is TCP and the connectionless protocols are UDP and ICMP. Under the TCP protocol, the transmission source initializes communication by sending the destination a packet with the SYN flag set. The destination then responds with a packet with the ACK flag set to acknowledge that it received the source's SYN packet, and with the SYN flag set. The source then sends another packet with the ACK flag set to acknowledge that the source received the destination's packet. The entire exchange of:

- SYN source to destination
- SYN-ACK destination to source
- ACK source to destination

is called the *three-way handshake*. Once this exchange is completed, a *connection* is established. Establishing a connection provides a more reliable communications

Continued

channel, but it does so at the cost of extra packet exchanges and internal bookkeeping to insure that all of the information is acknowledged. A formal, although different, exchange is used at the end of the communication to *tear down* the connection.

The most common methods of checking for ports on a remote system are *connect scans* and *SYN scans*. Connect scans attempt to establish a connection, as described here, from the host to possible ports on the destination host. SYN scans send the initial SYN packet of the three-way handshake to possible ports on the destination host and then receive (or don't receive) a SYN-ACK packet in response. However, instead of completing the connection with that ACK packet of the three-way handshake, the scanner simply moves on to send a SYN packet to the next target port. The destination eventually times out and stops waiting for the ACK packet.

Since SYN scans involve the exchange of only two packets, and connect scans require the exchange of four packets (three to establish the connection and a RST, or reset, to tear it down), SYN scans are faster. In addition, they are stealthier, since most operating systems are designed to recognize and log only successful connections. However, many NIDSs treat the stealthy SYN scans as hostile probes and will raise an alarm or even block the scanner from its targets. Rapid SYN scanning can also be a DoS attack, since it can consume large amounts of recourses on the target host, even crash some platforms.

Table 4.4 Advanced Tab Options

Do not Scan Fragile Devices

Scan network Printers	This option will force Nessus to scan all printers with a full set of tests that the scanner deems necessary. Older printers will often print all available paper during some of the tests, while newer printers will require a reboot depending on the embedded operating system. The default is to NOT scan network printers
Scan Novell Netware hosts	This option will force Nessus to scan all hosts deemed to be running Novell to be scanned with all plugins necessary. Older Novell NetWare installs are prone to crashing when having their servers fingerprinted. The default is to NOT scan Novell NetWare hosts.

Continued

Table 4.4 Continued. Advanced Tab Options

Global Variable Settings	
Probe services on every port	Nessus attempts to map each open port with a service. In some rare cases, this can cause the service to become unresponsive or have unforeseen side effects. This option is enabled by default.
Do not log in with user accounts not specified in the policy	Used to prevent account lockouts if your password policy is set to lock out accounts after several invalid attempts. This option is disabled by default.
Enable CGI scanning	Activates CGI checking. Disabling this option will greatly improve the time a scan will take to complete on a local network. The default value is enabled.
Network type	Allows the user to specify if the network being scanned utilizes public routable IP addresses, private non-internet IP addresses, or a mix of these values. Select "Mixed" if you are using RFC 1918 addresses and have multiple routers within your network. Mixed is the default value.
Enable experimental scripts	Causes plugins that are considered experimental to be utilized in the scan. This should not be used in a production network setting. The default value is disabled.
Thorough tests (slow)	This will cause NASL scripts to "work harder". For example when Nessus finds an open SMB file shares, the script can analyze 3 levels deep instead of the default 1 level. This will present the analyst with more results, and be more intrusive on the network, increasing the risk of denial of service. The default value is disabled.
Report verbosity	When Nessus creates the results report, more information will be provided with a higher setting. The default value is "Normal".

Continued

Table 4.4 Continued. Advanced Tab Options

Report paranoia	In some cases, Nessus cannot definitively determine if a host is vulnerable to a flaw or not. If the report paranoid is set to "Paranoid" then the flaw will always be reported in these cases of doubt. The setting of "Avoid false alarm" will not report the issue at all in the case of doubt. "Normal is the middle ground between these two settings. The default value is "Normal".
Log verbosity	A higher setting will cause more detailed information to be provided in the scan log. The log file can be found in $NESSUS/var/nessus/. The default value is "Normal".
Debug level	The two available levels is either "0" or "1". Set this option to "1" to enable debugging to assist with troubleshooting a Nessus scan. The default value is "0".
HTTP User-Agent	Specifies which browser type Nessus will impersonate while scanning http and https servers. The default value depends on which operating system the client is running on.
ICCP/COTP TSAP Addressing (Direct Feed Users)	This drop down menu item deals specifically with SCADA checks. It determines a Connection Oriented Transport Protocol (COTP) Transport Service Access Points (TSAP) value on an ICCP server by trying possible values. The default value for both start and stop are set to "8".
HTTP login page	
Login page	If the HTTP server on the target requires authentication, this option would specify the HTTP path (not the file system path) of the login page. Nessus will use this page to authenticate to the HTTP server before performing testing. Default value is "/"
Login form	If the HTTP server on the target requires authentication, this option would specify the HTTP form for login. Nessus will use this information to authenticate to the HTTP server before performing testing. Default is left blank

Continued

Table 4.4 Continued. Advanced Tab Options

Login form fields	If the HTTP server on the target requires authentication, this option would specify the form field names for login. Nessus will use this information to authenticate to the HTTP server before performing testing. The %USER% and %PASS% variables are defined in the Login configurations drop down in the Advanced tab, under HTTP account and HTTP password. Default is user=%USER%&pass=%PASS%
Login Configurations	
HTTP Account	Sets the %USER% value for logging into HTTP pages from the HTTP login page. Default value is blank.
HTTP password (sent in clear)	Sets the %PASS% value for logging into HTTP pages from the HTTP login page. During testing, the password will be passed as clear text. Default value is blank.
NNTP account	Sets the %USER% value for logging into Network News Transport Protocol (NTTP) servers. Default value is blank.
NNTP password (sent in clear)	Sets the %PASS% value for logging into Network News Transport Protocol (NNTP) servers. During testing, the password will be passed as clear text. Default value is blank.
FTP account	Sets the %USER% value from logging in FTP servers. The default value is "anonymous".
FTP password (sent in clear)	Sets the %PASS% value for logging into FTP servers. During testing, the password will be passed as clear text. The default value is "nessus@nessus.org" and will not be displayed.
FTP writeable directory	During FTP testing, Nessus may attempt to detect writable directories and/or upload test files to the FTP server. The directory specified here will be used as the upload/writable directory on the target FTP server. Default is set to "/incoming".
POP2 account	Sets the %USER% value for logging into POP2 servers. Default value is blank.

Continued

Table 4.4 Continued. Advanced Tab Options

POP2 password (sent in clear)	Sets the %PASS% value for logging into POP2 servers. During testing, the password will be passed as clear text. Default value is blank.
POP3 account	Sets the %USER% value for logging into POP3 servers. Default value is blank.
POP3 password (sent in clear)	Sets the %PASS% value for logging into POP3 servers. During testing, the password will be passed as clear text. Default value is blank.
IMAP account	Sets the %USER% value for logging into IMAP servers. Default value is blank.
IMAP password (sent in clear)	Sets the %PASS% value for logging into IMAP servers. During testing, the password will be passed as clear text. Default value is blank.
Misc information on News Server	
From address	Nessus will attempt to post a news message to Network News Transport Protocol (NNTP) servers, and will test if it is possible to post a message to upstream news servers as well. This field is the email address that Nessus will use to post a message to the news server. This message will delete itself automatically after a short period of time. The default value is "Nessus <listme@listme.dsbl.org>".
Test group name regex	The name of the news group(s) that will receive a test message from the specified address. The name can be specified as a regular expression (regex) so that the message can be posted to multiple news groups simultaneously. For example, the default value *"f[a-z]\.tests?"* will broadcast a mail message to all news groups with names that begin with any letter (from "a" to "z") and end with ".tests" (or some variation that matched the string). The question mark acts as an optional wild character. The default value is "f[a-z]\.tests?"

Continued

Table 4.4 Continued. Advanced Tab Options

Max crosspost	The maximum number of news servers that will receive the test posting, regardless of the number of name matches. For example, if the Max crosspost is "7", the test message will only be sent to seven news servers, even if there are 2000 news servers that match the regex in this field. Default value is "7".
Local distribution	Nessus will only attempt to post a message to the local news servers if this option is enabled. Otherwise, an attempt will be made to forward the message upstream. This is enabled by default.
No archive	If this option is selected, Nessus will request to not archive the test message. Otherwise, the message will be archived like any other posting. This is disabled by default.
Modbus/TCP Coil Access (Direct Feed Users)	This drop-down menu item is dynamically generated by the SCADA plugins available with the Direct Feed. Modbus uses a function code of 1 to read "coils" in a Modbus slave. Coils represent binary output settings and are typically mapped to actuators. The ability to read coils may help an attacker profile a system and identify ranges of registers to alter via a "write coil" message. The defaults for this are "0" for the Start reg and "16" for the End reg.
Nessus TCP Scanner	
Scan ports in random order	Used to circumvent some older IDS. Enabled by default.
Detect RST rate limitation	Certain systems limit how quickly they tear down the three-way handshake during scan detections. Nessus can detect that these RST packets are being rate limited and alter its scan. Enabled by default.
Detect firewall	Nessus attempts to determine if there is filtering between the scanner and the target. A combination of packet analysis and OS fingerprinting is used to find if reverse NAT is active. Default is enabled.

Continued

Table 4.4 Continued. Advanced Tab Options

Network congestion detection	Nessus will utilize Round Trip to Target (RTT) on open ports to detect if the network is congested or if rate-limiting hardware is at play. The default is enabled.
Ping the Remote Hosts	
TCP ping destination port(s)	Specifies a list of ports that will be checked with a TCP Ping, described later. When choosing a value, pick a range that is likely to not be blocked by routers or firewalls, like smtp and http. The Default value is "built-in".
Do an ARP ping	By enabling this option, the Nessus scanner will broadcast a request for the target's MAC Address. If a response is returned from one of the routers or the host, then the target is considered up. Default is enabled.
Do a TCP ping	TCP SYN packet is used as ping, sent to the port list described in destination ports above. If an SYN/ACK is returned (the port is listening), then the host is up. If a RST is return (the port is closed) then the host is up. Otherwise the host is considered down.
Do an ICMP ping	Option determines if a traditional ICMP request packet will be sent to determine if a host is up. The default is disabled.
Number of retries (ICMP)	Allows the user to set the number of attempts to try when conducting an ICMP ping. The default value is set to "6"
Do an applicative UDP ping (DNS, RPC…)	The UDP ping attempts to determine if a host is up by sending a single UDP packet. If an ICMP port unreachable message is returned, the system is up. If another UDP packet is returned, the host is up. Otherwise the host is down. Not as reliable as a TCP Ping. Default value is set to disabled.
Make the dead host appear in the report	If this option is selected, hosts that did not reply to the ping request will be included in the security report as dead hosts. Default is disabled.

Continued

Table 4.4 Continued. Advanced Tab Options

Log live hosts in the report	Select this option to specifically report on the ability to successfully ping a remote host. Default is disabled.
Test the local Nessus host	This option will include the local host in the Nessus scan. This is used when the host is within the target network range for the scan. The default is enabled.
SMB Scope	
Request information about the domain	Domain users will be queried instead of local users when this option is enabled. The default value is enabled.
SMB use domain SID to enumerate users	Specifies the SID range to use to perform a reverse lookup on usernames on the domain. The default setting is recommended. Start UID is 1000 and End UID is 1200.
SMB use host SID to enumerate users	Specifies the SID range to use to perform a reverse lookup on usernames on the local usernames. The default setting is recommended. Start UID is 1000 and End UID is 1200.
SMTP Settings	
Third party domain	All Simple Mail Transport Protocol (SMTP) test will be ran on all hosts within the scanned domain that are running SMTP services. Nessus will attempt to relay messages through the host to the specified domain in this option. It must be an outside domain address from the range being scanned. Default value is "example.com."
From address	The test message sent to the SMTP server will appear as if they originated from the address specified here. The default value is "nobody@example.com".
To address	Nessus will attempt to send messages addressed to the mail recipient listed in this field. The default value "postmaster@[AUTO_REPLACED_IP]" is used since it is a valid address on most mail servers.

Continued

Table 4.4 Continued. Advanced Tab Options

SNMP Settings	
Community String	It is recommended that if you know the community string of the devices in your network, you enter it in this field. Nessus will attempt guesses on both the Community string and the Private string during a scan, and will be used in subsequent scans via the knowledge base. If a Community string is not found, then a number of plugins will not be executed. Default value is "public".
UDP Port	Port to look for SNMP interactions on. Default value is 161 and should be left alone in most cases.
Service Detection	
Number of connections done in parallel	Sets how many simultaneous connections may be made to a target host. Default value is 10.
Network connection timeout	Number of seconds to wait for a TCP response before considering the connection to be timed out. Default value is 5.
Network read/write timeout	Number of seconds to wait for a TCP response on an established connection before considering the connection to be timed out. Affects how Nessus evaluates hosts that stop responding during an audit under the Network tab. Default value is 5.
Test SSL based services	Determines if SSL based services are to be tested on known SSL ports (e.g. 443), All ports, or None. Checking SSL on every open port can be disruptive for the tested network. Default value is "Known SSL ports".
UNIX Compliance Checks (Direct Feed Users)	This drop-down menu item provides the option to select 5 UNIX audit files to assign to the policy. Next to each item is a **Select** button that will open a window where you can browse to and select the audit file to use with this policy.
Unknown CGI arguments torture	This item "tortures" the arguments of the remote CGIs (Common Gateway Interface) by attempting to pass common CGI programming errors as arguments.

Continued

Table 4.4 Continued. Advanced Tab Options

Web Mirroring	
Number of pages to mirror	When enabled, Nessus will mirror web pages and then test for vulnerabilities. Pages will be mirrored in sequential order starting with the "Start page" until this number of pages are downloaded. The default value is 200.
Start page	Page to start mirroring. Default value is "/".
Windows Compliance Checks (Direct Feed Users)	This drop-down menu item provides the option to select 5 Windows audit files to assign to the policy. Next to each item is a **Select** button that will open a window where you can browse to and select the audit file to use with this policy.
Windows File Content Compliance Checks (Direct Feed Users)	This drop-down menu item provides the option to select 5 Windows File Content audit files to assign to the policy. Next to each item is a **Select** button that will open a window where you can browse to and select the audit file to use with this policy.

Once all the settings are configured properly for your new policy, simply click the Save button in the lower right of the Policy editor. If the option "share across multiple sessions" is enabled, then the policy will appear in the Policy pane and can be selected at any time when conducting a scan.

Target Selection

We are almost ready to start our first scan. In the last section, we told the Nessus scanner precisely what to scan for, now we need to tell the scanner where to scan. It is probably tempting to enable a bunch of plugins and unleash Nessus on every host on the network. This is not recommended. Unless you have very detailed knowledge of the devices on your network and know how they will respond to detailed interrogations, it is best to select a small subnet to target, no larger than a class C, to run you first scan against. It is also recommended that you run this scan while you are present, in front of the scanner.

Your best strategy for your first run is to select no more than five hosts as targets; preferably, targets that no one other than you rely upon. The platform for the Nessus server is probably a good choice. Any desktop systems you use can be included, too. You can use your root privileges on the server and root/Administrator privileges on your desktop(s) to profile those systems from the inside and compare them to Nessus' results without credentials. You will also avoid the risk of having to explain why you chose someone else's system as a target before you got any further on the learning curve.

The left pane, which we will call the Target panel, displays the list of targets we are going to scan. Under the Target panel are two buttons, the "+" button will add new targets, while selecting an existing target and clicking "−" will remove the target from the list. By clicking on the "+"the Targets editor will pop up, as in Figure 4.13.

Figure 4.13 Targets Editor

In the Target Editor, first select the scan type on the top of the interface. Each option will enable the appropriate entry fields below. Let's refer to Figure 4.13 again for example. By selecting the **Subnet option** button, we are now able to enter an IP address and the appropriate netmask. The IP range can be as small or as large as you want to make it. Be careful here because a typo can produce a range far larger than anticipated. Nessus will scan from the first IP to the last. So, instead of entering the subnet we did in Figure 4.13, we could have also entered a range of 192.168.16.1 for the start address and 192.168.16.255 for the end address. Once you have entered your selection, hit the **Save** button. The new target should now appear in the Target pane. This process can be repeated as many times as necessary to enter the full target list. Each time a target range is entered, a different "Scan" option can be selected. Please note, you could create the full target list ahead of time and enter them into a targets file. This is where "Hosts in file" option comes into play. Each target has to be on a separate line and can be either a single host, or a CIDR range (192.168.16.1/24). See the Tools and Traps for more information on CIDR notation. To use the host file, select the **Hosts in file** scan option then enter the path to the file or navigate to the file with "Select file…". Once everything is correct, select **Save** and the contents of the file described will load one per line into the Targets pane.

Just like with the plugins option pane when creating a policy, the check boxes to the left of the targets can be toggled on and off. Depending on how you entered the targets, each entry can be toggled, not each individual host, unless that is how you entered the targets.

Tools & Traps…

Classless Inter-Domain Routing

CIDR (Classless Inter-Domain Routing) notation is a compact and flexible way to define subnets. The notation has the familiar dotted-quad form of an IP address (IPv4 for purists), followed by a forward slash (/) and a number from 0 to 32 inclusive.
> For example:
> 192.168.16.1/24
> To interpret the notation:

1. Write the dotted-quad IP address as four strings of 8 binary bits.
2. Write another four strings of binary bits in which the first 24 bits are ones and the rest zeros.

Continued

3. Logically AND the two strings.

4. Convert the result back into decimal dotted-quad notation.

```
11000000 10101000 00010000 00000001
11111111 11111111 11111111 00000000
------------------------------------
11000000 10101000 00010000 00000000
192.168.16.0
```

The first 24 bits of the addresses on the subnet are fixed. The last 8 are free to vary.

The subnet addresses range from:

```
192.168.16.0 (11000000 10101000 00010000 00000000)
```

to

```
192.168.16.255. (11000000 10101000 00010000 11111111)
```

Similarly, we can read the notation 54.180.14.221/28 as:

```
00110110 10110100 00001110 11011101
11111111 11111111 11111111 11110000
----------------------------------------------------
00110110 10110100 00001110 11010000
54.180.14.208
```

Since the last 4 bits are free to vary, the subnet addresses range from:

```
54.180.14.208 (00110110 10110100 00001110 11010000)
```

to

```
54.180.14.223. (00110110 10110100 00001110 11011111)
```

Finally,

```
140.75.64.192/18
10001100 01001011 01000000 11000000
11111111 11111111 11000000 00000000
----------------------------------------------------
10001100 01001011 01000000 00000000
140.75.64.0
```

Since the last 14 bits are free, this subnet's IP addresses range from:

```
140.75.64.0 (10001100 01001011 01000000 00000000)
```

to

```
140.75.127.255 (10001100 01001011 01111111 11111111)
```

Starting the Scan

When everything is set correctly, click the **Scan now** button at the bottom center of Nessus client. The interface will change to other tab in the Nessus client labeled "Report". As the scan progresses, hosts will start populating the left pane with an expand icon to the left of the IP address or hostname, depending on how you set your policy.

New with this version of the client is the ability to start reviewing the results as the scan progresses. As the results from each plugin return, the target hosts will be displayed in either black, yellow, red. Black signifies that the host is up and nothing more than notes, or comments have been found. Yellow signifies that the host is up and plugins with the level of medium, or warnings have been discovered. And finally, red means the host has high, or serious vulnerabilities. By clicking on the **expand** icon to the left of the host you can see which port the different hosts were listening on. The same coloring scheme is used with the ports, or services, as with the hosts; black, yellow, or red.

Figure 4.14 shows a small test network scan in progress. As described above, host 172.16.168.16 was found to have a high, or serious, vulnerability. Select the port in question and view the results in the right hand pane. Use the scroll bar on the right if results move past the bottom of the screen. There is also a scan in progress indicator at the bottom of the screen. This version of the Nessus client has the ability to pause the scan in mid-stream by selecting the **Pause** button. Users can also stop a scan at anytime by selecting the **Stop** button.

Figure 4.14 Scan Report in Progress

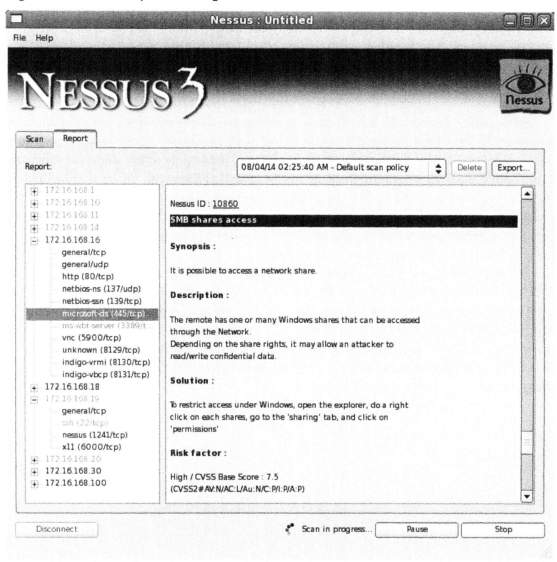

Once the scan is complete, we need to make sure to save the results. Select **File** in the upper left corner of the Nessus client, and navigate to "Save". The usual save interface for your operating system will appear. Enter a filename and click **Save**. Further exploration of the interface shows a drop down menu above the results pane. This drop down will show the date and time this target list was scanned and which policy was used. We have the option to delete a run out of this drop down list by selecting the date and time we want to dispose of and click on **Delete** to the right of the drop down. We can also export individual scan results by selecting the date and time from the drop down and click **Export**. The formats supported are *html*, *nbe*, and *nsr*. Make sure that once you select **Export** you enter the filename for the output, and select the proper format with the "Files of type" drop down. Click **Save** when ready. See Figure 4.15 for an example on exporting results.

Figure 4.15 Scan Report Export

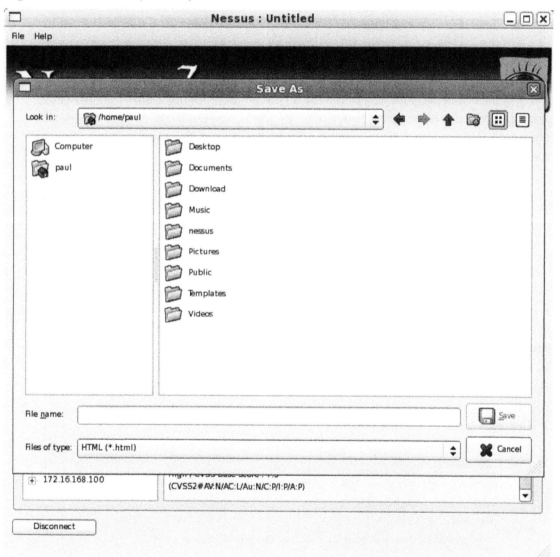

Nessus Command Line

The latest version of the Nessus client comes with a command line version that can execute many of the same options as the GUI. The command line is included even in the Windows version. Open command line prompt and type **nessuscmd –h** to see the available options. Command line options exist for:

- Port scanning
- Host discovery
- Selecting vulnerabilities
- Providing UNIX and Windows Credentials

Note that the Nessus server needs to be running on the local machine, or you have to also pass the connection information even if you are just running a port scan. It is also important that if you are going to actually execute a command, you need to invoke the commands with root privileges. Here is a list of the options the command line client will take for port scanning and host fingerprinting.

```
 -p <port_range> : Enable the port scanner and scan this port range
                   (use 'default' for the Nessus default port range)
 -sT : Perform a TCP connect()
 -sS : Perform a SYN scan
 -sP : Perform a PING scan
 -O : Enable OS Fingerprinting
Here is an example port scan with operating system identification invocation:
# nessuscmd -sS -O -p 1-1024 172.16.168.20
Starting nessuscmd 3.2.0
Scanning '172.16.168.20'…

Host 172.16.168.20 is up
Discovered open port imaps (993/tcp) on 172.16.168.20
[i] Plugin 11936 reported a result on port general/tcp of 172.16.168.20
+ Results found on 172.16.168.20 :
  - Host information :
    [i] Plugin ID 11936
      | Remote operating system : Linux Kernel 2.6
      | Confidence Level : 65
      | Method : SinFP
      | The remote host is running Linux Kernel 2.6
  - Port imaps (993/tcp) is open
```

The command line can also be passed options for individual plugins to be ran against the target list, as well login as credentials. Below is another example with the command line, this time we are showing a targeted scan against a host with credentials looking at the password policy for the system, Nessus Plugin ID 17651.

```
# nessuscmd -v 172.16.168.16 -i 17651 --smb-login Administrator
--smb-password password
Starting nessuscmd 3.2.0
Scanning '172.16.168.16'…

Host 172.16.168.16 is up
[i] Plugin 17651 reported a result on port microsoft-ds
(445/tcp) of 172.16.168.16
+ Results found on 172.16.168.16 :
  - Port microsoft-ds (445/tcp)
    [i] Plugin ID 17651
      | The following password policy is defined on the remote host:
      | Minimum password len: 0
      | Password history len: 0
      | Maximum password age (d): 42
      | Password must meet complexity requirements: Enabled
      | Minimum password age (d): 0
      | Forced logoff time (s): Not set
      | Locked account time (s): 1800
      | Time between failed logon (s): 1800
      | Number of invalid logon before locked out (s): 0
```

Summary

Nessus is very powerful and flexible. This makes it the popular tool that it is, and, at the same time, puts the responsibility of using it effectively on you. It's not a drop-in security fix. It takes practice to discover the best way to use it on any particular network.

Start small. Scan a few systems that you control and that no one else depends upon. Try different scanning options and plugins to see what they do. Do your reconnaissance. Scan the network and map it out before you start doing widespread vulnerability checking. When you start testing for vulnerabilities, make sure that you schedule your tests with anyone who might be affected.

Remember that your scanning strategy, like everything else security related, is a series of trade-offs. You might never want to run a potential DoS attack on your own network, but what would the cost be if someone else did it instead? Nessus runs more quickly and more safely if you tell it to trust the self-identification of systems and services, but what if they are lying?

With Nessus, you don't have to believe, you can test.

Solutions Fast Track

Preparing for Your First Scan

☑ *Do* select a small, preferably non-operational network or subnet to try out your first scans.

☑ *Do* discuss the potential risks of any scan with all relevant parties *before* you perform the scan.

☑ *Don't* forget that if there are DoS vulnerabilities on your network, someone else might find them if you don't.

☑ Always be aware of the following assumptions when you plan your scans:

☑ You know which IP addresses are being used on your network.

☑ You know *what* is using those IP addresses.

☑ You know what services are being offered at those IP addresses.

☑ A given service is running at the port commonly associated with it.

☑ A service at a given port is the service commonly associated with that port.

☑ You know how the firewalls and access control lists are configured on the network.

☑ You know what on your network is vulnerable to a DoS attack.

☑ Information from previous scans will be valid in the future.

☑ Any other assumptions that you can think of.

☑ Consider providing authentication information to Nessus if it might make the scan more effective.

☑ Check the source code of any plugins you will be using to make sure you understand how they work.

Starting the Nessus Client

☑ To start the client, type *NessusClient* in a terminal or select the Nessus Client icon.

☑ The "Connect" button allows you to authenticate your client to your Nessus server, after this, you will be able to select/edit policies and add/select targets.

Policy Options

☑ Recommendations for first scan:

■ Use port range 1–1024.

■ Enable safe checks.

■ Use the Nessus TCP Scanner.

■ Ping each host.

Policy Credentials

☑ Recommendations for first scan:

■ Leave windows credentials blank for you first scan, but enable for second on the same network to see differences.

Policy Plugins

☑ Nessus plugins are organized into functional families where each plugin represents one or more specific vulnerability tests that can be launched during a Nessus scan.

☑ There are a number of plugins and plugin authors, and so thorough research must be done in order to find the plugins that suit your specific needs.

☑ Plugins can be found through using the search utility at www.nessus.org, or using the plugin filter in the Nessus client.

Policy Advanced Options

- ☑ Recommendations for first scan:
- ☑ Ping the remote host options:
    - ■ Use ARP host ping.
    - ■ Use TCP host ping.
    - ■ Use ICMP host ping.
    - ■ Change number of retries (ICMP) to 3. On a small test network, packet loss is not an issue.

Target Selections

- ☑ Recommendations for first scan:
    - ■ Use the address range of a test network or nonoperational subnet, preferably containing the Nessus server.
    - ■ *Do not* scan operational systems.
    - ■ *Never* scan operational systems without notifying all potentially affected parties and obtaining appropriate prior approval.

Starting the Scan

- ☑ Click the **Scan Now** button.

Frequently Asked Questions

Q: I've started the Nessus scan, but it doesn't seem to be doing anything. What's wrong?

A: When you start the scan, the client will switch to the Report tab. Host listings should start being populated in the left pane. And the swirling "Scan in progress" indicator should be seen in bottom of the screen. If you don't see a list of targets at all, return to the left pane; make sure that you entered your targets correctly. If you see a list populating, but no additional targets are added to the left pane after a couple of minutes, make sure that your Nessus server actually has access to those targets. Remember that it's traffic between the Nessus *server* and the targets that's important. If your scan depends on an initial ICMP or TCP ping, and that ping is blocked, you may need to run without it. If everything is in order, you may want to investigate the targets themselves. Some host-based firewalls may hang a Nessus scan.

Q: I've found three plugins that all seem to test for the vulnerability I'm looking for. Should I use them all?

A: Almost certainly not. The plugins may well do different things. Examine the source code of each to determine exactly what each is doing and pick the one you want. If you don't know what a plugin does, you can't interpret the results it delivers. If you can't interpret its results, there's no point in using it. *If you don't understand it, don't use it.*

Q: I've selected all the Windows plugins and I'm running them on a large network full of Windows systems. I'm completing the scans on all my targets, but there are only a handful of results from each target. Shouldn't I be getting more information?

A: Most of the Windows plugins require read-access to the target's registry, at a minimum. Make sure that you provided appropriate credentials to provide such access on these systems. Make sure that the credentials are valid. You should also make sure that your network is not blocking SMB traffic between subnets.

Q: What are some common causes of failed Nessus scans?

A: Firewalls and traffic filters that block the scans; failure to provide appropriate credentials; misunderstanding the function of plugins.

Q: My first scan is taking too long. What could be the problem?

A: One of the purposes of your initial scans is to learn how to tune Nessus for your local conditions. You can reduce the number of targets, reduce the number of plugins, or use some of the "efficiency" features discussed in this chapter. Each of these approaches involves the risk of overlooking some important feature of your targets. That's why your first scan, ideally, is on a subnet you're very familiar with so that you can compare the Nessus results to what you already know about the systems.

Q: People are complaining that my scans are breaking their systems and making their printers spew garbage.

A: If this is happening during your first scanning session, you *really* need to reconsider your target range. *Don't scan anything important until you know what you are doing.* Also, make sure that your policy is set to not scan sensitive targets like printers in the "Advanced" tab.

## Chapter 5

Interpreting Results

Solutions in this chapter:

- **The Nessus UI Basics**
- **Reading a Nessus Report**

☑ **Summary**

☑ **Solutions Fast Track**

☑ **Frequently Asked Questions**

Introduction

Nessus is a tool designed to help you evaluate risk. "The proof of the pudding is in the eating," it's said, and ultimately the fruit of a vulnerability scanner is in the reports it outputs. For the Nessus scanner to be of any use, you must be able to read, interpret, and act on the data it generates. As anyone who's worked much with the Nessus scanner will attest, this is no simple task.

In this section, think of reading Nessus reports as learning a new language. We consider how the reports have a background, history, and context; and how one can, and must, understand these to fully understand what the reports are *actually* saying. We also pose some key questions that need to be asked as the reports are being read, warn of common traps and pitfalls, and describe additional sources of information that can compliment and complete the user-level reports.

We discuss two different GUI clients in this chapter, and evaluate the strengths and weaknesses of each with a view to getting the most out of reports.

The Nessus UI Basics

As you already know, the Nessus scanner architecture differentiates between the "server" and the "client" components. The Nessus client is responsible for generating and (in most cases) rendering the scan output. We consider two clients in this chapter:

- The Nessus 3 Client for Linux/UNIX
- The Nessus 3 Client for Windows

As far as reading the report output is concerned, both of these clients have simple and intuitive graphical interfaces. This chapter focuses more on understanding and interpreting the actual report content than the use of the point-and-click interface. Nevertheless, a brief overview of the features and functions of these two interfaces is offered for those readers who are not yet familiar with the tools at that level.

Viewing Results Using the Nessus 3 Client for Linux/UNIX and Windows

Written primarily by Renaud Deraison and distributed from nessus.org, the Nessus GUI Client for X Windows is the definitive client for Nessus. While perhaps not always as user friendly as some would like (especially for users not accustomed to UNIX GUI environments), the UNIX client is solid, complete, and comprehensive. The creators of Nessus, and Tenable Network Security, have taken great pains to make both clients as similar as possible.

Using the Basic Report Viewer

By default, the Nessus Report window is divided into two windows (as shown in Figure 5.1), showing the subnets included in the scan. Each IP address is shown in different colors, depending on the vulnerabilities discovered – Black for informational, Yellow/Orange for Medium and Red for High vulnerabilities. This gives you an immediate view of the troubles on your network. By clicking on each IP address individually, you get a quick summary of the issues on that particular device. The information displayed gives you the number of High, Medium, and Low vulnerabilities as well as the type of operating system and hostname.

Figure 5.1 The Nessus Client 3—Report Viewer

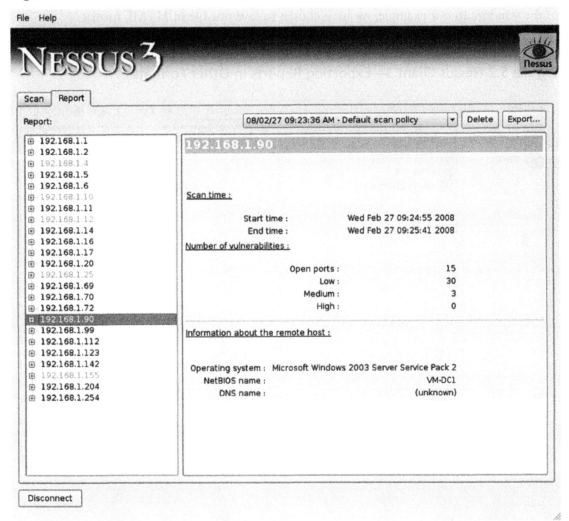

Clicking on the plus symbol next to the IP address you want to see presents a drill-down of the services available on the device and if there is any information or vulnerability (or vulnerabilities) associated with that service.

Saving and Exporting to Other Formats

By default, Nessus 3 saves scan results in a .nessus file containing all the information recorded in that session. This is an XML format file that contains the policy used for the scan, the IP addresses scanned and the results. Once Nessus has completed its scan, click on File | Save As and name your file. Nessus will automatically save this file as a .nessus file. You may wish to save your report in one of Nessus' older formats or as an HTML page. This is an easy process. Once you have saved your file as a .nessus file, you can, from the report window, click on the Export button; name your file in the Save As window and select the file type at the bottom of the window. In our example, we have chosen to save our file in HTML format.

Figure 5.2 Nessus Client 3—Exporting Reports in Other Formats

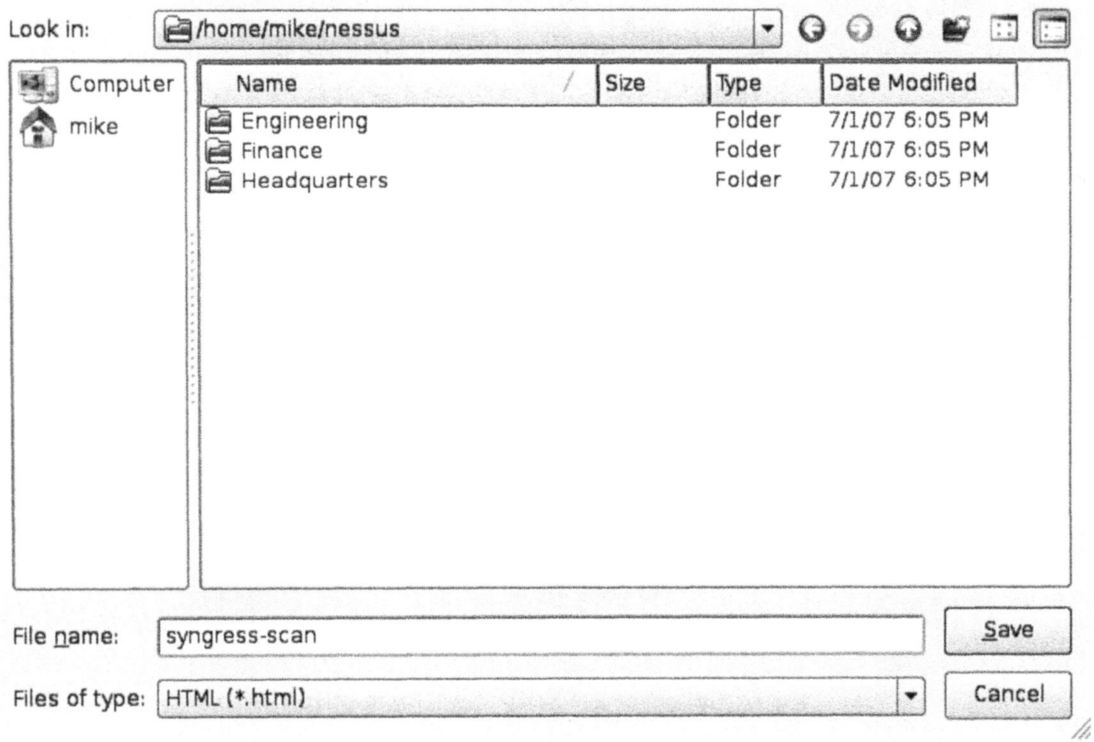

The format options include:

- **.nessus** The .nessus file format is an XML file that contains all the information pertinent to the scan and future scans run under the same policy. This file is self-sufficient and safer. It stores the range of IPs scanned, the information about the policy and the reports.

- **NBE** *Nessus BackEnd* reports that are pipe-delimited text files in which each vulnerability is reported on a new line, making them ideal for parsing using tools like *grep, cut*, and *awk*. NBE was also the format used for transporting reports between two different Nessus clients. With the .nessus format, the files are compatible with the Windows, Mac OSX and *nix versions of Nessus.

Tools & Traps...

.nessus File Fields

According to the Nessus documentation, the .nessus file consists of the following fields (*Nessus Client 3.2 File Format, v 3 2008/03/12*):

- **Targets** The Targets section can be populated with any combination of nothing, individual IP address(es)/hostname, address range or network.

- **Policies** This is the most robust section of the .nessus file. It is comprised of the plugin data and their set preferences. It can also contain scanning credentials. The plugin data can be enabled families or individual plugins. The Policies section is made up of "components". Each component has specific "elements". The policy will have a name and can have associated comments. The policy will also have Password Attributes that will tell Nessus how to store the passwords. Passwords can be stored in Clear Text, as a Mac OSX Keychain, with a Windows hash or, in the case of Linux, stored in the user's home folder with the UUID of the policy. If no selection is made for the Password Attribute, Nessus will store the passwords using the built-in encoding.

- **Preferences Component** Stores the information about preferences, broken into two elements: Server Preferences and Plugin Preferences.

- **Sever Preferences** This element stores the configuration information for the Nessus Server.

- **Plugin Preferences** This element will store specific configurations for how plugins are used.

Continued

- **Plugin Selection Component** This component contains the following elements: Family Selection and Individual Plugin Selection.

- **Family Selection Element** This element contains configuration information telling Nessus whether a plugin family is fully enabled, partially enabled or disabled. If a plugin family is fully enabled, all of the plugins in that family are enabled. If the family is updated with new plugins and the policy is used later, the new plugins will be enabled, too. With the partially enabled selection, only the information about the plugins that are enabled is stored in the Individual Plugin Element and if the plugins are updated, the new plugins will not be used. Finally, if the family is shown as disabled, none of the plugins will be used.

- **Individual Plugin Element** Information about the plugins from partially enabled families is stored here. Nessus then knows to use those plugins.

- **Reports** The Reports section contains all reports from scans, as well as the information from the Targets and Policies sections specifically associated with those reports. The Reports section is made up of a Report Host component and Report Item element.

- **Report Host Component** This component contains the results of the scan and a summary of the vulnerabilities for each host.

- **Report Item Element** The detailed results of each host's individual vulnerabilities are listed here.

The exact purpose and possible values of these fields are discussed in more detail when we cover the content of the Nessus reports later in this chapter.

- **NSR** The Nessus Report file format is no longer officially supported and has been absorbed into NBE. Essentially, the NBE file now contains all the fields in an NSR file in addition to some new ones. Later in this chapter, we describe the possible report types as being NOTE, WARNING, and HOLE, which map to the NOTE, INFO, and REPORT you'll see in the NSR output.

- **HTML** The HTML report format is a clean and browseable report of all the findings from the scan. The report is produced as a single HTML page, which is convenient for printing, e-mailing, and so forth, and lists the vulnerabilities grouped first by port number and protocol and then sorted by type. Later in this chapter, we describe the possible report types as being NOTE, WARNING, and HOLE, which maps to the Informational, Warning, and Vulnerability reports you'll see in the HTML table. Cross-references to external databases like Bugtraq, CVE, and the various vendor pages are provided as HTML links, which makes for easy browsing. We'll provide more on these external links later in this chapter.

Figure 5.3 The Nessus Client 3 – The HTML Report

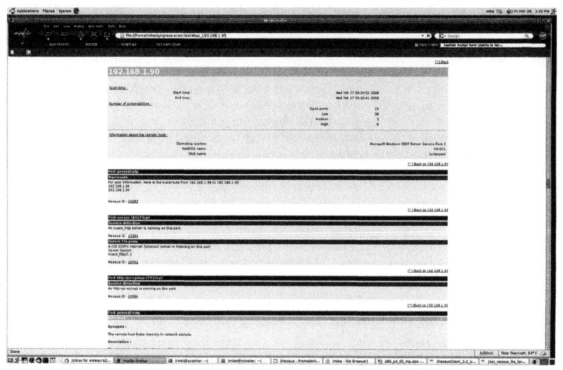

The HTML report for Nessus contains hyperlinks to each of the IP addresses discovered in the scan. The information regarding vulnerabilities for each device also contains a hyperlink to the plugin data stored on the Nessus Web site and a link to any external information. Each vulnerability has a *Synopsis*, which is a summary of the vulnerability, a more detailed *Description*, a *Solution* (if there is one) and a *Risk Factor*. We explore the precise meaning of risk factors later in this chapter.

Tools & Traps...

Writing Reports to a Database

Unlike the older NessusWX client, the Nessus Client 3 does not offer a "write to database" feature. However, older open-source project called "NNP"—The Nessus .nbe Log Parser—found at http://personal.crybe.com/solid/projects/, parses NBE files into SQL statements, and then uses these statements to insert data to a (MySQL) database. The authors of this project (Sergei Ledovskij and Miika Turkia) describe the program as "buggy." However, it's clear that they've given the problem some thought and there's much to use for beginners and advanced users alike. The parser works as a CGI that allows users to moderate the Nessus output stored in the database before generating a simple HTML report. Chapter 11 contains more detailed information for converting files to be used in databases.

Loading and Importing Reports

Clicking the Report tab from the NessusClient presents you with a different window from the Scan tab. From here, you can open old Nessus sessions and import old Nessus results. You don't have to be logged in to the Nessus daemon to do this. However, Nessus 3 can import old nessus files (such as .nbe or .nsr) or you can convert old Nessus files to the .nessus format from the command line. The following command can be used to convert files:

```
# /opt/nessus/bin/nessus -i in.[nsr|nbe] -o out.[nsr|nbe|html|txt|nessus]
```

The important switches are the –i signifying the input file (name.nsr or name.nbe) and the –o signifying the output file (in this case, you will want to name it name.nessus).

Selecting Import from the file drop down menu will allow you to select a previously saved report to load back into the interface. You don't have to be logged in to the Nessus daemon to do this, however, if the .nbe or .nsr file is not in your Nessus home directory, the Import selection will be grayed out. Your home directory will be whatever your home directory is in *nix (mine is /home/mike), but in Windows, your home directory will be contained within your My Documents folder. Within your My Documents folder, there will be a folder named Tenable and within that folder will either be a folder named Nessus or NessusClient.

You can always open previously saved .nessus files and the Nessus Client will allow you to search for these. With the Report tab selected on the Nessus Client, click on File --> Open and a window will appear allowing you to search for your .nessus file. This is shown in Figure 5.4.

Figure 5.4 Searching for .nessus files

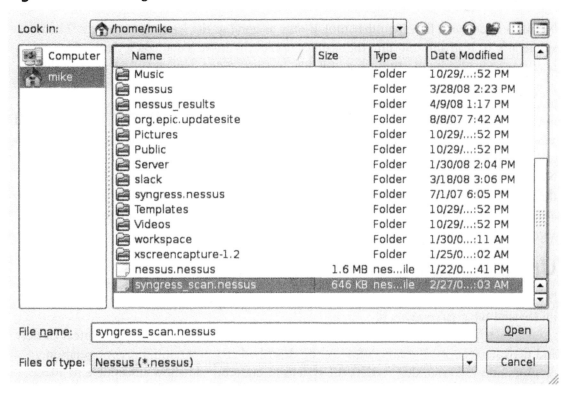

Using Multiple Tools to Improve Report Quality

The question of false positives is a serious problem in network-based vulnerability scanners and is covered extensively in this chapter and elsewhere in this book. As pointed out earlier, the older versions of the NessusWX client helped to address the problem by allowing you to mark selected issues as "false positives" and thus have them excluded from your final reports. Sadly, the newer clients don't offer such a feature. Multiple penetration testing tools allow you to import Nessus results and test to determine whether a vulnerability is a "false positive" or not. Commercial tools like Core Impact and free tools like Metasploit will allow you to import the Nessus results (currently the .nbe files) and test vulnerabilities. It should be part of your comprehensive testing program to test vulnerabilities and ensure the correct findings are reported.

Reading a Nessus Report

Nessus is a tool, and, like any other tool, is only as good as the hand that wields it. The better you're able to read and interpret the scanner results, the more value you'll derive from it. Learning to read scanner output is a little like learning a new language. As you grasp the grammar and the vocabulary, the slang and the colloquialisms, you'll find that a deep and rich pool of information becomes available to you. Of course, as with any language, there's much more to understanding Nessus reports than just knowing the vocabulary. To truly understand a language, you also need to understand something of the culture, history, customs, and traditions of the people who use it. Much the same is true if you want to get the most from Nessus reports. In this section, we examine the language of Nessus reports and how to read them. To fully grasp the language of Nessus reports, we also examine the definitions of *vulnerability* and *risk* and examine the logic that a scanner applies when determining whether a given vulnerability exists.

Understanding Vulnerabilities

Nessus is a "vulnerability scanner." To understand Nessus reports, it makes sense to first understand what *vulnerability* is.

Vulnerability is understood to mean "susceptible to attack." Hence, in the context of host and network security, a vulnerability can be described as a programming, configuration, or administration error that renders the system in question somehow susceptible to attack. While Nessus always scans specific hosts for vulnerability, one should bear in mind that an error on one host might render another host or the network in general, susceptible to attack. Such errors should also be considered vulnerabilities but can be much harder to spot, especially by an automated scanner. Bear this in mind as you analyze Nessus reports.

Information security theory teaches that three elements of information systems could be susceptible to attack:

- **Confidentiality** Some information is of strategic value to an organization and needs to be kept secret to maintain its value. If the confidentiality of the information is breached, the information loses its value. For example, a company's customer database is secret, and is a very valuable business asset. A telephone directory is public, and while it may still be an asset, it is considerably less valuable.

■ **Integrity** Information is only valuable if it is complete and correct. Moreover, it is often only valuable if it is also *perceived* to be complete and correct. For example, a company's financial figures for previous years are valuable business planning information, but only if it is accurate. If the information is found to be incorrect, it loses its value to the company. If improperly modified, information can be rendered useless, or worse, even dangerous. Furthermore, even if staff members distrust good information for some reason, they will place less reliance on the information in their decision making, and reduce the value of the information accordingly. Ironically, the same is true for the information generated by the Nessus scanner. If it's perceived to be inaccurate, it very quickly loses all its value. This is why the process of identifying and removing false positives is so important.

■ **Availability** Information has no value if it cannot be accessed when and where it is required. An extreme case of this is the physical destruction of information; for example, where hardcopy records are destroyed by fire. However, more subtle examples might include an unreliable computer network. If the information is not reliably available, its value is reduced.

The Nessus reports will indicate different vulnerabilities that might allow one or more of these elements to be attacked. While the Nessus NASLs will attempt to classify the vulnerability and explain its potential impact, you as the analyst will need ask yourself which, if any, of these elements is being put at risk, and what this implies for the specific target host, the network, and the organization in general. Later in this chapter, we discuss some key questions that you should ask yourself as you view the report. The questions will help you put the scanner output into perspective and fully understand its impact on the systems you're trying to protect.

Understanding Risk

We stated earlier that vulnerability implies susceptibility to attack. Clearly, the existence of a vulnerability does not necessarily imply that the system will be attacked, or that the attack will be successful. Risk is a much broader concept than vulnerability that factors in elements like the "value" of the system and the "probability" of an attack occurring. The introduction of these elements allows us to quantify risk and place it into perspective. With the risk more clearly quantified, we can compare the relative significance of the reports generated by a vulnerability scanner.

Damage & Defense...

Thinking about Attacking

Let's take a moment to look at risk and vulnerability from the perspective of an attacker. When we teach hacking courses, we tell students that an "attack" on a vulnerable system can take one of the following forms:

- **Shoot From The Hip** Remember, the attacker only needs to win once, meaning that if she can guess a password, or stumble onto a web administration backend directory, then that might be all that's needed to compromise your system. It's much harder to secure systems than to attack them. Never underestimate how lucky an attacker can get.

- **Data Mining** An attacker will collect any snippet of information they can get, regardless of its apparent value at the time—usernames, directories, background information, and the like. No snippet of information is considered irrelevant, and the true impact of information leakage often only becomes apparent when all the pieces are finally put together. We've achieved countless successful compromises simply by stringing together different snippets of seemingly innocuous information.

- **Exploit** In the classical sense, a vulnerability is "exploited" using a piece of software. Many programmatic errors, configuration errors, and so forth can be compromised in this way. Writing exploit code is both an art and a science, and only a very few have mastered it, leaving the rest to rely on code that is downloaded and used with very little real skill, knowledge, or control. As a result, exploit software is seldom a reliable attack vector. Have no doubt that it can and it does work, but be aware that many other attack vectors can be (and in our experience very often *are*) much more effective.

- **Brute Force** "If at first you don't succeed, force it!" Brute-force attacks are a much misunderstood attack vector. While not an "elegant" attack, the ease of automation and the anonymity offered by IP-based systems often makes brute-force attacks a viable option where other attacks fail. Try to look beyond traditional password guessing and explore other avenues for brute-force attacks: user enumeration, web directory guessing, session key highjacking, and so forth. We often demonstrate, for example, how e-commerce sites can be attacked by selecting a commonly used PIN number and cycling through all possible account numbers until one is found where that PIN has been used. In this manner, each account is only attacked once, thus bypassing security mechanisms such as account lockout.

■ **Combination Attacks** In our experience, most successful compromises rely on a combination of factors, blended from this list. The system leaks a username, a vulnerable service can be exploited, but only with a valid account, and so a password must be derived using brute force. Almost all the practical exercises in our hacking courses teach students to view attacks this way, and the thinking is consistently being affirmed by our real-life experience.

Use this thinking about attack vectors to put the risk represented by different vulnerabilities into perspective as you read through a Nessus scan report.

Understanding Scanner Logic

To understand what a scanner report is saying, we need to understand how a scanner actually thinks. Let's remind ourselves how a scanner's logic will typically work:

For each selected NASL script, the scanner will typically execute the following steps:

1. Ensure that all required NASLs are first executed, as specified by the "dependencies" list in the script.

2. Determine whether the affected service is running on the target. This is typically done by querying the Nessus Knowledge Base (KB) for the ports on which the affected service is running. If no relevant ports are found in the KB, the NASL script typically reverts to a default or might not execute at all.

3. Where possible, check whether the service banner suggests vulnerability. Mostly, this is done using simple regular expression matching.

4. If permitted by the "safe mode" setting, the NASL may attempt to verify that the vulnerability actually exists. This process varies dramatically from script to script, but in essence, we're dealing with some type of prompt-and-response test. The script sends a series of values over the network and then attempts to parse the target system's response for indications that it's vulnerable. In some cases, this process might repeat a few times, with different prompts, until the script can reach a conclusion.

5. The NASL will flag a report and set the "Risk Factor" according to the findings of (3) and (4), and the logic applied by the scriptwriter.

A little later in this section we discuss exactly what happens when a NASL script "flags" a report and examine all the elements of data found in a vulnerability report.

An understanding of the scanner's logic reminds us of some important truths. Some of these might seem obvious, but they bear mentioning nevertheless. Keep the following "reality checks" in mind as you read scanner reports:

- Each NASL is dependent on information it receives from other NASLs via the Knowledge Base. First, there's the obvious reliance on the NASLs listed as "dependencies." However, there's also a less obvious reliance on a set of NASLs that gather information, including things like the portscanners and find_service.nes. If any of these tests return incorrect or insufficient information for some reason, the NASL in question might fail, generating either false positives or even worse, false negatives. Take for example trojan_horses.nasl (NASL ID 11157) that attempts to detect Trojan horses by identifying open TCP sockets on ports commonly used by Trojans and on which the actual service cannot be identified. This script relies completely on previous NASLs that have listed "Unknown" services in the KB, the logic being that if something is listening on a given port and that "something" can't be identified using standard techniques, then that "something" might very well be malicious. The logic is sound in itself, but is thrown into disarray when ports are incorrectly listed as "Unknown" by *find_service.nes*. Many situations can result in this set of circumstances occurring, leading to a security report by *trojan_horses.nasl*. In this way, a perfectly secure host might be reported as already compromised by the Nessus scanner.

- Many tests are dependent on banner information. This is especially true where safe_checks is enabled, thus occasionally preventing the scanner from further prompt-and-response testing. Banners are often not updated when systems are patched, or can be masked or even modified to mislead scanners. Some, like Microsoft's IIS, never show version changes for the duration of the product's lifetime. One also sees this frequently from Sun Solaris systems, for example, where applying a patch from Sun does not always cause the affected service banner to be updated. This type of behavior by a vendor is commonly referred to as "backporting." In order to be 100% accurate, you'll need to check the patch level of the target system.

- Even when NASL scripts don't just rely on banners they're still conducted over the Internet or other networks that are often unreliable or can introduce "noise" in other ways. One example of this is transparent proxies that always respond to a TCP SYN request on web service ports, regardless of the actual target IP address. Due to this behavior, one can actually end up executing certain tests against the proxy, rather than the target server. This behavior can mislead the scanner into believing there is a web server service running on IP addresses that aren't even active.

- Even when network communications are clear and uninterrupted, the fact that we're testing over the network creates a "gap" that can make it almost impossible for a script to accurately determine the presence of a vulnerability. Imagine, for example, a script that tests for the presence of a buffer overflow vulnerability against Microsoft IIS 5. It's easy to detect the banner, but as the patch level isn't reflected in the banner, that tells us very little. The only remaining option is to actually emulate an attack and attempt to overflow the affected buffer—and that's where it gets tricky. How does the script tell if the overflow succeeded? Unless we're lucky and the service consistently fails when the exploit is run, it's extremely difficult to determine whether the exploit attack succeeded. In cases like this, NASL script-writers will often tend toward the side of caution and report the target as vulnerable. This is one of the chief causes for false positive reports. See *iis5_isapi_printer.nasl* (NASL ID 10661) as an example of a script that does a prompt-and-response test for a vulnerable element, but really can't determine whether the issue is present, or *msftp_dos.nasl* (NASL ID 10934) for an example of a script that would cause the service to fail as a test but is forced to fall back on an unreliable banner if safe_ checks is enabled.

- Finally, assuming that none of the previously described conditions occurs, one still has the human element to deal with. NASL writers are only human, and one often sees NASLs generating sparse or misleading reports. Consider *bind_query.nasl* (NASL ID 10539), for example. The NASL detects DNS name servers that allow "recursive" queries, and has been classified as "Serious" by the author. The script author cautions that this may not always be the case: "If this is your internal name server, then forget this warning." However, can you imagine how often this report will be generated by a Nessus scan against an ISP's network, where large numbers of "useable" DNS servers deliberately face the Internet? The NASL writer can never understand the context in which the scans are run, so *you* have to look through the report output to the core of what's being reported and interpret that information in the light of your own environment.

Notice that the points discussed here should be seen as "limitations" and not "errors" and that all these issues are endemic to *all* network-level vulnerability scanners. Nessus has consistently been shown to be one of the best vulnerability scanners there is and the examples in this list should do nothing to dispute assertion. Rather, they should serve to remind us that the scanner is only a tool and will never be able to do anything a skilled human technician cannot. Indeed, the better you understand the tool with all its strengths and weaknesses, the better it will serve you.

Key Report Elements

A Nessus scan "report" consists of a number of "issues," which are in turn classified as "Holes," "Warnings," or "Notes." If you look at a Nessus issue, regardless of the client you used or the report format, there will always be certain key pieces of information for you to consider. In this section, we review each element of a Nessus issue. Next, we will look at the different ways to view Nessus results. First, we list the elements in the order in which they appear in a pipe-delimited NBE format report:

- **Category** The first field of an NBE issue report is the category field, which is always either "timestamps" or "results." This value is not really a part of the report, but we mention it for completeness in case you're looking at an NBE file as you read this. In terms of reading Nessus output, you're only interested in lines with category "results."

- **Subnet** The subnet field is simply a truncation of the IP address that is performed by the Nessus client after the report has been received from the server. Nessus has no awareness of the actual subnet address in which the target resides, nor is there any mapping back to the original target specification even if the target was defined as a subnet. The subnet field simply performs a logical grouping of IP addresses by class C subnet address.

- **Hostname** The hostname field contains the IP address or DNS name for which the vulnerability is being reported. As an aside, you should note when starting your scan that DNS name and IP address are not necessarily interchangeable in terms of the behavior of the scanner, especially when scanning web servers.

- **Port** The TCP or UDP port number on which the vulnerability was discovered. The format is "port name (num/protocol)." Remember that Nessus dynamically detects what service is running on each scanned port. Thus, for example, it is not uncommon to see web server vulnerability reports on uncommon ports like 81 and 10000. However, this information is *not* shown in this field, and you should note that in the report, Nessus translates the port number shown in this field into the port name from the static /usr/local/share/nmap/nmap-service-probes file on the *nessusd* host. This field does not necessarily indicate the true function of that port or the findings of the *find_services.nes*. If no service name could be found by the server, the service name will be listed as "unknown." The keyword *general* tells us that the problem is not specific to a port but is a general TCP/UDP- or IP-level problem. For example, the script *os_fingerprint.nasl* (NASL ID 11936), which uses TCP fingerprinting techniques to determine the operating system of the target host, will report on port "general/tcp." A final point to remember is that Nessus executes scans per port. Thus, if you scan a host with multiple addresses or a service that listens on multiple ports (like HTTP and HTTPS), you'll see the same vulnerability report repeated for each port on which it was found.

- **Script ID** A unique NASL script ID number that is assigned by the Nessus core team to each new NASL plugin script when it is included in the distribution. The ID is often not displayed by the GUI clients, but is included in most of the "exported" report formats (like HTML). It provides the simplest and most direct link back to the original NASL. See the Tools & Traps sidebar for how to derive the NASL script name from the ID. The ID can also be used to search for the NASL on the Nessus web site—http://cgi.nessus.org/plugins/search.html—and to query the Open Source Vulnerability Database (OSVDB—www.osvdb.org) for additional vulnerability information. Finally, the ID should be used when communicating with other Nessus users, the Nessus core team, or the NASL writer to avoid any confusion or miscommunication.

Tools & Traps...

Searching through NASLs for Specific Script IDs

Nessus NASL scripts are stored in separate files with specific names like "http_version.nasl." The files are stored in the Nessus "plugins" directory—typically (but not always) /usr/local/lib/nessus/plugins. To verify (or change) the location of the plugins directory, examine the following line in the nessusd.conf file:

```
# Path to the security checks folder :
plugins_folder = /opt/nessus/ib/nessus/plugins
```

Given a specific script ID number, a simple *grep* command is often all that's required to identify the relevant .nasl file:

```
grep 10107 / opt/nessus/ib/nessus/plugins /*.nasl
```

Given that the list of plugins for a current Nessus version may now exceed 21,000, some distributions might have difficulties with this command—giving an evasive "Argument list too long" error. A simple way to work around this is to use the *find* command:

```
grep 10107 `find . -name "*.nasl"`
```

Note that the *find* command has been encapsulated in back quotes (ASCII code 96), which are used in UNIX shells to evoke command execution.
Another approach that should work is:

```
ls / opt/nessus/ib/nessus/plugins / | xargs grep 10107
```

This approach uses the xargs utility, which reads the filenames from the *ls* command and executes *grep* with the files as arguments.

- **Type** The report "type" is communicated by the Nessus daemon to the client via the NTP protocol as soon as a new issue is detected. Since the inception of NTP/1.1, a NASL writer who has detected a vulnerability literarily has three different function calls at her disposal: *security_note*, *security_warning*, and *security_hole*. With Nessus 3, these types are depicted using colors instead of icons in the report viewer, as discussed earlier.

  The definitions of these levels are a little sparse. However, Michel Arboi's "NASL Reference" paper offers the following guidelines:

  - **NOTE** reports "miscellaneous information."

  - **WARNING** reports a "mild flaw."

  - **HOLE** reports a "severe flaw."

- It's up to the NASL writer to select what report type to generate, and indeed many NASL scripts dynamically adjust the type based on exactly what was found and *how* it was found. For example, a vulnerability found with safe_checks off might the reported as a "HOLE," while the same vulnerability found with safe_checks on (using a simple banner grab) will be reported as a "WARNING." In generating the report, the NASL writer can also pass along some additional information. As of NTP/1.2, this can include the port number, protocol, and "data," which are included in the description you're shown by the client. Under the NTP protocol, the server will also pass the client the NASL ID number, which the client may choose to display. Notice the newest version of the Nessus report file outputs use similar terms in this field. Previous versions of the reports used different terms, which lead to some confusion.

- **Data** The "data" section is the actual human-readable text output of the script. Although always displayed as a single block of text, the data section logically consists of two parts. The first part (call it the "description") is the "static" part of the report—a generic description of the vulnerability that is included by the NASL writer by evoking the *script_description* function in the NASL. The second logical part of the data field (call it the "report") communicates additional information that was generated by the NASL as it executed. The NASL writer may use this facility to modify the text of the report on the fly, or to provide additional information on the vulnerability that was found. See *domino_default_db.nasl* (NASL ID 10629) for an excellent example of how this can be done. There is very little formal structure in the report data, and NASL writers are free to describe the vulnerability however they deem best. However, Nessus provides a number of sub-elements that you will often find included in vulnerability reports:

  - **Name** The NASL writer can specify a "name" or a "script_name" in the script, which gives a one-line synopsis of the problem the NASL is checking for.

- **Description** The description is simply the NASL report text. It's stored inside the script or generated dynamically by the script at execution time.

- **Bugtraq ID** A SecurityFocus Bugtraq ID (BID) number. This will allow you to reference the SecurityFocus vulnerability description at securityfocus.com; for example, www.securityfocus.com/bid/**xxx** or try http://cgi.nessus.org/bid.php3?bid=**xx**, where **xxx** represents the BID you are searching for. The Bugtraq mailing list, hosted by Symantec at SecurityFocus.com, is one of the most popular security disclosure forums on the Internet. Symantec makes a point of capturing, categorizing, and indexing newly discovered security vulnerabilities in the Bugtraq database. Each entry is assigned a unique BID number, which is referenced by the NASL.

- **CVE ID** CVE stands for "Common Vulnerabilities and Exposures" and is an initiative sponsored by the US-CERT at the U.S. Department of Homeland Security. According to the MITRE Corporation (the not-for-profit organization that manages the CVE database), the CVE is "a list of standardized names for vulnerabilities and other information security exposures—CVE aims to standardize the names for all publicly known vulnerabilities and security exposures." The ID looks like something like "CVE-2002-042" (a CVE entry) or "CAN-2003-666" (a CVE candidate entry), and it's a way of globally referencing vulnerabilities. Although the actual CVE database description of the vulnerability may seem a little sparse, that's because CVE provides more of a global key than a central repository. Using the CVE reference, you can exactly identify the specific vulnerability being tested by the NASL. CVE IDs can be cross-referenced at http://cve.mitre.org, or try http://cgi.nessus.org/cve.php3?cve=**xxx**, where **xxx** represents the CVE ID you are searching for.

- **Solution** The NASL writer may also include recommended remediation in the NASL output. Unlike commercial vulnerability scanners, Nessus does not offer an extensive database of "fixes" for the vulnerabilities it detects, nor does it offer to automatically fix the problem for you. When it comes to finding a solution for the problem being reported, you may very well be on your own. In fact, even when a solution is suggested by the NASL, it's highly recommended that you verify the recommendation and carefully test any changes in a test environment before applying them in production. Once you've applied your changes, you'll want to verify their effectiveness by running the scan again or using a tool like *nasl* to execute the NASL again.

- **Risk Factor** In addition to classifying the report as NOTE, WARNING, or HOLE, the NASL writer may include a Risk Factor in the vulnerability description. Typically, these ratings are restricted to Low, Medium, High, or Critical, but this isn't enforced in any way, so you might also come across ratings like Serious, Medium/High, or Medium [remote] / High [local]. Serious and Critical are used almost interchangeably. There isn't any "official" index for the different risk factors, so NASL writers apply their own definitions of the ratings. The only guideline is a rule-of-thumb that suggests that the report "type" should give an indication of the impact to a system in the case of a successful attack, while the Risk Factor should provide an indication of the likelihood of an attack succeeding.

We should remind ourselves of two important principles we learned earlier in this chapter: risk is a broad and complex question and probably can't be determined objectively by someone who's not familiar with your environment, and vulnerabilities should never be seen in isolation. You need to read the scan report in its entirety and interpret it in the context of your environment to get a real understanding of the level of risk with which you're dealing. Remember what was said about NASL being like a foreign language, and apply yourself to really "reading" the report to understand the risk to you. Consider creating your own "Impact Rating," using terminology with which your organization is comfortable. One crowd that's done quite a nice job of this is the Institute for Security and Open Methodologies (ISECOM) who publish a simple definition of different Risk Types in their *Open Source Testing Mythology* manual. Again, we present this only as an example that you could use when developing your own framework.

When looking at the reports using the Report View or the HTML output, you can see how these elements all come in to play. Figure 5.5 shows the output of a scan in the Report View. Notice the different color bars for the vulnerability headings showing the vulnerability severity. At the bottom of the vulnerability summary, you will also see the Risk factor and the Nessus ID.

Figure 5.5 Report View From the Nessus Client

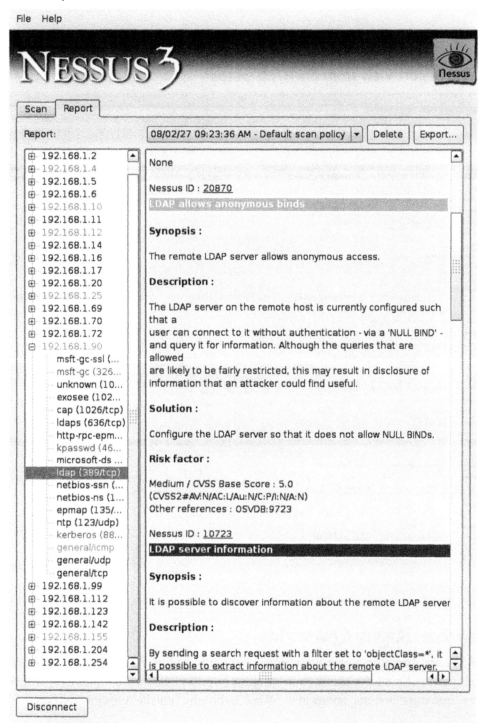

Figure 5.6 shows the same vulnerability in the HTML output. Notice they are exactly the same.

Figure 5.6 Report View from the HTML output

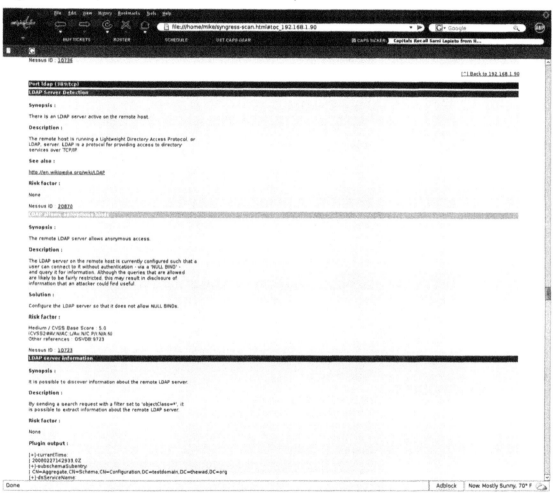

Asking the Right Questions

Imagine you are attending a presentation by a security vendor at a computer conference. As you listen, you're constantly asking yourself questions that help you comprehend what's being said. These questions include things like "What is this guy *actually* trying to tell me?" "What can I read between the lines?" "Is what she's saying really true?" "How does she know this?" and "What does this all mean to me?" Now imagine that the speaker's first language is not English and you have a good analogy for how you should approach reading a vulnerability scanner report.

In the previous section, we discussed what can be considered the "grammar" and the "vocabulary" of a Nessus report. However, as with any language, you need to read much deeper than that to really understand what's being said. As you read the report, regardless of how the output is being displayed, you need to be constantly asking yourself certain key questions about the content. Such questions will typically include:

- **What is actually being reported?** Bearing in mind that the NASL writer is not being paid to write lengthy descriptions of the vulnerability in question, and that the NASL writer might not be a native English speaker, it's up to you to ensure you fully understand what's *actually* being reported by the scanner. In reality, a NASL doesn't report the presence of a vulnerability. What it actually reports is the result of a specific prompt-and-response test. While the NASL writer has done what she can to assist you, it's up to you to determine whether the report really implies a vulnerability, and the impact of that vulnerability. Here are some steps you can follow to help you "read between the lines" of a Nessus vulnerability report:

  - **Read the NASL itself.** NASL is the true language of Nessus. If you want to understand the prompt-and-response test report, you'll have to read it in its native language. Be prepared to develop at least a rudimentary grasp of NASL syntax. (See also the Appendix at the conclusion of this book.)

  - **Read ancillary output.** NASL writers will often include part of the response to their test with the output they generate. This information can be invaluable in understanding why the vulnerability was reported and its actual impact. For example, *smb_enum_shares.nasl* (NASL ID 10395) is a very tidy script that (among other things) enumerates open shares on a computer. The script then goes on to list which shares were found. The presence of an open share, while reported by the NASL, would not necessarily be construed as a vulnerability. An open $IPC share, reported by the same NASL, could lead one to a complete listing of users and groups on the computer which could make an attack against the computer much easier.

Figure 5.7 shows how the script *smb_enum_shares.nasl* (NASL ID 10395) reports when it believes your computer has an open share. Under the heading "Plugin output:" it provides evidence of what was discovered. This information can be used to connect to the open administrative share with a blank password and pull information about the users and groups on the computer.

Figure 5.7 Reading the "Ancillary" Information in a Report

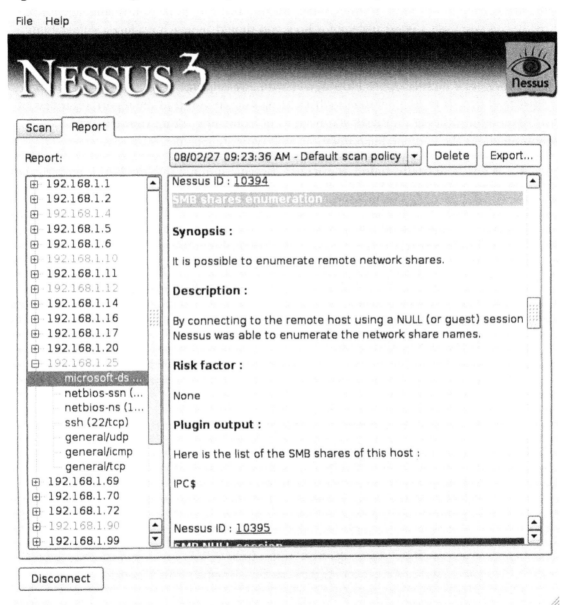

- **Read the report in context.** You should never read a NASL report on its own. Look at all reports for a given target to get the complete picture. A perfect example of this is the web server "false positive detector"—no404.nasl (NASL ID 10386). This script is designed to identify web servers that always respond with some form of success code to a request, regardless of whether that request can successfully be served, making accurate scanning of web servers extremely difficult. no404.nasl can often detect such behavior. The script writes a value to the Nessus KB that can be used by other scripts, but also generates a report warning you of the behavior. Now take a script like frontpage_chunked_overflow.nasl (NASL ID 11923), which checks for a buffer overflow in IIS FrontPage Server Extensions (FPSE). The current version of the script (1.10) works by making a carefully crafted HTTP POST to the affected URL and then parsing the response for an HTTP "200 OK" success code. Although this NASL does check that the remote host is in fact responding with a "Server: Microsoft-IIS/5.[01] (5.0 or 5.1)," it doesn't make use of the information provided by no404.nasl and therefore wouldn't automatically detect false positives. However, if you'd read the report generated by no404.nsal, you'd know that the web server was behaving strangely and view the NASL report with a little more suspicion. If you look even further, you might notice that there are no other FPSE-related issues. A typical report on a machine running FPSE will include at least NASL 10077—frontpage.nasl—which reports that the "remote web server appears to be running with the FrontPage extensions." If this report is missing, it sheds a report that FPSE is vulnerable, putting it into serious doubt. In this sense, none of the informational messages produced by Nessus is irrelevant, and there are many other examples that prove this.

- **Why was this report generated?** Once you understand what the NASL report is actually telling you, you might want to spend some time understanding why the script believes the target is vulnerable. If you've read through the script, it should be relatively easy to manually replicate the behavior of the script and trace its logic. For example, you might be able to retrieve the banner for a dated service that caused the report to be generated. Alternatively, perhaps you can observe how the web server responds with a "200-OK" result no matter what report you send it. Maybe you can use the DOS *net view* command and access the IPC$ share using a blank administrator password. Always remember, there's nothing the scanner can do that you cannot, and the scanner will always be disadvantaged because it cannot understand context, something you should be able to do very well.

- **Is this report accurate?** Now you're in a position to decide whether the report is accurate, or whether you're dealing with a false positive. Most of the reports will be accurate, and usually this is pretty obvious. However, a number of situations can cause false positives to be reported. By spotting these cases and weeding them out, you enhance the accuracy of the scan and ensure its credibility. This is especially important if you're going to be passing the report on to other technical people for remediation. Chapter 7 is dedicated to a discussion of how to spot false positives.

■ **What are the implications of this report?** Having weeded out reports that are blatantly false, and armed with both a solid understanding of the NASL and how it works, and a good understanding of the environment that you're scanning, you can apply your own impact rating to the issue being reported. Revisit some of the core concepts we discussed earlier in this chapter and use your knowledge of security fundamentals to put the NASL reports into perspective. Remember that there's no such thing as "zero" risk and focus your energies on mitigating the risks that are real and serious. The rating applied by the NASL writer should serve as a guide, but from our discussion of the definition of risk earlier in this chapter, it should be clear that risk is not something static. At the company, we work for we build software around the Nessus scanner that allows the analyst or the customer to adjust the risk rating as she deems appropriate for the system being scanned.

Factors that Can Affect Scanner Output

If we extend our analogy of Nessus output as a "language," then we've probably already covered many of the elements that make up a language—both the "technical" elements like grammar and vocabulary, and some "emotional" elements like culture, tradition, and the writer's personal background. One other factor that we haven't yet covered is the question of "history," which can have a huge influence on the actual meaning of the information that's being communicated. We view "history" in the context of Nessus reports as settings and variables that can impact scanner output. In this section, we explore some of the factors that can dramatically affect the contents of the report. You need to be aware of these as you read the report so that you can properly gauge the accuracy and the impact of the output.

Plugin Selection

Clearly, one of the factors that will have a big impact on the accuracy of your scan report will be the plugins you select. A detailed discussion of the plugin selection process is covered throughout this book. As with all elements of the scanner configuration, ensure that you understand the impact of the various plugin options—Enable All vs. Enable all but Denial of Service, and so forth. If the plugin doesn't execute, it can't identify the vulnerability. The use of the Nessus logs (/opt/nessus/var/nessus/logs/nessusd.messages) to verify that the plugin executed is discussed briefly a little later in this chapter.

Tools & Traps...

Locating the nessusd.messages File

The bulk of the Nessus logs are written to the nessusd.messages file. By default, this file can be found at /opt/nessus/var/nessus/logs/nessusd.messages. However, this needn't necessarily be the case. The actual target for Nessus logs to be written to is specified in the nessusd.conf file at:

```
# Log file (or 'syslog') :
logfile = /opt/nessus/var/nessus/logs/nessusd.messages
```

The "logfile=..." line specifies the location of a file to which the Nessus log output should be written. Alternatively, one can enter **syslog** or **stderr**, thereby causing nessusd to log either to the standard syslog or directly to stderr. If this is the, case no nessusd.messages file will be written into.

The Role of Dependencies

By default, if a script has dependencies, that script won't be run unless the listed dependencies have been completed. This is unless you configure the scanner to "Enable dependencies at runtime," in which case the scanner will load and execute any of the NASLs that are required for the NASLs you've selected. In the end, the output is determined by which tests are run, and the plugin list is actually built at runtime. Obviously, the construction of the plugin list will dramatically affect the output of the scan.

Safe Checks

Within many NASL scripts is a decision point that reads "if (safe_checks)," where the script decides whether it should depend on a simple banner check or execute a potentially destructive attack to determine whether the target is vulnerable to a given problem. Using safe_checks is much less likely to cause disruption of service (although, as of version 2.10, only 142 NASLs consider the option), but it's also much more likely to generate false positives. As such, selecting the safe_checks flag can dramatically affect the scan output.

Notes from the Underground...

Tests that Always Return Vulnerable

With safe_checks enabled, some tests will always return vulnerable. Read this comment by Renaud Deraison in response to a question about the accuracy of certain tests against Linux Red Hat:

Forum: SecurePoint - Nessus Archive

  Date: Mar 31, 14:57

  From: Renaud Deraison <nobody at nowhere.com>

On Wed, Mar 31, 2004 at 11:31:48AM -0500, MHewryk AT symcor DOT com wrote:

> Hi,

> I just wonder if nessus will consider the plugins

> upgrades for Fedora or RH ES 2.0, etc?

As far as I know, RedHat backports fixes into "their" version of OpenSSH/
Apache/whatever, but do not modify the banner of the server from the point
of view of the network, and they are still "thinking about it".

If you paid for RedHat ES/AS upgrades and are tired of getting false
positives from Nessus when scanning your systems, I recommend you email Mark
J Cox <mjc AT redhat DOT com> and tell them that you want RedHat to include
a tag in the banners of "fixed" programs, just like FreeBSD and many other
distributions are doing.

  -- Renaud

no404.nasl

As mentioned previously, the no404.nasl script is designed to detect web servers that push out a generic error message using the HTTP "200" success code, making them very difficult to scan for web server vulnerabilities. By storing a "snapshot" of the error that's returned in the KB, this NASL is able to help other scripts differentiate between truly positive HTTP responses and generic error messages. When this process works, it can have a dramatic impact on reducing the number of false positives from machines that exhibit this kind of behavior. Sometimes, Nessus fails to do this (for example, because the server has a "generic" error message that is simultaneously also random). Look for the no404.nasl report and examine the Nessus KB for the host in question to glean an understanding of how and how well no404.nasl is working.

Ping the Remote Host

Nessus gives you the option to first "ping" the target before scanning and then only continue the tests if the target responds to the ping. The scanner supports both ICMP (regular) and TCP pings, in which a number of TCP SYN packets are sent to the host on configurable destination ports. The risk here is that with firewalls and other network security devices, the ping packets may be filtered, causing the host to appear dead and be dropped from the target list. This risk is particularly real when TCP scans are used, as you need to select the ports on which the ping packets are sent. A machine that is active on the network but not listening on one of the selected ping ports might be missed.

Portscanner Settings

The portscan is the starting point and the basis for any vulnerability scan, and the choices you make when configuring the port scanner can have a huge impact on the scanner output. Nessus' capability, via find_service.nes, to accurately identify the actual service listening on an open port has largely done away with the problem of false negatives that used to result from services listening on nonstandard ports. However, if the portscanner misses open ports, they won't be queried by find_service.nes and might never be probed for vulnerabilities, thus resulting in false negatives—serious omissions in the vulnerability scanner output. Many NASL scripts will run against default ports regardless of what the portscanner found, but others will only run against relevant ports as found by the portscanner and stored in the Nessus KB. In such cases, it's critical that the portscanner is properly configured for accurate results.

The "Consider Unscanned Ports as Closed" scanner option has a big impact on how Nessus interprets the portscanner results. By default, Nessus considers unscanned ports "open," meaning if the portscanner didn't test them, they'll be assumed "open." Selecting this option, along with the "Optimize the Test" option, inverts this behavior, instructing Nessus to assume that ports are closed, thereby speeding the test up. Of course, it might cause Nessus to miss vulnerabilities and negatively impact the quality of the scanner output.

Proxies, Firewalls, and TCP Wrappers

In modern network security architectures, a number of systems can cause a portscanner to produce misleading results. As the Nessus scanner relies so widely on the portscanner output, an incorrect port scan can have a significant impact on scanner output. Inline HTTP proxy servers, proxy firewalls, LaBrea Tarpits, and TCP wrappers all respond to TCP SYN requests even when the port in question isn't necessarily open, and thus mislead the portscanner. Nessus keeps a record of this port as "open" in the KB and tries its best to run the appropriate tests against it. In most instances, Nessus' capability to accurately detect and identify active network services largely offsets the effect that incorrect portscanner results can have. Still, you need to be aware that if the network between the scanner and the target is acting strangely, then this will affect your scanner results.

Valid Credentials

A number of NASLs will attempt to log in to services using common or default credentials. If they succeed, the NASLs will store those credentials in the KB for other scripts to use, making those scripts much more accurate and powerful. The Windows Administrator password is a good example of this. If Nessus can determine what the password is, it can perform a number of tests against the Windows registry directly and thus give you a much more accurate impression of the patch level of the machine than it would be able to do purely from the "outside." The same is true for SNMP community strings. If you know (or have an idea of) what the passwords to various services are, it might be worth configuring these in the Nessus settings. At the same time, be aware of the "snowball" effect that can occur if Nessus coincidently guesses the correct password to any of the services being scanned.

KB Reuse and Differential Scanning

Nessusd allows one to store information about scanned hosts in the Nessus KB for later use. When scanning hosts for a second scan, one can select how much work should be redone, and how much Nessus should rely on the information gathered in the previous scan. One can even configure Nessus to report only on the differences between the information gathered in the current scan and the information stored from the previous scan. Obviously, the choices you make here will significantly impact the results that are displayed in the scan report.

And Many More…

Many more settings will impact the way the scanner behaves and can therefore impact the results. The better you understand these settings and how they're interpreted by the scanner, the better you'll be able to understand the scanner's output. Here's a brief list of some of the other settings that change the scanner's behavior in such a way that it could impact the output:

- **Optimize the test** By default, Nessus will launch all the plugins in the list, regardless of whether any of the required ports were found to be open. Selecting this option instructs Nessus only to launch a NASL script if the required ports and services were previously found and are stored in the KB. This option speeds the test up, but you might cause the scanner to miss potential weaknesses.

- **How to check if directories are writeable** This setting will determine how accurately Nessus can determine whether an FTP directory is writeable. Allowing

Nessus to depend on the directory permissions can often lead to false positives. One often sees this with the FTP servers on HP printers, for example.

- **Test SSL-based services** Nessus has the capability to scan web servers that are protected using SSL. This setting tells Nessus on which ports to search for SSL-enabled services. If you leave it on "Known SSL ports," the scanner will only search for SSL on standard ports like SSL, possibly causing it to miss SSL-enabled services running on other ports. Setting this value to "All" will cause the scanner to search all ports for SSL-enabled services.

Scanning Web Servers and Web Sites

You should note when starting your scan that DNS names and IP addresses are not necessarily interchangeable as targets, especially when scanning web servers that respond differently according to the "hostname" field in the DNS request header. When scanning web servers, it's often best to scan both the host IP address and the DNS names of each of the web sites residing on the server. While this leads to large-scale duplication of reports, it might also find vulnerabilities that are web site specific and won't be detected when just scanning the IP. You should also be aware that Nessus will sometimes automatically perform a DNS lookup of the IP address specified and use the hostname returned when sending requests to a web server. This can dramatically impact results.

Web Servers and Load Balancing

One often needs to deal with cases where the target is specified as something like "www.target.com," but the target address actually refers to a load balancer and not to the web server itself. Roughly put, there are three approaches to load balancing on web servers:

- **Reverse proxy** The load balancer accepts the HTTP requests from the client, forwards them to one of the web servers, receives the reply from the web server, and then forwards that back to the client.

- **HTTP redirect** Upon receiving the first HTTP request from the client, the load balancer responds with an HTTP "redirect" of some kind. The client then makes a new request, this time for the specified target, and continues to interact with that target for the remainder of the session.

- **DNS** Various kinds of DNS voodoo can be used to specify the IP address of the server to which the client should connect. The client resolves the web server name to the IP address specified, connects, and transacts with the same web server from the start.

It's easy to see how these approaches can cause strange results from a Nessus scan. When scanning in a load-balancing environment, ensure you understand how the load balancing is done and which element you're actually scanning.

Bugs in the Plugins

Remember that NASL scripts are just program code and are therefore susceptible to bugs, just as other code is. It's quite possible that under certain circumstances, a plugin can erroneously produce either false positives or false negatives because of simple programmer error. Make sure you update your plugin set regularly, if not every time you run a scan, and apply the principles taught earlier in this chapter to ensure that you understand each vulnerability report and why it was generated.

Tools & Traps...

Updating Nessus Plugins

It's essential to keep the Nessus plugins current, because new tests are being written all the time, and existing tests are continuously being enhanced and repaired. With Tenable's Nessus 3, once you have registered your installation of Nessus, you will receive automatic updates. You can check to determine if you are registered by issuing the command /opt/nessus/bin/nessus-fetch –check. There are basically four additional ways to update plugins:

- Download an individual NASL script from the web interface at www. nessus.org.

- Download a tarball with all the latest scripts for the current Nessus version. For Nessus 2.0.10, this can be found at www.nessus.org/nasl/ all-2.0.tar.gz.

- Run the script nessus-update-plugins, which ships with the Nessus install and is typically located at /opt/nessus/sbin/nessus-update-plugins.

- Some *nix distributions, like Debian, allow one to install a plugin set that *they* maintain via the native package manager. Be aware that these plugin lists are maintained by the OS distribution and may therefore lag a little behind the most current state.

Additional Reading

The output of the Nessus scan is always presented to you in the form of a report, in the format of your choice. To help you fully understand the report, however, there are some alternative sources of information that you can also explore. Furthering our language analogy, studying these sources can be likened to reading the history of a language or a people. It won't add to the report, but it might help you to better understand how the contents of the report were derived. There are a number of such sources that you should consider, each of which is considered in its own right elsewhere in this book, so reference to them is made here for completeness only.

Configuration Files

If the report you are viewing does contain the scanner configuration that was used, you can still learn about how the scanner was configured by looking in the various configuration files. In Figure 5.8, for example, you can very clearly see that for this scan:

- The Nmap portscanner is not enabled (10336=no), which is fine since NMAP is not required by Nessus.

- The portscan was limited to a default range of ports (port_range = 1–15000).

- Dependencies were loaded at startup (auto_enable_dependencies = yes).

- "Safe checks" were enabled (safe_checks = yes).

Knowing this information before reading the report will greatly assist you in understanding the output and evaluating the security posture of the target hosts.

Figure 5.8 This nessusrc File Shows What Can Be Learned by Reading the Scanner Configuration

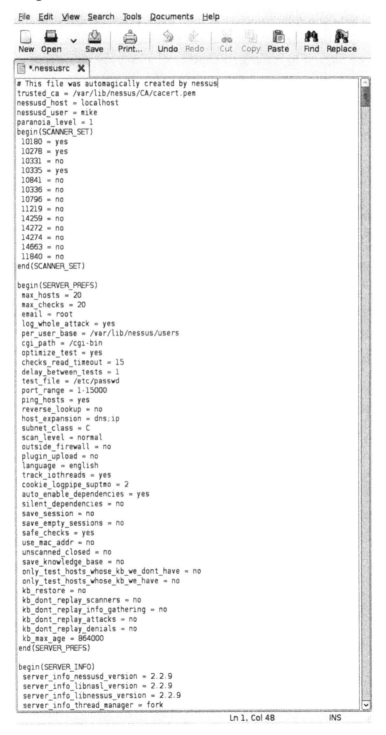

NASL

We've stated that NASL is the true "language" of the Nessus report. The NASL script describes the set of prompt-and-response tests that are performed to reach a conclusion on the existence of a given vulnerability. Only by reading and understanding the NASL script in question can you really "get behind the scenes" of a report and evaluate its accuracy and impact. There's no need to "speak" NASL fluently; all you're aiming for is a basic grasp of the content of a script. Use this book or the NASL guide at www.nessus.org/doc/nasl.html.

The Nessus KB

The Nessus KB is a temporary store used by Nessus to keep track of its progress and important information that'll be required later. For example, the KB will be used to store the list of open ports and the services that are believed to be listening on those ports. If "KB Saving" is enabled when the scan is run, the KB is saved to a text file that you can revisit when you read the report to help you understand what the scanner was "thinking." The KB for a given machine can usually be found at /opt/nessus/var/nessus/users/<your_nessus_user_name>/kbs/<target>. It's simple to read and is discussed in chapter 9 at length. By looking in the KB, you can learn valuable information such as what plugins were run, what services Nessus associated with the different open ports, and the content of the "generic" HTTP error message.

The Nessus Logs

If logging is enabled, the Nessus logfiles can also help you to better understand scanner output. The logs are covered in detail elsewhere in this book, so here are just a few specific categories of logfile entries that will often help shed light on the scanner findings:

```
user charl starts a new scan. Target(s) : 192.168.1.90, with max_hosts = 30
and max_checks = 10
```

This tells us that the scan was in fact launched against a specific target.

```
launching synscan.nes against 192.168.1.90 [24943]
```

This type of entry shows that a specific plugin was in fact launched. In this case, it's Nessus' own portscanner.

```
logins.nasl (process 24946) finished its job in 0.528 seconds
```

This type of entry tells us that the NASL completed without error. The time information can also be useful—a too-short completion time often suggests that the NASL didn't execute as expected.

```
Not launching swat_guessable_usernames.nasl against 192.168.1.90 none of the
required tcp ports are open (this is not an error)
```

This type of entry tells us that the specified NASL was never launched because the required ports were not identified.

```
Not launching apache_2_0_45.nasl against 192.168.1.90 because the key www/apache
is missing (this is not an error)
```

This type of entry tells us that the specified NASL was not launched because previously launched plugins did not identify an Apache web server on any of the scanned ports.

Forums and Mailing Lists

As an open-source product, Nessus enjoys support from a strong and vibrant user community. Renaud Deraison and the other members of the development remain actively involved in supporting and discussing the product and its use. Make use of this rich resource when using the product to learn about known bugs, quirky plugins, and advanced scanning techniques. While there are many resources on the web, the best place to start would probably be the Nessus site itself. Visit http://list.nessus.org/ or use a search engine to find what you're looking for. For more, please visit http://blog.tenablesecurity.com/.

Summary

Nessus is simply a tool that executes an extensive set of security tests over the network and can present you with the results in various different formats. To gain value from the scanner, you need to interpret the results of the tests yourself, and to do this, you first need to understand the tests and how they are executed.

In this chapter, we liken learning to understand Nessus scanner output to learning to speak a new language. You need to understand both the "technical" (vocabulary and grammar) and the "cultural" (history and tradition) elements. In practical terms, you'll have to familiarize yourself with a number of different areas, from the theoretical definitions of "vulnerability" and "risk" to the technical details of the NASL language and the various scanner configuration settings.

We discussed that the Nessus tests are really thousands of different little programs written by separate individuals, all with different backgrounds and perspectives, and suggested some steps one could follow to really "understand" what was meant by a given report and what implication that would have with you.

Finally, we explored the impact the different scanner settings could have on the scanner results and highlighted some specific settings that could significantly impact the results of your scan.

Solutions Fast Track

The Nessus UI Basics

- ☑ Nessus works on a client-server model.

- ☑ There are currently two open-source GUI clients available—Nessus Client for Windows and the Nessus Client for X. They are nearly exact.

- ☑ There is also a UNIX command-line client that is not discussed in this chapter.

- ☑ Both GUI clients discussed allow one to view scanner output, save and export reports in various formats, and import results from previously saved reports.

- ☑ Regardless of the client used, the Nessus scanner reports are detailed and complex and need to be carefully analyzed to be fully understood.

Reading a Nessus Report

- ☑ Nessus is a "vulnerability scanner." To understand Nessus reports, you need to first understand what "vulnerability" is.

☑ Risk is a much broader concept than vulnerability is. With the risk more clearly quantified, we can compare the relative significance of the reports generated by a vulnerability scanner.

☑ When analyzing Nessus reports, one should temporarily put on a "black hat" and consider what vectors of attack the information being reported would present to an attacker.

☑ Use this thinking about attack vectors to put the risk represented by different vulnerabilities into perspective as you read through a Nessus scan report.

☑ To understand what a scanner report is saying, we need to understand how a scanner actually "thinks." Understanding scanner logic is key to understanding Nessus reports.

☑ A Nessus scan "report" consists of a number of "issues," which are in turn classified as "Holes," "Warnings," or "Notes." If you look at a Nessus issue, regardless of the client you used or the report format, there will always be certain key pieces of information for you to consider.

☑ A Nessus report is a little like a newspaper report and needs to be read with a critical eye. As you read the report, regardless of how the output is being displayed, you need to be constantly asking yourself certain key questions about the content.

☑ Numerous settings and variables can impact scanner output and dramatically affect the contents of a Nessus report. You need to be aware of these as you read the report so that you can properly gauge the accuracy and the impact of the output. To help you fully understand a Nessus report, there are some alternative sources of information that you can also explore. Studying these sources won't add to the report, but it might help you to better understand how the contents of the report were derived.

Frequently Asked Questions

Q: Of the two Nessus clients discussed in this book, which do you think is the best to use?

A: This chapter focuses on the "content" of a Nessus report and steers away from the details of the various "point-and-click" interfaces. However, the standard HTML generated by the X client is our favorite for reading reports in, and the X client does give you a higher degree of control over the configuration settings. We also use raw NBE format a lot when reading reports, as it allows us to rip through "pipes," "greps," "awks," and "cuts" very quickly.

Q: If the Nessus reports are so open to interpretation and have to be read as carefully as you suggest, aren't there other vulnerability scanners that can produce more accurate and dependable results?

A: In short: No. We really don't believe there are. This is not to say that Nessus is *better* than all other scanners, only that Nessus is not *worse*. We have two reasons for saying this. First, Nessus has consistently compared favorably with all kinds of commercial products in numerous independent reviews. While other products might have better report content or offer some features that Nessus doesn't, the Nessus scanner will always rate among the top performers in almost every important area, and most significantly so in the area of accuracy. Second, the factors that make reading Nessus reports such a skill are common to all vulnerability scanners that perform tests over the network. The same type of "prompt-and-response" logic applied by Nessus is also applied by *every* other scanner of this kind, and thus the scanners all face the same challenges. Whichever scanner you use, you'd have to learn to really "read" its reports, just as you do with Nessus. All things being equal, the dedication and approachability of Renaud and his team, along with the enthusiasm of the Nessus user community and the "open" nature of the technology, might make it easier to learn than other products, once you put your mind to it.

Q: It's clear that the scanner configuration settings can dramatically impact the results of your scan. Is there then any "best" configuration to use?

A: Unfortunately, no. As you'll probably learn from this book, the scanner configuration will usually be a balance between accuracy and efficiency. The more accurate your scans, the bigger the impact, and the quicker you make the scans, the more chance you'll miss something. In terms of reading and understanding Nessus reports, the fact remains simply that you should have a grasp of the settings with which the scan was run when you read the report so that you can understand where the scanner is coming from. Without considering the scanner settings, you'll only ever have half the picture.

## Chapter 6

Vulnerability Types

Solutions in this chapter:

- **Critical Vulnerabilities**
- **Information Leaks**
- **Denial of Service**
- **Best Practices**

☑ **Summary**

☑ **Solutions Fast Track**

☑ **Frequently Asked Questions**

Introduction

When you run Nessus against your network, you might receive much more data than you bargained for. When staring at a massive report, how do you begin to know where to start fixing things, or where your real problems are? Being able to understand and classify reams of vulnerability data is one of the areas in which it's truly important to be able to identify and understand the different types of vulnerabilities that have been found. Having a clear idea of what vulnerabilities are out there and in what order they need to be addressed will help you define a plan for fixing your problems most effectively.

We will begin by classifying vulnerabilities into four broad categories: critical vulnerabilities, information leaks, denial-of-service (DoS) vulnerabilities, and best practices. Breaking down the types of vulnerabilities by type and potential impact makes it easier to realize what sorts of problems you have on your network, and to provide additional information and guidance to help determine what order the problems should be addressed.

Vulnerability classification is still an emerging field, and information security experts often have strong differences of opinion about the best way to deal with the thorny subject of classifying vulnerabilities. Some people maintain that it should be done by the affected service, by severity, or by which operating system is targeted. Still others take a more abstract approach, and it is this model that Nessus follows, classifying vulnerabilities by the potential impact of a successful exploit.

Critical Vulnerabilities

Critical vulnerabilities are your highest priority problems. These represent vulnerabilities that, if exploited, could lead to code execution, privilege escalation, system compromise, or similarly dire consequences. Critical vulnerabilities should be addressed immediately due to the imminent threat to your network.

When reviewing a Nessus report, critical vulnerabilities are indicated by entries with the high- and medium- risk levels. The risk levels are set by the plugin developer and are based on a worst-case scenario of the vulnerability being successfully exploited. Several factors are weighed when considering whether a given flaw is considered critical: the ability of an attacker to exploit the flaw remotely, the privileges obtained after a successful attack, and whether the vulnerability is being actively exploited in the wild. In general, your highest priority vulnerabilities will be those that are remotely exploitable, do not require an existing user account on the affected system, will yield privileged access, and can be automatically and reliably exploited.

Many system administrators are already familiar with a wide range of critical vulnerabilities, mostly due to the large number of worms that take advantage of these vulnerabilities to propagate. The Sasser worm exploited a buffer overflow in the Microsoft Windows Local Security Authority Subsystem Service (LSASS); the Witty worm exploited an overflow in the

ICQ protocol parser shipped with Internet Security System's IDS products; and the Slapper worm spread through a flaw in the OpenSSL library used in conjunction with the Apache web server.

For another example of a critical vulnerability, one that wasn't turned into an automated worm or virus, but is nevertheless a high-importance issue, consider the Solaris sadmind arbitrary command execution flaw. The default security settings of the sadmind RPC service allow a remote, unauthenticated attacker to execute arbitrary commands on a Solaris system as the root user. You can look at Nessus' reference page for this vulnerability at http://cgi.nessus.org/plugins/dump.php3?id=11841. Note that the risk factor is set to high, as befitting a vulnerability that would allow remote root compromise.

Notes from the Underground...

The 0-Day Market

As you might imagine, critical vulnerabilities are of the most interest to attackers, so much so that there's quite a market in the underground for new exploits, particularly those that have not been publicly disclosed or fixed by the vendor. Vulnerability scanners like Nessus will help you test your network quickly and comprehensively for known vulnerabilities, but keep in mind that new flaws are surfacing daily, many of which have been in private circulation for quite some time. This is one good reason why a vulnerability scanner is an important part of an in-depth defense, but should never be considered the final word on whether a system is vulnerable to attack.

Critical vulnerabilities are common targets for network worms, Trojan horse programs, and automated attack tools. If your network is full of critical vulnerabilities, just one well-written worm can spell disaster and widespread compromise. Even if you have a hardened border and good firewalls, all it takes is one infected user with a laptop to plug his system into your network to set off a cascade of automated attacks. The user might not even know that he's infected, but you'll certainly see the deleterious effects.

In addition to classifying critical vulnerabilities by their importance, we can also classify them by their type. Almost everyone who has worked a job that involves network security has heard of buffer overflows, but they're far from the only kind of exploitable vulnerability. Let's look at the different types of vulnerabilities that end up rated as critical.

- Buffer overflows
- Directory traversals

- Format string attacks

- Default passwords

- Misconfigurations

- Known backdoors

For this chapter's series of vulnerability explanations, let's assume that we have a well-meaning but clueless programmer/system administrator "Bob", and a devious attacker "Brian". This will give us a consistent framework for understanding how these vulnerabilities might be exploited, and how they found their way into our systems in the first place.

Buffer Overflows

Buffer overflows are perhaps the most famous type of critical vulnerability. They are caused by a programmer's failure to limit the amount of information that can be written in to a predefined buffer. When data is copied from one source (such as a network socket) into the buffer, an overflow can occur if the input data is greater than the size of the destination buffer. The programmer is responsible for checking the length value of the input prior to the copy operation.

If the length of input data is not checked, or the allocation routine for the destination buffer makes a mistake in the size of the input, the copy operation can result in memory corruption. Depending on where the destination buffer is stored in memory, this corruption can be used to hijack control of the vulnerable program. Although the exploitation details vary from platform to platform, nearly all buffer overflow flaws involving user input can result in the creation of a critical vulnerability.

For example, let's pretend that Bob has written an Internet chat system that requires users to provide their names when they connect. When developing this program, Bob uses a temporary 50-byte character buffer to store the name received from the connecting user. After all, nobody he knows has a name anywhere near that long, so it should be more than enough room.

Now, assume that Bob's program gets packaged, sold, and distributed for sale. A copy falls into the hands of curious Brian. Brian installs the server and uses the Telnet program to connect to the service. The service asks for his name, but instead of giving it Brian, he sends a long repeated string of the letter "A." To his surprise, the chat server immediately closes his Telnet session and refuses to accept new connections. Brian then runs the chat server again, this time with the help of a debugging tool. After sending the long string of "A" characters, the debugger shows that an exception occurred when trying to access the memory address 0x41414141 (the letter A has the hex value of 41).

Brian has seen this before. This appears to be a standard buffer overflow; the long name he provided has been copied over all other local variables in the vulnerable function, and has continued on to trash program state information in the process's stack memory. This can be exploited to execute arbitrary code on this system, such as an interactive command shell.

Nessus uses a variety of techniques to identify network services that are vulnerable to buffer overflow attacks. When the vulnerable service runs inside a single process, it is usually not possible to actually test for the overflow without crashing the service completely. To work around this limitation, Nessus employs techniques such as version fingerprinting, banner matches, and even partial overflows to determine whether a given service is vulnerable.

Buffer overflows in real software are often somewhat more complicated than this, but usually not by much—the basic principles remain the same. In the last few years, there have been buffer overflows discovered in products as diverse as gaim (OSVDB ID 3734, CAN-2004-0005), Mac OS X (OSVDB ID 3043, CAN-2003-1006), and Oracle (OSVDB ID 2449, CAN-2003-0727).

Directory Traversal

Directory traversal vulnerabilities are simply ways to access files outside a restricted directory structure. The best way to describe directory traversal attacks is by example. Let's assume our faithful but clueless Bob has installed an FTP server on his network. He has configured this server to only allow users to access the files in their home directories.

Brian has been given an account on this FTP server and is told to use it for backing up important files on his system. When Brian first connects to the FTP server, he notices that his current directory has been set to /home/brian. Being a curious-minded type, he tries to change his working directory to /home to see what other users have accounts on this system. The FTP server responds with an "Access Denied" message almost immediately; apparently, old Bob is trying to prevent people from snooping around on his server.

Like most modern operating systems, the system running the FTP server supports what are known as *parent paths*. A parent path is simply any path that references the special ".." directory name. This ".." directory always points to the directory above the current one. Brian realizes that this technique might apply against Bob's FTP server and gives it a whirl. Instead of sending a request to change into the /home directory, Brian simply asks the server to change into "..". To his glee, the FTP responds back with an OK and Brian is now able to see all of the files and directories in the /home directory.

If Brian is allowed to see the files in the /home directory, he might also be able to see system files. Consider the perils of allowing Brian to make a request like ".. /../../etc/ passwd". Depending on the system configuration, access to this file could result in Brian obtaining the encrypted password hashes of all users on the system (including Bob). The encryption method used by the passwd file can be broken through an exhaustive brute-force attack, something that at which any modern PC excels.

Nessus includes an impressive number of directory traversal plugins. These plugins test for traversal flaws in everything from web applications to Trivial File Transfer Protocol (TFTP) services.

The generic web server traversal check is responsible for discovering flaws in dozens of embedded web servers alone. Traversal flaws are one of the most common problems found with any protocol that maps user requests to local file paths.

In recent years, Apache (OSVDB ID 859, CAN-2002-0661), rsync (OSVDB ID 5731, CAN-2004-0426), and Microsoft's IIS (OSVDB ID 436, CVE-2000-0884) have all been found vulnerable to directory traversal attacks.

Format String Attacks

A format string vulnerability is another common error in the way in which user-supplied data is processed. It is common, in the C language, to use the *printf()* functions to create and manipulate character strings. These functions take an argument known as the *format specifier*, followed by a list of values. A format specifier is simply a template, with special sequences known as conversion specifiers used as placeholders for the parts of the template that change.

For example, a program that prints out "Hello NAME", where NAME is something determined at runtime, will use a format specifier such as "Hello %s". The "%s" is the conversion specifier for a NULL-terminated character string. When using this format specifier, the called function will expect a single argument after the specifier. This argument should be the memory address (pointer) of a null-terminated text string. The problem occurs when the format string specifier contains more conversion specifiers than there are arguments to the function. Instead of simply ignoring the extra "%" sequences, the function will take whatever happens to be in the process' stack memory and uses it as the argument for the specifier.

These vulnerabilities are often found when the format specifier string is created based on data supplied by the user. If the user data contains a conversion specifier, such as "%s" or "%d", the function will try to process arguments beyond what was provided by the programmer. In most cases, this will lead to garbled output or program crash. Talented attackers can craft their own sequence of conversion specifiers such that it results in arbitrary memory locations being written with whatever contents they choose. Format string vulnerabilities are often used to overwrite a function pointer with the memory address of user-supplied data (usually shellcode). After the *printf()* function is called, any calls to the overwritten function will result in the attacker's code being executed.

Let's assume that Bob modifies his chat server to record the user's name in a log file. The following snippet of code reads the name of the new user over the network and writes it into the log file:

```
char *userdata = ReadUserName();

char *logstring = malloc(strlen(userdata)+6);

snprintf(logstring, strlen(userdata), "User: %s", userdata);

fprintf(logfd, logstring);
```

If the userdata character array contains a conversion specifier, the *fprintf()* call will access whatever memory happens to exist on the stack. For example, if userdata contains "%p" (the pointer specifier), the log file will end up with something like this:

```
User: 0xbfff601a
```

This hex value just happens to be the next value in the process' stack memory. Using conversion specifiers such as "%d" and "%n", it is possible to cause arbitrary memory locations to be overwritten, one or two bytes at a time.

Nessus checks for format string vulnerabilities in a variety of ways. Often, a version match against the service banner is sufficient to determine if the remote service is vulnerable; other times, long strings of conversion specifiers, such as "%n", are sent to force the service to crash. A few applications will actually return the resulting string to the remote client; these are tested by specifying a harmless specifier and then looking for the signature in the output.

In recent years, there have been format string vulnerabilities in a number of major products, including Solaris' rpc.rwalld (OSVDB ID 778, CVE-2002-0573) and Tripwire (OSVDB ID 6608, CAN-2004-0536).

Default Passwords

It is astonishing and depressing how many systems are set up, configured, and deployed in the wild without anyone ever stopping to consider the peril of failing to change the password. Certainly, our bumbling Bob didn't consider necessary. Why, he set up his entire network without bothering to change the factory default passwords on any of the networking devices. All of his Cisco routers still have logins of "cisco" and passwords of "cisco", all of his wireless access points (WAPs) are still advertising an SSID of "linksys", and he's proud of it. He considers it a measure of system administration—all those passwords are so hard to remember, after all.

Enter Brian the war-driver, stage left in a tiny VW Beetle with a huge antenna on the roof. As he passes by Bob's place of employment, he detects a wireless network with a default "linksys" identifier. As an experienced war-driver, he's seen many different networks, and is reasonably familiar with the standard usernames and passwords of most of the major pieces of networking equipment out there. Encouraged by the default SSID of the WAP, Brian pulls out his laptop, associates to the access point, and finds that a local DHCP server is more than happy to issue him an IP address. Looking at the IP and his new gateway to the Internet, Brian tries to connect to the gateway via Telnet. He sees a login prompt, and tries "cisco" and "cisco" for the username and password. Just like that, he's in, and Brian now has a high degree of visibility and some degree of control over the router and Bob's connection to the Internet.

Once again, it can easily get worse. If Bob has also failed to change the enable password—the equivalent of the root account on a Cisco router—from its default setting, Brian might have easily just gained access to control the router entirely, which gives him a vast amount of power over Bob's network.

Nessus includes a massive set of plugins that test for common and default passwords. These plugins are able to identify default passwords on everything from SQL database servers to network printers. Default password vulnerabilities are extremely common on most sizable networks; most devices ship with default passwords preset, and not all system administrators are diligent about changing them immediately.

Misconfigurations

For example, Bob has just been tasked with providing FTP access to the company's primary web server, specifically to allow a web design firm to update the content. Recalling his bad experiences with his own FTP server, Bob decides to use the tried-and-true Microsoft FTP Server that ships with Internet Information Server (IIS). While this service has had a few security problems in the past, it is already installed and would take all of five minutes to set up. Bob adds a new user account for the web design firm, configures the FTP service to point to the web content, and sends the account details off to his boss.

Brian is bored. He has been poking around on various FTP servers all day, looking for a place to store some illegal files for a friend of his. Bob's FTP server happens to be in the same IP range that Brian is scanning. Brian attempts to log in to the server, using the default "anonymous" credentials, and is greeted with a directory listing of the company's web site. It appears that when Bob was configuring the new FTP service, he forgot to uncheck the "Allow anonymous access" option. The company's web site has now been completely exposed, allowing anyone on the Internet to read and possibly modify the contents. Brian creates a hidden directory in the web root and starts the slow process of uploading his illicit data to the server.

This particular misconfiguration is both extremely common and incredibly dangerous. One of the authors has seen an instance where the FTP service was used to backdoor the "secure login" page of a financial services organization. The intruder had simply downloaded the saved password log file once a day, for three months straight, until the backdoor was discovered. Anonymous FTP access is one of the many common misconfigurations that Nessus can detect.

Known Backdoors

The final type of critical vulnerability that we'll discuss, which Nessus checks for, are known backdoor programs. These range from the recently public to the well-known tools of crackers. And, given Bob's established lack of skill as a system administrator, it's quite likely that he has at least one system with a known backdoor on it. These backdoors are usually installed after an attacker has already compromised the system and wants to assure himself of having an easy and secret way to access the system later. Some backdoors, like Netbus and Portal of Doom, are quite well known. However, others are constantly being developed and discovered in the wild. Most often, a backdoor is a network service listening on an unexpected port on the compromised host, silently waiting for someone with the proper authentication credentials to log in. Many are silent upon connection until you send them the expected string, but some will actually prompt you for a login in identifiable and fingerprintable ways. Finding a known backdoor program listening on one of your systems is a critical vulnerability indicating not that you might be vulnerable to attack, but that you almost certainly have already been successfully attacked and compromised. Thanks to the global community of plugin developers, Nessus is able to detect and report a wide variety of backdoor programs. Plugins are being developed for each new backdoor as it is discovered.

Information Leaks

An information leak is a disclosure of information about your system. While it might seem at first that this isn't a big deal, in reality it can be one of the first steps of a devastating attack. Vulnerabilities classified as information leaks will allow an attacker to gather information about your system, and to, in effect, conduct network reconnaissance.

Many system administrators wrongfully dismiss information leaks as a minor problem. While it's true that they don't pack the punch of a remote root compromise or other critical vulnerability, information leaks are still very real threats to your system. Let's look at some of the possible issues that can come up when information is leaked.

Notes from the Underground...

Social Engineering with Gleaned Information

One of the primary threats when dealing with information leaks is the possibility that attackers can take a little knowledge and turn it into a lot of knowledge. If they manage to discover the name of a system user or employee through a vulnerability that leaks this information, they might be able to pose as that user to the help desk and try to get their password changed. They might be able to pose as that user to the physical security and get an official badge with their picture on it and some access rights. Moreover, they might just be able to start issuing arbitrary orders to other employees in that employee's name. Depending on how well trained your employees are about social engineering, it might go unnoticed.

Gleaning information from a system can greatly aid or speed a technical attack. For example, consider the Lotus Notes OpenServer Information Disclosure vulnerability, viewable online at http://cgi.nessus.org/plugins/dump.php3?id=10795. In the default configuration of a Lotus Notes OpenServer, a remote client is able to browse databases on that server via HTTP, potentially learning server versions, log files, and server statistics. Let's see what a talented attacker could do with that.

Knowing the version of a server will help greatly when mounting your attack. Instead of having to try exploits against all different possible versions of a server, you can limit your attack to exploits that you know will work against the version running. This will greatly speed up your attack, and allow you to maintain a lower profile in case network activity is being tracked by an intrusion detection system (IDS).

Being able to read the log files and server statistics will disclose even more valuable information. From the file sizes, you can often determine how busy a server is, when the peak periods of activity are, and, conversely, when the server is likely to be little used. You might also be able to gather usernames and authentication information—whether it's keyed or password, how many false tries are allowed before an account is locked, and so forth. This will give you a better idea of how to mount an effective and undetected attack against the integrity of the server.

Now that we understand how information disclosure attacks can be problematic rather than just a minor housekeeping detail of system administration, let's look at some different types of information leaks that you might run across, and consider how each might be used to gain further access to the system:

- Memory disclosure

- Network information disclosure

- Version information disclosure

- Path disclosure

- User enumeration

Memory Disclosure

One of the more common information leak vulnerability is memory disclosure. This problem occurs when a system forgets to clear a memory block before using it to construct a message that is sent to an untrusted party. Consider the memory block as a sheet of paper, and the message itself as the lead of a pencil. If the paper is not erased prior to a new message being written, any place on the paper that is not part of the new message could contain the contents of a previous message. The message in this case can be anything from an HTML page displayed by a web server to an ICMP packet on the network.

Memory disclosure flaws have been discovered in everything from the Windows NetBIOS service to the network card drivers used across a wide range of operating systems. The actual impact of a memory disclosure vulnerability depends on what the affected system is doing and what the disclosed memory is used for. In some cases, this can result in a remote attacker being able to capture passwords to and from the affected system.

For example, Linksys routers have a well-known vulnerability where they will respond to legitimate BOOTP requests with portions of the memory from their network cards in the payload (OSVDB ID TBD, CVE-2004-0580). Given enough packets, this can lead to an attacker being able to analyze the network traffic passing through the device.

Network Information

One of the first things that any new attacker is going to want to do is understand your network topology. There are several ways to go about this, but most of them rely on information leaks of some sort. When your attacker understands what resources you have on the network and where they are located, when he can chart the configuration and placement of firewalls, routers with access lists, and important servers and resources, then it's much more likely that he'll be able to launch a targeted attack, and it's much less likely that it will be noticed.

Several types of devices are commonly used to begin this type of network enumeration. Simple Network Management Protocol (SNMP) is a very popular choice for configuration management, and many networks never bother to change their SNMP strings from the defaults of "public" and "private". Therefore, when Brian first attempts to scan Bob's network, a quick sweep to see which devices speak SNMP and whether they'll respond to the "public" and "private" strings is probably well worth his time. If the attempt is successful, Brian might garner all sorts of information about these devices, from their IP addresses and configuration details to their administrators' names and phone numbers. The particular details of what information is available will vary greatly between equipment vendors and their supported Management Information Bases (MIBs), but most will yield a rich harvest to an intelligent attacker.

ICMP messages are another very common method of charting a network. Depending on what devices will respond to what sorts of probes, you can learn things like the local default router, the timestamp on the devices, what ports they are and aren't listening on (which will aid in discovering what services they're running), whether they will accept source routing (most devices will not, but you never know), and other such juicy information. This, too, is likely to be one of Brian's first tactics when scanning a network.

Version Information

Once hosts and basic network topology have been accounted for, the next step is to enumerate the services that are listening, and to determine as much information about them as possible. Many services will advertise their vendor and exact version in the banner that is presented upon connection. Apache web servers are fairly notorious for displaying detailed version information in the headers of every web page they serve. For example, here are the server headers provided by a typical Apache server:

```
HTTP/1.1 200 OK
Date: Sun, 10 Aug 2004 10:17:11 GMT
```

```
Server: Apache/1.3.23 (Unix) (Red-Hat/Linux) mod_ssl/2.8.3 OpenSSL/0.9.6b
Content-Type: text/html
```

As you can see, the information returned from the Apache server includes some specific version numbers, and the name of the Linux distribution on which it is running. A talented attacker can take one look at this server string and immediately know which exploits have a high probability of working. In this specific case, Brian might choose to exploit a vulnerability in the OpenSSL library to gain remote access to this system. The most commonly used exploit for this vulnerability requires the attacker to know exactly what version and Linux distribution the server is running on to succeed in the attack. Brian can easily determine what versions of Red Hat Linux included version 1.3.23 of the Apache server, and simply choose the relevant options in the exploit code.

Many other servers are equally verbose—name servers running BIND are susceptible to disclosing their version through the chaos txt query; most versions of the Secure Shell server will advertise their version information during the protocol handshake; and Exchange mail servers will provide the exact release build number in the SMTP greeting message. Many Nessus plugins depend on exposed version numbers to determine whether a given service is vulnerable. This technique is used in situations in which there is simply no other way to safely check for a given flaw.

Path Disclosure

Path disclosure is one of the most commonly overlooked information disclosure vulnerabilities. A path disclosure flaw exists when a network service can be forced to return the local file or directory path for a given resource. This information can then be used to successfully exploit other flaws that depend on knowing the file path.

For example, Bob's personal web site is hosted on a dedicated server at a large ISP. Bob has decided to start learning the PHP scripting language, which can be used to develop complex, dynamic web sites in a short period of time. The PHP interpreter is often configured to display errors directly to the user when a problem occurs in the PHP script. This error normally contains the full path to the PHP script, the line number, and type of error that occurred. Bob has decided to create a database backend for his web site; he makes the common mistake of placing the database username and password into a PHP script that is in the web root. To make matters worse, this PHP script simply ends in the ".inc" extension, which means that anyone who knows the path to this file can simply download it.

Brian has developed a slight vendetta against Bob at this point; he is tired of seeing this incompetent wonk getting a fat salary. Brian has been prodding at Bob's web site for quite some time, waiting for a chance to crack into the server and leave a nice message on the front page. As the weeks go by, Brian notices that a percentage of the web site content appears to be pulled from a database. Brian whips up a quick script to numerous parallel requests to one of the database-enabled pages on Bob's web site. After running this script for a few minutes, the requests start returning a PHP error message indicating that the database server has reached the maximum number of connections. This error message happens to include the file path to the PHP script that called the database connect routine; the same PHP script that ends in ".inc" and is sitting unprotected in the web root. Seeing this data, Brian figures out the virtual path in the web directory and downloads this file. Five minutes later, Brian is ecstatic to discover that the password Bob uses for the database server is the same one set for the root user account on the dedicated server.

User Enumeration

The last type of information disclosure we'll discuss is user enumeration. It's certainly in Brian's interests to be able to discover usernames of legitimate accounts on these systems. It greatly improves the ease of cracking passwords and gaining access that way, and will also increase the odds of successful social engineering. It will allow him to map out which users might have accounts on multiple machines, thereby giving some hint as to departmental or functional organization of the network. There are multiple ways to do this, depending on the operating system and the service. Some operating systems, like many variations of Windows, will allow you to connect to the Windows sharing services without requiring that you possess valid authentication credentials for that machine and make requests through that unauthenticated connection, including requesting local usernames.

Other services will not allow connections like that, but will have differences in response when a valid username is attempted versus an invalid one. A slightly more obscure example is the OpenSSH Username Validity Timing Attack (OSVDB ID 2140, CAN-2003-0190), where a failed login as a legitimate user fails after a delay, and a failed login as a nonexistent user returns immediately. Using this technique, it would be possible for Brian to try usernames until he saw one with a delay. That way, even if he didn't have the password, he would know that a legitimate user account existed on that machine with that name. As you can see, information leaks should be addressed whenever possible to prevent these types of attacks. They're not the glaring beacons of doom that critical vulnerabilities are, but they are one of the early targets of an attacker.

Denial of Service

Denial of service (DoS) attacks take an existing software service and make it unavailable to the users, usually by either consuming all its resources—whether processor, memory, or network—or sending it some type of malformed signal that the service does not handle gracefully. This can be costly, both in terms of productivity and sheer finance. When a networked service is unavailable, you might lose employee hours, work, effectiveness, and business. Customers or potential customers might be turned away from an unavailable site, and think less of your business because of it. The classic DoS attacks like WinNuke (a packet sent on port 139 that would cause the target machine to instantly bluescreen) and the Ping of Death (an oversized IP packet that exceeded the maximum size allowable of a packet) were just the beginning.

Currently, DoS attacks can be big business, or dirty business. Unscrupulous business folks have not hesitated at making sure that their competitors' networks were hit by a sudden and inexplicable stream of traffic that knocked them offline at just the wrong moment. This can be as grandiose as trying to extort payment from online sports bookies to ensure that they stay online and profitable during big betting events. "Nice server farm you've got here. Shame if something happened to it." Alternatively, it can be as petty as one person trying to knock the other offline entirely during the last few frantic minutes of bidding on a hotly contested item on eBay. In today's highly networked world, ensuring that you can access all your online resources whenever you want to is becoming ever more important.

In a more sinister approach, DoS attacks can also be used to cover a digital assault. If you know you need to do something that will cause someone's IDS to light up like a Christmas tree, taking out that IDS before you launch your noisy attack is clearly to your advantage. Alternatively, you can deliberately occupy the system administrators' time and attention by flooding one machine with network requests while you launch a low-and-slow offensive at a different machine, hoping that the extremely busy and stressed system administrators will not notice.

There are several avenues available to a DoS attack. They might attempt to drown your network connection in traffic, as in a distributed denial-of-service (DDoS) attack. This is the form of DoS with which most people are familiar, as the widespread DDoS attacks against major Internet sites like Yahoo.com, Microsoft.com, and sco.com have garnered a lot of press attention. However, it's not the form of DoS in which we are most interested. Nessus checks to see whether individual machines are vulnerable to DoS attacks through exploitation of the operating system or a service running on it. Through poor coding, software packages might allow excessive resource consumption, contain memory leaks, or just plain crash when they receive certain types of input. These are the DoS vulnerabilities that Nessus is concerned with, and the types of checks you'll see under this classification.

There is one important clarification to be made between different types of DoS checks. Some checks are merely banner grabs, looking for versions of software that are known to contain vulnerabilities that could lead to a DoS attack. Other checks will actually try to perform the DoS. In Chapter 8, we'll take a more in-depth look at the differences between these types of plugins.

Notes from the Underground...

Denial-of-Service Extortion Threats

An increasing and troubling trend in DoS attacks is the recent demands for payment to prevent attackers from launching a DoS attack on your system at a critical time. Silicon.com reports on the migrations of threats of this nature, from threatening online bookies right before a crucial match occurs, to threatening businesses to maintain their uptime and reputation (www.silicon.com/software/security/0,39024655,39120157,00.htm). Incidents of this nature are a growing concern for ISPs, businesses, and the security community, and are likely to continue to increase in frequency and severity.

Let's look at a recent example of a DoS attack, the Apache mod_ssl DoS of 2004, with Nessus-specific details available online at http://cgi.nessus.org/plugins/dump.php3?id=12100. A malformed SSL command (plain HTTP) sent to the HTTPS server running vulnerable versions of Apache with mod_ssl will trigger a memory leak, cause excessive memory consumption, and deny service to users trying to access the HTTPS server. This is a classic case of a DoS vulnerability through forced excessive use of local resources—in this case, memory utilization.

Best Practices

Best practices are a set of guidelines that define the industry recommended way to implement a given product or solution. While best practices vulnerability might not expose a currently exploitable hole, it highlights a configuration or setup that is not in conformance with the industry's agreed-upon ideal deployment. Nessus reserves the best practice category for vulnerabilities that are not an immediately exploitable threat, but should nevertheless be changed or updated as the current setup is depreciated or suboptimal.

There are many guides to best practices out there, as the following sidebar illustrates.

Tools & Traps...

Security Best-Practices Guides

There is a plethora of best-practices guides out there for network security and for system administration of various different types of systems. Here are a few, to give you an idea of the types of best practices being written:

- Cisco's "Network Security Policy: Best Practices White Paper" (www.cisco. com/warp/public/126/secpol.html) describes how to create a security policy, implement it, and respond to events.

- Microsoft's "Best Practices: Security Patch Management" (www.microsoft.com/ business/reducecosts/efficiency/manageability/patch.mspx) describes different ways to patch your Microsoft systems optimally.

- Razvan Peteanu's "Best Practices for Secure Development" (http://members. rogers.com/razvan.peteanu/best_prac_for_sec_dev4.pdf) describes how to develop applications in a secure fashion.

- ComputerWorld's "Best Practices for Wireless Network Security" (www. computerworld.com/mobiletopics/mobile/story/0,10801,86951,00.html) describes how best to securely deploy a wireless network.

There are many more best-practices guides out there. We urge you to seek out the relevant guides for the type of network and devices you have, and to read them to improve your security posture.

An example of a best-practices vulnerability is an HP printer that doesn't have a password set, as in http://cgi.nessus.org/plugins/dump.php3?id=10172. Although this does not match the classic definition of an exploitable vulnerability, the lack of authentication allows anyone to log in to the printer and change its settings, including its IP address. This is not configured ideally, and setting a password on the printer that only the rightful administrators know would greatly enhance the security of the printer. Following best-practices guidelines will make your network more secure against today's threats and against those that people in the industry see in the foreseeable future.

Summary

In this chapter, we looked at the different types of vulnerability classes that Nessus can analyze. Critical vulnerabilities are the most immediate and crucial threats to your network, and are often the basis for worms and viruses. Critical vulnerabilities include privilege escalation, local and remote root exploits, and other major problems. Information leaks do not directly threaten the security of your machines themselves, but divulge information that can be used to speed both technical and social attacks. Denial-of-service (DoS) vulnerabilities do not grant privileges or code execution to the attacker, but can be used to knock a functional machine offline, costing you wasted time, effort, and potentially affecting your customer's view of your reliability. Best-practice vulnerabilities follow the recommended guidelines of the product manufacturer and industry experts to produce the most proactively secure configuration and setup possible.

Solutions Fast Track

Critical Vulnerabilities

☑ Critical vulnerabilities are immediate threats to your network and systems security.

☑ The exploitation of a critical vulnerability could lead to execution of arbitrary code, unauthorized privilege escalation, or some similarly crucial and high-impact consequence.

☑ Nessus separates critical vulnerabilities as a classification to allow the most important vulnerabilities to be addressed first.

Information Leaks

☑ Information leaks can disclose system or user information to an attacker.

☑ Data gathered from information leaks can often be used to get a foot in the door and establish credibility for a later social engineering attack.

☑ Data gathered from information leaks can also be used to speed and fine-tune technical attacks, such as feeding harvested usernames to a password-cracking program.

☑ Data gathered from information leaks can also be used to target a specific vulnerability by disclosing the version of operating system or server software in use.

Denial of Service

☑ DoS vulnerabilities cause a normally available service to become unavailable. This can take the form of resource consumption, server downtime, or the crashing of operating systems.

☑ Although a DoS vulnerability is usually addressed soon after the attack traffic stops, it can still have a significant impact on business.

☑ DoS attacks can cause entire machines to crash, or require a hard reset in order to restore service.

☑ DoS attacks will not lead to direct compromise in and of themselves, but can be used to decrease the public's confidence in a business.

Best Practices

☑ Best practices are industry guidelines for implementation and maintenance agreed upon by the community.

☑ Although they are not reports of direct threats themselves, a best-practice recommendation would improve your security stance in the face of possible future threats.

☑ Savvy system administrators or security engineers will read best-practice guidelines as pertaining to their networks, and attempt to make proactive improvements.

Frequently Asked Questions

Q: If a vulnerability can cause a denial of service and/or remote code execution, is it usually classified as a DoS or as a critical vulnerability?

A: Usually in classification, the worst real possibility is considered the most important. Therefore, if the remote code execution is feasible, if there is proof of concept code, or if someone has shown how it could be done, the vulnerability is critical.

Q: Does the classification of a vulnerability in one of the four categories tell me everything I need to know about it?

A: No. In addition to which class the vulnerability belongs to, you should also consider which of your machines it's on, what defenses you have, how severe the vulnerability is, and what damage you could take if it were exploited. Some machines are more important than others, and some vulnerabilities will be more devastating than others.

Q: If a vulnerability is just a best practice, do I really need to care?

A: Yes, but how much will depend on your security policy and staffing. If you are very low on system administrator time, it's probably better to deal with the most important and most critical vulnerabilities first. Patch your gaping holes, and then get proactive.

Q: If a DoS vulnerability is exploited, will my machine restore itself when the attack traffic stops?

A: Some will, some won't. It depends entirely on the targeted machine and service.

Q: How do I know how much of a problem the information that I'm leaking is?

A: You might want to hire a penetration tester or security consultant to advise you, but consider whether any of that information could be used to identify avenues of further technical or social attack. How much? The damage is limited by mostly by your creativity in using the information available.

## Chapter 7

False Positives

Solutions in this chapter:

- **What Are False Positives?**
- **Why False Positives Matter**
- **Nessus and False Positives**
- **Dealing with False Positives**
- **Dealing with a False Positive**

Introduction

Just short of missing a vulnerability entirely, false positives (FPs) are any scanner's worst nightmare. A false positive is the inverse of a vulnerability that slipped past the scanner; the scanner reports a vulnerability when one doesn't exist. This chapter discusses what false positives are, why they are a major issue, categories of false positives, how to deal with false positives (specifically within the Nessus framework), and finally looks at some real-world examples on finding and eradicating false positives.

Nessus had a feature to maintain a record of false positives reported on a network. This feature has since become deprecated and discontinued. However, since it is important to understand the false positives on your network, the balance of this chapter is maintained for historical purposes. This can, perhaps, assist you in finding a solution to compile a list of false positives on your network and how to deal with them.

What Are False Positives?

Per *Wikipedia*—the Free Encyclopedia—"A false positive is when a test incorrectly reports that it has found what it is looking for" (http://en.wikipedia.org/wiki/False_positive). The encyclopedia correctly goes on to point out that false positives occur in all kinds of detection algorithms.

For a number of different reasons, network-based vulnerability scanners are particularly plagued by this problem. Aside from the often-vague definitions of a technical vulnerability, numerous variables and other external factors can affect the results of the test. As exploiting the actual vulnerability is seldom an option, and as a vulnerability scanner will always err on the side of caution, false positives are relatively common.

This issue is not unique to Nessus and will also affect every other scanner, whether commercial or open source. Indeed, as we will see later in this chapter, Nessus provides a number of checks and balances to ensure that false positives are kept to a minimum.

A Working Definition of False Positives

Although false positives are a known and recognized phenomenon in scientific testing, they have a very real and practical impact on the Nessus user.

For the purposes of this chapter, we're going to move a little beyond the strict, technical definition of a false positive, and also include reports that, while technically accurate, are misleading, irrelevant, or insignificant in the given context. Thus, we define two classes of "false positives":

- **Technical false positives.** These are false positives in the narrow, technical sense of the word where, for some reason, the test incorrectly returns a positive result. Specific categories of false positive found in this class include:

- **Buggy scripts.** These FPs are created when a plugin is not working correctly—due to a problem within the plugin, or within the Nessus scanner itself. Scriptwriters occasionally misunderstand the problem they're testing for, oversimplify the test, or simply make logical errors, which can cause the script to misbehave.

- **Check is technically accurate, but the service is actually patched.** A real-world example of this could be the plugin *msadcs_dll.nasl* (written by the author), which checks for the "RDS/MDAC Vulnerability." The script tests if the msadsc.dll DLL is located on the machine by sending an HTTP *GET* request for the DLL at its default location. If the DLL exists, it generates a report. However, the script has no way of knowing whether the DLL is patched, thus often resulting in a false positive. The same is true of the many scripts that rely on service banners (such as SSH, POP3, FTP, HTTP servers, and so forth). Very often, the service itself it patched, but still displays an old banner, referred to as a "backport." While Nessus does provide some mechanisms to help plugin writers counter this (see the plug-in script *backport.inc*), many plugins still see the old banner and still report the service as vulnerable, resulting in a false positive.

- **Check is positive due to the service misbehaving.** This typically happens when a custom-made (or home-grown) application is involved. For example, some add-ons for web servers could trigger certain plugins, resulting in an FP. Another example is plugins that check for a vulnerability by determining if a service still responds after a number of checks. The script *msftp_dos.nasl* is a good example of this: it connects to a Microsoft FTP server, logs in, and sends a string that causes a buffer overflow. It then attempts to send a HELP request and waits for a response. If the FTP server fails to respond to the second request, the NASL assumes it has crashed and reports it as vulnerable. Now, if the service becomes temporarily unavailable between the first request and the second request, the NASL can mistakenly interpret this as a crash and falsely report the server as vulnerable. A number of circumstances could lead to such a temporary unavailability of the service. One simple example is load. Security technologies, like shunning firewalls, can also create this type of behavior, as can regular firewall, transparent proxies, and intrusion prevention systems (IPSs).

- **Contextual false positives.** These are results generated by NASLs that are technically correct, but might not be significant, or *as* significant as the script suggests. Such results might therefore be considered false positives, but only in the context of the specific environment in which they're being run. There are various categories of contextual false positives:

  - **Check is positive, but issue is mitigated.** These are the cases where the scanner reports a problem, the problem really exists, but the owner of the network needs to live with the problem. An example of this is when a server cannot be patched, as the patch affects the normal operation of an application. In such cases, the network administrator or security officer might have implemented a workaround or some form of mitigation.

- **Check is positive but conditions apply.** This class of false positives also falls under the broader definition of the term. An example of this would be a script that correctly identifies a service that is vulnerable, but the attacker needs valid credentials to use the exploit. Basically, the plugin isn't smart enough to understand that the issue is there, but not exploitable. Depending on the level of security required for an environment, this might be a valid problem or could be classified a false positive. One should also take into account that some scripts do try to consider context. Take, for example, *wu_ftpd_site_exec.nasl*—a script that tests for a bounds-checking problem in some versions of wu-ftp. If script can log in to the server, it will run specific accurate tests for the vulnerability. Without credentials, the script will only parse the banner and test for vulnerable version numbers. The output of the NASL will inform you as to which of these methods was used.

- **Check is positive but not relevant.** Here we're referring to tests that are technically accurate but, because of the *context* within which they are run, can safely be ignored. For example, the Nessus scanner does not know if the scan is launched from inside or outside a network perimeter. Issues that could be interesting from an external point of view could be irrelevant if the scan was conducted from within the perimeter. For example, the NASL script *bind_query.nasl* (also written by one of the authors) tests for DNS servers that allow recursive queries to be performed. This behavior could be considered a vulnerability on the Internet, but is probably perfectly legitimate on the internal network. This NASL generates a "Serious' report," but points out that context is important: "If this is your internal nameserver, then forget this warning." The script *traceroute. nasl* simply displays the traceroute information from the scanner to the target. This information is also very likely to be irrelevant on an internal network.

Notes from the Underground…

"Vulnerable" vs. "Exploitable"

There is always some debate in the community as to whether a scanner should detect vulnerabilities or only issues that can actually be exploited. Our feeling is that a scanner's job is to detect *vulnerabilities*, and it is the analyst's job to determine *risk*.

In making this determination, the analyst will factor in questions like how difficult or easy the problem is to exploit. The scanner should always err on the side of caution—perhaps even paranoia.

For a less-experienced Nessus user, this differentiation can be hard to make. Such a user wants the scanner to say either "be worried" or "don't be worried." It is with such users in mind that we discuss the broader class of false positives referred to as *contextual false positives*.

Most false positives will fall in to one of these categories, each of which has its own challenges. In the next section, we provide ways to spot an FP, and how to deal with it.

Why False Positives Matter

Why are FPs such a big deal? Surely, it would be better if the scanner detects more holes (even if they do not exist) rather than missing something crucial.

You'll sometimes hear it said that the purpose of a security assessment is to help direct IT managers as to how they should invest valuable time, money, and human resources when it comes to security. The information generated by a vulnerability assessment, if accurate, can be a valuable decision-making tool. If the information is inaccurate, however, it will have exactly the opposite effect and end up wasting time, money, and human resources. Let's examine these issues individually.

False Positives Waste Your Time

The problem with false positives really stands out when one starts looking at a large number of hosts. Imagine scanning 200 hosts; each host with 5 FPs and 25 real problems (in other words, 20 percent of the reports are false positives). If we spent three minutes on each FP determining that it is indeed false, we have wasted 200 hosts × 5 FPs × 3 minutes = 50 hours or 2 days; compared to the 10 days we'll spend on the real problems. Running Nessus regularly on these hosts becomes a nightmare—we simply don't have enough time to go through every issue. One might argue that once one finds an FP on one host, you might classify it as an FP on all the hosts—reducing the time significantly. This is a dangerous assumption, as you might miss the one host where the scanner was not wrong, and this hole could be the one used by a hacker to compromise your network.

False Positives Waste Others' Time

Of course, FPs can also waste other people's time. If security people pass bad scanner information on to the technical people responsible for the hosts in question, then *those* people have to waste their time attempting to understand and fix a problem that doesn't exist. Often, the information is "bounced" several times between the technician and the security person before it is finally agreed that the report is "false" and can safely be ignored. This will always be a frustrating experience and does little to win support for the scanner, the scanning process, or the security team. We touch on this issue a little later in this chapter.

False Positives Cost Credibility

We all know that security is a process, and often a process that's not very welcome within business. Thus, the security officer is constantly engaged in a battle of hearts, in which she tries to win IT managers, technicians, and developers over to a "secure" way of thinking. Too many false positives can cause horrible setbacks in this process. The reason for this can even be described mathematically.

If we assume that there are X number of checks within the scanner, the scanner produces FP number of false positives, P number of real problems (positives), and N number of negatives—$FP + P + N = X$. Let us take this equation to the extreme: a report stating that a host is vulnerable to everything the scanner checks for (for example, $FP = X$) is just as useless as a report stating that the host is not vulnerable to any of the checks (for example, $N = X$). The other extreme—when there are no FPs and the scanner only reports real vulnerabilities ($P + N = X$, or $FP = 0$)—seldom occurs; it is a situation we strive toward.

This type of "bad" information will also quickly shed a bad light on the scanner, the scanner operator, and perhaps the entire security division. After a sufficient number of bad reports, the vulnerability assessment information will never again be taken seriously.

Generic Approaches to Testing

The mechanics of vulnerability testing have been debated on mailing lists and newsgroups for years. There are two methods to test for vulnerabilities. We'll call them "intrusive" and "nonintrusive." As we will see in the following sections, both approaches have pros and cons.

An Overview of Intrusive Scanning

The first way to test for a vulnerability is to actually exploit the vulnerability and determine if the exploit was successful. Let us look at an example. Imagine that a Microsoft IIS web server is vulnerable to the IIS WebDAV overflow (MS03-007). Exploiting this vulnerability under the correct circumstances leads to an IIS crash and full command execution with SYSTEM privileges. Renaud Deraison wrote a script that can check for this problem on a web server in an "intrusive" way: it sends the string *SEARCH/AAAA .... AAAA* (with 65535 As) to the web server within a WebDAV request. A vulnerable IIS server will crash on receiving this, and the script tests for this by checking if the HTTP server is "dead." It's an accurate way to test, but has the obvious drawback of leaving a trail of crashed IIS servers in its wake.

An Overview of Nonintrusive Scanning

There is another way to detect the WebDAV vulnerability described in the previous section—this time without actually exploiting it—and Renaud's *iis_webdav_overflow.nasl* can take this approach as well. Instead of actually sending data that will crash the IIS server, the script sends a WebDAV SEARCH request and parses the response for an HTTP 411 error code. If the error is received, the script reports a vulnerability, but with a disclaimer that "Nessus did not actually test for this flaw." In essence, this approach to testing relies on the fact that the server is IIS 5.0 and supports the WebDAV methods. It has no way of knowing whether the necessary service packs or hotfixes have been installed. Thus, this approach to testing can be significantly less accurate, but with the advantage that one doesn't have to keep rebooting IIS servers.

However, testing for vulnerabilities by actually exploiting them has other problems as well. In many cases, we cannot predict the behavior of a system when the exploit is run. In such a case, the scanner would not report the problem—although it actually exists (a false negative).

Moreover, many exploits leave the target server in an unpredictable state. An exploit that uses buffer overflow techniques can easily crash a server (or service). Nessus never uses exploit code, but rather tests for buffer overflows using random data. In a test environment, this might not be a problem, but crashing your company's production server will not win you any friends. Determining if the exploit actually worked is also not as easy as it seems. Let us assume that our exploit or method gives us the ability to execute any command on the target server, but we cannot see the output of the command (think SQL injection). How do we know if our command really executed? We could try to send Internet Control Message Protocol (ICMP) ping packets to ourselves, but what if the firewall (ours or theirs) blocks ICMP ping requests?

In addition, Nessus cannot use third-party hosts to test vulnerabilities—all the information needed to verify the existence of a vulnerability must travel between the target and the Nessus server. As such, Nessus is restricted from using some of the more advanced techniques used by exploit code in the wild.

It should be clear that intrusive tests aren't always better than nonintrusive tests. This cuts to the very heart of the issue of false positives—very often, there is simply not enough information available with which to indisputably determine whether a vulnerability exists.

Notes from the Underground...

Is Nessus a "Hacking" Tool?

It is important to note here that Nessus, unlike exploit codes, does not in any case install malicious content, malicious agents, or any other form of malware on the tested servers—an unfortunate misconception that we want to avoid in this book. To ensure all Nessus scripts are harmless, each plugin is reviewed by Renaud Deraison. This is further enforced by the fact the plugins themselves are open source, and open to scrutiny by the Nessus community.

The Nessus Approach to Testing

The Nessus scanner has the capability to use both methods of testing described in the previous section. The Nessus user can specify which approach she prefers by setting the *safe checks* configuration option. This option doesn't affect the behavior of the scanner, but should be considered by the individual NASL script when determining what approach to take. Bear in mind that the Nessus engine itself does not actually perform the checks—they are executed by third-party plugins. If the *safe checks* flag is set, the NASL may not use intrusive tests. If *safe checks* is *not* selected, the scanner will try to determine if the vulnerability exists, even if testing it could potentially crash the service. The Nessus engine only passes the setting to the plugin; the plugin decides what to do with it. Thus, many NASLs can test either "intrusively" or "nonintrusively" and select which approach to take based on the *safe checks* option. Not all NASLs have this capability, however, and the majority of scripts can only perform nonintrusive tests. At the time of this writing, there are approximately 4600 plugins, of which about 130 are "safe check" aware.

Setting plugins to use safe checks in Nessus is easy. The *safe check* option can be set as a property of an individual scan. Figure 7.1 shows the results of right-clicking on a scan, and selecting the Options tab in Windows Nessus 3 (Nessus 3.0.6 Build W319).

Figure 7.1 Results of the Safe Check Option

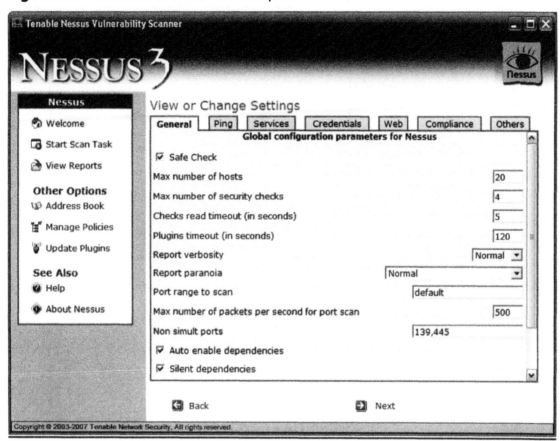

The same setting can be found on the UNIX client under Options in Figure 7.2. Getting to the options, however, is different. After launching the Nessus Client, click on the policy you want to edit, highlight it, and click on the **Edit** button at the bottom right corner of the window. This will launch the Edit Policy window. Click on the **Options** tab to find the Safe checks option.

Figure 7.2 UNIX Client, Scan Options

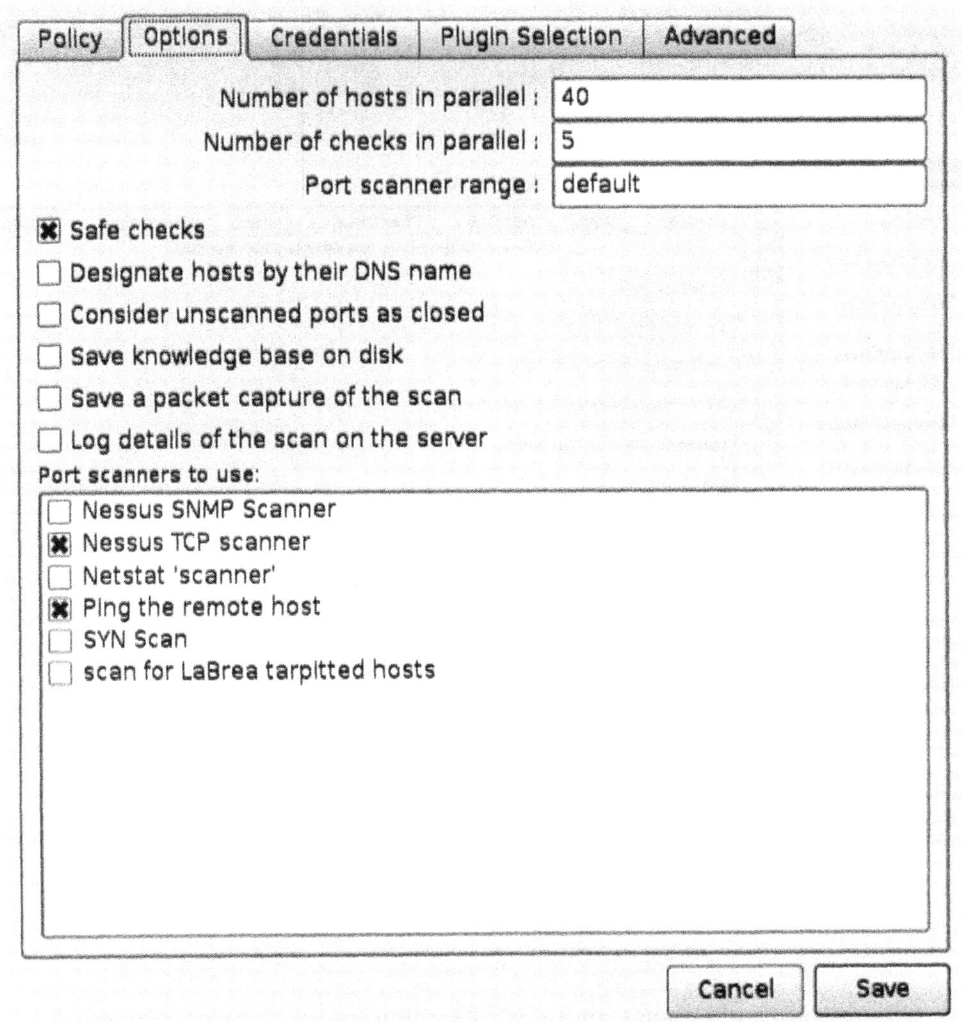

Policy	Options	Credentials	Plugin Selection	Advanced

Number of hosts in parallel : `40`

Number of checks in parallel : `5`

Port scanner range : `default`

- ☒ Safe checks
- ☐ Designate hosts by their DNS name
- ☐ Consider unscanned ports as closed
- ☐ Save knowledge base on disk
- ☐ Save a packet capture of the scan
- ☐ Log details of the scan on the server

Port scanners to use:

- ☐ Nessus SNMP Scanner
- ☒ Nessus TCP scanner
- ☐ Netstat 'scanner'
- ☒ Ping the remote host
- ☐ SYN Scan
- ☐ scan for LaBrea tarpitted hosts

[Cancel]   [Save]

Dealing with False Positives

It should be clear by now that scan reports will sometimes contain false positives, which need to be routed out for the scan information to be useful.

Notes from the Underground…

Asset Management and False Positives

Because false positives can be so troublesome, it is important to keep a handle on them and not allow them to create even more problems. Asset management is a key component to a good network security plan and Nessus can assist in that regard. Using Nessus as part of a regular scanning program can help you understand your network better, determine authorized devices on your network, and expedite remediation of vulnerabilities while accurately culling false positives from actual vulnerabilities.

Because the ability to track false positives within Nessus is no longer maintained, it is important to find a solution to track them outside the tool. Creating a database of devices on your network and the results of all scans for each of those devices is a good start. That way, once you have determined that a reported vulnerability on a device is, in fact, a false positive, that information can be kept in the database. This information can then be used to expedite remediation of vulnerabilities in the future. Please, do not forget to check the false positive on a regular basis to ensure nothing has changed and they are still "false."

Dealing with Noise

One of the biggest hindrances to spotting false positives is what we call "noise." These are reports that are technically correct but are uninteresting or irrelevant and make it hard for us to see the truly important issues. A Nessus report for hundreds of hosts, conducted from inside a perimeter, can be intimidating. One can very easily be lulled into marking real issues as FPs because the amount of data returned by the scanner is overwhelming. The first thing you want to do when trying to eliminate false positives is to move aside the "noise." The following steps can help to reduce several hundreds of possible vulnerabilities to a manageable amount of information to analyze:

1. **Identify vulnerabilities common to all hosts.** We have two different scenarios here: first, a specific plugin could misbehave in the particular environment, causing it to trigger on all hosts. A typical example is when dealing with a transparent proxy—the scanner will pick up port 80 open on all possible hosts, as the proxy picks up all the connections. The other scenario could be that all the hosts are vulnerable to a specific issue; for example, the Simple Network Management Protocol (SNMP) is

enabled with a commonly used community string. In such a case, one would not want to report the issue on each host, but rather globally on all hosts.

2. **Remove issues that are not applicable.** While the traceroute to a host might be interesting from outside the perimeter, it does not carry much information when the scan is conducted on the same network segment. Other issues that fall in this category could include predictable TCP sequence numbers, ICMP timestamp replies, and so forth.

3. **Remove some of the issues only classified as informational.** This really depends on the environment in which you work in—in some cases, you should retain these issues. Issues could include SSL cipher information, port identifications (for example, "a web server is running on this port"), and OS identification.

Once one's removed some of the "noise" in this way, one can start concentrating on the "real" issues; typically, medium, high, or critical issues that do not appear to be false positives. False positives still found in the remaining reports typically fall into the category of misbehaving services or patched services.

Analyzing the Report

From this point on, the detection of false positives is difficult and essentially requires one to examine and analyze each reported issue. Issues that prove to be FPs can be marked as such or removed from the list. Here's a simple method you can apply in this process:

1. **Understand your "environment."** Earlier we discussed a broad category of false positives we labeled "contextual," and explained how these reports are technically accurate but irrelevant or less relevant because of the specifics of the context within which the tests are run. For the purposes of this chapter, such issues are also classified as false positives. With sufficient knowledge of the systems being tested, many FPs are quickly identified and eliminated because it's clear that they can't be accurate or aren't relevant.

2. **Understand the problem.** We need to understand the vulnerability—why it is a vulnerability and how it could be exploited—even if we have to do it manually. Many forums, web sites, and mailing lists deal with vulnerabilities—in fact, when you start to Google for vulnerabilities, you might find yourself flooded with information. From all these sources of information, the following four sites have proven over the years to be current, reliable, and easy to use:

    a. **www.packetstormsecurity.net** Notice the search functionality at the top of the site. Enter some keywords of the vulnerability there and you will soon be on your way to papers, exploit code, and good descriptions of the problem.

b. **www.securityfocus.com** As the official Bugtraq mailing list archive site, it has been a favorite for ages. Click on the Vulnerabilities tab and enter the world of Bugtraq IDs (BIDs). A vulnerability can be found by searching on vendor and version, BID, CVE ID, title, or keyword. Every vulnerability has a Discussion, Exploit, Info, Solution, and Credits tab.

c. **www.osvdb.org** The Open Source Vulnerability Database, run and funded by individuals (unlike SecurityFocus, which has corporate backing) had humble beginnings, but has grown over the years to be an invaluable resource. The OSVB also uses identification numbers (OSVDBid); they are cross-linked to other IDs such as BID, CVE-ID, and ISS Xforce ID. The search functionality on the site allows searches to be performed on, among others, Nessus Script ID.

d. **www.securiteam.com** Backed by Beyond Security, SecuriTeam is known for their precise and thorough descriptions of vulnerabilities.

All of the preceding sites allow us to search for information on a specific problem, but the site's description of the problem might vary. Almost all of the Nessus plugins include a CVE ID. The CVE ID does not point to the actual issue, but rather acts as a standardized description dictionary of the issue. By searching on CVE number, we can find the standard description of the problem, and then use this description to search on the sites mentioned previously. A nice CVE ID and keyword search interface can be found at www.cve.mitre.org/cve/. Some sites like SecurityFocus and OSVDB allow us to search directly by CVE ID, Bugtraq ID, or keyword.

3. **Understand the plugin.** Once we understand the vulnerability and how the plugin works, we can begin to determine if it is indeed a false positive and into which category it would fall. To understand how a particular plugin works, you should understand the individual components and commands of the plugin. Plugins are written in a scripting language called NASL. A great source of information on this is the *Nessus Attack Scripting Language Reference Guide*, which can be found at www.nessus.org/doc/nasl.html. This document describes all the different function calls, operators, and basic syntax.

4. **Manually Verify the Results.**

a. **With the scanner.** After the environment has been changed, a patch has been applied, the scanner host (the box where Nessus is executed from) has been given elevated privileges, or scan options has been changed, we can simply run the scanner again.

b. **With other scanners.** While Nessus is one of the best scanners around, it is not the only scanner. Comparing results from different scanners is not a bad idea—in a perfect world, all scanners should have the same set of results.

c.   **With NASL.** With most installations of Nessus, you will find a command-line utility called NASL (on a FreeBSD standard installation, this utility is located in /usr/local/bin/, but could vary from installation to installation). This utility allows the user to execute basic plugins directly from the command line. In some cases, using NASL directly will not give you the desired results—the NASL utility does not have the same intelligence as the actual Nessus scanner. It won't, for instance, enable SSL within the plugin if you run an HTTP-based plugin against an SSL-enabled web server. Despite this, the NASL command-line utility provides us with a quick way to test a basic plugin.

d.   **By "hand."** If you've examined a NASL script and have a basic understanding of what it does, you can usually reproduce the test by hand. Here are some of the tools you'll commonly use for this:

    i.   **Telnet/Netcat** Some problems can be verified by simply connecting to the relevant port, sending a particular string to the service, and monitoring the output. This can easily be done using a telnet client (standard on both UNIX and Windows), or, for more advanced cases (for example, where binary data is involved), using Netcat. Source and binaries for Netcat can be found at http://netcat.sourgeforge.net.

    ii.   **Browser** Many HTTP(s) based problems can be reproduced by simply using a browser. Do not underestimate the power of a browser!

    iii.   **Using the relevant client** Of course, not all problems can be reproduced/tested using a browser or telnet. Obtaining the correct client for the service in question is always a good idea. For example, if the scanner reports VNC (remote administration software) with a blank password on a host, you might consider getting the VNC client and verifying that it is indeed the case.

    iv.   **Exploits** As a last resort, you can consider getting the actual exploit for the problem. Many web sites mentioned in the previous section also provide exploit code.

e.   **Manual on-host inspection.** One of the best ways of verifying if a problem really exists is to manually inspect the target—by logging in locally on the target. This is not always feasible, as the target might be physically in a different location, or you might not have credentials to access the host. By checking locally on the target you can easily find out if, for example, it is indeed not running a specific service pack.

> **NOTE**
>
> Keep in mind that some exploits could crash the server or service, that many exploits are "broken" on purpose, and that some exploits are intended to cause damage to your own (attacker's) system to discourage script kiddies from using them. In many cases, a service is only potentially or theoretically exploitable. This means that a vulnerability has been found, but that the proof of concept (or exploit) has not been released. Just because an exploit is not circulating "in the wild" does not mean that the service is not vulnerable and that the issue can be marked as an FP!

False Positives, and Your Part in Their Downfall

Nessus is an open-source scanner, and plugins are written by individuals all over the world. Although the Nessus team takes great care in plugin quality control, they are human. Because hosts can be installed in many different environments and services typically have many installation options, plugins are likely to cause a false positive in a "nonstandard" environment.

If you find that a plugin does not perform as it is supposed to, you can help make it better by describing the environment, server settings, and conditions where it caused a false positive. Providing this feedback will help raise the quality of the plugin (and therefore the entire scanner), making it work better for everyone. There are a number of ways to give feedback:

- Contact the author of the plugin. Almost all plugins contains the author's e-mail address.
- Describe the problem on the Nessus mailing list and monitor the list for a response.
- If all else fails, send an e-mail to bugs@nessus.org.

Be sure to check the Nessus FAQ and the mailing list archives before asking questions or giving feedback—it is very possible that someone else already raised the question or someone has responded to the same feedback.

Dealing with a False Positive

Once we have identified an FP, we can now "treat" it in a couple of ways. The following options come to mind:

- **Leave it as an FP.** We know a particular problem is an FP and we treat it as such. This approach works nicely in a small environment, when one only looks at one or two hosts, when there are not many results (typical when looking at a properly fire-walled environment), or when the results are not used by other people. As soon as we are looking at a larger number of hosts or issues, this becomes a problem—for example, "I cannot remember if problem XXX on host YYY is really an FP any-more." Reports used by more than one person are also a problem—person A might know that issue X is an FP, but person B has no idea of knowing unless she verifies it manually (again).

- **"Fix" your host or environment.** Even if you know your host is not vulner-able to a particular issue, try to understand the way the plugin tests for it and try to fix it. This could be as simple as recompiling a service or changing a banner. This way, the plugin will behave as it should and will never generate an FP on the host again.

- **Disable the plugin.** When disabling a plugin, you need to keep in mind that the plugin will be disabled for all hosts in the scan—while it might generate FPs for some hosts, it might work perfectly for others. In totally disabling the plugin, you could risk missing some real vulnerabilities on other hosts.

- **Treat or change the particular plugin yourself.** This is a very dangerous option. The plugin was written in a particular way. The fact that it generates an FP on your host does not mean it contains bugs; rather, your host or environment is misbehaving. Rather, contact the author of the plugin to explain your environment—most authors are happy to adapt the plugin.

Disabling a Nessus Plugin

Disabling a plugin for a particular scan is easy. We will show you how you can do this using both the UNIX and Microsoft clients. For our example, we will assume that the plugin with ID 10722 (LDAP allows null bases) is causing a false positive.

Disabling a Plugin with Nessus 3

Using the Nessus 3 Windows client:

1. Start the client and define a new scan. Go to Start Scan Task -> Enter the target you want to scan and enter the device IP address or host list as in Figure 7.3.

Figure 7.3 Client Started with a New Scan Defined

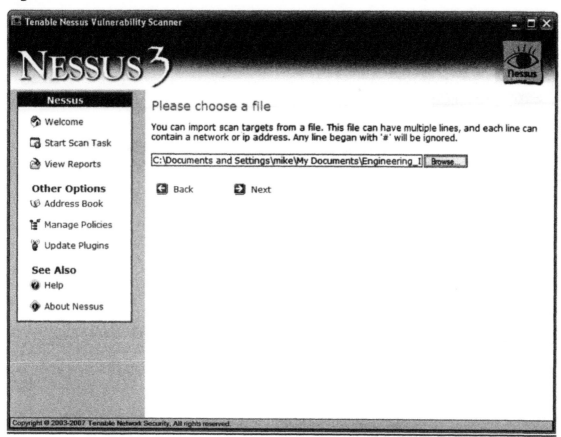

On the menu in the left side of the window, click on Manage Policies → click on Create new policy → enter the name of your policy (we will use Syngress disabled) → Click OK and that will bring you back to the Manage Policies window. Click on Edit Plugins as shown in Figure 7.4.

Figure 7.4 Selecting the Plugins

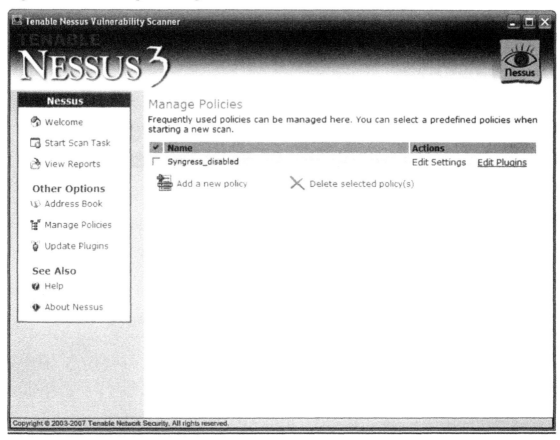

2. **Find the plugin you want to disable.** This is not always as easy as one might think, as the description of the plugin and the output of the plugin might not match. In addition, version Nessus 3 does not give the user the ability to search per plugin ID, neither does it show it when the plugin is selected. After some searching, we find our plugin in the "remote file access" section, as shown in Figure 7.5.

Figure 7.5 Plugin within the Remote File Access Section

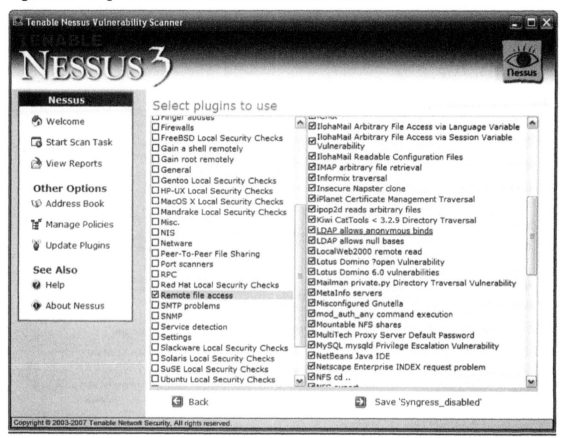

3. **Disable the plugin.** The plugin is currently "in use." To disable it, we unselect this box. After clicking **Close**, we view the plugin set again and voilà – it appears to be disabled, as shown in Figure 7.6.

Figure 7.6 Disabling the Plugin

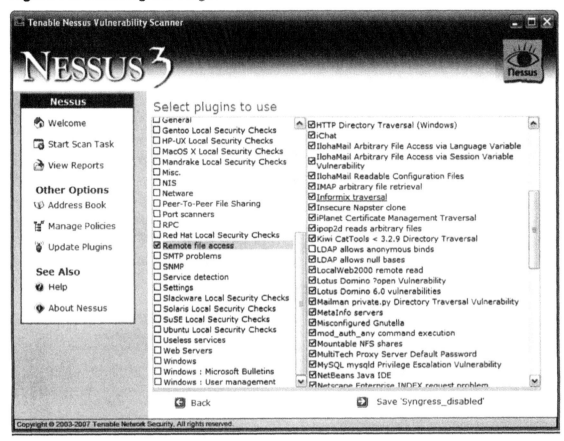

Scans run from this session will now ignore this check.

Disabling a Plugin Under Unix

Disabling the plugin in the Nessus UNIX client is even easier:

1. **Start the client and log in.** After launching the Nessus Client, click on the policy you want to edit to hightlight it and click on the **Edit** button at the bottom right corner of the window. This will launch the Edit Policy window. Go to the **Plugin Selection** tab, as shown in Figure 7.7.

Figure 7.7 Plugins Tab

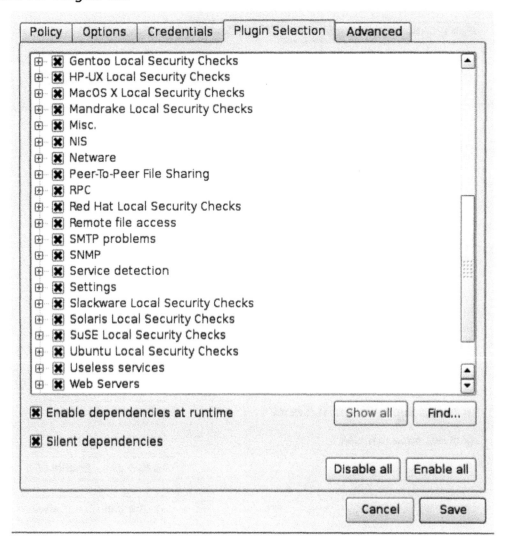

2. **Find the plugin to disable.** Here we will use the Find functionality to assist us in finding the plugin. We click on **Find**, select **ID**, and enter the plugin ID 10722 (LDAP allows null bases) in the **Contains** field. You can also search for a plugin based on **Name** or **Family**. When we click **OK**, the category and plugin are displayed (see Figure 7.8).

Figure 7.8 Finding the Plugin to Disable

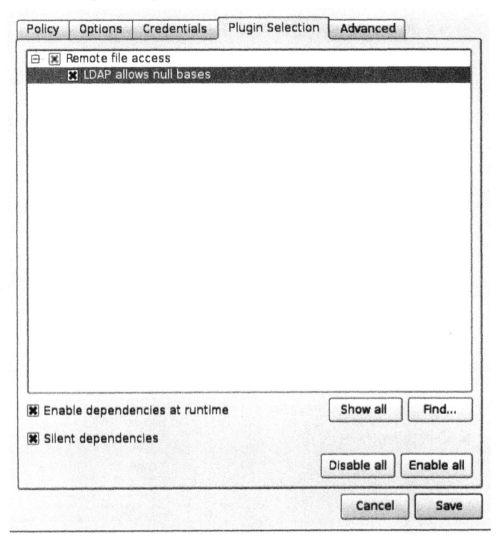

3. **Disable the plugin**. We now know that the plugin is in the *Remote file access* section. We clear the **Pattern** box, unselect **ID number** again, and click **Enable all (but dangerous)**, so we can select all the plugins. Scrolling down, we find the **Remote file access** section. We double-click on it, and all the plugins in this family appear. Deselecting the box to the left disables the plugin (see Figure 7.9).

Figure 7.9 Disabling the Plugin

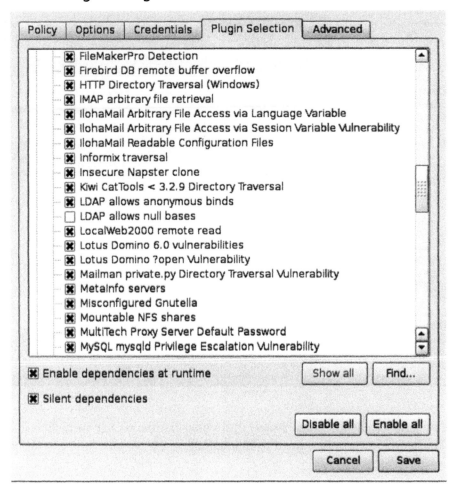

The plugin will be disabled for all scans done from the client. To enable the plugin, click on it again, and the button will appear to be going into the screen (the difference between a checked and unchecked plugin is minimal—look closely).

Marking a Result as a False Positive with NessusWX

The NessusWX client has the functionality to mark a result as an FP after a scan has completed. Once an issue has been marked as a false positive (by simply ticking the **FP** box), it is identified with a red cross next to it. Here we assume that we want to define the traceroute to an internal host as a false positive as it is not relevant to our environment. In Figure 7.10, these areas are highlighted.

Figure 7.10 Issue Marked as a False Positive

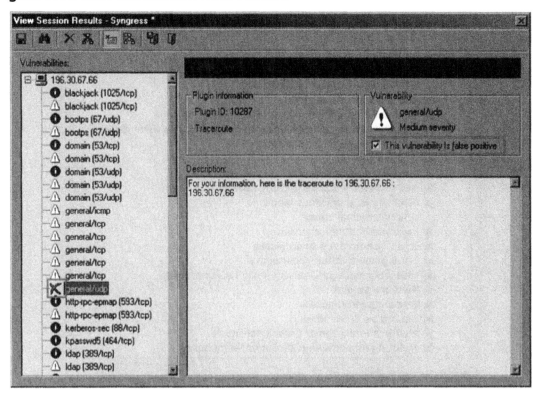

When an issue has been marked as an FP, the user has the choice to include it in HTML reporting or database export, as shown in Figure 7.11.

Figure 7.11 User Choice to Include the Issue in HTML Reporting or Database Export

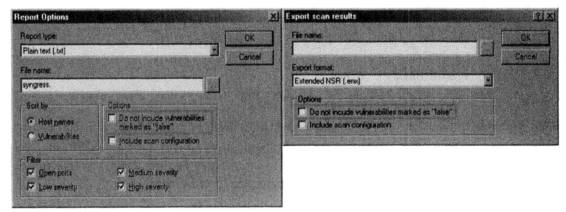

When these boxes are ticked, the issues marked as FPs are simply not included—they are not displayed in the report or database export as false.

False Positives and
Web Servers—Dealing with Friendly 404s

Of all the services running on computers today (over the Internet), web servers are probably the most common. When looking externally at a network today, one finds that the majority of ports are used for HTTP or HTTPs and SMTP. The web service has become one of the most developed services—administrators and vendors are constantly looking to improve the performance and security of web servers. It then comes as no surprise that about a third of all Nessus plugins deal with web servers. Because of the complex nature of web servers, we will spend some time on FPs and web servers.

Let us look at how a web server works—a client (browser) requests a file in an HTTP request. The web server tries to find the file and return it to the client. If the file does not exist, the server reports an error (error 404 means "file not found"). If the file is protected by some means of access control list (ACL), the server responds with error 403 (forbidden). When a problem occurs when the server tries to serve the file (or execute the CGI script), it might send back error 500 (Server Error). There are many error codes, each for a different situation. If the web server can find the file, it has the permission to serve it, does not cause an internal error on the server, and returns the file with a code 200. Code 200 means that the server could respond to the request. For a complete list of status codes, refer to RFC 2616 (Hypertext Transfer Protocol—HTTP/1.1), section 10—Status Code Definitions. While the RFC describes how web server should behave, experience shows that not all vendors strictly conform to the RFC.

Let us first look at how most web server checks work. Most plugins will look for the presence of a particular script. If the server returns a 200 code, the plugin assumes that the script is present, and (if it has *safe_check* capabilities and the *safe_check* option is set) reports the issue. Other scripts might look for a 302 Redirect—the common factor is that they look at server response codes. So, what is the problem?

The following example shows what could happen. The web administration interface called Webmin listens on TCP port 10000. Webmin was written in such a way that it does conform to RFC 2616; it replies with a 200 status code every time, if the file exists or not. Figure 7.12 is a screenshot of a request for the root document.

Figure 7.12 Telnetting to a Webmin Interface

```
Trying 192.168.0.1...
Connected to syngress.edited-site.com.
Escape character is '^]'.
GET / HTTP/1.0

HTTP/1.0 200 Document follows
Date: Sat, 11 Sep 2004 13:23:34 GMT
Server: MiniServ/0.01
Connection: close
Set-Cookie: testing=1; path=/
pragma: no-cache
Expires: Thu, 1 Jan 1970 00:00:00 GMT
Cache-Control: no-store, no-cache, must-revalidate
Cache-Control: post-check=0, pre-check=0
Content-type: text/html; Charset=iso-8859-1

<!doctype html public "-//W3C//DTD HTML 3.2 Final//EN">
<html>
<head>
<meta http-equiv="Content-Type" content="text/html; Charset=iso-8859-1">
<title></title>
</head>
<body bgcolor=#cccc99 link=#0000ee vlink=#0000ee text=#000000
onLoad='document> []
```

It does not matter what we request, we always get a 200 OK response. Let us request a nonexistent file and see what happens (see Figure 7.13).

Figure 7.13 Another 200 OK Response

```
                              xterm
Trying 192.168.0.1...
Connected to syngress.edited-site.com.
Escape character is '^]'.
GET /nothereatallnononever HTTP/1.0

HTTP/1.0 200 Document follows
Date: Sat, 11 Sep 2004 13:34:03 GMT
Server: MiniServ/0.01
Connection: close
Set-Cookie: testing=1; path=/
pragma: no-cache
Expires: Thu, 1 Jan 1970 00:00:00 GMT
Cache-Control: no-store, no-cache, must-revalidate
Cache-Control: post-check=0, pre-check=0
Content-type: text/html; Charset=iso-8859-1

<!doctype html public "-//W3C//DTD HTML 3.2 Final//EN">
<html>
<head>
<meta http-equiv="Content-Type" content="text/html; Charset=iso-8859-1">
<title></title>
</head>
<body bgcolor=#cccc99 link=#0000ee vlink=#0000ee text=#000000
onLoad='document.forms[0].pass.value = ""; document.forms[0].user.focus()'>
```

If a plugin relies on the 200 status code to generate a positive (as it does with a couple of CGI checks), this host would always show up as positive. In the same way, some web servers are configured to reply with 200s (a status code that means the file is there) when a client requests a nonexistent file—it typically happens when a web server renders a "friendly" 404 message. This makes it very difficult for the plugins to determine if the file is really there, or if the web server is simply replying to all requests with a 200.

To counter this problem, Renaud and H.D. Moore wrote a plugin called *no404.nasl*. The plugin checks for a collection of files it knows will never reside on the target server (all files start with "NessusTest"). It then inspects the output of such requests; again trying to match it against known responses. When the plugin finds that the server responds with a nonstandard error message, it records the response and stores it in the Knowledge Base. Subsequent plugins can now use this—if they check for a specific offensive script or file, the dependency on the *no404* plugin will ensure that intelligence is applied. If the server responds in the same way it did when a nonexistent file was requested, the plugin assumes the file does not exist on the server rather than blindly follow the error code.

The use of *no404* dramatically improves the accuracy of the scanner when faced with nonstandard web servers.

Summary

The presence of FPs in scanner reports is probably one of the main reasons why people stop using a particular scanner. If the signal-to-noise ratio is high enough, one can lose track of the signal completely—which is as bad as having no signal at all. In this chapter, we defined different categories of false positives, looked at how Nessus deals with false positives, how to find a false positives, and what you can do to make Nessus a better scanner. The Nessus framework gives administrators and security personnel the option to investigate the inner workings of the scanner in intricate detail. This, combined with clever frontends, the option to toggle between scan modes (safe scanning), and plugins that are written to be as FP aware as possible are all moves in the right direction when dealing with FP issues. Online resources such as the OSVDB, PacketStorm, and SecurityFocus provide tons of details on how each vulnerability works and how to test for it. Armed with an open-source scanner and these resources, an analyst should be able to deal effectively with false positives.

Solutions Fast Track

- ☑ A false positive occurs when a scanner (such as Nessus) does a test for a vulnerability and incorrectly finds it to be vulnerable.

- ☑ False positives waste time (yours and anyone to whom the report is passed).

- ☑ False positives can be broadly categorized as technical or contextual. Technical false positive refer to problems with the scanner or plugin, while contextual false positives are more related to the environment and the perspective of the analyst running the scanner.

- ☑ Spot false positives by looking for results that do not make sense, like finding a Microsoft IIS problem on a UNIX server or finding problems related to patch levels when you know the patch is installed.

- ☑ Try to understand the problem. Refer to the original problem on mailing lists, web sites, online forums, or the web sites listed in this chapter.

- ☑ Determine if the false positive is generated because of your environment, or if the plugin misbehaved.

- ☑ Manually test if the problem really exists using other scanners, manual verification using a browser, telnet, Netcat, or an exploit.

- ☑ If you are sure that the plugin is not working, disable the plugin, or mark the result as a false positive in the scanner's result.

- ☑ Provide feedback on plugins that consistently generate false positives to the author of the plugin, or write to the Nessus mailing list.

Frequently Asked Questions

Q: What is a false positive?

A: Technically, a false positive occurs when a scanner (such as Nessus) does a test for a vulnerability and incorrectly reports its findings.

Q: How do FPs influence the quality of a report?

A: The more FPs in a report, the less the report reflects the actual truth; the more time is wasted on trying to correct the false findings. This wastes time and resources.

Q: Can Nessus be configured or customized to remove tests that generate known false positives?

A: Before a scan is started, each plugin within Nessus can be disabled. Entire families of tests can be disabled. After the scan is complete, the analyst can even decide to mark a finding as a false positive and exclude it in the scanner report (NessusWX client).

Q: I know a specific plugin generates a false positive. How do I report it?

A: You can report a plugin that generates a false positive to the author of the plugin or write to the Nessus mailing list.

Q: I know a specific plugin generates a false positive. How do I change it?

A: Although it is not recommended that you change plugins, you can (Nessus and all the plugins are open source). Be aware that the plugin was written in a specific way for a specific reason; don't meddle with it if you are not comfortable with NASL. In addition, remember that every new installation of Nessus will still contain the old version of the plugin.

Chapter 8

Under the Hood

Solutions in this chapter:

- **Nessus Architecture and Design**
- **Host Detection**
- **Service Detection**
- **Information Gathering**
- **Vulnerability Fingerprinting**
- **Denial-of-Service Testing**
- **Putting It All Together**

☑ **Summary**

☑ **Solutions Fast Track**

☑ **Frequently Asked Questions**

Introduction

To really understand Nessus, you have to know how its internal logic works and how it behaves on your network. This chapter describes how each stage of a Nessus scan is performed, with particular attention to the internal programming design of Nessus. Once you understand the logic behind the code, you will find it easier to diagnose problems relating to your scan, to create custom plugins, and to answer questions about why Nessus did or did not find a particular vulnerability. In this chapter, we look at the logical and behavioral guts of Nessus, how it works, and how it scans. We also give you a glimpse on how Nessus uses the Nessus Attack Scripting Language (NASL) to accomplish these tasks. By taking this view, you will end up with a much deeper understanding of Nessus under the hood, and be able to more easily understand where and how additional Nessus plugins should fit into the logic of the program.

Like many other vulnerability assessment tools, Nessus divides the process of detecting vulnerabilities on the network into a few major milestones, where each is dependent on the success of a previous major milestone. This process is further segregated by the plugins themselves. Each plugin that is part of a major milestone might require additional minor milestones to be passed prior to it being successful in testing the vulnerability that it will later report. Behind each major milestone, you can find one or more plugins, depending on the complexity of the major milestones. A major or minor milestone doesn't necessarily indicate vulnerability. Some of the major and minor milestones used by Nessus are required for the sole purpose of allowing other plugins to detect vulnerabilities; such is the case with Microsoft HotFixes enumeration (this minor milestone is officially called "Installed Windows Hotfixes"). The port-scanning milestone is usually done by a single plugin, while the Microsoft HotFixes enumeration requires about eight or more different plugins to succeed.

A few of the major and minor milestones are so essential that they cannot be avoided by disabling the plugins that are responsible for a specific milestone. However, you can save precious time by providing the milestone with results it will eventually generate.

Nessus will go through two preliminary, but very important to the success of the scan, major milestones before it goes on to doing vulnerability testing: host detection, the detection of whether a certain host is "alive" or "dead," can be also referred to as "online" and "offline," respectively; and service detection, the detection of what ports are responsive on the remote host and the type of application or service running behind those ports. These two major milestones are essential to the success of a Nessus scan; not detecting a certain host as "alive" or not detecting a certain port as open and its underlining service might cause us to falsely believe we are immune from vulnerabilities.

Following these two major milestones, Nessus will go about into its information-gathering milestone. During this milestone, each application or service discovered during the previous service detection milestone will be examined to determine its application name and version. This allows Nessus to, as early as possible, decide which vulnerabilities it needs to check against the application or service it discovered. In addition, during this stage, Nessus will enumerate the products, service packs, hotfixes, patches, and so forth installed on the remote host.

This information can then be used by numerous plugins to save precious time and bandwidth required versus each plugin having to find the data without using the milestone as its dependence. The final two major milestones are vulnerability testing and denial-of-service (DoS) testing. During these two major milestones, numerous plugins are launched against the server. Which plugins are launched against a certain port depends on the previous major milestone in offering information on the type of products installed, whether a required service pack or patch was installed, and whether a perquisite is met, such is in the case of a valid username and password for authentication discovered during testing conducted by Nessus' information-gathering milestone.

As you can see, knowing what are the milestones and knowing what they do will allow you to quickly spot problems that might prevent you from using Nessus to its fullest as a vulnerability assessment tool. Knowing these inner workings will also allow you to determine why certain vulnerabilities were not discovered, how to write new plugins to detect missing vulnerabilities, or how to improve existing plugins to better detect vulnerabilities of which you are aware.

Nessus Architecture and Design

Before we dive into explaining how milestones work, a brief explanation of Nessus' system processes generation and handling is in order. Skipping this section will not affect your understanding of the different Nessus milestones. However, reading it will give you some insight into how Nessus manages the different scans and plugins, why Nessus requires a certain amount of memory and CPU to run, and why Nessus launches dozens and up to hundreds of subprocesses when it scans several IP address in parallel.

Nessus uses an individual process model—each client connection to the Nessus server will result in a new process to handle that connection. Furthermore, within each connection, the scan launched is host based. When the nessusd daemon receives a list of machines to scan, it forks its process and spawns a new iteration for each host. In addition, each plugin is launched in its own process every time it is used. Consequently, we see a new process for each plugin, per host, per scan.

Launching a sniffer on the network and capturing the traffic originating from the nessusd daemon to the tested network might mislead the common observer to think that Nessus initiates a scan of a network range with a ping sweep (also referred to as an ICMP sweep), followed by a full portscan of each machine, followed by a full attempt to detect services, and finally for each of the services detected by the corresponding plugins. This type of traffic might appear to have originated from a single process launched by a single nessusd daemon; this is not the case with Nessus. The packets seen can be directly related to which plugins are enabled and to the different milestones that we discuss in the sections that follow.

Instead, Nessus launches n instances (where n is the number of machines you're scanning) of a ping probe, one per forked branch, followed by n instances of service detection, and so forth. As we review the process that Nessus goes through to scan each host and determine what vulnerabilities are present on it, keep in mind that we are following one forked branch per host.

Questions have been raised about the efficiency of this programming model—there is a common belief that calling *fork()* is slow and unwieldy, because when a process is forked, a new copy of the process and its attendant memory must be cloned and copied into memory. However, Nessus uses a copy-on-write memory model. This means that when a process is forked, the only things actually written into memory are the differences between the old process and its child. This is quite efficient.

The nessusd daemon and client for UNIX is written in C; however, to simplify things, the plugins can be written in NASL, the Nessus scripting language. Originally, plugins were also written in NASL, although current development is favoring a movement toward NASL plugins in favor of the C plugins, as they are easier to debug, maintain, and write.

Without any dependence on the language in which the plugin was written, Nessus will invoke each plugin with its own built-in wrapper. The wrapper provides an environment that gives the plugin any information it might require, dependency fulfillment, and programming/networking interface. This allows the plugin writer to concentrate on writing the plugin instead of trying to make sure a certain dependent plugin has launched, how to transfer data between two plugins, or how to open a socket through which to send data.

Generally speaking, Nessus will launch the plugins according to the plugin ID. Nessus' internal plugin scheduler performs a few optimizations, dependencies, and reordering of the launch of plugins according to a few rules. The first rule is that no portscanning or DoS plugin will launch in parallel with other plugins; this includes all plugins that are marked with the ACT_SCANNER, ACT_KILL_HOST, ACT_FLOOD, or ACT_DENIAL category. This rule was introduced to prevent Nessus from launching a port scanner while trying to crash a host, or launch two DoS plugins in parallel, making it impossible to know which actually caused the server to fail. The second rule is that if a plugin has a dependency, its dependency will need to be launched prior to the plugin being dependent on it. This allows plugins to use the results gathered by other plugins for their own needs; information might include port numbers, service types, registry information, authentication settings, and so forth.

To better illustrate how the dependencies rule the success of the plugins, we will give two examples. The first example plugin is the *Buffer overrun in Windows Shell* vulnerability, whose plugin filename is smb_nt_ms04-024.nasl. Manually going over the source code of the plugin might make you believe it only depends on a single plugin; however, using the plugin_depend. pl tool you can quickly see that this isn't the case:

```
The plugin smb_nt_ms04-024.nasl depends on:
Filename: smb_hotfixes.nasl, Category ACT_GATHER_INFO, Requires Ports 139 445
Filename: netbios_name_get.nasl, Category ACT_GATHER_INFO, Requires Ports
Filename: smb_login.nasl, Category ACT_GATHER_INFO, Requires Ports 139 445
Filename: smb_registry_full_access.nasl, Category ACT_GATHER_INFO, Requires
Ports 139 445
Filename: smb_reg_service_pack.nasl, Category ACT_GATHER_INFO, Requires Ports 139 445
Filename: smb_reg_service_pack_W2K.nasl, Category ACT_GATHER_INFO, Requires
Ports 139 445
```

```
Filename: smb_reg_service_pack_XP.nasl, Category ACT_GATHER_INFO,
Requires Ports 139 445
Filename: cifs445.nasl, Category ACT_GATHER_INFO, Requires Ports 139 445
Filename: find_service.nes, Category ACT_SCANNER, Requires Ports NONE
Filename: logins.nasl, Category ACT_SETTINGS, Requires Ports NONE
Filename: smb_registry_access.nasl, Category ACT_GATHER_INFO,
Requires Ports 139 445
```

As you can see, this plugin might appear simple, containing only four lines of NASL code. However, as it depends on other plugins, its functionality is actually divided throughout different plugins. Further, the success of this plugin greatly depends on the success of previously launched plugins.

The second example plugin is the *osTicket Attachment Code Execution* vulnerability, whose plugin filename is osticket_attachment_code_execution.nasl. Going over the dependencies of this plugin reveals an intricate tree of dependencies:

```
The plugin osticket_attachment_code_execution.nasl depends on:
Filename: global_settings.nasl, Category ACT_INIT, Requires Ports
Filename: http_version.nasl, Category ACT_GATHER_INFO, Requires Ports
"Services/www" 80
Filename: no404.nasl, Category ACT_GATHER_INFO, Requires Ports "Services/www" 80
Filename: osticket_detect.nasl, Category ACT_GATHER_INFO, Requires Ports
"Services/www" 80
Filename: find_service.nes, Category ACT_SCANNER, Requires Ports NONE
Filename: http_login.nasl, Category ACT_GATHER_INFO, Requires Ports
"Services/www" 80
Filename: httpver.nasl, Category ACT_GATHER_INFO, Requires Ports
"Services/www" 80
Filename: www_fingerprinting_hmap.nasl, Category ACT_MIXED_ATTACK, Requires Ports
"Services/www" 80
Filename: webmirror.nasl, Category ACT_GATHER_INFO, Requires Ports
"Services/www" 80
Filename: logins.nasl, Category ACT_SETTINGS, Requires Ports NONE
Filename: DDI_Directory_Scanner.nasl, Category ACT_GATHER_INFO, Requires Ports
"Services/www" 80
```

Again, the success of this plugin is dependent on the success of multiple other plugins that are executed before this plugin can be launched.

The third rule that Nessus takes into account is that it will first launch all the ACT_INIT plugins. Currently, there is a single plugin marked as ACT_INIT. This plugin's purpose is to set the global settings that will have almost no effect on the behavior of other plugins; rather, it only affects the type of feedback the nessusd daemon will send to the user. This plugin also tells Nessus whether to launch two additional plugins (referred to as experimental_scripts)—the web server fingerprinting plugin and the anti Nessus detection plugin—and whether to do a run through all of the plugins, which means that the test will take longer to complete.

After Nessus finishes launching its single ACT_INIT plugin, it proceeds to the ACT_SCANNER plugins. Currently, four plugins fall under this category: the ping plugin, which is part of the host detection milestone; the Nmap wrapper plugin, which is part of the service detection milestone; and two other plugins that try (at this stage of the scan) to determine whether scanning the remote host in question would be a waste of time. This waste of time might occur for two reasons: 1) the host is a generic IP redirector, those IP addresses (also referred to as top-level domain wildcards) that when contacted will redirect all traffic to a predefined address; and 2) the host being tested is part of the LaBrea tarpitting, a product that takes unused IP addresses and creates virtual servers that are attractive to worms, hackers, and security scanners. More information on the product can be found at http://labrea.sourceforge.net/labrea-info.html.

After Nessus has finished with its ACT_SCANNER plugins (it now knows whether a host is "alive" and what ports and services are available on it), it runs its ACT_SETTINGS plugins that affect the type of test Nessus will conduct. Skipping any of the ACT_SETTINGS plugins will diminish the number of vulnerabilities you detect, as these types of plugins allow you to define such things as SMB username, password, and domain. SMB is a protocol used by Microsoft and others for its file-sharing and printing services, to enable certain HTTP intrusion detection system (IDS) evasion techniques, and other settings.

From this point, Nessus will launch the plugins according to their script ID number, lowest number first. This will not happen in most cases, as the plugin dependency rule will take precedence and certain plugins will be launched first. This usually means that all the ACT_GATHER_INFO plugins will launch prior to ACT_ATTACK, ACT_MIXED_ATTACK, and so forth, as these plugins are more sophisticated and require the results of other plugins before they can be launched successfully.

Nessus concludes the scan by launching the two ACT_END plugins. One of these two plugins will go over all the known open ports, and report which ports now appear to be closed, due to a plugin or due to the port-scanning activity. The other will go over all those ports considered unknown, meaning that the service behind them could not be detected by Nessus port scanners, plugins, or any other means. It then asks the reader of the results file what that type of port is used for. The second plugin is done mainly as a feedback method to the Nessus development team, rather than actually giving security-related information to the person using Nessus.

Host Detection

Let's look at the first milestone of a Nessus scan, the process of identifying which systems in the target range are actually "alive." As mentioned earlier, this milestone is especially important, because if a certain host appears to be "dead," Nessus will end that particular scanning thread, and report no vulnerabilities for it.

The plugin in charge of determining whether a certain host is "alive" is ping_host.nasl. This plugin is a modular plugin, and can determine whether a remote host is "alive" by several means.

The means of detection can be controlled via the Nessus client interface. Several means of detection allow you to determine whether a certain host is "alive" by methods that cannot be easily blocked by firewalls. This allows you to determine that a certain host is "alive" even if it isn't answering ICMP Echo requests (also known as ping test), or even if it has almost all its ports set on the firewall to DROP (not return any data to the user).

The plugin supports four approaches to determining whether a certain host is "alive." The first approach is to do an ICMP Echo test. During this, an ICMP Echo request is sent to the server; if it responds with any type of IP-based packet, it will be marked as "alive." To enable this option, you need to check the **Do an ICMP ping** check box under the **Advanced** tab (Ping the remote host is selected on the drop-down menu) as demonstrated in Figure 8.1.

Figure 8.1 Setting for ICMP ping

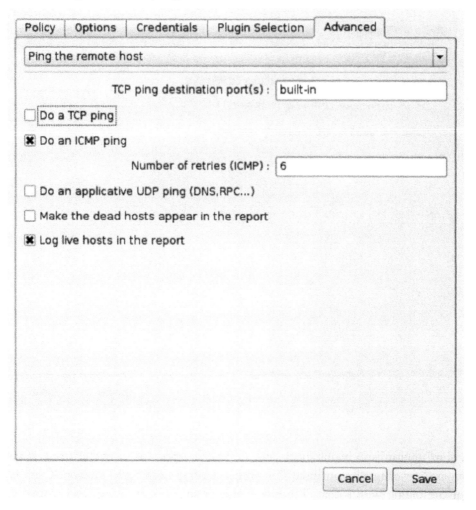

The second approach is to do a TCP ping. During this, a TCP SYN packet is sent to the remote server with a certain destination port and source port. The list of source ports can be predefined via the Nessus GUI by providing semicolon delimitated numbers in the edit box or using the built-in Nessus selection of ports **TCP ping destination port(s)** under the **Advanced** tab. To enable TCP ping, check the **Do a TCP ping** check box. This is shown in Figure 8.2.

Figure 8.2 Setting for TCP ping

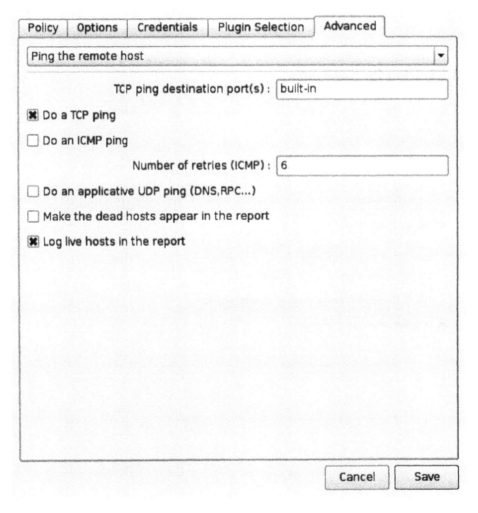

The third option is to enable both, and the fourth option is to enable none. If you enable both, you are "covering all your bases," or simply leaving nothing to chance. If you enable none, you are telling Nessus that all hosts—range or single—are "alive" and require testing.

Not enabling any will benefit those who cannot reliably determine whether a certain host is "alive," but will hinder those who don't want to spend time on nonexistent hosts.

For each approach, Nessus marks all the IP addresses that were not detected as "alive" with **Host/ping_failed**. However, this doesn't mean that that host name will not proceed to the next milestone service detection. Only after the next milestone returns with no open ports will Nessus assume that the remote host is in fact "truly dead," as it will check the Knowledge Base items **Host/dead** and **Host/ping_failed** for the **true** value, and once it sees it is in fact true, will stop the scan from continuing.

Damage & Defense...

Firewalls

By default, most firewalls DROP packets. This means that any request sent to them on a port for which they don't have a rule will not trigger any response from the destination server. This makes it is especially hard to detect whether a certain host is "alive" if it is also not responding to ICMP Echo requests. Therefore, the success of a TCP ping relies on the ability to choose those TCP ports that are not blocked by a DROP packet rule.

Several port numbers can be used, but we suggest 21 (FTP), 22 (SSH), 23 (Telnet), 25 (SMTP), 80 (HTTP), 110 (POP3), 135 (NetBIOS), 139 (NetBIOS), 143 (IMAP), 443 (HTTPS), 445(NetBIOS), 1723 (PPTP), and 3389 (Terminal Services). This pretty much covers any Internet-based server you can find and any internal server.

Note that exaggerating the number of the TCP ports you probe will increase the time required to determine whether a certain host is "alive."

This milestone can be very time consuming when you provide Nessus with range of IP addresses, subnets, or even entire classes of IP addresses. To save time, you can limit the type of host detection to TCP ping or an ICMP ping, limit the number of ports you use for TCP ping, or prepare beforehand a comma-separated list of IP addresses to Nessus to use instead of a range.

Using Nmap, a very popular tool used for port scanning and mapping available from www.insecure.org/nmap/, you can easily accomplish the last option. Another option is to generate a list of IP addresses from your DHCP server's database; in the case of ISC's DHCP server, the list of IP addresses is stored in a text-based leases file, which can be easily converted to an comma-separated IP address list. Basically, any source of "live" IP addresses will save you time on the host detection milestone.

Service Detection

After a list of hosts is established, the next step is for Nessus to determine what services are running on them. To do this, Nessus uses the plugins of type ACT_SCANNER. As there are different types of port-scanner technologies, different plugins can take rule in this phase. In previous versions of Nessus, most people would use nmap_wrapper.nes, or nmap.nasl. Both plugins provided a seamless interface to all of Nmap port-scanner's configuration parameters; the difference is that nmap.nasl is written NASL, while nmap_wrapper.nes is written in C. Other C-implemented port-scanners include SYN Scan, synscan.nes, and the TCP Connect scan nmap_tcp_connect.nes. However, with the most release of version 3, Nessus no longer included Nmap as its default port scanner. Instead, it uses its own built-in version of a port scanner. It is still possible to use Nmap with Nessus, but Tenable recommends using the built-in scanner for better performance.

Damage & Defense...

Running Nmap

In order to use Nmap with Nessus 3, you must download nmap.nasl from http://www.nessus.org/documentation/nmap.nasl. Once you have downloaded the script, you must copy it to your plugins directory (usually /opt/nessus/lib/nessus/plugins). If you have Nessus running, close it and kill all Nessus processes. Make sure Nmap is in your $PATH and then relaunch Nessus. If you have done this correctly, you will see the client displaying Nmap as the new port scanner.

Running either the nmap wrapper or the built-in Nessus scanner will allow you to control the port-scanning stage. Both plugins allow you configure such parameters as Host Timeout, Min/Max RTT Timeout, and Min/Max Ports Scanned in Parallel, and provide these plugins with an external file that will contain all the results for the port scan. The ability to use this file allows you to quickly skip over the port-scanning phase into actually testing the vulnerabilities.

Tools & Traps…

Nmap and the Full-Connect Scan

Nmap, authored by Fyodor and found at www.insecure.org/nmap/, is one of the most popular scanning tools online. It boasts a wide variety of scan types that will allow you to test for listening ports in a multitude of ways. A full-connect scan is the noisiest and most obvious variety of TCP scan available. You send a TCP packet with the SYN flag set to each port, and if you receive a proper SYN/ACK response, you send a packet with the ACK flag set to complete the TCP three-way handshake and connect to the service listening on the port. While this is an obvious way to check what ports are listening on a machine, Nessus is not designed to be stealthy, just efficient.

The results from any port scanner you choose to use will be stored in the Knowledge Base as Services/known entries. Once the complete list of ports is compiled, Nessus will launch its service detection plugins to try to detect the type of service sitting behind each open port.

Damage & Defense…

An Obstacle for Assessment Tools

One of the most common problems that vulnerability assessment tools face today is that as the number of products expands and unassigned port numbers are becoming increasingly scarce, products are choosing almost random port numbers for their product. This means that you might find a web server residing on port 10000, an SMTP server on port 2500, and so forth. This hinders the capability of Nessus to detect vulnerabilities, unless it has an internal mechanism that is able to detect the type of service residing behind a certain port.

Nessus uses two plugins to do this job: find_service.nes and find_service2.nasl. find_service. nes is written in C, and find_service2.nasl is written in NASL. These two plugins detect the type of services to which a certain port answers. These two plugins are intelligent enough to auto detect whether a certain port is SSL protected, and guess the type of service running behind them using fingerprinting techniques. The fingerprinting technique used by find_service.nes is to send each of the ports it knows is open a predefined string, *GET / HTTP/1.0*, followed by Nessus going over the response received from the server as a reply to the predefined string. The predefined string list Nessus uses to determine the type of service is extensive and constructed in an intricate nesting of *if else* statements, so that it will seldom mismatch the type of service behind a certain port.

Over time, the list of services that find_service.nes detects grew, and updating this plugin required the user to recompile it each time. This triggered the creation a new NASL plugin, find_service2.nasl. This plugin, like its sister plugin, tries to detect all those ports that find_service.nes was unable to detect. It does this by sending a different predefined string, *HELP*, and checking the response.

After one of these plugins detects the type of service residing behind a certain port number, it will mark it in the Knowledge Base under Known/tcp/portnumber and Services/servicetype. For example, Webmin's web interface residing on TCP port 10000 will be marked in the Knowledge Base as Known/tcp/10000 and Services/www, respectively. This information will be then used by any plugin with the port dependency of either port 10000 or Services/www under its NASL tag of script_require_ports.

Unless you specifically tell Nessus that any unscanned port should be considered closed by marking the check box under **Edit Policy | Option | Consider unscanned ports as closed**, any additional port that is requested by a plugin will be tried even if it wasn't supplied in the port range. The default port range used by Nessus is 1–1024. If you supply Nessus with a port range of *1*, a single port, you will still obtain results, as the following ports will be probed for their existence:

```
2, 3, 4, 7, 9, 11, 13, 15, 19, 21, 22, 23, 25, 27, 35, 37, 53, 79, 80, 81, 90,
98, 109, 110, 113, 119, 135, 137, 139, 143, 209, 256, 257, 258, 259, 264, 360,
389, 406, 443, 444, 445, 512, 513, 514, 515, 524, 543, 548, 554, 593, 617, 625,
628, 631, 873, 900, 901, 999, 1080, 1100, 1192, 1214, 1220, 1241, 1281, 1311,
1313, 1314, 1352, 1433, 1521, 1541, 1570, 1665, 1720, 1723, 1755, 1812, 1995,
2000, 2001, 2002, 2082, 2200, 2223, 2224, 2301, 2381, 2501, 2525, 2533, 2543,
2601, 2602, 2603, 2604, 2605, 2710, 3000, 3050, 3067, 3104, 3128, 3135, 3306,
3372, 3690, 4000, 4001, 4002, 4080, 4105, 4242, 4321, 4661, 4662, 4663, 4711,
4899, 5000, 5003, 5009, 5010, 5060, 5432, 5554, 5556, 5631, 5679, 5680, 5800,
5801, 5802, 5900, 5901, 5902, 6000, 6001, 6002, 6003, 6004, 6005, 6006, 6007,
6008, 6009, 6050, 6112, 6129, 6346, 6515, 6667, 6680, 6699, 6723, 6777, 6789,
6790, 6969, 7000, 7001, 7003, 7070, 7100, 7101, 7161, 7210, 7323, 7777, 7778,
7779, 7786, 8000, 8001, 8002, 8008, 8010, 8080, 8081, 8082, 8100, 8129, 8181,
8383, 8390, 8443, 8500, 8765, 8888, 8987, 8999, 9000, 9001, 9090, 9099, 9100,
9400, 9669, 9999, 10000, 10005, 10082, 10168, 12345, 12754, 13666, 14002, 14238,
15104, 15858, 17300, 17990, 20000, 20034, 20168, 21227, 21317, 21544, 21554,
22273, 27960, 30100, 32000, 32123, 33270, 33567, 33568, 34012, 36794, 42800,
44334, 51051, 60008, 65301
```

This range doesn't mean that you will find vulnerabilities on a web server listening on port 8000, as 8000 is probed only by a limited set of plugins. The rest of the web server-related plugins will look for the Services/www entry, and as this entry is only provided by the find_service.nes and find_service2.nasl plugins, most tests will not test this port for vulnerabilities.

> **NOTE**
>
> A shortcoming of not providing an inadequate, too-short or lacking port range is that any unofficially assigned port number, such as the use of port 13201 for a web server, will not be probed for vulnerabilities related to web servers. This is because the find_service.nes and find_service2.nasl plugins will not be launched against that port, which in turn will not be detected as a web server.

After Nessus identifies services, it can then go about gathering more information about what products are listening on those ports and their vulnerabilities.

Information Gathering

At this stage, Nessus uses the previous two milestones to obtain information about each host and service. The category for plugins in this milestone is ACT_GATHER_INFO. The plugins in this category are by definition constrained and verified to not cause any harm to the remote server, as they only do service queries, application fingerprinting, and general remote version analysis.

The ACT_GATHER_INFO set of plugins is by far the most common type of plugin. Out of 20791 available plugins (as of the time this book went to press, with Nessus version 3.0.0 build 2G161_Q), 3543 (or 85 percent) are information-gathering plugins. Even though they are called information gathering, they can in fact return whether a remote host is vulnerable to a certain vulnerability. The idea behind name information gathering is that the plugin can be run safely without the possibility of causing harm to the service against which it is launched. This is accomplished by passively detecting the presence of vulnerabilities, by either capturing the version given by the remote host, or by testing the vulnerability in an harmless way, such as sending a cross-site scripting attack and looking for our scripting code in the result.

Before any information-gathering plugin is launched, its port requirements are checked and verified that they have been fulfilled. Setting the script_required_ports NASL tag marks the port requirements for each plugin. Some types of services might reside on more than one port; in those cases, the plugin will refer to the type of port instead of the port number. One very good example for this is the use of port 80 and its corresponding service name, Service/www, in all the plugins that test web servers for vulnerabilities.

Some information-gathering plugins only gather information that will be later used by other plugins to determine whether a remote server is vulnerable. These plugins are usually launched at the beginning of the scan, as other plugins use the information to successfully detect the presence of the vulnerability. One of the more prominent plugins that belongs to this family is the NetBIOS and registry-related plugins; specifically, *Using NetBIOS to retrieve information from a Windows host* and *SMB log in*. Any plugin that requires registry access to determine whether a remote host is vulnerable to a certain vulnerability will fail unless these two plugins are launched and are successful. The first plugin will capture the NetBIOS name of the host being tested. The second plugin determines whether the guest or user-provided SMB username, password, and domain do in fact allow Nessus to connect to the remote host.

If the first plugin is successful, it will enter SMB/name in the Knowledge Base. The *SMB log in* plugin will then use this to try to log on to the remote host. Once the *SMB log in* plugin logs on to the remote host, it will mark the SMB/login, SMB/password, and SMB/domain entries in the Knowledge Base with appropriate data that will allow subsequent plugins to log on to the remote host. If both plugins are successful, a few other plugins can use the information that they provided to determine whether the remote host is missing any Microsoft Security patches (MSXX-XXX). To save time, a new NASL was recently introduced, *Installed Windows Hotfixes* (also known as smb_hotfixes.nasl), that enumerates all existing registry keys, patches, and service packs on a remote Windows machine. The enumerated data is stored in the Knowledge Base under SMB/Registry/HKLM. Time and bandwidth are saved by storing this information in the Knowledge Base; 44+ plugins use this information when checking whether a certain service pack or patch exists.

The smb_hotfixes.nasl is dependent on five other plugins that require the success of *Using NetBIOS to retrieve information from a Windows host* and *SMB log in* and other plugins before they can assist smb_hotfixes.nasl in gathering all available service pack and patch information from a remote host.

Registry access isn't the only type of vulnerability testing that requires SMB logon to work; some tests look for files and more specifically for their content to determine whether a remote host is vulnerable. One such example is *Putty Modpow integer handling*, also known as putty_version_check.nasl. This plugin will try to access the content of putty.exe in several locations by way of Windows' file-sharing capabilities. Once it has accessed putty.exe, it will look for its version information, which it will then use to determine whether a remote host contains a vulnerable version of putty.exe.

Such plugin sophistication is not limited to Windows-based tests; introduced in version 2.1.0 are local tests that allow the use of an SSH client certificate to enumerate all installed packages on a remote UNIX machine. The list of local tests contains over 1800 plugins, the majority of them falling under local tests for RedHat. All local tests are preformed by a single plugin, Use *SSH to perform local security checks*, also known as ssh_get_info.nasl. This plugin will connect to a remote host, determine its flavor of RedHat, FreeBSD, Mandrake, SuSE, MacOS X, or Solaris, and then use the operating system's internal mechanism to enumerate all installed packages and their corresponding version. Once this information is stored in the Knowledge Base, any of the 1800 plugins can simply query for the existence of a product and its version to determine whether the host is vulnerable.

It might look like most plugins are not doing any actual testing, but this isn't completely true. Some plugins will connect to a web server, for example, and capture the version banner the server returns from which they will determine whether it is vulnerable to attack. Others will connect to every web server they see, determine whether a certain PHP script exists on it, and then query that script with a special URL to try to trigger a known response. For these plugins to be successful, the response from a vulnerable script must differ from that of an immune script, or a false positive will occur.

Damage & Defense...

Version Banners

Relying solely on version banners is highly susceptible to false positives; this is especially true for those products that are backported, and their version remains the same while a patch to fix a certain vulnerability is introduced. If you use Nessus to scan for vulnerabilities, any test that solely relies on banners will return an extensive amount of false positives on such systems as Debian, FreeBSD, RedHat, and so forth. To counter those cases, the Nessus Project recently introduced an include file called backport.inc that lists backported versions of products. If such a backported version is detected, no false positive will be triggered.

Most information-gathering tests so far appear passive; they connect, send small amounts of data back and forth, and then determine whether the remote host is vulnerable by looking at the response. A more complicated information-gathering plugin is *Raptor/Novell Weak ISN*, also known as raptor_isn.nasl. This plugin checks for Raptor firewalls that have poor Initial Sequence Number (ISN) randomization, thereby making them more vulnerable to a successful TCP hijack or TCP injection attack. This script generates two successive IP packets, identical except for their randomly created IP IDs, TCP sequence numbers, and window sizes. The plugin will then send both packets to the Raptor firewall while monitoring the response it receives from the server.

If the plugin gets both packets back, it will check the ISN by comparing the TCP sequence number against the acknowledgment in both packets. If they match, the remote firewall is vulnerable to a weak ISN attack.

Vulnerability Fingerprinting

After a thread finishes the information gathering for a given host and writes its findings to the Nessus Knowledge Base, it runs through any attack plugins it's configured to use. These can include plugins in the ACT_ATTACK, ACT_MIXED_ATTACK, and ACT_DESTRUCTIVE_ATTACK categories. These plugins will run in this order, and will highlight specific vulnerabilities present in the target(s). Because of the potentially problematic nature of some of these checks, they can be turned off while scanning. All of these represent a more aggressive attack pattern than the informational plugins described previously; they will actually execute an attack on the server, rather than just trying to determine if that version is vulnerable.

By definition, any plugin that tries to circumvent some defenses, without any adverse effect on the system availability, will be categorized as ACT_ATTACK. One such plugin example is *MS SMTP DoS*, also known as mssmtp_dos.nasl. This plugin will connect to the Simple Mail Transfer Protocol (SMTP) server, and send the proper SMTP sequence **HELO** followed by **MAIL FROM**, **RCPT TO**. Currently, this type of traffic cannot be distinguished from any other SMTP traffic. However, when the attack sequence starts, Nessus will send a **BDAT** command, which is defined as an alternative to the SMTP's command DATA, followed by a **b00mAUTH LOGIN**, which allows us to determine whether a remote server is vulnerable by examining the response we receive. An immune server should respond with **503 5.5.2 BDAT Expected**; however, a vulnerable server will not respond in this way, allowing us to determine that this server is vulnerable to attack.

NOTE

This vulnerability was discovered in 2002 in Microsoft's SMTP server. The flaw involves how the service handles a particular type of SMTP command used to transfer the data that constitutes an incoming mail. By sending a malformed version of this command, an attacker could cause the SMTP service to fail. This would disrupt mail services on the affected system, but would not cause the operating system itself to fail.

For additional information regarding this vulnerability, see www.securiteam.com/windowsntfocus/5XP0L2A6AS.html or www.securiteam.com/exploits/5AP0O1P6MK.html.

Not all ACT_ATTACK plugins try to trigger a problem in the remote server; some just try to determine if some type of attack is feasible. To determine the feasibility of an attack, most ACT_ATTACK plugins rely on the results of previously launched NASLs. One such plugin is *DB4Web directory traversal*, also known as db4web_dir_trav.nasl.

This plugin directly relies on the success of the no404.nasl, httpver.nasl, http_version.nasl, and webmirror.nasl plugins. These plugins in turn rely on the DDI_Directory_Scanner. nasl, http_login.nasl, www_fingerprinting_hmap.nasl, and logins.nasl plugins. This dependency tree allows the db4web_dir_trav.nasl plugin to accurately detect the presence of the vulnerability without "falling prey" to servers that act in a similar way to DB4Web.

The no404 plugin is a very important part of the effort Nessus makes to reduce the number of false positives it generates. The purpose of no404 is to try to determine what information can be used in the response of a web server to determine that it doesn't contain a certain file. The httpver.nasl's plugin's purpose is to determine whether the remote web server supports the extended HyperText Transfer Protocol (HTTP) protocol—version 1.0 or version 1.1, which is the extended one. The http_version.nasl plugin's purpose is to determine the vendor of the web server running on the remote host, so that Apache tests will not be launched against Microsoft's IIS web server. Finally, the webmirror.nasl plugin's purpose is to determine which Common Gateway Interfaces (CGIs), also known as user-driven pages, are available on the remote server.

By taking into account all the data provided by the plugins on which the webmirror.nasl plugin is dependent, the script can be very accurate in determining whether a remote host is vulnerable. The plugin, for example, can know which type of operating system the DB4Web is running under, whether the remote host supports HTTP/1.1's keep-alive connection so it can speed up the test, and whether it responds with the error code 404 for files you request that do not exist, again allowing you to speed up the test and increase its accuracy.

Damage & Defense...

Nessus Speed

Nessus has greatly improved the speed at which it can test web servers by improving its internal mechanisms responsible for querying a remote web server for the existence of certain files. The internal mechanisms support HTTP/1.1's keep-alive, allowing Nessus to use a single open socket for all its web queries, instead of constantly opening new sockets and closing them after a test has finished.

However, this might adversely affect servers that do not properly support HTTP/ 1.1's keep-alive standard; one such example is Novell. Novell has sent an advisory regarding this problem to its customers in TID2966181. However, such an incident is rare; this issue was reported in June 2003.

If that's an ACT_ATTACK, what's an ACT_MIXED_ATTACK? ACT_ATTACK plugins are safe to use even when safe checks are enabled—they are unlikely to take down your server. An ACT_MIXED_ATTACK is a script that can be used with the safe checks off in a potentially destructive fashion, or with the safe checks on as a potentially safe attack—although with less certainty of assuring you that your server is vulnerable or not. Let's look at an example of this type of check: the *ntpd overflow* plugin, also known as ntp_overflow.nasl.

In this plugin, the test starts by determining whether the Network Time Protocol (NTP) is enabled on the remote host. This is then followed by verifying whether safe_checks() has been enabled. If it has, it will initiate a subsection of code that will try use NTP's internal provided information to determine the version of NTP server running. If it falls under the version range that is known to be vulnerable, the script will mark the vulnerability as present. This, as mentioned previously, can be problematic when servers are backported to include fixes for vulnerabilities. The problem of backported is avoided if safe_checks() are disabled; in that case, an actual attack will be mounted against the NTP server, a buffer overflow attack, and the resilience of the NTP server is tested. This makes the test much more accurate, and more generic, as it allows you to discover vulnerabilities in products that weren't considered vulnerable prior to the test being conducted.

The third category of vulnerability assessment plugins that the Nessus daemon will run through when trying the attacks is the ACT_DESTRUCTIVE_ATTACK plugins. These will not be tried unless safe checks are turned off, as they always have the potential to do something destructive to the target system, such as lock out accounts, crash services, or exploit a running service.

One example of such a plugin is the *SMB log in with W32/Deloder passwords*, also known as smb_login_deloder.nasl. This plugin will try to determine whether a remote host has been compromised by the W32/Deloder worm. The worm will try to modify an existing account, usually administrator, with a predefined set of passwords. Trying a list of passwords on a certain username can cause that account to become locked out, which is why this plugin is marked as destructive.

For each of these classes of attacks (ACT_ATTACK, ACT_MIXED_ATTACK, and ACT_DESTRUCTIVE_ATTACK), Nessus will run through all the available and appropriate attacks as noted in the Knowledge Base, and then move on to the next class. When all the vulnerability fingerprinting is done, Nessus will look at one last class of vulnerabilities before generating a report.

Denial-of-Service Testing

Nessus also has the capability to test a server or a network against known DoS vulnerabilities. It is usually inadvisable to do this against a production network during business hours, as you might cause excessive delays if your DoS scans show your network to be vulnerable (by downing it). Plugins labeled ACT_DENIAL, ACT_FLOOD and ACT_KILL_HOST can simulate a real DoS attack.

The DoS checks are the last milestone in the scan of hosts just in case they are successful. It would be poor design to knock your Web server offline at the start, for example, thereby missing scanning it with all the other plugins and tools available to find vulnerabilities. Moreover, even within the class of DoS testing, the host-killing checks are last, so as not to deprive other checks of their host's uptime for as long as possible. Let's look at the options for these types of tests:

Here's a simple case, the *Microsoft's SQL TCP/IP denial of service* also known as mssqlserver_dos.nasl. This particular vulnerability from 1999 caused the Microsoft SQL server to crash, this occurred when it received a packet whose payload contained more than two null characters.

The plugin relies on the results of *Microsoft SQL TCP/IP listener is running* (also known as mssqlserver_detect.nasl) prior to beginning its DoS job. The plugin starts its work by checking whether TCP port 1433 is open. If it is, the plugin establishes a TCP connection to that port and sends a six-NULL bytes packet. To confirm whether the attack was successful, the plugin will try to reconnect to TCP port 1433; if it is unable to connect, it will report that the vulnerability has been confirmed to exist.

Since Nessus version 2.1.00, a new category was introduced—ACT_FLOOD. Plugins in this category require the capability of Nessus to send a constant stream of data to a remote host in order for the DoS to occur. Because such attacks can use large amounts of bandwidth, they have been marked for easy exclusion as category ACT_FLOOD.

For an example of a flooding DoS attack, let's look at the *MacOS X Directory Service DoS* plugin, also known as macos_x_directory_svc_dos.nasl. This plugin attempts to cause the MacOS X's directory services to no longer respond to any connection by flooding it with more than 250 connections. The attack itself is no more bandwidth consuming that opening and closing a socket; however, 250 connection attempts are unusual for a "normal" plugin. The final category to discuss is ACT_KILL_HOST. This includes all those plugins that try to kill the operating system and not any specific product. An example is the *Linksys Gozila CGI denial of service*, also known as linksys_gozila_cgi_DoS.nasl, which attacks the CGI on a Linksys device.

The attack consists of single connection to the web server available on the Linksys device and requesting the Gozila.cgi with no parameters. Unlike the previous example, you can see that we are not wasting bandwidth; we can trigger the issue with a single request. The difference between ACT_KILL_HOST and ACT_FLOOD is that we will use the function *end_denial* at the end of the plugin, which will try to confirm whether the remote host is still alive. Nessus determines whether a remote host is still alive by trying to connect to one of the remote host's TCP ports, and seeing if such a connection is possible.

Putting It All Together

Throughout this chapter, some data in the Knowledge Base was used for the benefit and improvement of the functionality of every plugin. This is by no means accidental. The Knowledge Base has become one of the most important features that Nessus has in its arsenal that make it usable, extendable, and accurate. One plugin can concentrate on grabbing data from the registry, while others concentrate on taking that data and deducing from it whether you are vulnerable. However, the Knowledge Base is not a flawless implementation.

The Knowledge Base is unfortunately a one-way communication; a plugin will be unable to use it for two-way communication with other plugins running simultaneously. Nessus writes to the Knowledge Base from the plugin process to the host-specific process over a socket pair. Processes always get their own copy of the Knowledge Base once they are spawned from the main process, and any updates to the Knowledge Base will not affect their copy. This implementation has pros and cons. One of the obvious pros is that no shared data is used, and as such, no locking and unlocking mechanism is required, which will speed up the entire process of scanning hosts. In addition, any process that will, even by mistake, not unlock one of the entries in the Knowledge Base will have no effect on any of the other processes. One obvious con is that two plugins running simultaneously will not be able to use the Knowledge Base as a means of talking to each other, and in theory make the testing procedure work better. Another con is that multiple copies of the Knowledge Base are kept, thereby requiring more memory than storing a single copy of the Knowledge Base that every plugin will use.

As you can see from the way the Knowledge Base is implemented, Nessus' process model ensures that a problem in a specific plugin will not cause the entire scan (or even the scan of a particular host) to fail or stale. This includes those instances where a plugin might SEGFAULT, causing a segmentation fault to the process running it or any other problem, such as the case where a plugin takes too long to complete.

The Knowledge Base is stored under the configuration directory of Nessus, under the path hierarchy of /opt/nessus/var/nessus/users/[user used to logon to Nessus]/kbs/[IP or hostname]. For example, in our installation, the Knowledge Base information for host 192.168.1.62 is stored under /opt/nessus/var/nessus/users/mike/kbs/192.168.10.69. Knowing where the Knowledge Base is stored, and knowing how to parse the content found, will allow you to debug any problems that might arise. Nessus by default will not store any Knowledge Base information after the scan is completed. To keep a copy of the Knowledge Base after the scan is completed, check the **KB | Enable KB saving** check box.

Once you have such a Knowledge Base entry, parsing it is not a big problem. The data format used in the Knowledge Base files is textual, and can be easily parsed by a Perl script. For each entry written in the Knowledge Base, Nessus stores the time, in milliseconds since 1970.

This is followed by the type of Knowledge Base entry. There are five types available: ARG_STRING defined as 1, ARG_PTR defined as 2, ARG_INT defined as 3, ARG_ARGLIST defined as 4, and ARG_STRUCT defined as 5. The most common types are strings and integers; in both cases, the data is stored in strings, so the number "1" will be stored as "1" and not as its binary counterpart 0x01.

The next thing to follow is the name of the Knowledge Base entry, which is delimitated from the value by the equal sign (=), and the value's end is marked with a new line. This means that each line will be the entire Knowledge Base entry; if new lines exist within it, they will be replaced with the string | n, to avoid confusion.

Some lines in the Knowledge Base are informational some are scan settings, and others contain vulnerability values. The first step when trying to determine why a certain scan has not completed successfully would be to verify that the plugin was in fact launched. For example, let's assume we are trying to see if our *SMB log in* plugin was launched against our host. The first step is to find out that the *SMB log in* plugin's number is 10394. Once we know this, we can look for the entry *Launched/10394* in the Knowledge Base; if it exists, the plugin was successfully launched. Next, we can determine whether the plugin was successful by determining whether it called one of the security_hole, security_note, security_warning, and so forth functions. This is determined by looking for the *Success/10394* entry. You can see what type of vulnerabilities were discovered by looking for entries that start with *SentData/[plugin id]*; each of these entries is a single result like you can find in other types of results files Nessus can generate. Any data that is shared between plugins will be saved with its corresponding Knowledge Base name and value.

During the scan, Nessus will generate a temporary report file in the NBE format. This temporary file is created under the /tmp directory. This file contains the temporary results discovered for the period of the scan; once the scan is completed, this file will be converted to whichever format you desire. The file-naming convention is random enough to hinder the possibility of a symbolic link attack—an attack that can be used in those cases where temporary filenames can be guessed beforehand and symbolically linked to another file, but have the constant convention of "nessus-" followed by six random bytes.

Notes from the Underground...

(plugin_depend.pl)#!/usr/bin/perl

```
# This Perl script receives a filename as its first parameter.
# This filename is considered to be a NASL, for each of the dependencies
# listed in it it will open them, and find any additional dependencies,
# once it is done with all the dependencies it will print them as a list.
```

Continued

```perl
#
# Coded by Noam Rathaus of Beyond Security Ltd.
# It is released under the GNU Public Licence (GPLv2)
#
use strict;

my @OpennedList;
my @Dependent;
my $debug = 0;
my $Filename = shift;
plugin_open($Filename);

print "-----------\n";
print "The plugin $Filename depends on:\n";
foreach my $Depend (@Dependent)
{
  plugin_show($Depend);
}
print "------\n";

sub plugin_show
{
  my $Filename = shift;
  my $Category;
  my $RawPorts;
  my @Ports;
  if ($debug)
  {
    print "Filename: $Filename\n";
  }
  my $Buffer;
  if (open(BASE_PLUGIN, $Filename))
  {
    while (<BASE_PLUGIN>)
    {
      $Buffer .= $_;
    }
```

```
      close(BASE_PLUGIN);

   if ($Buffer =~/script_category\(([^\)]+)\)/gs)

   {

     $Category = $1;

   }

   if ($Buffer =~/script_require_ports\(([^\)]+)\)/gs)

   {

     $RawPorts = $1;

     while ($RawPorts =~/([^\,]+)\,?/gs)

     {

       push @Ports, $1;

     }

   }

 }

 print "Filename: $Filename, Category $Category, Requires Ports @Ports \n";

}

sub plugin_open

{

 my $Filename = shift;

 if ($debug)

 {

   print "Filename: $Filename\n";

 }

 my $Found = 0;

 foreach my $Openned (@OpennedList)

 {

   if ($Openned eq $Filename)

   {

     if ($debug)

     {

       print "Already opened\n";

     }
```

Continued

```perl
    return;
  }
}

push @OpennedList, $Filename;
my $Buffer;
if (open(BASE_PLUGIN, $Filename))
{
  while (<BASE_PLUGIN>)
  {
    $Buffer .= $_;
  }
  close(BASE_PLUGIN);
  if ($Buffer =~/script_dependencies?\((([^\)]+)\);/gs)
  {
    my $Dependencies = $1;
    while ($Dependencies =~/"([^"]+)"/gs)
    {
      my $TempDepend = $1;
      my $Found = 0;
      foreach my $Depend (@Dependent)
      {
        if ($Depend eq $TempDepend)
        {
          $Found = 1;
          last;
        }
      }
      if (!$Found)
      {
        push @Dependent, $1;
      }
    }
  }
}
```

```perl
   if ($debug)
   {
     print "Depends:\n";
     foreach my $Depend (@Dependent)
     {
       print "$Depend\n";
     }
     print "—\n";
   }
 }
 foreach my $Depend (@Dependent)
 {
   plugin_open($Depend);
 }
}
```

Summary

In this chapter, we saw how the internal logic of the Nessus server works when scanning. We discovered that each machine is assessed and scanned independently in a host-based model. We looked at the many different types of plugins that are available for the Nessus server, and the order in which they are checked and run for each host. We discovered the many configurable options that will allow us to optimize our scans for our network and our scheduling.

Solutions Fast Track

Nessus Architecture and Design

☑ Nessus uses an individual process model—each client connection to the Nessus server will result in a new process to handle that connection; in addition, within each connection, the scan launched is host based.

☑ Generally speaking, Nessus will launch the plugins according to the plugin ID. This order does not occur in reality, as Nessus' internal plugin scheduler performs a few optimizations, dependencies, and reordering of the launch of plugins according to a few rules.

☑ The nessusud daemon and client for UNIX is written in C; however, to simplify things, the plugins can be written in NASL, the Nessus scripting language.

Host Detection

☑ Each host is assessed independently, up to the maximum number of hosts that might be concurrently scanned.

☑ You can use TCP pings, ICMP pings, or both for host detection.

☑ TCP pings are the default choice for host detection.

Service Detection

☑ By default, a full-connect TCP portscan is used to determine what ports are listening on any given machine.

☑ Once the open ports have been established, the nessusd daemon will depend on the find_service.nes binary and the find_service2.nasl script to identify what service is running on each port.

☑ Find_service.nes depends on direct output of the service, whereas find_service2.nasl uses the HELP command to retrieve useful data.

Information Gathering

☑ Plugins used for information gathering run right after services have been identified for each machine.

☑ Information-gathering plugins can probe the machine, grab banners, send crafted packets, and so forth, but they will not perform any active attack.

☑ There are far more plugins to gather information than any other type of plugin.

Vulnerability Fingerprinting

☑ Plugins capable of performing actual attacks will be used for vulnerability fingerprinting.

☑ There are three types of vulnerability fingerprinting plugins: attacks that are unlikely to cause actual harm, attacks that can be potentially destructive, and attacks that can be configured either way.

☑ The use or nonuse of destructive attacks in a scan is regulated by the use of safe checks.

Denial-of-Service Testing

☑ Denial-of-service (DoS) testing is performed last in any given thread. This is to ensure that if the host is knocked offline or the service does go down, all other vulnerabilities that would be findable have been found.

☑ Flooding attacks are present in Nessus 2.1, but not yet present in the mainline Nessus code train.

☑ The last attacks to be performed are those that might knock the entire host offline, thereby preventing any further testing.

Putting It All Together

☑ When all threads have completed scanning, Nessus will check the contents of the temporary NBE it created during the scan and generate a report from the data collected there.

☑ Data from each machine, by default, is grouped individually in the report, so you will see a full assessment of the vulnerabilities of each machine, one at a time.

☑ The Knowledge Base information can be stored on the machine in a form of a file, allowing easy debugging of possible false positives.

Frequently Asked Questions

Q: Why is it important to understand what all these plugins do?

A: Nessus is modular by design. If you want to write your own plugins for extended scanning, it's a good idea to have an understanding of the architecture of Nessus so you know what type they are and where to add them. You wouldn't want to accidentally put a destructive or DoS plugin before all the informational checks; you could lose valuable data that way.

Q: So, what is this Knowledge Base thing?

A: The plugin Knowledge Base is where Nessus stores the information it gathers as it goes through a scan. At any point, the Knowledge Base will contain information about what on the network Nessus has discovered so far.

Q: What if I do things in the wrong order?

A: Unless you are writing your own plugins, Nessus will automatically select the correct order for plugins to run based on the class of plugins to which they belong. If you write your own, just make sure that you assign them to the appropriate class.

Q: Will the Nessus server behave the same way when scanning if I use a local client or a remote one?

A: The scanning behavior will be the same. All that comes from the server; the client just selects options for the server and the scan and then sets the server free to do its job.

Q: Where can I find out more about NASL and its syntax?

A: You can read the appendix in this book, or look online at www.nessus.org/doc/nasl2_reference.pdf.

Q: Why are things scanned in a particular order?

A: Maximum gain of information for minimal disruption. The hosts are identified and fingerprinted and the servers are identified first for efficiency reasons. Then, the information-gathering phases, attack phases, and DoS phases are ordered that way to ensure that the best data is gotten out of a scan before the machine or service is knocked offline, if you have configured options that allow it.

## Chapter 9

The Nessus Knowledge Base

Solutions in this chapter:

- **Knowledge Base Basics**
- **Information Exchange**
- **Limitations**

☑ Summary

☑ Solutions Fast Track

☑ Frequently Asked Questions

Introduction

In 2000, Nessus introduced the then "experimental" Knowledge Base saving feature. The original Nessus Knowledge Base was an in-memory list of data gathered during a vulnerability assessment. With the release of Nessus 1.0.5, however, Nessus servers gained the capability to save the Knowledge Base to disk for use in future scans. Now, in version 3.0.6, this feature has been around for several years and is very useful for performing contrast assessments over short periods of time.

The merits of the Nessus Knowledge Base, or KB, are obvious. The Knowledge Base allows Nessus to use information gleaned from a past scan of a system to enhance, and speed up, the scan being performed. Even more important, though, is that one plugin can use data gathered by a previously run plugin, decreasing the number of interactions with each host and making plugin development easier. A perfect example of this is the current implementation of Microsoft HotFix checks. In the original implementation, each check made a connection to the remote registry to examine its relevant key/value pairs. The "Installed Windows Hotfixes" check released in 2004 instead makes a single remote registry connection and proceeds to populate the Knowledge Base. Subsequent Nessus Attack Scripting Language (NASL) scripts need only query the local Knowledge Base to glean this information.

The goal of this chapter is to get the reader familiar with the workings of the Nessus Knowledge Base. The chapter highlights how the Knowledge Base works and how you can use it to maximum benefit.

It should also be noted that many plugins use the knowledge base to store information on username and password pairs gained during the scan. An example of this is the SMB username and password that the nessus user can enter on the "Edit Policy-->Credentials" section of the Edit Policy Dialog. It is used through the Knowledge base call kb_smb_login() and kb_smb_password().

Knowledge Base Basics

This section (as its title implies) is aimed at covering the basics of the Nessus Knowledge Base. We will discuss briefly how the Knowledge Base is implemented and how it can be used and configured by the user.

What Is the Knowledge Base?

The Nessus Knowledge Base is quite simply the list of information gathered about a host being tested. It allows plugins, or tests, to share information about the target system allowing for both more intelligent testing and more conservative use of bandwidth and processing power. Please keep in mind, as we discuss *plugins*, *tests*, and *scripts*, that these terms are interchangeable in the world of Nessus. The Knowledge Base feature allows Nessus to restrict tests to only those that are pertinent to the host being tested. For example, Nessus currently contains several thousand distinct tests for CGI abuses. (The Common Gateway Interface, or CGI, is a standard for external gateway programs to interface with information servers such as HTTP servers). These tests would be pointless against a server that does not have a running HTTP daemon. To conserve bandwidth (and to distinguish itself from many of the regular brute-force scanners available today), Nessus will first determine if a web server is running on the server (on port 80 or any others within its configured scan range) and will set a key within the Knowledge Base for "Services/www" with its value being the corresponding discovered httpd port; for example, "Services/www/8181/working=1". Tests that require a web server to be present will first make a call to the Knowledge Base to determine the value for "Services/www" before continuing.

As stated, Knowledge Base saving has been compiled in by default since version 1.1.0. As of the current version (3.0.6), the Knowledge Base is vital to many of the plugins in the Nessus library, and can not be disabled while maintaining Nessus' functionality as a comprehensive scanner.

The Knowledge Base is considered "fresh" for a user-configurable period of time. During the specified time, the Knowledge Base will be consulted for information about the host. This will affect the actions performed by the scanner on subsequent scans within the specified time window. In short, Nessus can be configured to only conduct vulnerability tests against ports reported to be open by the Knowledge Base. This reduces the traffic generated by the scanner (effectively preventing the scanner from first doing a portscan of the target host), but introduces the possibility that the scanner could "miss" a port that has opened between the time the Knowledge Base has been created and the current scan. These options are covered in more detail later in this chapter.

A word about the "Policy.xml" file

As of the NessusClient 3.0.6 version, many settings are not directly accessible from the client interface. The Nessus Engine still uses these settings, however. The master definition file for the settings is located (by default) at: "/opt/nessus/var/nessus-client/Policies.xml", but the NessusClient file is kept on a per-user basis. This file is located in "<user home directory>/.nessus-client/" and is named "Policies.xml" as well.

This file contains a section for each Policy you have defined in the GUI. In order to be sure you are modifying the correct policy, it is a good idea to use a XML editor to make your changes. This will ensure that the formatting is good, and that you are operating under the policy that you think you are working on. If you choose not to, please be aware that the policies are organized under the <PolicyName> tag in the "Policies.xml" file. So, for example, if you have a Policy called "Nightly Scan", the preferences tags you will need to alter for that policy are located under the <PolicyName>Nightly Scan</PolicyName> tag set.

A practical example: If you want to change the maximum time that the Nessus Knowledge Base is saved, you will need to modify the file: "<user home directory>/.nessus-client/Policies.xml". It is recommended that the user use a formatting XML editor in order to preserve file integrity and make it simpler to track which Policy one is operating upon. XML files (like the Policies.xml file), are particularly sensitive to formatting errors. The format of the Policies.xml is simple XML file. For example, the entry to change the maximum age of the saved knowledge base entries would be as follows:

```
            <Policies>

                ...

                  <Policy>
<PolicyName>Nightly Scan</PolicyName>
...
<Preferences>
<preference>

                            <name>kb_max_age</name>
                              <value>864000</value>
                  </preference>
...

                  </Preferences>

          ...
</Policy>

          ...
</Polcies>
```

The ellipsis (…) represent other information in the "Policies.xml" file. This information may be quite large and can usually be collapsed by a good XML editor to make things simple to read.

An interesting note about the kb_max_age key. The time is calculated in seconds, so 864000 is exactly 10 days (864000 / 60 = 14400 minutes / 60 minutes = 240 hours / 24 hours = 10 days). Many other keys to modify Knowledge base behavior are specified in the Policies.xml file also.

Where the Knowledge Base Is Stored

The Knowledge Base is stored on the Nessus server and is created by default in the /opt/ nessus/var/nessus/users/<username>/kbs directory, where <username> refers to the Nessus user who initiated the test. These directory locations can be configured by passing compilation options to the configure scripts during the install process for versions of nessus prior to 3.0. Releases of Nessus greater than 3.0 are standardized on the /opt/nessus directory. Each host tested results in the creation of its own Knowledge Base file, which is named for either the IP address or the fully qualified domain name (FQDN) of the tested host.

```
[root@nessus]# ls /opt/nessus/var/nessus/users/nessus-user/kbs/192/168/0/
192.168.0.1    192.168.0.123    192.168.0.100    192.168.0.50
womwom.sensepost.com        packetstormsecurity.org
```

Using the Knowledge Base

Options pertaining to the Knowledge Base can be found under the Options tab of the Edit Policy Dialog of the GUI Nessus client. For this chapter, we are going to address both the previous version, as well as the current version. The reason for this is to bridge the gap for the knowledgeable user from the previous version(s) to the current version.

Figure 9.1a gives the user a single option to enable the saving of the knowledge base to disk. Additional configuration options are not configured using the GUI, where previous versions did as illustrated in Figure 9.1b.

Figure 9.1a Configuration Options (NessusClient version 3.0.6)

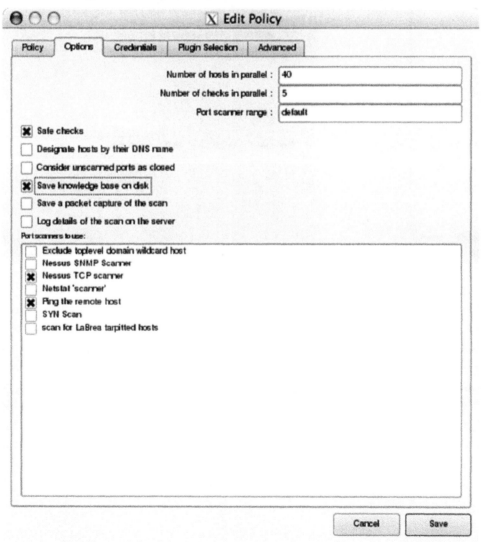

Figure 9.1b Configuration Options (NessusClient version 3.0.5 and earlier)

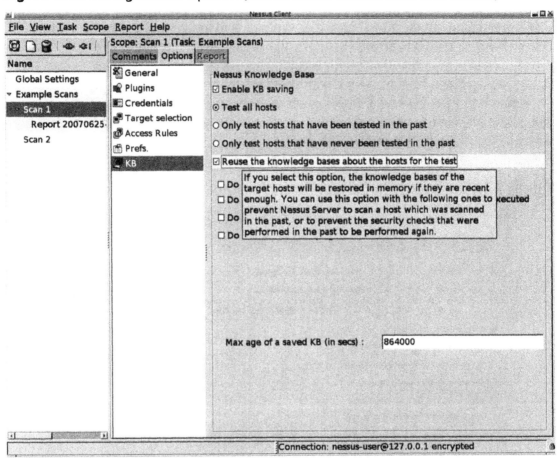

The check box highlighted in Figure 9.1a is the option that enables Knowledge Base saving on the Nessus server. This setting is not selected by default in either the 3.0.6 version, or the older series. The previous versions, prevented the user from making changes to the Knowledge Base-specific configuration options that follow unless Checking the box brings us to the screen in Figure 9.2.

Figure 9.2 Knowledge Base Saving Enabled (NessusClient version 3.0.5 and earlier)

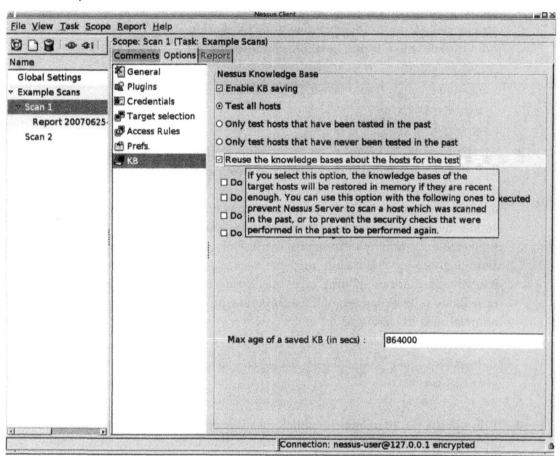

Even with the Knowledge Base saving option activated, the Nessus client defaults to a "neutral" configuration. As you can see in Figure 9.2, the default settings cause the Knowledge Base to be saved, but do not allow it to affect subsequent scans. Therefore, the Nessus server will write the Knowledge Base to disk, but will never consult it for subsequent scans on the same hosts.

The following options, selected via option buttons in previous versions or via the "~/.nessus-client/Policies.xml" in current versions, allow the user the option to scan all hosts, scan only hosts without a valid Knowledge Base, only hosts that have a valid existing Knowledge Base, or block scanning with plugins which would cause Denial of Service attempts. These options can be used in different situations to great effect. In the NessusClient version 3.0.6 and later, the key names are given as well with text excerpts. For example:

■ An administrator performs a scan on an entire subnet to determine the key critical hosts. The Knowledge Bases of non-critical hosts are removed from the /kbs directory. With the option to "Only test hosts that have been tested in the past," the scanner will not try to discover new hosts in the subnet on subsequent scan runs and thus will only test the hosts the administrator has chosen as key hosts.

```
<preference>
  <name>only_test_hosts_whose_kb_we_have</name>
  <value>yes</value>
</preference>
```

■ An administrator performs a scan on an entire subnet and generates his results. A few days later, he discovers that new hosts have been added to the subnet. Running the scanner with the "Only test hosts that have never been tested in the past" option instructs the scanner to run tests only on the new hosts that it finds, serving to both enumerate new hosts and to list vulnerabilities found in those new hosts. This option is powerful in a number of scenarios. For instance, consider that a company can only afford high network utilization once per week. And so, once per week, the administrators run a scan over all hosts. They then scan each day for any hosts that were missed due to being powered off, taken home, or newly introduced into the environment since the last scan.

```
<preference>
  <name>only_test_hosts_whose_kb_we_dont_have</name>
  <value>yes</value>
</preference>
```

■ It is important to highlight the pitfalls of network topologies such as those using DHCP when using the previous Knowledge Base saving settings, and possibly overcoming this pitfall by using the MAC address setting option.

■ Policy dictates that all hosts will be fully scanned, but after scanning them they are discovered that they are sensitive to several DoS attacks. Preventing hosts which are sensitive to DoS scans from being scanned by using the option to prevent DoS scans from re-running would be very useful to prevent a lot of extra work by the system administrators.

```
<preference>
  <name>kb_dont_replay_denials</name>
  <value>yes</value>
</preference>
```

■ The Administrator decides to only do a "contrast scan" to see if the vulnerabilities that have been sent to the system level administrators have been fixes. The option to avoid scanning with the IP scanner but instead to scan for vulnerabilities based on the existing Knowledge Base entries.

```
<preference>
  <name>kb_dont_replay_scanners</name>
  <value>yes</value>
</preference>
```

■ The Administrator decides to only do a "contrast scan" as above, but instead just wants to test the attack plugins only. As such the following will allow that to happen (there was no GUI options for this in previous versions).

```
<preference>
  <name>kb_dont_replay_info_gathering</name>
  <value>yes</value>
</preference>
```

■ The Administrator decides to only do a "contrast scan" as above, but instead just wants to test the information gathering plugins only. As such the following will allow that to happen (there was no GUI options for this in previous versions).

```
<preference>
  <name>kb_dont_replay_attacks</name>
  <value>yes</value>
</preference>
```

In previous versions (NessusClient 3.0.5 or earlier), the last four check boxes in Figure 9.2 are grayed out, precluding the user from selecting them. Selecting the "Reuse the Knowledge Bases about hosts for the test" check box allows the user to select these four check boxes (see Figure 9.3). In current versions (3.0.6 and later) of the NessusClient, the following changes must be made to the "~/.nessus-clients/Policies.xml" file:

```
<preference>
  <name>kb_restore</name>
  <value>yes</value>
</preference>
```

NOTE

Please note that this is absolutely necessary if you want to use the Knowledge Base specific options. If this option is not enabled, no other Knowledge Base Scanning Options will work as anticipated.

Figure 9.3 Knowledge Base Reuse (NessusClient Versions prior to 3.0.6)

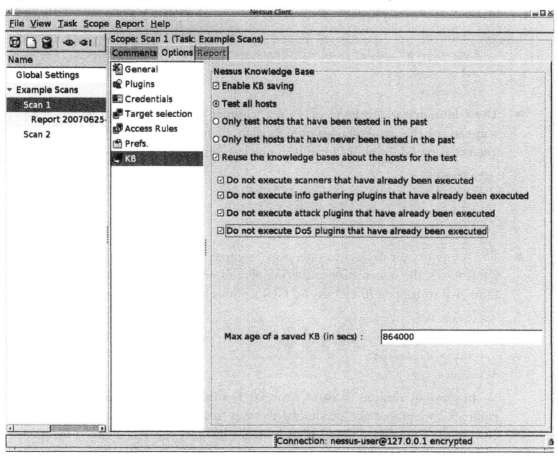

The four check boxes correspond directly to the following Nessus plugin categories:

- ACT_SCANNER
- ACT_GATHER_INFO
- ACT_MIXED_ATTACK, ACT_DESTRUCTIVE_ATTACK, and ACT_ATTACK
- ACT_DENIAL, ACT_KILL_HOST, and ACT_FLOOD

Users familiar with NASL will notice that there are two other categories at the time of this book's publication: ACT_INIT and ACT_SETTINGS. Both of these serve to set global variables used by other plugins, but not to actually interact with systems, and thus cannot be deactivated by use of the Knowledge Base.

The remaining text info box in Figure 9.4 allows the user to enter the maximum age in seconds for a Knowledge Base. After this number of seconds, the information in the Knowledge

Base is considered stale and must be rediscovered. Again, this setting is important to decrease the odds that the Knowledge Base does not decrease the accuracy of a scan by using data that has become inaccurate as the target systems' configuration changes over time.

Figure 9.4 Knowledge Base Age (NessusClient version 3.0.5 and earlier)

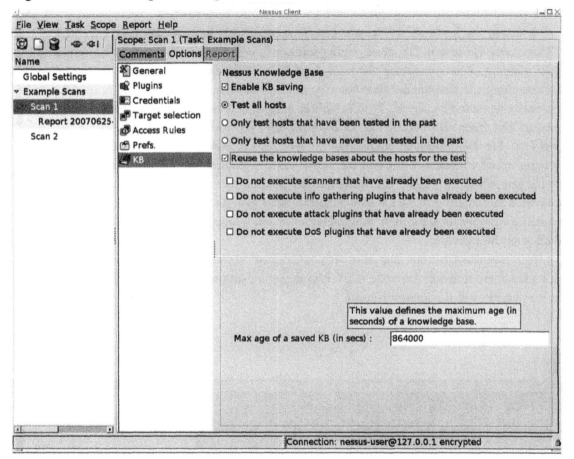

As can be seen in Figure 9.4, the default maximum age for a saved Knowledge Base is 864000 seconds, or 10 days. In previous versions (prior to 3.0.6) if no value is specified here, a more conservative default of 3600 seconds, or one hour, is used. In versions 3.0.6 and newer, the maximum age defaults to 864000 (10 days). The maximum age of the Knowledge Base is the maximum lifetime, in seconds, of a Knowledge Base. After this lifetime passes, the entire Knowledge Base is considered obsolete and is disregarded by the scanner and thus regenerated on the next scan.

In order to set the maximum age of the Knowledge Base entries in versions of the NessusClient 3.0.6 and later, you must modify the "~/.nessus-client/Policies.xml" file as illustrated below.

```
<preference>
  <name>kb_max_age</name>
  <value>864000</value>
</preference>
```

Selecting the first option "Do not execute scanners that have already been executed" (Policies.xml file option "kb_dont_replay_scanners") will result in the scanner running without port scanning or ping scanning the target host. This lowers the resultant noise on the network by consulting the Knowledge Base for a list of hosts and open ports on those hosts. All data normally generated by the ACT_SCANNER plugins will be pulled from the Knowledge Base instead. The three check boxes that follow limit the execution of information gathering, attack, and DoS (Denial of Service) plugins respectively. An administrator who has just added new plugins either manually or through the nessus-update-plugins script might choose to select all of the check boxes to ensure that only the new plugins are executed. This is only advisable, of course, if you have performed a scan using the older plugins recently enough for the data to be trusted. Don't just look for new vulnerabilities or you'll miss hosts that have very old vulnerabilities on the network!

It is important to note that as of version 3.0.5 of Nessus, the ability to do differential scans has been removed from the GUI. It is at present unknown if this feature will be restored in the future or if it is gone for good.

Tools & Traps…

Knowledge Base Saving: Caveats

A few caveats must be kept in mind when reusing saved Knowledge Bases. One can easily picture a host that starts a vulnerable web server after it has been scanned. If the saved Knowledge Base is used to avoid rescanning the host, then it is a certainty that the new service will not be discovered and probed for vulnerabilities. The saved Knowledge Base function should therefore be used with caution and is best used against relatively tightly controlled subnets when testing for a few select vulnerabilities. It is also important to use a relatively short maximum lifespan.

A second caveat, and a very real danger, that should be considered is that of sensitive information disclosure through access to the Knowledge Base files. With the increasing use of the Nessus Knowledge Base, we are quickly reaching the point where access to the Knowledge Base files is worth as much as access to an actual Nessus report. By default, the /opt/nessus/var/nessus/users directory (which stores the Knowledge Base files) restricts access to the Knowledge Base files to the root user. Relaxing the permissions on this directory could result in inadvertently sharing sensitive data with other users on the same machine or attackers who can gain even low levels of illicit privilege on the system.

Information Exchange

As mentioned earlier, the primary aim of the Nessus Knowledge Base is to facilitate the sharing of information between tests (plugins) to remove redundancy during testing. We will now quickly examine exactly how the Knowledge Base can be used within NASL scripts. After reading this section, the reader should be able to use calls to write to and read from the Nessus Knowledge Base to improve his or her scripts.

How Plugins Use the Knowledge Base to Share Data

This section uses examples to illustrate how entries can be written to and read from the Knowledge Base using the various Knowledge Base related calls. This topic is probably best explained by example. For an illustration, let's say we run a "clean" scan (in other words, no existing Knowledge Base) against the target womwom.sensepost.com. The scan completes, finding a host of vulnerabilities present on womwom.sensepost.com's web server. Examining the Nessus Knowledge Base created for this host (/opt/nessus/var/nessus/users/nessus-user/kbs/womwom.sensepost.com) reveals about 14900 lines of text. One must bear in mind that about 14800 lines of the Knowledge Base can be attributed to the Nessus server committing to the Knowledge Base its list of port statuses (open or closed), and successfully launched tests against the target. These entries are then used in subsequent tests to ensure that plugins are not rerun if Knowledge Base saving is enabled and the appropriate check boxes have been selected. There would be more lines in the Knowledge Base file if the test had not excluded potentially destructive plugins.

A quick *grep* for the expression "*3 Port*" in the newly created womwom.sensepost.com Knowledge Base file will give us an example of data stored in the Knowledge Base.

```
[root@nessus]# grep "3 Ports" womwom.sensepost.com
1182801060 3 Ports/tcp/25=1
```

```
1182801060 3 Ports/tcp/22=1
1182801060 3 Ports/tcp/111=1
1182801060 3 Ports/tcp/443=1
1182801060 3 Ports/tcp/631=1
1182801060 3 Ports/tcp/1241=1
1182801060 3 Ports/tcp/1234=1
```

An Nmap scan against the same host confirms our Nessus results.

```
[root@blowfish]# nmap -sT womwom.sensepost.com

Starting nmap 4.20 ( http://www.insecure.org/nmap/ ) at 2007-06-24 23:43 EDT
Interesting ports on womwom.sensepost.com (XXX.XXX.XXX.XXX):
Not shown: 1696 closed ports
PORT        STATE       SERVICE
22/tcp      open        ssh
25/tcp      open        smtp
111/tcp     open        rpcbind
443/tcp     open        https
631/tcp     open        ipp
1234/tcp    open        hotline
1241/tcp    open        nessus
Nmap run completed -- 1 IP address (1 host up) scanned in 0.385 seconds
```

The results match, which also lets us know that Nessus' TCP scanner is working. Next, a host of plugins like find_service.nes and find_service2.nasl then attempt to determine the service running behind these open ports. Once a plugin has determined the running service, it makes a call to the Knowledge Base by using NASL's register_service(port, proto) call. This call defines two items in the Knowledge Base:

- Known/tcp/port = proto
- Services/proto = port

For illustration, we make a simple alteration to the nasl that confirms the existence of a Nessus daemon running on a host (nessus_detect.nasl). All we need to do here is add the following lines:

```
-snip-
# nasl modified for simple test
register_service(port: port, proto: "FooBar");
-snip-
```

Running the scan again against the host womwom.sensepost.com returns the exact same portscan result as before. A *grep* (or *egrep* in this case) for Services or Known (identified services) in the new Knowledge Base file returns the following:

```
[root@nessus]# egrep "Known|Services" womwom.sensepost.com
1182801060 1 Known/tcp/111=portmapper
1182801060 1 Services/portmapper=111
1182801060 1 Services/www=443
1182801060 1 Known/tcp/443=www
1182801060 1 Services/unknown=111
1182801060 1 Services/www=631
1182801060 1 Known/tcp/631=www
1182801060 1 Services/smtp=25
1182801060 1 Known/tcp/25=smtp
1182801060 1 Services/ssh=22
1182801060 1 Known/tcp/22=ssh
1182801060 1 Services/unknown=1241
1182801060 1 Services/www=1234
1182801060 1 Known/tcp/1234=www
1182801060 1 Services/nessus=1241
1182801060 1 Services/FooBar=1241
1182801060 1 Known/tcp/1241=nessus
1182801060 1 Known/tcp/1241=FooBar
```

Also worth noting here is that the Nessus scanner has managed to correctly identify and register the web server running on port 1234:

```
1086043083 1 Services/www=1234
```

NASL also provides the set_kb_item(string: name, string: value) and get_kb_item(string: name) functions to set and retrieve single key-value pairs from the Knowledge Base. The function get_kb_list(string: name) is almost the same as the get_kb_item function, except, as its name suggests, it returns a list to the calling script. To demonstrate how a NASL would make use of these functions, we create two simple dummy plugins (sense.nasl and post.nasl). It's important to note that as of version 3.0.6, the "script_cve_id" directive is now required in order to compile and run a plugin successfully. If you are using the usual "rc" scripts to run the nessus daemon, it is likely that you will miss the plugin warnings. See the chapter on NASL to learn about error checking and NASL script (or check the file /opt/nessus/var/nesus/logs/nessusd.dump in order to see nessusd's complaints).

sense.nasl:

```
# This script written to demonstrate kb writing <haroon@sensepost.com>
if(description)
{
  script_id(123123);
  script_cve_id("CVE-2007-9990");
  script_version ("$Revision: 1.2 $");
```

```
 name["english"] = "sense";
 script_name(english:name["english"]);
desc["english"] = "
Pointless test in order to set a kb item.
We will set a key of Wierd/non_existant/key
with a value of Moo
Risk factor : Info";
 script_description(english:desc["english"]);
 summary["english"] = "Sets pointless KB item";
 script_summary(english:summary["english"]);
 script_category(ACT_GATHER_INFO);
 script_copyright(english:"This script is not worth Copyrighting (nwC)
2004 haroon meer");
 family["english"] = "Misc.";
 script_family(english:family["english"]);
 script_dependencie("find_service.nes");
 exit(0);
}
 set_kb_item(name: "Wierd/non_existant/key", value:string("Moo"));
```

Once this plugin has been run, we can peek ahead to check for a successful Knowledge Base write by manually *grep*'ing the resultant Knowledge Base file:

```
[root@nessus]# grep Wierd womwom.sensepost.com
1182801060 1 Wierd/non_existant/key=Moo
```

So far, so good! Now we write another simple (and pointless) NASL to read the value from the Knowledge Base and display the results.

post.nasl:

```
# This script written to demonstrate kb reading <haroon@sensepost.com>
if(description)
{
 script_id(223123);
 script_cve_id("CVE-2007-9991");
 script_version ("$Revision: 1.2 $");
 name["english"] = "post";
 script_name(english:name["english"]);
```

```
desc["english"] = "
Pointless test in order to read a kb item.
We will retrieve the value for the key
Wierd/non_existant/key_

Risk factor : Info";
   script_description(english:desc["english"]);
   summary["english"] = "reads pointless KB item";
   script_summary(english:summary["english"]);
   script_category(ACT_ATTACK);

   script_copyright(english:"This script is not worth Copyrighting (nwC)
2004 haroon meer");
   family["english"] = "Misc.";
   script_family(english:family["english"]);
   script_dependencie("sense.nasl");
   exit(0);
}

   val = get_kb_item("Wierd/non_existant/key");
   security_note(data:"We extracted the following key from the KB for
this host" + val, port:0);
```

The post script simply creates a value called "val," which is populated by the value returned from the Knowledge Base using the get_kb_item("Wierd/non_existant/key") call. The last line simply returns the string through the report viewer. Note also the script_dependencie("sense.nasl") line that needs to be included in our post.nasl script. This ensures that the sense.nasl will be run prior to the running of post.nasl should the configuration be set to include dependencies at run time.

As of version 3.0.6 the Nessus has gotten smarter. It will now run plugins upon which other plugins are dependant, if the "Enable dependencies at runtime" is checked. The companion "Silent dependencies" will prevent warning messages when selecting plugins with unsatisfied dependencies. Figure 9.5 illustrates the two check boxes. Both of these check boxes are located on the "Edit Policy" dialog under the "Plugins" tab. Previous versions allowed the explicit examination of dependencies, but this is no longer needed, thanks to the dynamic dependency calculations.

Figure 9.5 NASL Script Dependency Options

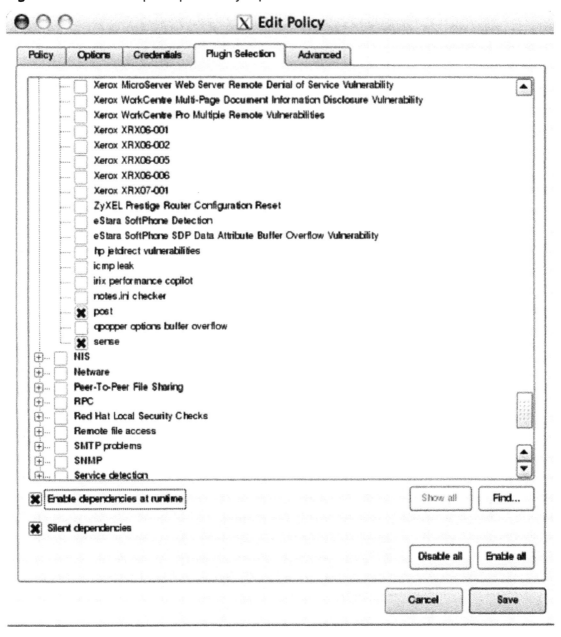

The result of the scan is shown in Figure 9.6 for the sake of completeness, but illustrates that post.nasl successfully read the key/value pair written to the Knowledge Base by sense.nasl.

Figure 9.6 Nessus Report Viewer (Single Knowledge Base Key/Value)

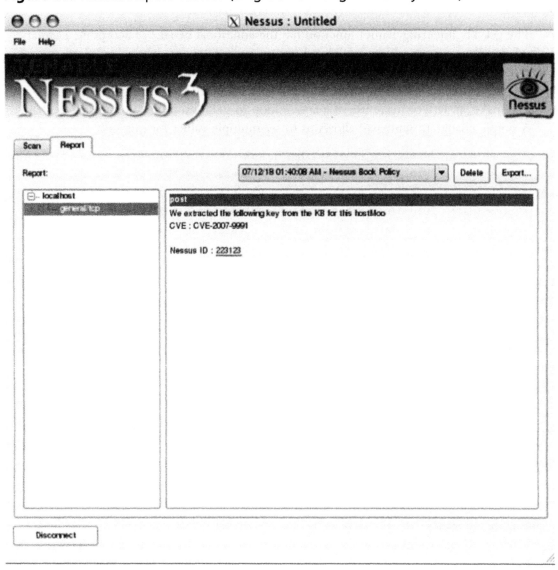

It is important to note that in the present version of Nessus (3.0.6) a cached copy of the plugin code (compiled) is kept. This cached copy of a NASL plugin can keep changes from being affected in nessusd. Nessusd will use the existing cache in /opt/nessus/var/ nessus/ with the file names plugins-code.db and plugins-desc.db. These two files should be removed if the plugin author makes changes, or as of version 3.0.6 you can also use "nessusd –t" to only recompile the plugins which have changed since the last full compile cycle. When in doubt:

```
[root@nessus]# rm /opt/nessus/var/nessus/plugins-code.db
[root@nessus]# rm /opt/nessus/var/nessus/plugins-desc.db
```

The get_kb_list(string: name) function has the additional benefit of accepting a literal Knowledge Base entry name or a wildcard (for example, "Services/www" or "Services/w*"). Since the Knowledge Base might hold multiple lines with the same key, the function get_kb_list() returns a hash. The requesting NASL then needs to either wrap the request in a call to make_array(), or make use of a *foreach* loop to iterate through all items in the hash.

A simple change to sense.nasl allows us to set multiple values for our key:

```
set_kb_item(name: "Wierd/non_existant/key", value:string("Moo"));
set_kb_item(name: "Wierd/non_existant/key", value:string("Doe"));
set_kb_item(name: "Wierd/non_existant/key", value:string("Ray"));
set_kb_item(name: "Wierd/non_existant/key", value:string("Me"));
set_kb_item(name: "Wierd/non_existant/key", value:string("Far"));
set_kb_item(name: "Wierd/non_existant/key", value:string("So"));
set_kb_item(name: "Wierd/non_existant/key", value:string("La"));
set_kb_item(name: "Wierd/non_existant/key", value:string("Ti"));
set_kb_item(name: "Wierd/non_existant/key", value:string("Doe"));
```

While this example is highly contrived, there are many cases where multiple plugins add a key-value pair to the Knowledge Base resulting in this type of situation. The corresponding change that needs to be made to our post.nasl is made incredibly easy thanks to NASL's make_list() function.

```
-post.nasl-
val = make_list(get_kb_list("Wierd/non_existant/key"));
  foreach item (val)
  {
    answer = answer + ", " + item;
  }
  security_note(data:"We extracted the following keys from the KB for this host"
+ answer, port:0);
-post.nasl-
```

The *foreach* loop used here iterates through the array and merely appends the new array element to the answer variable. This answer variable is then reported to the user (see Figure 9.7).

Figure 9.7 Nessus Report Viewer (Multiple Returned Values)

The Type of Data that Is Stored

Theoretically, the Nessus Knowledge Base can be used to store just about any type of data that one comes across during an assessment. Most plugins restrict themselves to writing data to the Knowledge Base that is worth sharing with other plugins. For example:

- **Information about the scan** ("What tests did I run?")
- **Information about a test** ("Did the test succeed?")

- **Information about the target** ("Open Ports/Service Banners/Service Descriptions")
- **Information about the results** ("3 Info messages and 1 Critical during this scan!")

The value of a key begins immediately following the equal sign and is terminated by the newline character.

```
1086051533 1 ftp/banner/21=BLEH_BLEH_ BLEH_BLEH_ BLEH_BLEH_ BLEH_BLEH_ BLEH_
BLEH_ BLEH_BLEH_ BLEH_BLEH_ BLEH_BLEH_ BLEH_BLEH_ BLEH_BLEH_ BLEH_BLEH_ BLEH_BLEH_
BLEH_BLEH_ BLEH_BLEH_BLEH
1086051588 1…
```

Dependency Trees

The simplistic sense.nasl and post.nasl examples used earlier in this chapter served to introduce the concept of script dependencies in the Knowledge Base. With more complex tests that are built on top of more layers of protocols, keeping track of these dependencies becomes a little more challenging. We now examine the smb_lanman_browse_list.nasl script to explain the concept of NASL script dependency trees.

The smb_lanman_browse_list.nasl script has the relatively modest goal of obtaining the remote host's browse list. Before this script can successfully run, however, it requires the completion of the following two scripts: netbios_name_get.nasl and smb_login.nasl. With the option to "enable script dependencies at run-time" set, the scanner will attempt to launch those plugins if they have not already run. netbios_name_get.nasl in turn requires cifs445.nasl, while smb_login.nasl requires netbios_name_get.nasl, cifs445.nasl, logins.nasl, and find_service.nes. cifs445.nasl is in turn dependent once more on find_service.nes. This might seem convoluted, but it's actually a reasonable dependency tree that shows that the plugin authors are abstracting the process appropriately, working to both avoid duplicating code between plugins and to create a framework for building other SMB/NetBIOS-related plugins.

Limitations

While the Knowledge Base is an invaluable addition to Nessus' architecture, it does have some shortcomings inherent in its current design. This short section is aimed at ensuring that the user is aware of the possible complications that could arise when making use of the Nessus Knowledge Base.

Using get_kb_item and fork

We explained earlier the use of get_kb_list() when dealing with multiple key/value pairs. When the singular get_kb_item() is used to retrieve a list, the plugin forks for every additional returned value. This technique has both pros and cons, allowing us to write really small tests when dealing with multiple keys, but at the same time adding a level of complexity that we need to be careful of. Returning to our post.nasl after having created multiple entries in the kb using sense.nasl, we have:

```
-post.nasl-
# This script written to demonstrate kb reading <haroon@sensepost.com>

if(description)
{
  script_id(223123);
  script_cve_id("CVE-2007-9991");
  script_version ("$Revision: 1.2 $");
  name["english"] = "post";
  script_name(english:name["english"]);
desc["english"] = "
Pointless test in order to read a kb item.
We will retrieve the value for the key
Wierd/non_existant/key
Risk factor : Info";
  script_description(english:desc["english"]);
  summary["english"] = "reads pointless KB item";
  script_summary(english:summary["english"]);
  script_category(ACT_ATTACK);
  script_copyright(english:"This script is not worth Copyrighting (nwC)
2004 haroon meer");
  family["english"] = "Misc.";
  script_family(english:family["english"]);
  script_dependencie("sense.nasl");
  exit(0);
}
  security_note(data:"We extracted the following keys from the KB for
this host" + get_kb_item("Wierd/non_existant/key"), port:0);
-post.nasl-
```

Note that this time, we call security_note() just once. The call to get_kb_item(), however, will return a list, causing the plugin to fork for every unique key/value pair returned. This results in the report shown in Figure 9.8.

Figure 9.8 Nessus Report Viewer (Multiple Key/Value Pairs)

This forking needs to be kept in mind when dealing with sockets. A call to open a socket made prior to the fork will potentially result in multiple children trying to write to the same socket at the same time.

Tools and Traps…

Knowledge Base Saving in a DHCP Environment

Astute readers will have spotted the inherent danger of saving Knowledge Base files based on IP addresses or DNS names on a network running the Dynamic Host Configuration Protocol (DHCP). In such cases, it is possible for hosts on the network to be out of sync with the data contained in the Knowledge Base. For example, hosts A, B, and C are scanned and their respective Knowledge Bases are stored. During the lifetime of these Knowledge Bases, however, the hosts' DHCP leases expire and are redistributed to other hosts. This then leads to the new hosts inheriting the Knowledge Bases of the hosts that previously had their IP addresses! This is almost certainly the worst kind of inaccuracy possible when using the Knowledge Base, but also the easiest to guard against.

In a DHCP environment, the user/analyst should turn on the **Designate hosts by their MAC address** option under the **Scan options** tab (in NessusClient versions 3.0.5 and below, or enable it in the scan "Policies.xml" file under the section "use_mac_ addr" (as below).

```
<preference>
  <name>use_mac_addr</name>
  <value>yes</value>
</preference>
```

Selecting this check box or enabling this Policy.xml option will cause Nessus to save entries into the Knowledge Base using the host's Ethernet MAC address instead of its IP address. Since MAC addresses are unique physical numbers tied to the hosts' network cards by the hardware manufacturers, they serve as excellent unique identifiers when IP addresses aren't reliable. Remember, though, that MAC addresses are at Layer 2, the data link layer, and are thus only useful on a LAN. You can't communicate with a host through a router and still discover the host's MAC address. You'll need to place a nessusd server on each network for which you want to identify hosts by their MAC addresses.

Summary

The Nessus Knowledge Base gives power to both the analyst writing tests, and the administrator running the scanner. The security analyst will benefit from being able to write more efficient, less bandwidth-hungry tests, while the administrator benefits from decreased network traffic while maintaining his security posture at acceptable levels. The decision to use Knowledge Base saving and to limit future scans based on data stored within the Knowledge Base is a tricky one, however, and should be carefully examined before execution.

The bulk of the settings governing the use of the Knowledge Base during a scan can be found under the KB tab of the Nessus Setup GUI on the client. Theses settings can be used to enable or disable Knowledge Base saving, and to guide what the scanner can do with the stored Knowledge Base data and for what period of time. A Nessus user might choose to scan or ignore hosts with existing Knowledge Bases and might choose to run different permutations of the NASL script families based on the information stored in the target host's Knowledge Base.

Making use of the Knowledge Base to store data that should persist (at least for the duration of the scan) makes good sense and is a technique that has been used to increasing effect as time goes on. Simply making use of the correct calls to retrieve these stored values and being aware of the Knowledge Base's possible limitations is important when writing NASL scripts.

Solutions Fast Track

Knowledge Base Basics

- ☑ The Knowledge Base is the list of information gathered on a single tested host.

- ☑ This information is referenced during the running scan and can be configured to serve as a data store for subsequent scans on the host for a configurable period of time.

- ☑ Selecting the Enable KB Saving option under the KB tab will by default save Knowledge Bases per host but will still redo all subsequent scans from scratch unless other options are set.

- ☑ The scanner can be configured to ensure that only "New Hosts" (hosts that are discovered by the scanner that do not have a corresponding Knowledge Base) or "Old Hosts" (hosts that do have Knowledge Bases) are tested.

- ☑ One can choose to ignore scan categories on hosts with valid Knowledge Bases.

- ☑ It is important to delete the /opt/nessus/var/nessus/plugins-code.db and the /opt/nessus/var/nessus/plugins-desc.db when updating plugins, otherwise, the old plugin code will be used instead of the new code. Nessusd must also be restarted in order to compile (cache) the new code. As of version 3.0.6 you can also use "nessusd –t" to only recompile the plugins which have changed since the last full compile cycle.

Information Exchange

☑ Entries are stored and retrieved from the Knowledge Base in the form of key/value pairs.

☑ The scanner can be configured to dynamically "Enable dependencies at run-time" to ensure that plugins are ordered well, such that key values are set in one plugin before they are required by another.

☑ Values can be written and read by making use of set_kb_item() and get_kb_item()/ get_kb_list() calls, respectively.

Limitations

☑ Using get_kb_item() to retrieve a set of values in a single call causes the NASL to fork for every returned value. This could cause complications if multiple children attempt to communicate with the same socket opened prior to the *fork()*.

☑ One should consider the fact that scanned hosts could change within the window period of a Knowledge Base's lifetime, potentially causing a scanner to overlook issues until the Knowledge Base expires. It is thus important to set short-enough lifetimes for the Knowledge Bases via the GUI **KB** tab or the "Policies.xml" file section "kb_max_age".

☑ DHCP'd environments are prone to complications with reusable Knowledge Bases, but this can be mitigated somewhat by making use of Ethernet MAC addresses instead of IP addresses as Knowledge Base filenames. When using this replacement mechanism, remember that every host you want to scan must have a nessusd server running on its local network (LAN).

Frequently Asked Questions

Q: Is there a difference between using get_kb_item() and get_kb_list()?

A: Yes. get_kb_item() will fork for every new key/value pair returned (when dealing with multiple returned entries), while get_kb_list() will not.

Q: Is it dangerous to always keep my Knowledge Base valid for the default 10 days?

A: *Dangerous* is a relative term. The risk that one must live with (if limiting the actions of certain tests) is that the target host might have changed within that time window in its configuration, vulnerability set, or even IP address!

## Chapter 10

Enterprise Scanning

Solutions in this chapter:

- **Planning a Deployment**
- **Configuring Scanners**
- **Data Correlation**
- **Common Problems**

- ☑ **Summary**
- ☑ **Solutions Fast Track**
- ☑ **Frequently Asked Questions**

Introduction

Enterprise vulnerability scanning is quite complicated, and as such requires a certain amount of planning, preparation, and adjustment. The key factors for effectively scanning the enterprise for security vulnerabilities are easy administration, periodic scanning, and accurate results.

There is no trivial way to take a scanner such as Nessus and use it to scan the entire enterprise network. Simply pointing it toward the network and scanning will not be enough. This chapter shows some of the caveats that make this process difficult. You'll learn, for example, why simply scanning the entire network from a single point is often not viable. This involves exploring distributed scanning, differential reporting, report correlation, and automated updating.

At this point in the book, we expect that you are most likely already using Nessus for regular security testing, and are looking to take it up a notch—from maintaining a list of hosts you regularly scan, to scanning your entire enterprise and using the results to improve your enterprise's security status.

Planning a Deployment

In the following section we will help you outline your plan for deployment.

Define Your Needs

Before scanning your enterprise network for security holes, you must remember that simply scanning anything that has an IP address will not bring you the expected benefits unless you can handle the huge number of vulnerabilities that are likely to appear in the report.

Our experience shows that on a typical vulnerability scan in a medium-to-large enterprise, each host scanned returns an average of 3 high-risk, 5 medium, and about 10 low-risk vulnerabilities. Quick math will show that scanning a small subnet of 100 hosts will return around 300 high-risk vulnerabilities and about 1,800 vulnerabilities in total. This computation doesn't take into account that some vulnerabilities might be the same on different computers, or that the same vulnerability might exist on different ports on the same machine.

According to an old Chinese proverb, "if *what we know* is the contour of a circle, and *what we do not know* is the inside of that circle, the *more we know* the less *we know that we do not know*." We therefore must prepare beforehand so we're not overwhelmed by the amount of information we will receive once we start scanning the network. We will divide the preparation into three parts: planning, preparation, and segmentation.

Planning

Some companies consider their customer database their most critical asset. Others consider the CEO's laptop most sensitive. Others still will mark their file server as the important one. Just as this is different for each company, each company's security needs are different, and so is the understanding of what "enterprise scanning" requires.

The easiest way to identify your most critical assets is to answer the following question: How much money and time will you lose if "something bad" happens to that asset? The definition of "something bad" is your worst-case scenario; this might be the deletion of a critical file or perhaps your database falling into the hands of your competition. Once you answer that question, you will see that scanning anything and everything doesn't necessarily solve the problem of scanning your most critical assets, as too much information is just as bad as too little. If you fail to notice vulnerabilities in your most critical assets because the report overflows with data about your least important hosts, you've simply missed important vulnerabilities for a pitiful reason.

When customers say they are uncertain of what is critical and what is not, it is good practice to revert to this list of items, ordered with more critical resources first:

1. Centralized servers (DNS, mail, file, database)

2. Financial servers and workstations

3. Management servers and workstations

4. Servers and workstations containing marketing data and plans

5. Sales servers and workstations

6. All remaining hosts

This list is a good starting point in identifying what the company management should worry most about an attacker compromising.

Scanning the right assets in the right way (most important first, or, alternatively, the most critical more frequently) will help you understand what is required to protect your critical machines.

This will prevent you from being overwhelmed by information and subsequently giving up the idea of scanning your enterprise. We have seen many cases of companies that reached the unfortunate conclusion that vulnerability scanning is "impractical," just because they were scanning the wrong parts of the network or just too much of it. This made it impossible for them to realize the obvious benefits if the vulnerability scanner was used properly. They threw away a tool that would be perfectly useful if it was simply tuned to only examine the most critical systems.

New security holes surface daily, and in order to be effective, you should plan to run your scans on a regular basis. It would be impractical to try to handle dozens and sometimes hundreds of reports illustrating the security vulnerabilities of the enterprise network without first prioritizing which reports are most important.

By the end of this section, you will be able to develop a list of critical assets (identified by hostnames, IP addresses, or even IP ranges) ordered by how important they are to your organization. Next to each asset, list what their acceptable "bill of health" is. You might decide that some servers must be completely free of vulnerabilities, while others might have medium- and low-risk vulnerabilities only. At the very least, do not accept any "high-risk" vulnerabilities on any of the critical assets. In addition, write down a point of contact for each asset, as this will be required once you start generating reports and need someone to address the issues found, and the frequency with which you will scan the asset. Table 10.1 shows one way of organizing the list of assets.

Table 10.1 Asset List

Asset Name	IP Ranges/ Hostnames	Expected Results	Manager Name and E-Mail	Frequency of Scans
HR database	192.168.1.50–250	No open ports No vulnerabilities	Joe Smith joes@acmecorp.net	Daily
R&D file servers	192.168.1.3–10	No open ports except file sharing and HTTP No high or medium vulnerabilities	John Williams johnw@acmecorp.net	Every other week

When it comes to the frequency of scans, we prefer *more* versus *less*. By *more*, we mean that running the scan once a day is preferable to running it once a month. Although this might sound extreme (we can imagine you're now thinking, "Do I really need to scan my network on a daily basis?"), you need to remember the recent Sasser worm. The Sasser worm hit the Internet just three weeks after the vulnerability was discovered. This means that a monthly vulnerability scan could have missed this vulnerability altogether, and as a result you would have missed the need to install this critical patch. This vulnerability discovery to worm creation window has actually been steadily shrinking. We cannot stress enough how important the frequency of your scans is to their success in preventing worm outbreaks at your site.

NOTE

Here are some vulnerability statistics from ICAT, available at http://nvd.nist.gov/statistics.cfm.

In the first month of the year 2008, 442 new vulnerabilities have been discovered and reported. In 2007, the total count was 6,690, in 2006 it was 6,607, and in 2005, the total number 4,929, and in 2004, 2,456 new vulnerabilities were revealed. In the year 2003, the total count was 1,007, and in the year 2002, the total number of vulnerabilities discovered was 1,308. Year 2007 holds the record for the last four years with 6,690.

The CERT reports, available at www.cert.org/stats/, show even higher figures. The number of vulnerabilities reported to CERT in the year 2007 was 7,236; in 2006 was 8,064; in 2005 was 5,990; in 2004 was 3,780; in 2003 was 3,784; in 2002, the number was 4,129; and in 2001, the count was 2,437.

According to SecuriTeam.com, an online vulnerabilities database, an average of about five new vulnerabilities are discovered each day. The total number of new vulnerabilities reported on the web site during the first five months of the year 2004 was over 750.

Most network administrators and security managers are extremely busy people who will find it difficult to handle a dozen or more scanning results a day, especially when they need to give these results the required attention. We will therefore show you in later sections ways to reduce the amount of reports generated to just one or two. Each of these reports will only show the changes since the last scan (if any) by using differential report generation.

Preparation

In many organizations, different managers are in charge of different assets. Each of these managers needs to be prepared for the vulnerability scans on his or her assets. In fact, in most cases, the scans will find vulnerabilities in the assets for which the managers are responsible, so it's a good idea to prepare them for the potentially bad news. Furthermore, vulnerability scans are very "noisy"—the relevant network and system administrators need to be prepared to see abnormal log entries, higher CPU and memory consumption, and an increase in network traffic during the scanning phase.

Notes from the Underground...

The Importance of Prior Notification

One of the authors was once present during a vulnerability scan that was done without prior notification to some of the system and database administrators. During the scans, some of the Solaris systems and the Oracle databases exhibited strange and abnormal log entries, all caused by the fact that the vulnerability scanner was sending

Continued

unusual requests as part of the vulnerability assessment. Not knowing that a scan was in progress, the administrators immediately assumed the database was failing and started to run corrective measures.

You might be able to guess what happened next. The corrective actions, which were trying to fix a nonexisting problem, corrupted the database and destroyed the information stored on that machine. Hours of labor could have been saved if the administrators had been notified in advance of the pending scan and that unusual events would potentially occur during that time.

A good way to make sure everyone is aware that you are implementing enterprise-scaled vulnerability assessment is to invite the different managers to a meeting where you present the following:

- An overview of Nessus' capabilities.

- Different aspects of Nessus' effects.

- Live scans of a test environment, preferably a machine or subnet of low importance. This will better illustrate how the scan affects the machines and demonstrate the scanning process.

This last point, the demonstration of a live scan, should probably involve a look at the log messages generated on the target machines and might include a look at the network traffic through a sniffer like tcpdump or Ethereal.

By the end of this section, all of your asset managers should be aware of your intention to regularly scan them. They should understand that these scans will result in vulnerabilities being highlighted, which will then need to be addressed.

Finally, remember the politics of the situation. If you want a manager to be most responsive to vulnerability data, or any data presented by the security team, it's important to work hard to avoid an adversarial relationship. Approach the manager with a helpful tone and do what you can to make the process easier. Otherwise, you might find that either vulnerability scanning gets shut down or the results ignored. You can often help managers most by giving them a preliminary report, allowing them the chance to fix vulnerabilities and get a second scan in one to three day's time. This helps managers show that they are responsive and that vulnerabilities get a short lifespan on their watch.

Segmentation

As discussed earlier, your network contains different kinds of assets, each of which might have a different type of confidential material on it. The scan results, and scanning in general, might reveal sensitive information, such as usernames, weak passwords, hidden directories, and, of course, security vulnerabilities in those assets. To minimize information leakage, you should consider segmenting your scans, breaking them up so no one report contains information about the entire enterprise.

Segmentation allows you to test each of your assets while not providing confidential information about one set of assets to a manager of another set. In computer security, we're always thinking about risk avoidance and risk mitigation. In this situation, we're trying to decrease both the probability that sensitive information leaks and how much information a single leak can carry. Giving information about one asset's vulnerability to eight people instead of two roughly quadruples the risk. Remember, that person might turn against the organization, potentially criminally. He might drop the report on the ground inadvertently; he might get mugged. It's far easier to deal with these events if the report that's used maliciously contains less information.

There's more than just vulnerability information at stake, though. Nessus can be configured with or discover sensitive information, including logon information for Windows, brute-forcing results, SNMP community names, and so forth, and as this type of information can show up in the vulnerability reports, you should segment the results in such a way that only the people who need access to each piece of information actually receive it. Another benefit of segmentation is that it allows you to use load-balancing techniques to optimize the scan based on your network topology and host concentrations.

Network Topology

Your organization's network topology largely affects the quality of the results you receive. For example, results from scanning the internal network (or MZ network) from your DMZ network will differ from a scan done from your internal network. Each of these scans is equally important, and the different results provide insight into your network's security situation. The difference is mainly caused by the effect that firewalls and other network devices have on the scan, as they allow or block connections, route or reroute traffic, according to a predefined rule set.

Therefore, a critical question to answer during the planning phase is, "what do you want to find?" Are you trying to see what a normal employee would be able to do to your file server, or what a night cleaning crewmember could do without having a valid username and password combination? Are you trying to find out what an Internet attacker would be able to do to your web server, or what a hacker could do if he successfully compromises the DMZ?

Each of these questions is equally important and requires a different type of deployment.

NOTE

At first glance, it might seem logical to install a scanning server on each of your different networks (DMZ, MZ, privileged network, etc.) and run VA scans from each to the rest of the organization. However, that would probably be a waste of time, as high-risk vulnerability on a sensitive host, no matter who has access to that network, should always be considered critical. Hiding a vulnerability doesn't fix it—it will eventually resurface. Network segmentation is an added protection, but should not be an alternative to fixing vulnerabilities.

The actual benefit of scanning the network from different points of view is in providing you with a feel of what needs to be addressed immediately and what can wait. For example, a high-risk vulnerability on your web server connected to the Internet needs greater attention than a high-risk file-sharing related vulnerability on the same web server does, as no outsider should have access to the related file-sharing port.

When segmentation is involved, we always recommend separating your network topology into two parts—internal and external—before dividing it further. "Internal" refers to the networks that are accessible only to employees, while "external" consists of all the hosts that are accessible from the Internet.

Your external topology should be scanned from an external server, imitating as much as possible an external attacker. The internal topology should be scanned from an internal server with full network access, imitating to the greatest extent possible an internal attacker.

NOTE

You should remember that when you receive the results for the external scans, every vulnerability should be accounted for, as it has been proven in the past that something considered a medium-risk vulnerability can quickly develop into a high-risk problem. In addition, low-risk vulnerabilities sometimes indicate that something is wrong: unnecessary services are installed on a hardened server, or incorrect rules are configured on the firewall. For example, your scan might find an unnecessary portmap or rpcbind process on a UNIX box and rank that as a low priority. A week later, when researchers release a remote-root vulnerability in Sun's rpcbind, the risk due to that unnecessary service is much higher. It's better to address even low-priority issues early, before the vulnerability escalates or a new one is discovered.

Bandwidth Requirements

One of the more important aspects of enterprise scanning is that unlike a one-time penetration test, typically done quarterly or even annually, enterprise scanning is done on a daily, weekly, or monthly basis. As such, network effects of the scan, such as bandwidth utilization or intrusiveness of the scans, are especially important.

Unfortunately, no network can provide us with unlimited bandwidth, and no two points on the network can use the complete bandwidth allowed by the network hardware without affecting other points on the network. Therefore, you must take into consideration that scanning your network will affect your network's overall performance. To complicate things even further, inter-office communications infrastructure tends to be even more restricted, and instead of 10/100/1000Mb per second, we can expect those communication lines to be 1Mb per second or less. In any case, this bandwidth needs to be shared with our coworkers—saturating the connection with our vulnerability scan will result in inaccurate scan reports due to packet loss, and lost of connectivity and functionality to our coworkers. Although Nessus does not consume much bandwidth if properly configured, scanning across a low-bandwidth and high-latency connection is not recommended unless there are no other alternatives.

How can we handle the problem of scanning multiple physical locations? One easy solution is to place a server in each location to make sure the available bandwidth between the scanning server and the network being scanned is at least 10Mb.

However, a better solution would be to first understand how much bandwidth Nessus requires, and enumerate any locations that do not meet these requirements. Before we lay out the bandwidth requirements, let's look at what affects bandwidth consumption. One simple rule of thumb is that a host with no open services requires far less bandwidth to scan than a server hosting multiple web servers, each running on a different port. The fewer services a host has, the fewer plugins Nessus will need to launch against it; thus, the lower bandwidth the Nessus scans will consume.

We have used freely available open-source tools to verify the bandwidth requirements needed for an average host. The tools are very easy to obtain, and require no knowledge of programming and very little technical skills. First, we need to use the ever-popular packet-capturing tool tcpdump (available from www.tcpdump.org). You can use simple capturing filters to capture only those packets originating from the scanning computer to the scanned host. We also use further filtering of the captured packets to prevent the capture file from becoming too large and difficult to handle.

For example, testing a port-80 scan using the filter `host 192.168.1.243 and port 80` allows the capture of all traffic originating from and destined for port 80. After capturing the entire Nessus session, you can generate statistics on the captured traffic. To do so, open the capture file using Ethereal (available from www.ethereal.org) and choose **Statistics | Summary**. Alternatively, if you want to create more in-depth graphs and statistics, you can use the tool tcpstat (available at www.frenchfries.net/paul/tcpstat/) with gnuplot (www.gnuplot.info).

Tcpstat is able to take raw tcpdump files and generate numerical data from them. This numerical data combined with gnuplot allows you to take any numbers and crunch them into a graph.

We used the following steps to capture packets, take the capture file and convert it to numerical data, and generate from it an easy-to-analyze graph. We start with our packet-capturing command:

```
tcpdump -w iis.dump "host 192.168.1.243 and port 80"
```

Once a substantial amount of data is captured, we convert it to statistical information using:

```
tcpstat -r iis.dump -o "%R\t%B\n" 1 > iis.total.data \
tcpstat -r iis.dump -f "dstport 80" -o "%R\t%B\n" 1 > iis.up.data \
tcpstat -r iis.dump -f "srcport 80" -o "%R\t%B\n" 1 > iis.down.data
```

We then generate the corresponding graph by opening gnuplot and typing the following at the prompt:

```
set term png small
set data style lines
set grid
set yrange [-10:]
set title "IIS Bandwidth"
set xlabel "seconds"
set ylabel "KBytes/s"
plot "iis.total.data" using 1:($2/1024) smooth csplines title "Total"\
    , "iis.up.data" using 1:($2/1024) smooth csplines title "Up"\
    , "iis.down.data" using 1:($2/1024) smooth csplines title "Down"
```

The result of gnuplot will appear on the screen, and can be redirected to a file. For example, writing these lines to a file called gnuplot.script and running `gnuplot gnuplot.script > picture.png` will generate a file called picture.png containing the desired graph.

Now that we know how to generate the information, let's understand the different phases of Nessus scans and how much bandwidth they generate using the method just illustrated.

Portscanning Phase

During the portscanning phase, Nessus 3.0 and later use an internal scanner to determine what ports are open on a particular host. The tcp-connect uses a single TCP 72-byte packet with its SYN flag set, is Nessus' default method to detect open ports. This packet is sent to each of the ports you configure Nessus to scan. Nessus by default will scan all ports between 1 and 15,000.

The number of packets sent depends on the latency of the scanning host, the network, and the host being scanned. On a very low latency and high-bandwidth network, this portscan can take roughly 1.5 seconds.

Doing some quick math brings us to:

$$15,000 \times 72 = 1,080,000 \text{ bytes}$$

The response packets require roughly the same amount of bandwidth. Dividing that by 15 seconds brings us to 720,000 bytes per second, or 720KBps. Although this isn't very high, multiplying this by a few dozen hosts will generate enough traffic to temporarily bring a 100Mbit (roughly 12.5Mbytes per second) network to its knees. In addition, this large amount of packets will strain the firewalls and network devices responsible for connecting your scanning host with the host being scanned.

Moreover, not all traffic is created equal. We see in Figures 10.1 and 10.2 that the portscan phase generates average traffic—this average is controlled by how long we wait for a response from the host being portscanned. We will use this waiting time to reduce the bandwidth requirements, by setting the value to 1 millisecond (with the value of *Maximum wait between probes (ms)*). In addition, notice that there is a minimal difference between the bandwidth consumption of a TCP Connect() scan and a SYN scan. The interesting dip below zero packet/second can be attributed to GNUPlot's smoothing of the curve.

Figure 10.1 Portscan (1–15000)

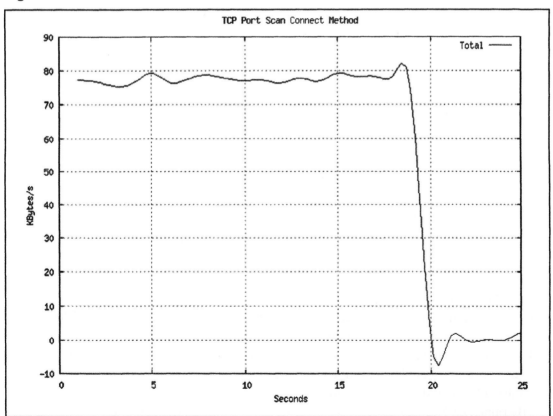

Figure 10.2 Portscan—SYN (1–15000)

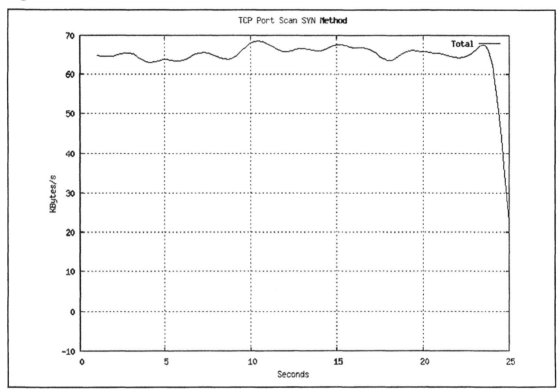

We can easily control how fast the portscan proceeds and the average bandwidth being consumed by choosing settings other than the defaults Nessus uses. Of course, these changes will affect the time it takes to portscan the host, but at the moment, we are more concerned about bandwidth utilization than scanning speed. Note that our goal in enterprise scanning is an optimal configuration where no interaction with the scanning server is required after our early tuning, and thus we can just sit back and receive reports, while Nessus scans at its own speed consuming predetermined bandwidth. The process is automatic, and we don't really care how long it takes, just that the results are accurate and as unobtrusive as possible.

Testing Phase

During this phase, Nessus takes each port reported open and runs a service detection process on it to determine the service type of that port (for example, HTTP, SMTP, POP3, etc.). For each service detected, Nessus will then run its arsenal of plugins. The more ports and applications you have on your machine, the more bandwidth consumed. However, since you can control the number of plugins that are run simultaneously, you can easily control the utilized bandwidth during this phase.

By launching Nessus against a default IIS web server and analyzing the traffic generated, we can see that the upstream bandwidth required averages 30KB per second, while the downstream is an average of 239KB per second. Running a similar scan against a default Apache web server will return different results: for the upstream an average of 13KB per second, and for the downstream an average of 73KB per second.

An average is one thing but when we observe the scans in progress, a more elusive bandwidth requirement issue hides behind it, as there are impressive bandwidth peaks going well over the 500KBps for Apache and over the 1,000KBps for IIS. However, in both cases, they are the downstreams—the responses from the server. This means that asymmetric connections can be used while it might appear that this was not the case before.

There is one obvious difference between `Apache Scan (port 80/www)` and `IIS Scan (port 80/www)`. The `IIS Scan (port 80/www)` is a slow starter, while the `Apache Scan` appears to consume an average bandwidth throughout the scan. With version 3.0.5 and later, both scan types have been dramatically improved in terms of speed.

This difference in bandwidth consumption is due to the type of plugin "sophistication" Nessus uses—when the web server is detected to be Apache, Nessus will run certain tests, whereas if IIS is detected, those tests will not be run.

You should note that HTTP is not a special case—most protocols are just as bandwidth intensive as HTTP, if not more. For the sake of comparison, NetBIOS (the protocol used when scanning for vulnerabilities affecting ports 135, 137, 139, and 445) will yield a higher bandwidth usage on an unpatched Windows 2000 system when it is provided with a username and password combination in comparison to when it is only allowed to use NULL (anonymous) sessions.

The provided username and password allow Nessus to use two important functionalities—registry access and remote share access—which in turn result in more plugins becoming relevant. These two functionalities are time consuming (making the scan take longer to complete) and consume a great deal of bandwidth. However, given valid credentials, they provide very important information; for example, notification of backdoors, worm infections, and policy breaches, including expired passwords, locked accounts, administrative group members, and so forth.

So, what does this all mean? It means that Nessus' bandwidth requirements aren't negligible, and that in most cases they cannot be dismissed as unobtrusive. Furthermore, the different types of operating systems (OSs) and applications being checked affect how much bandwidth is consumed.

There are now two big questions: How can we minimize the average bandwidth being consumed, and where can we place the scanning server without affecting the network's bandwidth utilization?

The first question is easy to answer. You can minimize the average bandwidth consumed by configuring Nessus to run fewer tests in parallel by tweaking the value *Number of checks to perform at the same time* via the graphical user interface GUI or by setting the value of *max_threads* found in nessusd.conf.

The best time to employ this tweaking, changing the value of *max_threads*, is whenever there are more than several hosts we want to scan, preferably with the same network mask, or at least on the same physical network (provided they are not separated by network devices or firewalls). Doing so accomplishes two important things. First, it minimizes the strain a scan will have on the network, and second, it minimizes the load on the scanning server itself. At the moment we are more interested in the first goal. The subsequent question will be better explained in the section *Configuring Scanners*, where we explain how to spread the scan over several physical servers, while not necessarily increasing the maintenance workload. We will do this by managing the servers from a centralized location, automating them so they update themselves send the generated reports back to that central location.

Automating the Procedure

Before installing Nessus daemons on several computers, we must first create a test plan that will answer the following questions:

- How do we verify that the scanners do not cause harm to our network?

- How do we monitor the bandwidth usage that might be incurred by our scanning?

- How do we verify that the scanners are working properly and are in fact finding vulnerabilities?

Similar to the Hippocratic Oath taken by physicians, the most important part of the enterprise scanning is to make sure the network does not suffer from being scanned. The network can suffer due to unresponsive applications, high CPU, memory usage, or by traffic congestion. Our scanning servers can cause any of these problems.

These effects will need to be prevented. To avoid problems in applications or bandwidth congestion, you need to prepare some sort of test lab where several non-production servers will go through the same scanning as you are planning to use.

The test lab will allow you to verify the effects on your network of setting the port range, plugins to run, network scan speed, and so forth. This test lab will create a scanned environment that is as real as possible, allowing you to detect issues that might arise in the actual scans and solve them before they can cause problems in your real environment.

The test lab will also ensure that you are not running scans with incorrect settings. For example, running Nessus with a port range of 1–1024 and telling it to regard all other ports as closed will have an adverse effects on the results of your scan. Any service above port 1024 will be considered closed—numerous applications use ports higher than 1024: Oracle, MySQL, MSSQL, IRC, and Proxies, to name a few. Those applications will not be tested for vulnerabilities, and you might never notice.

To avoid such incorrect settings from affecting the results of your scans, you will need to create self-made "honeypots" that you know are vulnerable to a certain extent. These honey-pots will be used to verify that Nessus is in fact running correctly. We do not need to actually use commercial honeypots—all we require is to understand our network structure enough and expect certain vulnerabilities to appear. For example, if we know a certain Windows machine wasn't patched with the latest MSXX-XXX patch, we can use one of Nessus' tests as a marker that our scans are working correctly and that we are able to access the registry to detect that missing patch.

We assume from now that you created your test lab, ran some Nessus scans, verified that they are not affecting your test lab's network, and you are running them as correctly as possible finding all the vulnerabilities that appear in the test lab servers. Does this mean that we are finally ready to scan the enterprise? Again, we must reiterate that you are still missing a crucial part of making Nessus work correctly—this important part is what makes the difference between recurring vulnerability assessment and one-time vulnerability assessment.

One of Nessus' most important features is its capability to update tests amazingly frequently. Nessus is installed with an easy-to-use script that will update the plugin library used by the scanner. The script, trivially called nessus-update-plugins, downloads a file from the www.nessus.org web site, extracts its content to the plugin folder, and restarts the Nessus daemon, making the update process as smooth and automated as possible.

However, the script's behavior leaves more to be desired. How can you verify that the update process was successful for every Nessus daemon you have on the network? How can you make sure all Nessus daemons are in fact up to date? How can you roll out any custom-made plugins you create? How can you avoid the Nessus daemons downloading a big file from the Internet, possibly slowing the Internet connection? And, how can you avoid giving direct access to the Internet to each of these Nessus daemons?

All of these questions can be answered using a more centralized approach to updating the Nessus engine. The required materials for centralizing the plugin-updating mechanism are a web server and some scripting skills. The update mechanism is composed of five stages:

1. Download the update.
2. Unpack the update.
3. Install the update.
4. Delete the plug-in caches.
5. Restart the Nessus daemon.
6. Report success.

Each stage will be done as much as possible in a single operation, making the update mechanism as redundant and safe as possible. In addition, it will guarantee that if a stage fails, the centralized server is informed. To implement the download stage, we suggest you either use the wget utility (which features the ability to Proxy, HTTP Authenticate, Resume, Retry, and many other nifty features) or implement a file downloading script via some external libraries, like Perl's amazingly popular LWP module.

We suggest you modify the downloading process so it does not download the same file each time it updates, as nessus-update-plugins does, but rather have some type of versioning mechanism where you can keep track of what version the Nessus daemon last attempted to update.

The version does not have to be more than a simple counter increasing by one each time you decide to roll out an update to your Nessus daemons, or perhaps a timestamp. After the download is complete, the updating mechanism will inform the web server that it was successful in downloading the update.

Our next stage is extraction and installation of the update. You do not have to separate the two stages, although it is recommended that you verify that the extraction was successful before trying to overwrite files—some extraction programs will partially overwrite the files if the archived file was corrupted, making your installation unstable or even unusable.

The installation of new plugins (unlike overwriting existing plugins) has no effect until the Nessus daemon is restarted; therefore, we must restart the Nessus daemon before continuing.

Restarting Nessus via a HUP signal (as is done by nessus-update-plugins) has no effect on the scan that is currently in progress—the scan will continue scanning as if nothing had happened.

This is both and bad. It's good because it doesn't stop our current scan, but it is bad because it doesn't reload any new scripts, making the current scan only partial (without all the new or updated plugins). We cannot avoid this, but we can modify our update mechanism to recognize such an event and alert us that a scan was in progress while the update was running, so that we can make a decision on whether we want to rerun that scan.

You can easily verify whether a scan is currently in progress by obtaining the list of running processes on the Nessus daemon and looking for the string *testing* (followed by the IP being tested). If this string appears, a scan is currently in progress. If not, you can safely signal a HUP at the end of the update mechanism or even restart the Nessus daemon service.

Once the Nessus daemon restart process has completed by either a HUP signal or a full-fledged stop and start, the script should again report to the web server that it has successfully restarted Nessus. The cautious administrator might also want to verify that Nessus has successfully HUPed/restarted by checking the */var/log/messages* (or any other file configured by the nessusd.conf file) for the string *nessusd x.x.xx started* (if Nessus was started/restarted) or for the string *Caught HUP signal – reconfiguring nessusd* (if Nessus was HUP'ed).

Unfortunately, we can't cover the aspects of automatically updating each Nessus daemon, including its libraries, and binaries using a mechanism similar to the one discussed previously, as it is too complex to be covered here. However, we can suggest using other means of updating that are equally good and relatively safe. By using Debian's apt-get, you can constantly check whether the Nessus you are using is up to date. Debian's unstable distribution is updated with the latest version of Nessus. At the time of writing, Nessus 3.0.5 is available by Debian. By simply running the command `apt-get -t unstable update`, followed by `apt-get install -t unstable nessusd nessus`, whenever a new version is available it will be installed on the machine.

Nessus' client provides two different ways of determining configuration and version information on a remote Nessus daemon. One is the -p parameter that allows you to obtain a list of the server and plugin preferences. The parameter can also work from a remote location where the only requirements are a username and password or client-side certificate (depending on the authentication mechanism used by the Nessus daemon). The other is the -P (uppercase) parameter that allows you to obtain a list of plugins installed on the server. This parameter, as the previous one, can be used from a remote location.

Instead of using the -p and -P parameters on your own and parsing the results returned, we recommend using the update-nessusrc script (available at www.tifaware.com/perl/update-nessusrc/). This easy-to-use Perl script takes an existing configuration file and is able to display the differences between your configuration file and the remote Nessus daemon. The differences include version changes, different plugin settings, and new, removed, or changed plugins. Unfortunately, the update-nessusrc script does not support command-line parameters that control the host to which it connects or change the username and password combinations it uses. However, by modifying the updated-nessusrc script and adding support for such a parameter, you can make the script incredibly handy.

The Nessus daemon keeps track of its actions through the log files. These log files can therefore be used to maintain a good record of what was scanned, when it was scanned, and how long it took. As going over the Nessus daemon log file manually is no easy task, we suggest using nessustail.pl (available from Nessus' nessus-tools package). The tool is a very easy-to-use Perl script that will comb through the message log created by the Nessus daemon and highlight potential problems such as segfaults, interruptions, HUP signals, and plugins that were too slow to finish.

Configuring Scanners

We'll now look at specific ways to deploy distributed scanning in terms of scanning topologies, examining the advantages and disadvantages of each.

Assigning the Tasks

Once we have decided what we want to scan, we need to start dividing the scans between the different hosts. When we divide the scans, we need to make sure we do not breach the confidentiality of the different departments by placing a single server scanning administratively separate networks, we do not cause too much traffic across the network by placing the server in a single place and scanning the whole network from it, and that we can still control the servers placed around the network even if they are in the different parts of the network.

There are three possible distributed scanning topologies you can use: *Star*, *Flat*, and *Islands*. Each topology has its advantages and disadvantages. We will start with the islands topology, as it is the easiest to explain. The islands' goal is to install Nessus daemons that are completely isolated from each other, thus maintaining the highest form of separation between the different departments. In the islands topology, there is no single point of control to the servers, and each network has its own Nessus client connecting to the server.

Advantages of the islands topology include:

- Information cannot leak between departments.

- Any problems with one server's scans does not affect the others.

- Each server can have an independent administrator. This administrator doesn't gain any additional access to other servers or other scanning servers.

- No additional firewall or networking devices rules need to be placed between the departments or between the Nessus client and the server.

- The different servers can provide different points of view of the same hosts (for example, DMZ vs. MZ).

Disadvantages of the islands topology include:

- Maintenance overhead because there is no centralized management.

- Higher hardware costs, as more servers are required.

- No centralized updates server can be created.

- Data cannot be correlated between different servers, or brought in to a centralized database for report consolidation.

The next topology we will discuss is the flat topology, which provides real increases in scalability over the islands topology, although it raises bandwidth requirements. In the flat topology, the Nessus daemons are installed all over the network. The network itself is fairly open between the departments and allows traffic to flow unobstructed. In this type of topology, the Nessus client can be used to manage the servers practically from any location. As the network is wide open, a single Nessus daemon can scan several departments.

Advantages of the flat topology include:

- A single server can scan the entire network.

- Management can be done virtually from any point of access on the network.

- A centralized update server can be used to update all the different Nessus daemons.

- Reports can be consolidated between the different servers.

- No additional firewall or networking devices rules need to be placed between the departments or between the Nessus client and the server.

Disadvantages of the flat topology include:

- Information may leak between two reports, as servers can house more than a single network vulnerability report.

- As a single server can be used to scan the entire network, it becomes a single point of failure with regard to the enterprise's vulnerability scanning.

- A single server cannot provide different views of the network's vulnerabilities (for example, DMZ vs. MZ).

- A single server causes higher bandwidth consumption across the organization compared to distributed servers.

The last topology we will discuss is the star topology. In this topology, the Nessus daemons are servers spread cross the organization that are all connected (in addition to their normal network access) to a management network. In this topology, we can manage all the servers from the management network, and can use this network to transfer data between the servers and to update these servers. However, the servers themselves cannot interconnect, as the management network allows only access to the centralized network.

Advantages of the star topology include:

- Information cannot leak between departments.

- Bandwidth consumption is divided between the servers.

- It provides different views of the network's vulnerabilities (for example, DMZ vs. MZ).

- A centralized update server can be used to update all the different Nessus daemons.

- Reports can be consolidated using a centralized server housing all the data.

Disadvantages of the star topology include:

- Management can only be done from a single point.

- Higher hardware costs are incurred, as more servers are required.

- Reports cannot be consolidated by interconnecting two servers.

- Additional firewall and network devices rules need to be placed between the departments and the management network.

- A single administrator would have control over the entire set of Nessus daemons, with the ability to inadvertently breach the different departments' confidentiality.

System Requirements

The Nessus daemon by itself isn't a large memory or CPU consumer. An idle Nessus daemon, with no clients attached, will consume virtually no CPU time, and around 14MB of memory. A disconnected Nessus client memory consumption is around 12MB. Once a connection is made, the daemon's memory consumption will jump to around 14MB, and the client's memory consumption will jump to around 40MB. Any additional Nessus client connecting to the daemon will consume an additional 1.5MB of memory.

Using these figures, we can safely assume that the Nessus daemon can hold a few dozen open connections with Nessus clients. However, the numbers given do not provide an accurate picture, as they do not include the memory consumption requirements needed once a scan starts. The memory consumption will vary greatly during the portscan phase and the plugin running phase, as different plugins are loaded, executed, and unloaded.

The tcp connect process requires around 0.5MB of memory for each host it portscans with TCP connect() scan and OS fingerprinting. By default, Nessus issues scans for up to 255 hosts in parallel, which means that a heavily used network can easily consume all available memory during the portscanning phase.

This calculation doesn't take into account the fact that the Nessus daemon will spawn an additional process for each host it scans, consuming roughly an additional 2.5MB of memory per host scanned. This process is responsible for launching the different plugins (the NASL and NES files).

Running the Nessus client with a Nessus daemon, where we configured the Nessus daemon to run one plugin at a time, will cause the Nessus daemon to consume roughly 16MB of memory in total. Using the same configuration, but configuring it to run two plugins at a time, will make the memory consumption jump at times to 20MB, but the average memory consumption will remain around the 16MB mark as Nessus waits for the two plugins it has launched to finish prior to launching two new ones. This is true even if the first plugin finishes several minutes before the second plugin.

Table 10.2 illustrates the memory consumption of the Nessus daemon vs. the number of simultaneous plugins being used (when scanning a single host). Note these results may not be accurate across all implementations of the nessusd binary. The numbers were obtained by snapshoting the process through "ps xal" under each test case on a Linux system with a system C library of glibc 2.6 and Nessus 3.0.5. In short, your mileage may vary.

Table 10.2 Memory Consumption of the Nessus Daemon

Number of Plugins	Peak Memory Consumption	Average Memory
1	18MB	16MB
2	22MB	20MB
3	24MB	22MB
4	26MB	23MB
8	34MB	28MB
16	48MB	44MB
32	84MB	76MB
64	104MB	94MB

NOTE

You will need to modify the value of `max_checks` in the nessusd.conf file to go over the 10 plugins mark. To go over the 64 marker on older (pre-version 3) versions of nessusd, you will further need to modify the nessus-core/nessusd/pluginlaunch.c file and change the value of MAX_PROCESSES from its default value of 32 to whatever you desire and then recompile.

The calculation for more than one host is a bit more difficult, and requires a long trial and error process to get the memory consumption requirements. As a rule, the `nessusd` process requires an average of about two times as much memory for any additional host for the peak memory requirement, and about one and a half times the memory needed for the average memory. We do recommend, however, as memory is a relatively inexpensive component, to equip the scanning servers with at least 1GB of RAM to answer most of your memory needs for scanning. You need to remember that you do not want to scan too many hosts in parallel, or use too many plugins in parallel, as both of these are bandwidth consumers. The Nessus daemon consumes plenty of CPU but it is not a CPU hog, as the utilization of CPU consumption depends on two main factors: the number of hosts being tested and the number of plugins being launched. As more hosts are tested and more plugins are launched in parallel, the CPU time for processing of the network data increases, and with it, the CPU loads. As in many other tasks, increasing memory has a greater effect on Nessus' speed than using a faster processor.

NOTE

Older versions of the Nessus daemon does not support Symmetric Multi Processing (SMP) in its native code, and will not benefit from it more than any other nonnative-SMP program running on the computer. Newer versions can use the operating systems lightweight process threading capabilities (also called Native POSIX Threading) to enhance performance. Multi-CPU machines can enhance the performance of post version 3 nessusd processes. While this is a compelling argument to install it on a multi-purpose machine, the utilization of the system IO bus and network are limiting, and sometimes crippling on large scans, even with the dramatic enhancements in version 3. We therefore recommend running the Nessus daemon on a dedicated machine, instead of installing it on a multipurpose server.

Scanning for a Specific Threat

Every once in a while, a new threat arises in the form of a critical advisory. The new vulnerability may affect more than one host on your network, but you are not certain which ones. It would appear that your viable solution would be to scan your entire network for all vulnerabilities and filter out that new vulnerability in which you are interested. However, scanning the entire network is neither simple nor quick.

We suggest this alternative. Scan your network with a limited set of plugins, which allows you to scan your entire network in a very short timeframe while trimming down the amount of vulnerabilities found to just those about which you are concerned. The only shortcoming of this type of scan is that you will need to make sure that all the plugin dependencies are met—open ports, dependent plugins, and so forth.

The dependencies requirement can easily be met by setting the parameter `auto_enable_dependencies` to yes in your configuration file and choosing the plugin numbers you are interested in enabling. As an alternative to changing your configuration file, you can use the tool update-nessusrc mentioned in the previous section. One of the tool's parameters is `--includes` followed by ID numbers. These ID numbers are the plugin IDs. Plugin IDs are unique identifiers for the specific test you are interested in using. For example, if we want to test for Microsoft's MS04-011 (incidentally, this patch addresses the vulnerability that the Sasser worm exploits), we need to first locate the appropriate plugin filename. In our case, there are several related plugins—we choose to use the registry-based smb_nt_ms04-011.nasl. Inspecting the file smb_nt_ms04-011.nasl, and looking for the entry `script_id` will reveal that the script's ID is 12205. We will use this number to run `update-nessusrc -c "" -f "" -r "" -i "12205"` `basic`, where `basic` is the default Nessus configuration file, `12205` is the relevant script ID, `-c` sets the name of the categories you want to enable, and `-f` sets the name of the families you want to enable.

> **NOTE**
>
> Remember that before you start scanning using this configuration file, you need to set the `auto_enable_dependencies` to `yes`. Failing to do so will return scan results that are misleading, as some of the tests plugin 12205 depends on will not execute.

In some cases it is better to meet (or avoid meeting) the plugin dependencies on your own, as the dependencies directly affect the behavior of certain plugins and the "path" (or method) that is used to discover a certain vulnerability. However, this is only recommended to those who are fully aware of the consequences of not meeting a given dependency—the most problematic outcome is that you might completely miss the presence of the vulnerability you were looking for.

Notes from the Underground...

Testing New Plugins

When you want to test your newly acquired or created plugin that depends on other plugins for such things as registry access, the NASL command-line interpreter will be insufficient, as it does not support Knowledge Base access or meeting of dependencies. The only viable solution in this case would be to run that test using a configuration file that specifically requests this newly formed plugin as the only plugin to execute, and that you mark the `auto_enable_dependencies` to `yes`.

We can easily illustrate the difference between meeting the dependencies and failing to do with an example of plugins that have the `script_exclude_keys` entry in them. Each plugin that has the `script_exclude_keys` entry in it will not be executed if a plugin has previously set the key this entry lists to exclude, such as in the case of `tcp_chorusing.nasl`.

NOTE

The `tcp_chorusing.nasl` plugin checks whether a remote Windows 95/98/Me machine answers to the same packet more than once—this will happen if it has more than one TCP/IP stack bound on that adapter.

The `tcp_chorusing.nasl`'s plugin logic is as follows: If the key SMB/WindowsVersion (which `tcp_chorusing.nasl` excludes) is set, the remote host is a Windows XP/2000/2003, and as such is certainly not vulnerable to this attack. However, if the key is not set, it will go about testing the vulnerability against the remote machine, using a real attack packet. Therefore, plugins partially answering to the dependency required by the test (plugins that set a value to SMB/WindowsVersion) will cause the plugin to test each host it finds on the network for the vulnerability.

In addition to the exclude behavior, certain plugins read Nessus' internal information Knowledge Base and act according to the information given there. Therefore, if we want to control the plugin's behavior, we will need to prevent the Knowledge Base information from being written. One way of doing this is to stop certain plugins from running by not meeting or only partially meeting their dependencies.

Notes from the Underground...

The Nessus Community and Plugins

Unlike other commercial vulnerability assessment tools, Nessus enjoys a large community of plugin developers and plugin maintainers. However, as there is no paid quality assurance team making sure the plugins are accurate, false positive free, and informative, the Nessus community requires your assistance. The most helpful feedback you can provide the Nessus community is its ability and inability to detect vulnerabilities, and, if possible, new plugins that detect those vulnerabilities. It is important to note that if you do find a problem with any of the Nessus plugins, you should report as much information regarding the host being tested and e-mail all the information to the bugs@nessus.org.

Best Practices

In the following section we will outline the best practices you should keep in mind.

Divide and Conquer

It is important to avoid sensitive information unintentionally appearing in reports that are available to less-classified personnel. Both the Nessus configuration file and the reports generated might contain sensitive information such as usernames, passwords, domain names, and so forth. As different divisions of your company are exposed to different types of sensitive information, you should run a separate scan for each division to keep reporting tools separate.

Segregate and Limit

In some companies, a different person from the one who installed the Nessus daemon might control the Nessus client. In such cases where it is not possible to further separate the Nessus daemons between the different networks, it is important to create daemon-based rules to prevent users from scanning networks and hosts that they don't need to.

The Nessus daemon's internal configuration file allows creation of rules that allow this segregation and limitation to be done easily. A rule is basically composed of an action: *reject*, *accept*, and *default* followed by an IP and associated network mask. The rules can be server-wide, user based, or client based. As we do not have control over the client-based rules, you should mainly concentrate on server-wide and user-based rules.

NOTE

Client-based rules are set by the Nessus client and offer no protection from someone using your Nessus daemon to scan a host it shouldn't.

Server-wide rules block a certain range of IPs from being scanned by the server. They are relevant to all users who connect to the Nessus daemon, and cannot be overridden by choosing a different user. User-based rules block a certain range of IPs, as before, from being scanned by the server, but they are dependent on the user who logged on to the system. A certain user might be able to scan host A, and another might not—it all depends on the username used to log on to the Nessus daemon.

We recommend placing a limited range of IPs that hosts can scan on each of the Nessus daemons you install, and extending that range as required. These rules will prevent the scanning host from accidentally being used to scan the entire network or even a single host you didn't intend to scan, such as sensitive servers, production networks, and so forth.

Certificates for the Forgetful

The Nessus daemon supports two authentication methods: password-based and certificate-based. We will not discuss why one is better than the other, but from our experience, certificates are easier to move and handle, and are more secure against snooping and capturing, while passwords can be captured, guessed, forgotten, and so forth. As such, we recommend that you install your entire Nessus daemon installation base with certificate authentication instead of password-based authentication. Both have no implications on anything but the logon phase where the Nessus client connects to the Nessus daemon.

Speed Is Not Your Enemy

Having a faster connection with lower latency between your scanning server and the host being scanned improves the speed at which you can scan the host and the reliability of your results.

A host scanned over a low-bandwidth WAN connection with a high percentage of packets lost will produce a greater percentage of both false positives, usually from denial-of-service (DoS) tests, and false negatives, which generally come with web-based tests.

It is therefore important to make sure that you conduct your scans through an optimal network connection, and that this connection offers as much bandwidth as you require and introduces as little latency as possible.

Keep a Watchful Eye

It is easy to lose track of the last time you received the results from a particular scan. Sometimes, a scan will only return partial results. This is especially true when you are working with large-scale networks where a momentary reset of a router, firewall, or other network device might cause hosts to disappear, artificially thinning your reports.

It is critical to always be aware of what vulnerabilities have been fixed and what new vulnerabilities are present as a result. Tracking these vulnerabilities and including them in the reports you receive can help you make certain that everything is working properly.

Data Correlation

In this next section, we'll focus on data correlation, especially in regards to the reports that are developed.

Combining Reports

Obviously, the most important part of Nessus isn't the scan itself, but rather the scan's results. While reading dozen of Nessus reports using the Nessus GUI can prove difficult, you can easily solve this problem by building your own vulnerability database. A comprehensive database often contains reports about all of the servers that were found to be vulnerable, along with the vulnerability identification numbers, descriptions, and risk factors. Once you've entered the data into a database, it's easy to query it and reveal which parts of the network are the most vulnerable, which vulnerabilities affect most of your servers, which servers contain a particular worm's affected vulnerabilities, and so forth.

Preparing Your Database

Before we can begin, we will need to prepare the database. For this section, our examples will use MySQL as our database server, because it is freely available for both the Linux and Windows operating systems, and is easy to use. However, any other database server can be used, instead. No matter which database server you choose, it will need to hold at least one database and one table where your information can be stored. You can easily parse Nessus' NBE (Nessus BackEnd) file format with any program that can interpret content that is delimitated by the pipe sign (|).

The fields the Nessus' NBE returns are IP address, affected port, script ID, vulnerability type, and description. To begin, we will first need to create a table that contains these fields. We will start by using the following SQL query:

```
CREATE TABLE ScanResults (
                        ID INT AUTO_INCREMENT,
                        IP TEXT,
                        Port TEXT,
                        PluginID INT,
                        Type TEXT,
                        Description TEXT,
                        PRIMARY KEY ID (ID)
);
```

You might need to modify the script depending on your database configuration.

The aforementioned table will be used to hold our scan results, which we will parse using the following Perl script:

```perl
#!/usr/bin/perl
# nbeparser.pl - Nessus NBE parser
# Thanks to A.M.I for helping with the Voodoo
use strict;
use DBI;

my $db = "nessusdb";
my $dsn = "DBI:mysql:database=$db;host=localhost;port=3306;mysql_read_default_file=
/etc/mysql/my.cnf";
my $user = "nessusdb";
my $pass = "nessusdb";

my $dbh = DBI->connect($dsn, $user, $pass, {'RaiseError' => 1});

my $filename = shift;
open(NBE, "$filename") || die "File not found\nYou need to provide this program
with a valid filename to parse.\n";

while (<NBE>)
{
  my $line = $_;
  if ($line =~/results/) # only pull results from the nbe file.
  {
    our @values = split(/\|/, $line);
    # only pull full results lines (not just portscan entries)
```

```
   if ($values[5] ne '')
   {
     my $SQL = "INSERT INTO ScanResults SET IP='".$values[2]."',
        Port='".$values[3]."', PluginID='".$values[4]."', Type='".$values[5]."',
        Description=".$dbh->quote($values[6])."";

     print "$SQL\n";

     my $sth = $dbh->prepare($SQL) or die "Cannot prepare statement:
        $DBI::errstr\n";
     $sth->execute() or die "Cannot execute statement: $DBI::errstr\n";

     $sth->finish();
   }
 }
}
$dbh->disconnect();
close(NBE);
```

You can run this script on a system that has a Perl interpreter installed by typing the following at a command line. Root or administrator privilege will not be necessary, so make sure to run this command as an ordinary user:

```
nessus-user $ ./nbeparser your_real_report_name.nbe
```

If the script has successfully completed, you should now have your own Scan Results table that contains the outcome data of the Nessus report file whose name you specified on the command line; in this case, `your_real_report_name.nbe`. From here on, you should be able to query your database and find the information that you need from this report.

This script is not a perfect solution, however. It is, in fact, a very simplistic piece of code and is therefore unable to handle tasks that are more complex. For more complex (especially enterprise-scalable) applications, you'll need to write your own. We'll outline the limitations here to help you realize when you've outgrown the script. First, this script can't verify whether the results you seek are already there. Moreover, it can't tell you the date that your results were generated. Additionally, the resulting database table does not differentiate between different reports' filenames. Therefore, a unique line is generated for any entry found in the results file. Thus, if you accidentally run the script on the same results file, duplicate entries will appear in your database. What this comes down to is that the table is too simplistic to support any form of differentiation of data. This means that it is difficult to discern which vulnerabilities are old problems and which ones have recently appeared.

Outside of differentiation, this script will not work in a model where you scan the same targets from multiple points. For example, it isn't possible to show the same target's vulnerability results from the DMZ and the privileged network. In short, it's just a basic structure to get you started.

Adding additional columns can solve some of these problems, but before we do that, let's look at some queries we can execute to find useful information from the database. Let's start by finding which vulnerability affects the most computers on our network. We first need to find out what script IDs we have affecting our network, so we will execute:

```
select DISTINCT PluginID from ScanResults;
+----------+
| PluginID |
+----------+
|    12205 |
|    10394 |
|    10400 |
|    10150 |
|    11011 |
+----------+
```

We then need to take each PluginID and count the number of entries it has in the database. We will use the following SQL statement:

```
select COUNT(*) from ScanResults WHERE PluginID='11011';
+----------+
| COUNT(*) |
+----------+
|        8 |
+----------+
```

After going through all the different PluginIDs, we can conclude that PluginID 11011 is the one that affects the most machines in our network.

If we look up this plugin's description, we learn that this test detects whether the remote servers support NetBIOS, and that we forgot to eliminate the same host being affected more than once by this vulnerability. We will recount using this SQL statement:

```
select COUNT(DISTINCT IP) from ScanResults WHERE PluginID='11011';
+--------------------+
| COUNT(DISTINCT IP) |
+--------------------+
|                  4 |
+--------------------+
```

It seems almost all of our vulnerabilities appear in all four hosts we scanned, and that we don't have a single vulnerability that we need to give special attention to before the others. This is in fact false—if we take into account the severity of the vulnerabilities, one vulnerability will be more important to highlight than the others.

Let's start by finding how many High/Medium/Low risk vulnerabilities we have in the database. For the sake of simplification, we will consider a *Serious* risk factor as equal to *High*.

We can count the number of vulnerabilities according to their risk factor by executing the following SQL statement:

```
select COUNT(*) from ScanResults WHERE Description LIKE '%Risk factor : High%' OR
Description LIKE '%Risk factor : Serious%';
+----------+
| COUNT(*) |
+----------+
|        1 |
+----------+
select COUNT(*) from ScanResults WHERE Description LIKE '%Risk factor : Medium%';
+----------+
| COUNT(*) |
+----------+
|        4 |
+----------+
select COUNT(*) from ScanResults WHERE Description LIKE '%Risk factor : Low%';
+----------+
| COUNT(*) |
+----------+
|        1 |
+----------+
```

We can easily see that we have a High/Serious risk factor vulnerability. We can cross-reference this by counting the vulnerabilities that occur more than once on our network by using the SQL UNION statement. We will come back to this in the next section, which covers differential scanning.

Now that we know we have a High/Serious risk factor vulnerability, we can pull its PluginID and search for an explanation about this vulnerability either from the description that comes with that entry in the database or by going to http://cgi.nessus.org/plugins/dump.php3?id=XXXXX and replacing XXXXX with the PluginID.

```
select PluginID from ScanResults WHERE Description LIKE '%Risk factor : High%' OR
Description LIKE '%Risk factor : Serious%';
+----------+
| PluginID |
+----------+
|    12205 |
+----------+
```

Going to http://cgi.nessus.org/plugins/dump.php3?id=12205 shows that the plugin that reports this vulnerability is named *Microsoft Hotfix KB835732 (registry check)*, and that this problem is solved by installing the patch available from www.microsoft.com/technet/security/bulletin/ms04-011.mspx.

One of the greatest benefits of using a database is that you can easily compare two different results that were generated from two different network locations; for example, DMZ vs. privileged network. We first need to modify our database table to include an *Exposure* column, and insert the results gathered from the different sections of the network.

We start by adding a new column named *Exposure*:

```
ALTER TABLE ScanResults ADD Exposure TEXT;
```

We will mark all existing records with the word *Privileged*, using the following statement:

```
UPDATE ScanResults SET Exposure='Privileged';
```

Now we should restart the scan, and insert the results using this script. However, before we rerun the scan, we will add to the SQL statement the string:

```
Exposure='DMZ'
```

Resulting in:

```
my $SQL = "INSERT INTO ScanResults SET IP='".$values[2]."', Port='".$values[3]."',
PluginID='".$values[4]."', Type='".$values[5]."', Description=
".$dbh->quote($values[6])."', Exposure='DMZ'";
```

We will now have the same table as before, but with new entries that illustrate the state of vulnerability from an internal network (privileged) and from an external network (DMZ). The first neat thing we can do is compare the results we received from the privileged network with that of the DMZ and see which vulnerabilities we solved by segmentation alone.

The following SQL statement can be used to find out which vulnerabilities "disappeared" due to scanning from the two different locations:

```
SELECT CurrentScan.IP, CurrentScan.Port, CurrentScan.PluginID FROM ScanResults AS
CurrentScan LEFT JOIN ScanResults ON (CurrentScan.PluginID = ScanResults.PluginID
AND CurrentScan.Port = ScanResults.Port AND CurrentScan.IP = ScanResults.IP AND
CurrentScan.Exposure != ScanResults.Exposure AND ScanResults.Exposure = 'DMZ')
WHERE CurrentScan.Exposure = 'Privileged' AND ScanResults.Exposure IS NULL;
```

```
+---------------+------------------------+----------+
| IP            | Port                   | PluginID |
+---------------+------------------------+----------+
| 192.168.1.4   | netbios-ssn (139/tcp)  |   11011  |
| 192.168.1.13  | netbios-ssn (139/tcp)  |   11011  |
| 192.168.1.138 | netbios-ssn (139/tcp)  |   11011  |
| 192.168.1.243 | netbios-ssn (139/tcp)  |   11011  |
+---------------+------------------------+----------+
```

The following SQL statement will reveal which new vulnerabilities have "appeared" due to scanning from the two different locations:

```
SELECT ScanResults.IP, ScanResults.Port, ScanResults.PluginID FROM ScanResults AS
CurrentScan LEFT JOIN ScanResults ON (CurrentScan.PluginID = ScanResults.PluginID
AND CurrentScan.Port = ScanResults.Port AND CurrentScan.IP = ScanResults.IP AND
```

```
CurrentScan.Exposure != ScanResults.Exposure AND ScanResults.Exposure =
'Privileged') WHERE CurrentScan.Exposure = 'DMZ' AND ScanResults.Exposure IS NULL;
Empty set (0.00 sec)
```

The following SQL statement will reveal which vulnerabilities "persist" between the two different locations:

```
SELECT ScanResults.IP, ScanResults.Port, ScanResults.PluginID FROM ScanResults AS
CurrentScan LEFT JOIN ScanResults ON (CurrentScan.PluginID = ScanResults.PluginID
AND CurrentScan.Port = ScanResults.Port AND CurrentScan.IP = ScanResults.IP AND
CurrentScan.Exposure != ScanResults.Exposure AND ScanResults.Exposure = 'DMZ') WHERE
ScanResults.Exposure = 'DMZ' AND CurrentScan.Exposure = 'Privileged';
```

```
+---------------+-----------------------+----------+
| IP            | Port                  | PluginID |
+---------------+-----------------------+----------+
| 192.168.1.243 | microsoft-ds (445/tcp) |   12205 |
| 192.168.1.13  | microsoft-ds (445/tcp) |   10394 |
| 192.168.1.243 | microsoft-ds (445/tcp) |   10400 |
| 192.168.1.4   | microsoft-ds (445/tcp) |   10394 |
| 192.168.1.4   | netbios-ns (137/udp)  |   10150 |
| 192.168.1.243 | microsoft-ds (445/tcp) |   10394 |
| 192.168.1.138 | microsoft-ds (445/tcp) |   10394 |
| 192.168.1.13  | netbios-ns (137/udp)  |   10150 |
| 192.168.1.243 | netbios-ns (137/udp)  |   10150 |
| 192.168.1.4   | microsoft-ds (445/tcp) |   11011 |
| 192.168.1.13  | microsoft-ds (445/tcp) |   11011 |
| 192.168.1.138 | netbios-ns (137/udp)  |   10150 |
| 192.168.1.138 | microsoft-ds (445/tcp) |   11011 |
| 192.168.1.243 | microsoft-ds (445/tcp) |   11011 |
+---------------+-----------------------+----------+
```

Even though the example is simplistic, you can see the benefit you receive from using the database as your information-generating tool. Scanning the hosts from the DMZ revealed that all our firewall was doing was blocking port 139, which as you can see is insufficient in blocking most vulnerabilities.

There are other means of inserting data into a database; specifically, NessusWX (available from http://nessuswx.nessus.org), Nessus' Windows-based client. NessusWX can generate SQL statements that you can paste into your SQL server, or directly insert entries into a MySQL-based database. We find NessusWX's capability to use a SQL server better than storing the results in a file, but as the data cannot be manipulated before it is entered, we prefer using our own scripts to insert data into the database.

Differential Reporting

Differential reporting and the trend analysis information you can generate from it allows you to easily spot changes on your network. Differential reporting allows you to compare one scan against another, and receive only the changes caused when a new vulnerability has been discovered, a new host is added to the network, or a new service is operating. This allows you to reduce the size of the report you receive, and the overload generated due to it, while still allowing you to be successfully alerted to new security problems on your network.

You can generate differential reports using either of two methods: scan normally and use a database to generate differential data, or use Nessus' built-in differential reporting features through the configuration. Choosing the latter only requires marking the scan as differential, by either editing the configuration file used by Nessus or setting the `save_knowledge_base`, `kb_restore`, and `diff_scan` entries to `yes`. Alternatively in versions of the Nessus Client older than 3.0.0, you can change these values via the GUI by activating the **KB | Enable KB saving**, **Reuse the knowledge bases about the host for the test**, and **Only show differences with the previous scan** options. In current versions (newer than 3.0.0) you will need to modify the client configuration XML file. Please see the chapter on the Knowledge Base for full details.

Once the scan has completed, the results you receive are only those new vulnerabilities, ports, or hosts that weren't present in the previous scan. The shortcoming from this type of scan is that you cannot generate any additional information from the results; for example, what was fixed, what vulnerabilities are still present although found a certain timeframe ago, and so forth. Another disadvantage of this type of differential data is that it is hard to determine what has changed. Some plugins return dynamic data, such as the plugin that retrieves the SMTP banner. Since the banner might contain the current time, it will be different between every two scans you conduct and will constantly appear in the differential results, even though nothing actually changed with regard to that vulnerability.

You can partially minimize this effect by excluding the information-gathering plugins from being launched again against the hosts in versions of the Nessus Client older than 3.0.0 by choosing **KB | Do not execute info gathering plugins that have already been executed**, or by setting the `kb_dont_replay_info_gathering` entry in the configuration file to yes. In current versions (newer than 3.0.0) you will need to modify the client configuration XML file. Please see the chapter on the Knowledge Base for full details. However, this would defeat the purpose of scanning the computer for all possible vulnerabilities, including any information-gathering plugins (consider, for example, a situation where an information-gathering plugin was enhanced—you will never get to see these enhancements since the new version will never run). Furthermore, it risks keeping outdated information in the Knowledge Base.

NOTE

By default, Nessus keeps records in the Knowledge Base for a period of 10 days. If you are interested in waiting more than that between differential scans, in versions of the Nessus Client older than 3.0.0 change the value of **Max age of saved KB (in secs)** found under **KB** tab, or modify the value of `kb_max_age` from 864000, which equals 10 days, to any other value. In current versions (newer than 3.0.0) you will need to modify the client configuration XML file. Please see the chapter on the Knowledge Base for full details.

Now that you know how to use Nessus' built-in feature for differential scanning, we'll look at how to use your database to generate similar and better differential information from the same scans. In the previous section, we implemented the table structure. In this section, we'll take things a step further by modifying the table to include an additional column to accommodate our differential scan data. This column, that we'll label ScanDate, will enable us to set the date at which the report is generated. We'll do this by implementing the following SQL statement:

```
ALTER TABLE ScanResults ADD ScanDate DATE;
```

In addition, we will need to modify the nbeparser.pl script, from the previous section, so that it includes the ScanDate column. The value to which we will set the ScanDate will be the reserved word NOW(). MySQL will, in turn, convert this to the date and time at which an entry was inserted. This change to the script will result in:

```
my $SQL = "INSERT INTO ScanResults SET IP='".$values[2]."', Port='".$values[3]."',
PluginID='".$values[4]."', Type='".$values[5]."', Description=".$dbh->
quote($values[6]).", ScanDate=NOW()";
```

Now, we'll generate two separate scans. The first scan will be conducted today, without making any changes. Next, we will alter our network so that it appears that one of our hosts is no longer responding. Additionally, we will turn off a few of our services on another one of our hosts. This will enable us to create a second scan that will now appear as if it is being completed one day after our first scan. Once we've imported results from both scans into our database, we can start to derive meaning from the resulting data. From here on, we will assume your database contains results for scans that were completed for the same range of IP addresses.

Let's begin by pulling any scan dates with which we can work. This can be easily accomplished by using the following SQL statement:

```
select DISTINCT(ScanDate) from ScanResults;
+------------+
| ScanDate   |
+------------+
| 2007-12-15 |
| 2007-12-16 |
+------------+
```

Now, we can provide a list of hosts that were discovered during the scan and a list of hosts that were absent using the following SQL statement:

```
SELECT DISTINCT(CurrentScan.IP) FROM ScanResults AS CurrentScan LEFT JOIN
ScanResults ON (CurrentScan.IP = ScanResults.IP AND CurrentScan.ScanDate !=
ScanResults.ScanDate AND ScanResults.ScanDate = '2007-06-15') WHERE CurrentScan.
ScanDate = '2007-06-16' AND ScanResults.IP IS NULL;
Empty set (0.00 sec)
SELECT DISTINCT(CurrentScan.IP) FROM ScanResults AS CurrentScan LEFT JOIN
ScanResults ON (CurrentScan.IP = ScanResults.IP AND CurrentScan.ScanDate !=
ScanResults.ScanDate AND ScanResults.ScanDate = '2007-06-16') WHERE CurrentScan.
ScanDate = '2007-06-15' AND ScanResults.IP IS NULL;
+--------------+
| IP           |
+--------------+
| 192.168.1.52 |
+--------------+
```

The first statement returns a list of the new hosts that appeared on the network, and the second statement returns a list of IPs that have dropped off the network. As you can see, host 192.168.1.52 is absent from the second scan's results.

We can now create similar lists for both ports and vulnerabilities. Let's start by using the SQL statement that will retrieve the new ports that differed between our two scans:

```
SELECT DISTINCT(CurrentScan.Port), CurrentScan.IP FROM ScanResults AS CurrentScan
LEFT JOIN ScanResults ON (CurrentScan.Port = ScanResults.Port AND CurrentScan.
ScanDate != ScanResults.ScanDate AND ScanResults.ScanDate = '2007-06-15') WHERE
CurrentScan.ScanDate = '2007-06-16' AND ScanResults.Port IS NULL;
Empty set (0.05 sec)

SELECT DISTINCT(CurrentScan.Port), CurrentScan.IP FROM ScanResults AS CurrentScan
LEFT JOIN ScanResults ON (CurrentScan.Port = ScanResults.Port AND CurrentScan.
ScanDate != ScanResults.ScanDate AND ScanResults.ScanDate = '2007-06-16') WHERE
CurrentScan.ScanDate = '2007-06-15' AND ScanResults.Port IS NULL;
+--------------------+---------------+
| Port               | IP            |
+--------------------+---------------+
| mysql (3306/tcp)   | 192.168.1.243 |
| x11 (6000/tcp)     | 192.168.1.52  |
```

```
| loc-srv (135/udp)    | 192.168.1.243 |
| ssh (22/tcp)         | 192.168.1.52  |
| unknown (1029/udp)   | 192.168.1.243 |
| ftp (21/tcp)         | 192.168.1.243 |
+---------------------+---------------+
```

Here it's easy to spot that host 192.168.1.243, which is present in both scans, had some ports from the first scan close before our second scan was run. Additionally, we can see that host 192.168.1.52 had a port open in the time period between the scans. Moreover, this host is absent from our second scan. However, these two facts are not equal in importance. Simply put, if host 192.168.1.52 is no longer there, its open and closed ports are meaningless to us. Once we recognize this, we can easily filter out host 192.168.1.52 from our results by creating a more complex SQL statement:

```
SELECT DISTINCT(CurrentScan.Port), CurrentScan.IP FROM ScanResults AS CurrentScan
LEFT JOIN ScanResults ON (CurrentScan.Port = ScanResults.Port AND CurrentScan.
ScanDate != ScanResults.ScanDate AND ScanResults.ScanDate = '2007-06-16') WHERE
CurrentScan.ScanDate = '2007-06-15' AND CurrentScan.IP NOT IN ('192.168.1.52') AND
ScanResults.IP IS NULL;
```

```
+---------------------+---------------+
| Port                | IP            |
+---------------------+---------------+
| mysql (3306/tcp)    | 192.168.1.243 |
| loc-srv (135/udp)   | 192.168.1.243 |
| unknown (1029/udp)  | 192.168.1.243 |
| ftp (21/tcp)        | 192.168.1.243 |
+---------------------+---------------+
```

In the NOT IN clause, we place any IPs that previously appeared as being absent from the previous scan, thus filtering them out from the information in which we are interested. A very similar SQL query can show the vulnerabilities that have been addressed:

```
SELECT DISTINCT(CurrentScan.PluginID), CurrentScan.IP, CurrentScan.Port FROM
ScanResults AS CurrentScan LEFT JOIN ScanResults ON (CurrentScan.PluginID =
ScanResults.PluginID AND CurrentScan.ScanDate != ScanResults.ScanDate AND
ScanResults.ScanDate = '2007-06-15') WHERE CurrentScan.ScanDate = '2007-06-16' AND
CurrentScan.IP NOT IN ('192.168.1.52') AND ScanResults.PluginID IS NULL;
```

```
+----------+---------------+------------+
| PluginID | IP            | Port       |
+----------+---------------+------------+
|    11580 | 192.168.1.254 | general/udp |
+----------+---------------+------------+
```

```
SELECT DISTINCT(CurrentScan.PluginID), CurrentScan.IP, CurrentScan.Port FROM
ScanResults AS CurrentScan LEFT JOIN ScanResults ON (CurrentScan.PluginID =
ScanResults.PluginID AND CurrentScan.ScanDate != ScanResults.ScanDate AND
```

```
ScanResults.ScanDate = '2007-06-16') WHERE CurrentScan.ScanDate = '2007-06-15' AND
CurrentScan.IP NOT IN ('192.168.1.52') AND ScanResults.PluginID IS NULL;

+----------+---------------+------------------------+
| PluginID | IP            | Port                   |
+----------+---------------+------------------------+
|    10916 | 192.168.1.243 | microsoft-ds (445/tcp) |
|    12054 | 192.168.1.243 | microsoft-ds (445/tcp) |
|    10915 | 192.168.1.243 | microsoft-ds (445/tcp) |
|    12209 | 192.168.1.243 | microsoft-ds (445/tcp) |
|    10481 | 192.168.1.243 | mysql (3306/tcp)       |
|    10914 | 192.168.1.243 | microsoft-ds (445/tcp) |
|    11890 | 192.168.1.243 | loc-srv (135/udp)      |
|    10913 | 192.168.1.243 | microsoft-ds (445/tcp) |
|    10092 | 192.168.1.243 | ftp (21/tcp)           |
+----------+---------------+------------------------+
```

With these two statements, you can spot which new vulnerabilities appeared (in this case, a vulnerability whose script ID is 11580) and which vulnerabilities appear to have been addressed (in this case, vulnerabilities with script IDs 10916, 12054, 10915, 12209, 10481, 10914, 11890, 10913 and 10092).

This wealth of information can be very useful for an administrator when handling a large network, as some vulnerabilities might take longer to fix, in which case seeing them appear and reappear in every report you receive might degrade your ability to understand this as well as your ability to follow the reports as a whole. In contrast, showing you only the changes between the two scans, while giving you the ability to generate a complete report at will, gives you the best of both worlds, seeing the data both in full and differential formats.

Another feature that we can incorporate using simple SQL queries is the ability to see vulnerability trends, or how long a certain vulnerability has been around on the server in question, as data can be easily fetched by its scan date. To better illustrate this, we added some data into the database, after starting new services on the machine 192.168.1.243.

We start by requesting a list of all the unique PluginIDs we can find in the table:

```
SELECT DISTINCT(PluginID) FROM ScanResults

+----------+
| PluginID |
+----------+
|    11834 |
|    12264 |
|    10287 |
|    10916 |
|    10342 |
```

```
|    12054 |
|    11835 |
|............................|
|    11580 |
|    10719 |
+----------+
```

Then we use an SQL statement that will show for a particular PluginID and an IP, how long that vulnerability has been present:

```
SELECT IP, Port, ScanDate FROM ScanResults WHERE PluginID='10481'
ORDER BY IP, Port;

+---------------+------------------+------------+
| IP            | Port             | ScanDate   |
+---------------+------------------+------------+
| 192.168.1.243 | mysql (3306/tcp) | 2007-06-15 |
| 192.168.1.243 | mysql (3306/tcp) | 2007-06-17 |
+---------------+------------------+------------+
```

We specifically chose a vulnerability that was there, disappeared, and reappeared. As you can see, this vulnerability appeared to have been fixed, but resurfaced later—a very valuable piece of information. Why has this vulnerability resurfaced? Was some kind of firewall rule changed? Was this vulnerability only partially addressed? This information would be hard to come by if you didn't use this type of differential information gathering.

NOTE

You can use, as we did in this query, the ORDER BY directive of SQL to prevent the same vulnerability from appearing on the same IP, but on different ports, from confusing the trend the SQL statement returns.

We now want to generate some graphs from the data we collected. We'll do this by using MySQL's capability to generate on-the-fly comma-separated value (CSV) files and the SQL statement's power to return the number of entries it has for a specific row. The following SQL statements will return for each risk factor the number of entries divided by the different scan dates. We also added the raw data returned by each of the SQL statements:

```
SELECT ScanDate, COUNT(ScanDate) FROM ScanResults GROUP BY ScanDate
INTO OUTFILE 'vuln.total.data';
```

```
+------------+-----------------+
| ScanDate   | COUNT(ScanDate) |
+------------+-----------------+
| 2007-06-15 |              77 |
| 2007-06-16 |              55 |
| 2007-06-17 |              54 |
+------------+-----------------+
```

SELECT ScanDate, COUNT(ScanDate) FROM ScanResults WHERE Description LIKE '%Risk Factor : High%' OR Description LIKE '%Risk Factor : Serious%' GROUP BY ScanDate INTO OUTFILE 'vuln.high.data';

```
+------------+-----------------+
| ScanDate   | COUNT(ScanDate) |
+------------+-----------------+
| 2007-06-15 |              10 |
| 2007-06-16 |               6 |
| 2007-06-17 |               6 |
+------------+-----------------+
```

SELECT ScanDate, COUNT(ScanDate) FROM ScanResults WHERE Description LIKE '%Risk Factor : Medium%' GROUP BY ScanDate INTO OUTFILE 'vuln.medium.data';

```
+------------+-----------------+
| ScanDate   | COUNT(ScanDate) |
+------------+-----------------+
| 2007-06-15 |              10 |
| 2007-06-16 |               7 |
| 2007-06-17 |               7 |
+------------+-----------------+
```

SELECT ScanDate, COUNT(ScanDate) FROM ScanResults WHERE Description LIKE '%Risk Factor : Low%' GROUP BY ScanDate INTO OUTFILE 'vuln.low.data';

```
+------------+-----------------+
| ScanDate   | COUNT(ScanDate) |
+------------+-----------------+
| 2007-06-15 |              25 |
| 2007-06-16 |              21 |
| 2007-06-17 |              18 |
+------------+-----------------+
```

All you need to do now to generate a nice graph from this data is to use the following gnuplot script:

```
set term png small
set data style lines
set grid
```

```
set yrange [ -10 : ]
set title "Vulnerability Trends for IP 192.168.1.243"
set xlabel "Date"
set ylabel "Number of Vulnerabilities"
set xdata time
set timefmt "%Y-%m-%d"
set xrange ["2007-06-15":"2007-06-17"]
set format x "%d-%m"
set yrange [0:]
plot "vuln.total.data" using 1:($2) title "Total"\
  ,"vuln.high.data" using 1:($2) title "High"\
  , "vuln.medium.data" using 1:($2) title "Medium"\
  , "vuln.low.data" using 1:($2) title "Low"
```

The utility will generate a graph similar to what is shown in Figure 10.3.

Figure 10.3 Trend for 192.168.1.243

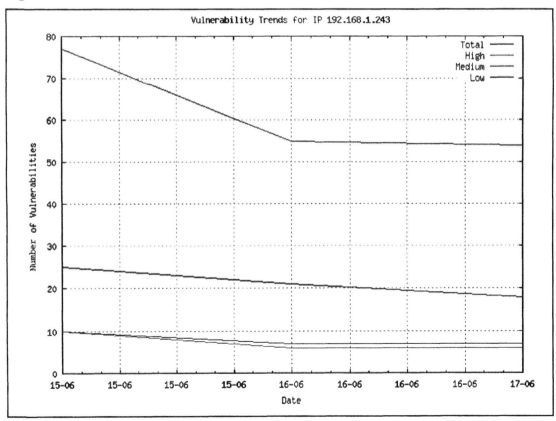

The more extensive data you have, the more interesting and useful this graph becomes. Taken over time, this graph illustrates how vulnerabilities are progressing for this particular host. Continuing our data mining, we would now like to count the number of vulnerabilities divided by dates and IPs by issuing the following SQL statement:

```
SELECT ScanDate, IP, COUNT(IP) FROM ScanResults GROUP BY IP, ScanDate;

+------------+---------------+-----------+
| ScanDate   | IP            | COUNT(IP) |
+------------+---------------+-----------+
| 2007-06-15 | 192.168.1.243 |        31 |
| 2007-06-16 | 192.168.1.243 |        15 |
| 2007-06-17 | 192.168.1.243 |        17 |
| 2007-06-15 | 192.168.1.254 |        18 |
| 2007-06-16 | 192.168.1.254 |        19 |
| 2007-06-17 | 192.168.1.254 |        17 |
| 2007-06-15 | 192.168.1.4   |        21 |
| 2007-06-16 | 192.168.1.4   |        21 |
| 2007-06-17 | 192.168.1.4   |        20 |
| 2007-06-15 | 192.168.1.52  |         7 |
+------------+---------------+-----------+
```

The only piece of information we are lacking is those vulnerabilities that are persistent. A vulnerability can be declared persistent if it persists for a long time and is present in every scan. Thinking graphically, we mean that the vulnerability's line starts on one end of our graph and proceeds to the other without segmentation. By performing the following query, we can get a perspective for each plugin we tested for, when it was first detected, and how many hosts were affected:

```
SELECT ScanDate, COUNT(ScanDate), PluginID, Port FROM ScanResults
GROUP BY ScanDate, PluginID, Port ORDER BY PluginID, ScanDate;

+------------+----------------+----------+-------------------------+
| ScanDate   |COUNT(ScanDate) | PluginID | Port                    |
+------------+----------------+----------+-------------------------+
| 2007-06-15 |              1 |    10028 | domain (53/tcp)         |
| 2007-06-16 |              1 |    10028 | domain (53/tcp)         |
| 2007-06-17 |              1 |    10028 | domain (53/tcp)         |
| 2007-06-15 |              1 |    10092 | ftp (21/tcp)            |
| 2007-06-17 |              1 |    10092 | ftp (21/tcp)            |
|..........................................................................|
| 2007-06-16 |              2 |    12053 | general/tcp             |
| 2007-06-17 |              2 |    12053 | general/tcp             |
| 2007-06-15 |              1 |    12054 | microsoft-ds (445/tcp)  |
```

```
| 2007-06-15 |              1 |     12209 |   microsoft-ds (445/tcp) |
| 2007-06-15 |              3 |     12264 |   general/icmp            |
| 2007-06-16 |              3 |     12264 |   general/icmp            |
| 2007-06-17 |              3 |     12264 |   general/icmp            |
+------------+----------------+-----------+--------------------------+
```

You can easily spot in this query output what vulnerabilities appear more than others, and what vulnerabilities are particular to certain hosts.

To summarize, as the data is in a relational database, you can generate a multitude of SQL statements to go through this data and analyze it. The data can be further extended to contain such columns as *assignee*, the person in charge of fixing a particular vulnerability, *ignore* allowing you to ignore certain results from future reports, and so forth. We explain the *ignore* column in better detail in the next section.

Filtering Reports

The previous section focused on the benefits of differential reporting and how to generate differential reports. In this section, we look at how to filter out wrong or misleading content from your reports. This will enable you to filter out enterprisewide false positives and irrelevant vulnerabilities, generate reports containing less information than the original database, and divide the reports based on the type of operating system. In other words, you will be able to locate the relevant data that you seek.

As before, we'll be using a MySQL database containing the single table with its differential data that we created in the previous section, and the Perl script that we used to insert the data into the table. We will start by generating a table of IPs vs. operating systems with a simple SQL statement:

```
SELECT IP, MID(Description, LENGTH('The remote host is running ')+1, LOCATE(';',
Description)-LENGTH('The remote host is running ')-1) AS OS FROM ScanResults WHERE
PluginID='11936' GROUP BY IP, OS;
+---------------+------------------------------+
| IP            | OS                           |
+---------------+------------------------------+
| 192.168.1.243 | Microsoft Windows 2000 Server |
| 192.168.1.4   | Microsoft Windows XP          |
+---------------+------------------------------+
```

This SQL statement looks through the database for all the records of the Nessus plugin *OS Identification*. When such entries are found, they are grouped together. The result from the *Description* column is made a bit more readable by using MySQL's string handling functions.

NOTE

OS detection algorithms, whether they are ICMP based or use a fingerprinting technique, are rarely accurate or consistent. Therefore, if you want to better generate reports divided by OS types, we suggest that you build an additional table where you can enter and maintain IP vs. OS information manually.

You can also limit your data to a certain IP or IP range. As our table contains numerous records, we will need to eliminate all extraneous data, fix the most critical issues, and then handle those issues that remain. We can use simple queries to filter out IPs, by using *IP='192.168.1.254'* as our query string. Alternatively, we can use a range of IPs by using *IP IN ('192.168.1.52', '192.168.1.254')*. Furthermore, we can create a subset of the network by using an *IP LIKE '192.168.1.%'*.

At times, you might need to scan a large part of the network, but not the entire network. In such an instance you can use Nessus' capability to parse the value of an IP/netmask pair into a list of IPs. This will create a list of IPs that fall under that range. The same can be done for 192.168.1-2.1-2, which will return the list 192.168.1.1, 192.168.1.2, 192.168.2.1, 192.168.2.2. This list can then be taken to the SQL queries *WHERE* section, and provided as is.

To save time, use the table from Table 10.1 and insert it into the MySQL table. Be sure to select the relevant IPs by asset instead of only by the IP. Now, be sure to use the following table structure for your records:

```
CREATE TABLE AssetList (
                  ID INT AUTO_INCREMENT,
                  AssetName TEXT,
                  IPs TEXT,
                  ExpectedResult TEXT,
                  Contact TEXT,
                  Frequency TEXT,
                  PRIMARY KEY ID (ID)
);
```

After entering the details into the table, use the IP addresses found in the *IPs* column to filter out the data in the ScanResults table.

Most enterprise networks are bound to have a few irrelevant vulnerabilities. Nessus was built to report everything, and then let someone else sort through the results. That way, it's possible for you to define what is important and what is not. This makes it possible for you to be sure that you do not miss any vulnerabilities, because Nessus will not ignore any. However, when you are dealing with a large-scale network, this can result in a few hundred irrelevant vulnerabilities. For example, items like administrative privilege vulnerabilities will appear when Nessus is provided with the administrative credentials required to remotely access the workstations' registry.

As all our data is in the database, we can quickly weed out these records by explicitly deleting the records from our database where a certain PluginID is equal to a certain number, or by adding a new column to the ScanResults table that marks the record as irrelevant. The second option enables you to reactivate those entries in the future as changes occur in the corporate policy regarding that vulnerability.

Additionally, some vulnerabilities are simply false positives, caused by a variety of issues. Unfortunately, fixing these false positives requires time and effort. The quickest fix requires a familiarity with Nessus' scripting language and the ability to find and repair the underlying problem. Therefore, we must adopt an approach similar to the solution we used with the irrelevant vulnerabilities described in the previous two paragraphs. To do this, we must mark those vulnerabilities that are false positive as irrelevant. We will also need to locate and fix the root cause of the false positive, by e-mailing bugs@nessus.org, reporting it online at http://bugs. nessus.org/, or e-mailing the Nessus mailing list (available at http://list.nessus.org). Alternatively, you can fix the offending NASL on your own, or contact the NASL's author—a contact e-mail address is usually available at the top of each Nessus Plugin.

Third-Party Tools

In this section, we highlight some third-party tools you can use to assist your deployment, maintenance, and usage of Nessus.

Extracting Information from a Saved Session Prior to Version 2.2.0 of Nessusd Using sd2nbe

In versions of the Nessus daemon prior to 2.2.0, it has the capability to store information about scanning sessions in a file for resuming interrupted scans. This option is normally used to recover sessions; however, it is not limited to that. You can take the information saved in the session and convert it to an NBE data file using the sd2nbe tool available from www.tifaware. com/perl/sd2nbe/. Once the session information is in NBE format, we can open it using the Nessus client or convert it to HTML or XML.

Nessus Integration with Perl and Net::Nessus::ScanLite Prior to Version 3.0.0

Prior to version 3.0.0 of the Nessus server a package called Net::Nessus::ScanLite existed to assist in automating scanning. Building a wrapper to the Nessus command-line client to automate your deployment and to automatically schedule scans could be done through this package.

You can use Net::Nessus::ScanLite, a Perl module that allows you to implement your very own Nessus client. The Perl module is almost a complete command-line Nessus client, supporting all of the Nessus client features and offering an API to easily use the results of a scan. Later versions of Nessus (3.0.0 and later), do not use the same underlying protocols to communicate between client and server. As of the writing of this book, no other packages could be located by the author to take the place of the Net::Nessus::ScanLite package.

Using simple scripts, you can connect to the Nessus daemon, grab the results, and dump them directly into the database without generating a single file. You can also extend this to create a complete Perl-based web interface where you choose what IP to scan. That same Perl-based web page can call the script that runs Nessus, and return the results. This tool is available from http://search.cpan.org/~jpb/Net-Nessus-ScanLite-0.01/.

Users who have trouble installing the necessary dependencies can use the automated CPAN installation, which takes care of all the dependencies required.

NOTE

As this is a book written by security professionals who are paid to be paranoid, we'll always suggest using the nonautomated installation mechanism that allows you to check PGP signatures instead. The following automated process does not check PGP signatures, and its documentation admits to weak security:

"There's no strong security layer in CPAN.pm. CPAN.pm helps you to install foreign, unmasked, unsigned code on your machine. We compare to a checksum that comes from the Net just as the distribution file itself. If somebody has managed to tamper with the distribution file, they may have as well tampered with the CHECKSUMS file. Future development will go towards strong authentication."

(Source: http://search.cpan.org/~jhi/perl-5.8.0/lib/CPAN.pm#SECURITY)

As this documentation reminds you, an attacker who compromises the CPAN servers can replace the Perl module that you're installing while also replacing the checksum on the same server. The only way to avoid having a vital piece of your security infrastructure compromised by an attacker's hostile code is to check that code's PGP signature before installing it. Avoid using easy methods that ignore this risk, especially on your organization's security infrastructure. Exercise best practices to avoid this infrastructure compromise or you might find yourself losing control of the system, and your job!

Executing the following commands will install the module:

```
# perl -MCPAN -e shell
cpan> install Net::Nessus::ScanLite
```

A very easy way to manage multiple Nessus daemon installation is by using a web interface. Several such web interfaces have been written as open-source projects. One such project is the Vulnerability Scanning Cluster (VSC). The VSC interface was written in PHP and uses the MySQL database as its backend for storing information. VSC allows users to manage hosts by hierarchical order, to select different scanning policies, to schedule future and recurring scans, and to view scan results. The tool is available from www.sourceforge.net/projects/vscweb/.

Nessus NBE Report Parsing Using Parse::Nessus::NBE

If you already have several Nessus reports in NBE data format and want to process them without much hassle, you can use the Parse::Nessus::NBE module. This module handles the regular expressions work for you, leaving you to simply request different types of information within the reports. Parse::Nessus::NBE can locate banners, open ports, plugins, numbers of vulnerabilities, web directories discovered, NFS-related issues, OS types, SNMP related issues, OS type statistics, service statistics, and vulnerability statistics.

This tool is available from http://search.cpan.org/~dkyger/Parse-Nessus-NBE-1.1/. Again, new users can use the following automated CPAN installation to handle the required dependencies, but should remember the resulting risk to their organization's security infrastructure. Those choosing this method can execute the following commands to install:

```
# perl -MCPAN -e shell
cpan> install Parse::Nessus::NBE
```

Common Problems

Several problems might arise while you are using the Nessus daemon to scan your network. These problems are not necessarily related to bandwidth or a vulnerability, but rather to a product vendor's improper handling of abnormal and unexpected traffic being directed at their product.

In this section, we divide the problems that might surface when scanning your network with Nessus into the following categories: aggressive scanning, volatile applications, and printer carnage. Toward the end of this section, we also describe another shortcoming that might show up when running Nessus against your enterprise's workstations. These workstations might be turned off during some part of the scan or change their IPs due to a restart, and the results pertaining to these workstations need to be addressed differently.

Aggressive Scanning

The type of portscan performed on your network has an effect on the stability of numerous types of hardware and software. We need to remember that while the main goal of the portscan phase is to detect open ports, it needs to do so while making sure that the software and hardware being scanned will "survive" the portscan, so that we can detect vulnerabilities in that software/hardware and do not needlessly reduce their uptime.

The Nessus daemon uses its own internal engine for scanning as over the 3.0 version. As such, it supports a new set of scan features namely: SYN, Connect, SNMP Scanning, a "Tarpit" scanner, and the Netstat scanner. Some of these scanners are not traditional scanners, but specific service scanning tools designed to probe for specific conditions. The more traditional TCP Connect and SYN scans do most of the network heavy lifting. Each scan type has a different effect on the software and hardware being scanned. As we are not testing the vendor's product endurance to portscanning but rather searching for vulnerabilities, we will want to use the closest thing to a normal user's connection: TCP connect(). Other scan types can cause inadvertent DoS conditions.

NOTE

Even though TCP connect() is considered the slowest scan type, it emulates in closest resemblance what a normal user would go through to connect to a remote host's ports.

Volatile Applications

Not all of the possible problems stem from portscanning alone. Many applications are easily affected by Nessus' interaction on the ports on which they listen. Application developers expect the program connecting to it to behave in a certain way, according to the predefined protocol. A web server developer may assume that the client is always a web browser; an FTP server developer is likely to consider an FTP client to make incoming connections. This means that the QA process of the program is likely to run a client that behaves in a normal way, and doesn't send unexpected content.

The Nessus plugins are far from perfect in this respect. They were built to detect vulnerabilities. A vulnerability stems from the combination of a misbehavior on the part of the client and the server's poor reaction to that misbehavior. As such, Nessus plugins are likely to misbehave from the server's point of view. In addition, many of the Nessus plugins do not just assume a vulnerability exists because of the remote server type and version, but rather actually try to probe more deeply, usually attempting to exploit the problem.

By attempting to exploit vulnerabilities, Nessus tends to create fewer false positives, as a system that isn't vulnerable won't be successfully exploited. This is more accurate simply because it simulates the attacker's interaction with a vulnerability. Checking for vulnerabilities by attempting their exploitation also leads to detecting vulnerabilities in products not previously known to be vulnerable. One such example is the infamous AUX/LPT/COM1 DoS vulnerability. This vulnerability stems from the fact that when you request one of these reserved names as a filename from a remote web server, the server's attempt to access that filename will cause it to hang and subsequently disrupt the web server's service to clients. As this vulnerability affects more than a single server, the same plugin that detects it on Vendor X's product can detect it on Vendor Y's product as well, as the attack works for both products in a similar manner.

This behavior, however, affects a wider range of products than that which the Nessus plugin was built to detect, causing problems when you scan products that are relatively obscure, went untested by security analysts, weren't properly upgraded to prevent such problems, and so forth. These machines might crash when scanned or their applications might stop responding, requiring a restart of the affected applications or even the entire server.

Another issue that can arise from badly written products is the effect a certain plugin might have on the tested machine when not conforming to the vendor's specified protocol. From the point of view of the person who developed an application, anyone connecting to his or her port is trying to access the developer's service and thus knows what product is listening on that port, and as such will use the proper syntax. This isn't necessarily the case when a vulnerability scan is communicating with that port, especially in those cases where the scanner doesn't even know what application is listening. Before you disregard this, think about how many different web servers exist, from mainstream servers to small server programs on network printers that don't even respond to every HTTP command.

A badly written protocol implementation might be waiting for a *QUIT* command, and if such a command does not arrive, it might fail to close the connection (such as is the case with some SMTP servers). Due to this, Nessus' plugins launched against that port that fail to send the *QUIT* command will create a new connection that the product will never close. Over the course of multiple plugins that interact with the product's port, the scan will cause the product to create multiple sockets, consuming valuable resources and overloading the machine it is run on, and also possibly causing the failure of the server altogether.

This issue can also manifest itself during the portscan, as no data is sent to those ports. A badly written application might try to read a set size of bytes from the socket, and as no data is sent, the product will freeze waiting for more bytes or otherwise fail.

In most of the cases we mention here, where the product fails, the behavior is in fact a problem in the product and not in the Nessus scanner, and the product's failure to handle unexpected input without failure should itself be addressed as a vulnerability. For example, older Cisco routers might still hang when receiving Nessus' UDP scan packet on their syslog port, UDP 514. However, such unexpected behavior may end up causing the program to fail without your knowledge of the cause. Therefore, it is important to make sure that the majority of your critical products are properly tested for robustness to portscanning and testing during the testing lab phase discussed earlier. One of this book's authors used Nessus' to scan a Cisco router and caused it to hang so badly that it lost its configuration, requiring a router administrator to enter the configuration line by line at the router's console. All this from a single UDP 514 packet! This type of failure could have been prevented with a router firmware patch deployed proactively and served as a DoS vulnerability, but it disconnected a network for 30 minutes. This problem should probably be found in a lab, instead of on the production network.

Another issue that might occur due to Nessus launching plugins against a specific product is that the product might not be designed to receive numerous simultaneous connections. You need to remember that Nessus makes scans run faster by launching more than a single plugin against each host. Badly written products may not support such multiple connections, and may as a result fail to address new connections or even crash. This type of behavior is difficult to predict and might occur even if you have done previous tests in a test lab, as the problem may require particular circumstances only likely in production use, such as high CPU load or network utilization.

Printer Problems

One of the most common problems occurs when scanning network appliances, especially printers. Scanning a printer can waste money in a form that isn't easily replaceable or recoverable. Some printers using old firmware versions handle portscans amazingly badly—they begin to print huge amounts of garbage, wasting large amounts of paper and ink or toner. This is because the printer wastefully thinks that the scan is someone trying to print something.

Printers aren't the only piece of network appliance affected by such scans. Voice over IP (VoIP) products, billing devices, automated teller machines (ATMs), time clock machines, parking systems, and basically any other product that answers to IP traffic but wasn't coded to handle unexpected input well or tested for security vulnerabilities by the manufacturer may display erratic behavior during the scan. The effects a scan would have on such devices aren't always wasteful as in the case of a printer, but going through your corporate building and restarting all the time clock machines is something you will want to avoid.

NOTE

Think of the situation in which your scan brings down all the time clock machines in your organization during the night, and you are violently awakened at 6:00 A.M., after the shift changed and find out that no one can clock in. Not only will this cause havoc in the corporation, it will also get you out of bed earlier than expected.

At least in the case of printers, the Nessus daemon now incorporates a test to specifically detect whether the IP being scanned is a printer, and, if this is the case, prevent the scan from testing that IP's printing-related ports. Still, we suggest that you avoid testing network devices whenever possible, unless you can verify that scanning these devices doesn't cause them to misbehave.

Scanning Workstations

Scanning workstations is very tricky. Workstations are restarted frequently, and might not be available during scanning hours, especially when scans occur in the middle of the night. In addition, scanning workstations might affect their reaction speed; the workstation might change its IP address due to Dynamic Host Configuration Protocol (DHCP) usage, and its vulnerabilities should usually be rated differently from servers' vulnerabilities.

We still believe that scanning workstations is an essential part of your organization's way of addressing the security issues on your network. Despite the inherent challenges, we recommend that you put forth the extra effort and scan workstations as part of your regular network security scanning.

If the corporate servers are secure, but you have over 10,000 workstations wide open to attack, your network cannot be considered secure. A single worm entering the internal network can affect these workstations and thus the rest of the network, by disturbing them due to the worm exploiting the vulnerability and as an effect bringing the network down due to the resultant excessive worm traffic. This is no imaginary scenario: MSBlaster and Sasser are just recent examples of worms that affected both corporate servers and workstations. Networks that made sure their servers were secure were still affected by the worm attacking their workstations.

The issue isn't just limited to these worms that affect only Windows-based machines. UNIX machines have been attacked by a small number of worms as well. Additionally, worms that attack IIS, Apache, OpenSSL, Microsoft SQL Server, and others will affect development networks as well. A worm attacking your development network still affects your corporate servers, where the loss of revenue occurs immediately when a developer is unable to update a production server application because his workstation has to be taken offline for worm removal.

NOTE

Another reason why development machines are so important to scan is that they often run experimental versions of operating systems or applications, typically without recent service packs, as those machines get reinstalled frequently. You should make sure those machines are protected from the rest of the network if they cannot be secured.

One of the problems mentioned previously is that workstations might not be available for scanning. This is especially true for employees who work in shifts, or turn off their workstations once they leave the office. For these workstations, scanning during off-peak hours is futile, as the machines cannot be scanned when they're off. However, these workstations are no less critical than those computers that are kept constantly on.

NOTE

You have to remember that the weakest link in your network's security is the computer that an attacker can compromise most easily. The CEO's secretary's computer is sometimes as valuable as the CEO's computer in terms of intellectual property. Additionally, most firewall policies grant much more privilege to an arbitrary internal computer than they do to outside computers. Attackers who compromise a single internal machine and use it to attack others are in much better shape than when they had no internal access.

Another problem is that workstations tend to have a weaker CPU and less memory compared to servers. As such, they will be more affected by Nessus' scans. The Nessus scan on those hosts will cause them to consume more resources than usual. As this cannot be avoided, we suggest considering running the workstations scans at off-peak hours, while keeping in mind that you need to instruct the employees to avoid turning off their computers when they leave.

Another problem that rises from large-scale corporate networks is the frequent use of DHCP. The protocol is used in most corporations to avoid the need to statically assign IP addresses to each workstation on the network. This in turn causes a problem for someone trying to understand what host was vulnerable at the time of the scan, as the IP it was allocated might be now, at the time of reading the vulnerability report, assigned to a different computer. This problem can be easily avoided by instructing the Nessus daemon to report vulnerabilities by the MAC address, or Ethernet card hardware address, of the vulnerable computer instead of by its IP address. This feature can be activated via the configuration file's `use_mac_addr` entry.

The last point to consider about workstation scanning is that not all vulnerabilities can be measured in the same way as when you're scanning a corporate server. A workstation wide open for file sharing might not be as critical as a corporate server having the same vulnerability. This is because a workstation's stored information is usually less valuable than that of the corporate server, and this is true in most cases where a centralized server stores all the information (documents, spreadsheets, and so forth). The problem is much harder to solve, and requires better planning of what tests you want to perform on the workstation and what data you want to filter out from the reports prior to going over them.

Summary

Once a security an officer concludes that enterprise scanning is needed, he or she is usually baffled by the big questions: "How do I do it? And how much effort must I put into that?" These two questions are answered in detail in the Enterprise Scanning chapter. We all know that planning your deployment is important, and this is the case with Nessus.

Nessus requires preparation of your network for the bandwidth requirements of the scanner. Measuring these requirements is not always easy, but with a few tricks and the right third-party tools, you can measure these requirements, and understand the effect they will have on the network.

Bandwidth utilization is greatly affected by the different types of topologies you use to deploy the scanning servers. The different topologies also affect the hardware requirements and the necessary preparations for the day when you will need to scan a specific vulnerability instead of using the complete arsenal of vulnerability tests at your disposal.

As simply scanning your network is not enough, you need to place these results in some centralized location and start sorting out the relevant data. Once the data is placed in a database, we can use it to correlate the different results provided by the differential exposure to vulnerabilities from multiple locations throughout an organization. We can also use the database to see how the vulnerabilities have progressed over time. Most importantly, once the data has been placed in a single location, we can filter out any false positives and irrelevant vulnerabilities.

You are not obliged to do everything from scratch—several third-party tools exist that you can use to ease your usage of Nessus in the organization. These tools are free to use and you can extend them to further suit your needs. As with everything in life, there are several common problems with running Nessus in your organization. Some problems can be easily avoided, while others can be detected beforehand in the test lab so that their impact can be minimized.

Solutions Fast Track

Planning a Deployment

- ☑ Make a list of your network's assets, who is responsible for them, and to whom the results should be mailed.

- ☑ Invite all the network's assets owners and managers to an overview of Nessus' capabilities, and the effects they have. Give a live demonstration.

- ☑ Use a test lab to determine the network bandwidth requirements your organization can afford.

- ☑ Automate the server's process of scanning and updating.

Configuring Scanners

☑ Choose a topology that suits your needs.

☑ Buy any additional hardware you require.

☑ Practice scanning for a specific threat, as in the case of a critical Microsoft advisory.

Data Correlation

☑ Use a database instead of files to store all the results.

☑ Correlate the results you receive from scans to help you concentrate on the most serious vulnerabilities.

☑ Generate differential results from the data stored in the database.

☑ Generate complex results using sophisticated SQL statements.

☑ Filter out from the database irrelevant vulnerabilities and false positives.

☑ Use third-party tools to ease the use vulnerability assessment in your organization.

Common Problems

☑ Avoid problems caused by scanning too aggressively.

☑ Test relatively unknown software and hardware in a test lab to avoid unexpected problems.

☑ Try to avoid scanning printers to save paper resources.

☑ Scan your workstations during working hours to avoid illusive hosts, or instruct your employees to leave their workstations turned on for the night.

Frequently Asked Questions

Q: Is it feasible to scan my entire enterprise network periodically?

A: The question is not whether you should scan your entire network, it is whether you can afford *not* to scan it. Not knowing what vulnerabilities you have in your network is certainly not going to help you secure the organization. This chapter should give you some ideas on how to manage this obviously challenging task.

Q: How often should those scans run? You discuss daily/weekly scans, but we can hardly cope with our current rate of quarterly network audits!

A: As noted earlier, the Sasser worm started spreading in just over three weeks after the vulnerability was discovered. This "window of exposure" is getting smaller and smaller all the time, and demonstrates the need to perform vulnerability scans on a weekly basis. The real question is how to handle the wealth of information you will start receiving once the scans are configured to run automatically and frequently. The answer is technological: differential reporting, data mining through databased results, and eliminating false positives, using the techniques outlined in this chapter.

Q: When dealing with other departments, I have difficulties explaining why a certain vulnerability needs to be addressed. This is especially true when dealing with knowledgeable technical people such as system administrators and programmers. How can I convince them that the problem is indeed serious and should be dealt with promptly?

A: As a person in charge of security in your company, you probably have a good understanding of why security is a concern. We found that this is not always the case with other technical people who do not deal with security issues daily. However, this approach can be reversed. Security is an interesting subject for most technical people, and in many cases system administrators or programmers will be extremely happy to participate in a security workshop that explains the concepts and demonstrates the risks. By exposing potentially resistant staff to the subject and raising their awareness to the risks, you will increase the level of cooperation and will find it easier to communicate any security concerns. People tend to cooperate better once they have a better understanding of what the challenges are—this can usually be done without training them to be security experts… Focus on cooperating with them, educating them, and framing your discussions within both the risks and the business needs. Finally, as much as possible, understand the technology and risks yourself, so you can explain them to others realistically and convincingly.

Q: How scalable are the solutions presented in this chapter? Will they work in my complicated network?

A: This chapter is based on our own experience overseeing implementations of enterprise wide vulnerability scanning solutions. If you break the huge task of scanning your entire enterprise into smaller tasks (like we did in this chapter) and then further distribute the tasks as appropriate among the different networks you have, you will see that although not trivial to set up, once the setup is working, the benefits are tremendous. Applying techniques such as distributed scanning and report correlation make it possible to use the Nessus scanning tool across the enterprise.

Q: Some of the perl modules outlined here seem pretty useless for current versions of Nessus. Is there anywhere I can go for help getting this type of automation working?

A: This is a tricky question to answer, but we know that it will be asked. The answer lies in waiting for the need to be fulfilled by Tenable. Without information on how the new protocol works between the Nessus Client and the nessusd, the community at large can not product perl modules to speak correct "nessus language" to the nessusd. Without the ability to talk to the server program, we must use the "nessus" command line command and appropriately configure the "~/.nessus-client/Policies.xml" file. By setting options in this file, we can affect the behavior of the nessusd scanning process. Tenable may in the future publish a tool or API for sending remote commands to the nessusd again, but as of the writing of this book, they have not.

Q: Why do the authors of the perl modules not update them?

A: The answer to this question lies in the closing of the nessusd source code. When Tenable closed the source code to the nessusd, two things happened. The first is a technical thing, namely that perl developers (or any other for that matter) could not longer look at the source code and derive information from it. The second thing that happened is that legal copyright protection came into force for the nessusd and it's communication mechanisms. Under the DMCA (Digital Millennium Copyright Act) the process of reverse engineering, or figuring out how something works from it's behavior, is considered illegal. Since most developers have no interest in being incarcerated, they choose not to reverse engineer the software or protocols in order to update their Perl modules. In answer to what can be done about this: on the first count, persuade Tenable to release the protocol specifications to the community, or two, if you live in the US, write your senator or congress person and express your displeasure with the law.

Chapter 11

NASL

Solutions in this chapter:

- **Why NASL?**
- **Structure of a NASL Script**
- **An Introduction to the NASL Language**
- **The Nessus Knowledge Base**

☑ **Summary**

☑ **Solutions Fast Track**

☑ **Frequently Asked Questions**

Introduction

When I initially announced the use of the Nessus Attack Scripting Language (NASL) within Nessus, many users disapproved, since it was not a "known" language such as Perl or Python. Over time, the use of a dedicated language turned out to be a good design decision, since it gives us, as developers, full control of the virtual machine used by the individual plugins. The use of NASL dramatically simplifies the maintenance of the plugins; bug fixes and enhancements can be applied to the NASL interpreter itself, avoiding the need to modify each and every plugin. For example, each of the network-related functions—such as connecting to a system or receiving data from it—are defined at the scripting engine level, not the plugin level. If we want to improve the way in which network connections are made, we only need to modify the NASL interpreter, and not the thousands of plugins that use these functions.

In this chapter, I explain why the NASL language was written, how it works, and why it is best suited for vulnerability detection. Then I explain how to write a NASL script for use within Nessus, how the Knowledge Base (KB) can be used, and how the contribution process works if you want to submit your own plugins to the community.

Why NASL?

In 1998, the first version of Nessus was released with around 50 security checks, otherwise known as "plugins." These plugins were implemented as shared libraries, written in the C programming language, and renamed to have a .nes file extension. The goal of this approach was to separate the scanning engine (nessusd) from the security checks it performs. This separation provided Nessus with a modular and easily extensible architecture. At the time, using shared libraries to write plugins made a lot of sense; it allowed us to quickly create new plugins based on existing C programs.

A few months after the initial release of Nessus, I had written nearly 200 plugins this way. Compiling these plugins would take up to 30 minutes on my 200MHz Pentium PC (which was a beefy computer at the time). During that same time, I was investigating ways to help people upgrade the plugin set without having to recompile the entire Nessus package. In short, the C plugins were showing their limits, as they were slow to install and complicated to upgrade.

I wrote a small script called "plugins-factory" (which is still included in the Nessus distribution but fortunately is not used) that would take a C plugin and compile it into a shared library (.nes). The idea behind this was to write a plugin update script that would download the latest C plugins from the web, compile them, and then install them. Due to the obvious security implications, the idea never went anywhere.

After looking into the currently available scripting languages, Perl stood out as the best language to use for Nessus plugins. However, Perl had several pitfalls at the time:

- Large memory footprint

- Sending and receiving raw packets was not well supported

- No reliable way to control the underlying virtual machine

This last point was, by far, the most important. From a high-level view, every security check in a scanner basically does the same thing; it connects to some port on the remote host, "does some stuff," and then deduces if the remote host is vulnerable to a given flaw. The best way to tune every security check is not to edit them individually, but to tune to the virtual machine that executes them. For example, when we added SSL support to Nessus, we did not have to modify any of the existing plugins; we only modified the way the socket functions work underneath. Another concern with using Perl as the plugin language was that almost all advanced functionality was only available through external modules. These modules each have their own set of required packages and system libraries. I was afraid that users would contribute really nice plugins, but the external package requirements would complicate the installation process. By having a dedicated language, I decided to make life a bit more difficult for contributors, but much simpler for end users. This is how the Nessus Attack Scripting Language was born.

I started to write a language, tentatively called "NASL," whose goals were the following:

- Each script must be self-contained (in one file)

- Easy to install for the end user

- Easy to learn for the contributors

- Small memory footprint

- Designed for network security checks

- Strong security

- Easy to modify and extend

- Support multiple languages

The result was a library now referred to as "nasl1," which had some pitfalls (for example, it was really slow and would be too lax regarding syntax errors), but overall, it did its job properly. Over 1000 security checks were written in this first version of NASL. Initially, speed was not much of a concern; it will always take more time to establish a TCP session than the NASL interpreter would spend parsing the plugin code.

However, as the number of plugins increased over time, and as people started using Nessus to scan more and more hosts, nasl1 was eventually considered too slow for the task. The original code was difficult to extend, and the decision was made to simply rewrite it.

In 2001, the libnasl library was rewritten by Michel Arboi to extend the language and fix the pitfalls that existed in nasl1. This rewritten library was dubbed "nasl2," and became the biggest new feature in Nessus 2.0. With Nessus 3.0 the nasl language was rolled into the main engine, and is considered to be in it's third version. Some of the features of the nasl language are:

■ **Self-contained scripts** Each NASL script contains both the code that checks for the flaw and a description of the plugin itself. Initially, I had considered using an external file for the description, but dismissed this idea due to the complexity it would introduce.

■ **Easy to install for the end user** NASL is a self-contained package that can be configured to use the OpenSSL library. Any user with a copy of the GNU C Compiler (gcc) and GNI Bison (bison) could easily build and install the NASL language interpreter.

■ **Easy to learn for the contributors** NASL looks very much like C, with some Perl-isms. If you have ever programmed or scripted in the past, the learning curve is small. The big difference between C and NASL is the lack of pointers and memory management.

■ **Small memory footprint** A typical Nessus check will only require a few hundred kilobytes of memory, which means that more plugins can be launched at the same time.

■ **Designed for network security checks** NASL is designed to establish connections, send data, and parse the results. It comes with a number of function libraries that implement high-level protocols. Example protocols include SMB, NFS, RPC, SMTP, HTTP, and many more. All these libraries are written in NASL.

■ **Strong security** NASL checks cannot access the local file system, execute system commands, or connect to third-party hosts (they can only establish connections with the remote host currently being tested). Additionally, the lack of pointers and memory management results in a language that is not vulnerable to buffer overflows. This makes NASL a very strong language for developing security checks and reduces the time it takes to publish new plugins. We do not have to worry about the security of the scanner itself when writing a new plugin.

■ **Easy to modify and extend** The current implementation of the NASL interpreter is very clean from a code perspective. This makes the addition of new operators or built-in functions very easy, while maintaining backward compatibility with older implementations of the library.

■ **Support for multiple languages** NASL was initially designed to support a great number of languages, but the limitations of ASCII encoding were not taken into account. At this time, only the French language implementation has made much progress. Many languages, such as Japanese, cannot be represented in the extended ASCII character set. The number of new plugins being written every day, as well as the frequent modifications to old plugins, would place large demands on any translation effort. We have investigated ways to have better support for non-English languages, but at this time, that goal has been delayed.

Why Do You Want to Write (and Publish) Your Own NASL Scripts?

The Nessus engine (nessusd) is not a vulnerability scanner; it's a network engine that launches a set of plugins against every host on the network. The Nessus engine is responsible for launching plugins in the right order, facilitating communication between the plugins, and managing the resources they require.

What this really means is that as a user, you have the ability to write plugins that perform network security checks, and almost any other type of network-wide test (such as policy compliance). For example, if your corporate policy is to use Apache 1.3 instead of Apache 2.0, you can easily write a plugin that verifies that every system with an active web server is indeed running the correct version of Apache. If your company requires the use of SSH.com's SSH server instead of OpenSSH, writing a compliance check is also very simple. Finally, if you deal with Windows hosts and your corporate policy is to deploy patches using Microsoft's Software Update Services (SUS), you can easily write a plugin that will warn you whenever a Windows host is not configured to use your company SUS server.

You might also want to write your own security checks because Nessus.org has not published a check for a vulnerability with which you are dealing. Although the Nessus project does its best to provide plugins for as many vulnerabilities as possible, many situations would result in a plugin not being written. When a flaw is reported in a product with a very small user base, the Nessus plugin developers might choose to spend their time working on a plugin that applies to a larger group of people instead. Unsupported shareware products and software that provides a specific function to a niche industry are both candidates for exclusion. This is not to say that if someone submitted a plugin that it would be rejected, just that these are a lower priority than the dozens of critical flaws discovered in mainstream products every week.

The best way to submit your plugin is to post it to the *plugin-writers* mailing list (please refer to Chapter 12). Your plugin will be reviewed and potentially included with the Nessus distribution. Once your plugin has been accepted, the Nessus development team will automatically maintain it. This means that if the NASL API changes (and it is constantly being improved), your plugin will be updated and will continue to work with newer versions of Nessus. Publishing your plugin allows you to write it once and let a team of dedicated people maintain it in the future.

Structure of a NASL Script

A NASL script is divided in two sections. The first section is called the "script description" and contains NASL code that is used by the Nessus engine. This code contains information such as the unique plugin identifier, a short name for the plugin, its dependencies, and other attributes that are used to control how and when this plugin is launched. This section defines what the users will see in the client interface as well as what ends up in the final report. The description and name fields in this section are just as important as the test code itself; if end users are not able to determine what this plugin does or understand the significance when they review the report, they might inadvertently ignore a serious vulnerability on their network.

The second section is called the "script body." This code is the actual meat of the plugin; it is responsible for testing the actual vulnerability and reporting any relevant data. How this section is written depends on quite a few factors. Some plugins will gather data and report it, others will query saved data and trigger alerts based on the contents, and a handful will just configure other parameters of the scan and exit.

Internally, this means that the Nessus engine actually executes every script in two different ways. When the Nessus engine first starts, it will set the "description" variable to TRUE and then execute every plugin once. This allows the engine to build a dependency tree and provide a list of available plugins to the Nessus client software. During the actual scan, each plugin is launched once for each target on the network, with the "description" set to FALSE. If for some reason the description section does not contain an `exit()` call at the end, the engine will continue processing the plugin. To prevent any problems during the initialization phase, the engine will disable all network-related functions, reducing the impact of buggy plugins.

The Description Section

This section must call the following functions:

- **`script_id(<number>)`** The unique ID number of this plugin. Each plugin is attributed a unique ID that that will not change over time. Traditionally, Nessus scripts use the 1xxxxx space (10000, 10001, and so on…). If you intend to develop private scripts that you do not intend to distribute, it is recommended you use the 9xxxxx ID space.

- **`script_name(english:"<name>")`** The short name of the script, it should be relevant to the tested vulnerability.

- **`script_description(english:"<description>")`** A concise description of the flaw tested for by the plugin, how it can be resolved, and the potential risk. If the plugin generates dynamic output (for example, it reports the version number of a remote service), this description should explain what the script does. Plugins that generate dynamic output specify argument to the "data" parameter of the `security_hole()`, `security_note()`, and `security_warning()` functions in the script body. A good description is around 10 to 20 lines long, contains a solution, and a risk factor. Although the description is "free form," we highly recommend that it include the solution and risk factor, as it helps user prioritize the report. The following example is from Nessus plugin #11591:

```
desc = "The remote host is running 12Planet Chat Server - a web based chat
server written in Java.

The connection to this server is done over clear text, which means that
```

an attacker who can sniff the data going to this host could obtain the
administrator password of the web site, and use it to gain unauthorized
access to this chat server.

Solution : None at this time
Risk factor: Low";

- **`script_summary(english:"<name>")`** A one-line description of what the plugin actually does.

- **`script_category(<category>)`** The script category is used by the Nessus engine to determine when the plugin should be launched. The following categories exist:

  - **ACT_INIT** The plugin fills the Knowledge Base and must be launched before anything else.

  - **ACT_SCANNER** The plugin is a port scanner or a "pinger" that determines if the remote host is alive.

  - **ACT_SETTINGS** The plugin processes user-specified preferences that might affect the rest of the plugins (some preferences are stored in the Knowledge Base).

  - **ACT_GATHER_INFO** The script will gather information about the remote services (for example, it grabs the banner, determines what service is running on which port, and so on…). Most of the scripts in this category fill the Knowledge Base with data that is used by other scripts.

  - **ACT_ATTACK** The script nonintrusively tests for a flaw and is likely leave "noisy" logs on the tested system.

  - **ACT_MIXED_ATTACK** The script will perform an intrusive check if "safe checks" are disabled (for example, attempt to reproduce a buffer overflow condition), and will perform a nonintrusive check if "safe checks" are disabled. The nonintrusive check might have a higher chance of false positives.

  - **ACT_DESTRUCTIVE_ATTACK** The script might disable the remote service while performing the test. Scripts in this category will be disabled if the "safe checks" option is set.

  - **ACT_DENIAL** The goal of the script is to disable the remote service. Scripts in this category will be disabled if the "safe checks" option is set.

  - **ACT_KILL_HOST** The goal of the script is to crash the tested system. Scripts in this category will be disabled if the "safe checks" option is set.

  - **ACT_FLOOD** The script might crash the tested system and potentially affect the network itself. Scripts in this category will be disabled if the "safe checks" option is set.

- **ACT_END** The script must run after every other script has finished.

- `script_copyright(english:"<copyright>")` A one-line sentence that states who holds the copyright on this script.

- `script_family(english:"<family>")` The family to which the script belongs. A plugin might fall into more than one family. For example, if a buffer overflow was found in Microsoft's IIS web server, it could logically be placed into both the "Gain a shell remotely" and "Windows" families. When these situations come up, the rule of thumb is to associate the plugin with the family to which the vulnerability is closest. For example, a flaw in IIS is would be placed into the "Windows" family, since it is an integral part of the Windows operating system. By the same logic, a buffer overflow in a Novell product would be placed into the "NetWare" family. Selecting the proper family is often a difficult task, since one flaw might affect various operating systems and services. This becomes particularly complicated when dealing with a flaw in an application library that is used by a wide variety of products. We have been investigating other categorization techniques, but have not developed a better method at this time.

If you intend to share your script with the community, avoid creating your own family name and use one of the following standard names instead:

- **Backdoors** The plugin tries to detect backdoor services and Trojan horse programs. This family also applies to vendor-installed maintenance accounts and other "official" backdoors.

- **CGI abuses** The plugin looks for flaws in a web application (PHP, CGI, and so forth).

- **CGI abuses : XSS** The plugin looks for flaws in a web application (PHP, CGI, and so forth) which expose Cross Site Scripting vulnerabilities.

- **CISCO** The plugin looks for flaws in a product made by Cisco.

- **CentOS Local Security Checks** The plugin looks for local security issues in a CentOS Linux system.

- **Databases** The plugin looks for flaws in database products (Oracle, Sybase, MS SQL, mysql, postgresQL, etc.).

- **Debian Local Security Checks** The plugin looks for local security issues in a Debian Linux system.

- **Default Unix Accounts** The plugin looks for accounts which are enabled, and have a default password when the system is newly installed.

- **Denial of Service** The plugin looks for flaws that would result in a denial of service (DoS) if exploited.

- **FTP** The plugin looks for flaws in a File Transfer Protocol (FTP) service.

- **Firewalls** The plugin looks for flaws specific to firewalls and proxy servers.

- **Gain a shell remotely** The plugin looks for flaws that would result in arbitrary code execution, such as buffer overflows and format string attacks.

- **Gain root remotely** The same as "Gain a shell remotely," but affecting services running as the root user (the most powerful account on UNIX systems).

- **General** The plugin performs a task that is not directly related to vulnerability detection, such as service discovery.

- **Gentoo Local Security Checks** The plugin looks for local security issues in a Gentoo Linux system.

- **Misc.** The plugin does something that does not fit into one of the other families.

- **NetWare** The plugin looks for flaws affecting Novell NetWare products.

- **Peer-to-Peer file sharing** The plugin detects various peer-to-peer (P2P) file sharing services.

- **Remote file access** The plugin looks for flaws that can be exploited to obtain remote file system access.

- **SMTP Problems** The plugin looks for flaws in Simple Mail Transfer Protocol (SMTP) services.

- **Service Detection** The plugin looks for services which are open to the network.

- **Settings** The plugin sets variables for other plugins.

- **Slackware Local Security Checks** The plugin looks for local security issues in a Slackware Linux system.

- **Ubuntu Local Security Checks** The plugin looks for local security issues in a Ubuntu Linux system.

- **Windows** The plugin looks for flaws related to the Microsoft Windows operating system.

- **Windows : Microsoft Bulletins** The plugin looks for flaws related to the Microsoft Windows operating system.

The following functions are not strictly required, but should be used as needed:

- `script_bugtraq_id(ID1, ID2,...)` Associates the plugin with one or more Bugtraq ID values. Bugtraq identifiers are managed by SecurityFocus (www.securityfocus.com/bid). This information is incorporated in the final report.

- `script_cve_id("CVE-XXXX-YYYY", "CVE-XXX2-YYY2",...)` Associates the plugin with one or more CVE identifiers. CVE is a vulnerability dictionary that is managed by the Common Vulnerabilities and Exposures project (http://cve.mitre.org). This information is incorporated in the final report.

- `script_xref(name:<name>, value:<value>)` Associates a plugin with an arbitrary reference type and value. Currently, this function is used to link Nessus plugins with IAVA (U.S. Government) and OSVDB (www.osvdb.org) identifiers, as well as standard HTTP URLs. This information is incorporated in the final report.

- `script_timeout(timeout)` Specifies the number of seconds that the plugin is allowed to run before it is killed. This prevents a buggy plugin or slow service from causing a scan to hang indefinitely. If this function is not called, the default of three minutes will be used. If your particular plugin will take longer than this, make sure that this function is called. Calling this function with the parameter of zero (0) will allow the script to run indefinitely.

- `script_dependencies("name1.nasl", "name2.nasl",…)` Defines a list of other plugins that must run before this one. This is particularly useful if your plugin requires information from the Knowledge Base that is placed there by another plugin. Be careful when adding dependencies, because it is possible to create a circular dependency tree that will result in *bad things* happening inside the Nessus engine (a recursive function will consume all available stack space). You may notice that some plugins also call script_dependencie(); this is the older syntax for this function and behaves exactly the same way.

- `script_require_ports(port1, port2,…)` Instructs the Nessus engine to not launch this plugin if *all* of the listed ports are closed.

- `script_require_keys(key1, key2,…)` Instructs the Nessus engine to only launch this plugin if *all* of the listed Knowledge Base keys are defined.

- `script_exclude_keys(key1, key2,…)` Instructs the Nessus engine to only launch this plugin if *all* of the listed Knowledge Base keys are *not* defined.

An Introduction to the NASL Language

If you are familiar with C, Perl, or PHP, you should have no problem picking up the NASL language. Since NASL was designed to perform network checks, the language is focused on string manipulation and networking. Everything else was designed to be out of your way; you do not need to worry about memory management, pointers, or operating system peculiarities. NASL was designed to run from within the Nessus engine and does not have the capability to read data from the console or otherwise interact with the host system (with a few exceptions in the case of "trusted" scripts). In a way, you can view a NASL script as an elaborate configuration file that tells the Nessus engine what to do. You can launch scripts in a stand-alone mode, using the command-line NASL interpreter, but some functions are dependent on the environment provided by the Nessus engine. For example, scripts run from the command line are not able to automatically negotiate SSL-wrapped services or manipulate the Knowledge Base. The `display()` function is available for debugging purposes; it is one of the few functions designed for use outside of the Nessus engine.

Writing Your First Script

When writing NASL scripts, it is common practice to test them with the *nasl* command-line interpreter before launching them as part of a Nessus scan. The *nasl* utility is part of the Nessus installation and takes the following arguments:

```
nasl [options] script1.nasl [script2.nasl…]
```

Each option that the NASL interpreter can use is listed below with it's corresponding category:

- Security

  - **-S** : `Generate a signed .nasl file` – This creates a signed .nasl file to allow greater access to resources through the Nessus Engine. A RSA Public/Private keypair is required to sign a script.

  - **-X** : `Run the script in 'authenticated' mode` – This allows greater access to resources through the Nessus Engine without a signed script.

- Parser Tools

  - **-L** : `'lint' the script (extended checks)` – This checks the script rigeriously for syntax errors and parser errors. It also tests all elements of a script, not just those which will run under given cases. It is a good idea to use this options before releaseing a plugin.

  - **-V** : `Show the script ID, script name, etc.… (use twice for description)` – This option dumps informaiton about the plugin that would be put in the report output. It also displays the information that would be included in the .nsr or .xml report output (numeric cross references, Bugtraq ID number, etc.).

  - **-T <tracefile>** : `Trace the script execution` – This forces the interpreter to write debugging information to the specified file. This option is invaluable when diagnosing problems in complex scripts. An argument of "-" will result in the output being written to the console.

- Script Execution Environment

  - **-t target** : `Execute the scripts against the target(s) host` – This option sepcifies the IP address or hostname against which you would like to test your script. The NASL networking functions do not allow you to specify the destination address when establishing connections or sending raw packets. This limitation is as much for safety as for convenience and has worked very well so far. If this option is not specified, all connections will be made to the loopback address, 127.0.0.1 (localhost).

- **-k <file>** : `Load the KB file <file> in the KB` – This causes the interpreter to load the Knowledge Base (KB) file associated with the target host. This only works if the target host has a KB file, and it has not expired.

- **-D** : `Run the 'description part' only` – This runs the description portion of the plugin only. No network code is executed and the same conditions apply to the script as would apply if the Nessus Engine were running the plugin with the description variable set to TRUE.

- **-s** : `Specifies that the script should be run with 'safe checks' enabled` – This causes the interpreter to run the script in safe mode. Any plugins marked as ACT_DESTRUCTIVE_ATTACK, ACT_KILL_HOST, ACT_DENIAL, or ACT_FLOOD will not run.

- Other

  - **-h** : `Shows this help screen` – This does the obvious and show the terse help for the nasl command.
  - **-v** : `Shows the version number` – This displays the version number of the nasl interpreter and exits.

For our first NASL script, we will write a simple tool that connects to an FTP server (on TCP port 21), reads the banner, and then displays it on screen. The following NASL code demonstrates how easy it is to accomplish this task:

```
soc = open_sock_tcp(21);
if (! soc) exit(0);
banner = recv_line(socket:soc, length:4096);
display(banner);
```

Let's walk through this small example:

```
soc = open_sock_tcp(21);
```

This function opens a TCP socket on port 21 of the current target (as specified with *nasl –t*). This function returns NULL on failure (the remote port is closed or not responding) and a non-zero file descriptor on success.

```
banner = recv_line(socket:soc, length:4096);
```

This function reads data from the socket until the number of bytes specified by the "length" parameter has been received, or until the character "\n" is received—whichever comes first.

As you can see, the function `open_sock_tcp()` takes a single, non-named argument, while the function `recv_line()` takes two arguments that are prefixed by their name. These are referred to as "anonymous" and "named" functions. Named functions allow the plugin writer to specify only the parameters that he needs, instead of having to supply values for each parameter supported by the function. Additionally, the writer does not need to remember the exact order of the parameters, preventing simple errors when calling a function that supports many options. For example, the following two lines produce identical results:

```
banner = recv_line(socket:soc, length:4096);
banner = recv_line(length:4096, socket:soc);
```

Save this script as "test.nasl" and execute it on the command line:

```
$ /usr/local/bin/nasl -t ftp.nessus.org test.nasl
** WARNING : packet forgery will not work
** as NASL is not running as root
220 ftp.nessus.org Ready
```

If you run *nasl* as a nonroot user, you will notice that it displays a warning message about "packet forgery." NASL scripts are capable of creating, sending, and receiving raw IP packets, but they require root privileges to do so. In this example, we are not using raw sockets and can safely ignore this message.

Now, let's modify our script to display the FTP banner in a Nessus report. To do so, we need to use one of the three special-purpose reporting functions: `security_hole()`, `security_warning()`, and `security_note()`. These functions tell the Nessus engine that a plugin is successful (a vulnerability was found), and each denotes a different severity level. A call to the `security_note()` function will result in a low-risk vulnerability being added to the report, a call to `security_warn()` will result in a medium-risk vulnerability, and `security_hole()` is used to report a high-risk vulnerability. These functions can be invoked in two ways:

```
security_note(<port>)
```

or

```
security_note(port:<port>, data:<report>, proto:<protocol>)
```

In the first case, the plugin simply tells the Nessus engine that it was successful. The Nessus engine will copy the plugin description (as registered with `script_description()`) and will place it into the report. This is sufficient for most plugins; either a vulnerability is there and we provide a generic description, or it is not and we do not report anything. In some cases, you might want to include dynamic text in the report. This dynamic text could be the version number of the remote web server, the FTP banner, the list of exported shares, or even the contents of a captured password file.

In this particular example, we want to report the FTP banner that we received from the target system, and we will use the long form of the `security_note()` function to do this:

```
soc = open_sock_tcp(21);
if (! soc) exit(0);
banner = recv_line(socket:soc, length:4096);
security_note(port:21, data:"The remote FTP banner is : " + banner, proto:"tcp");
```

If you execute this script from the command line, you will notice that the "data" parameter is written to the console. If no "data" parameter was specified, it will default to the string "Successful." When this plugin is launched by the Nessus engine, this data will be used as the vulnerability description in the final report.

Now that our plugin code has been modified to report the FTP banner, we need to create the description section. This section will allow the plugin to be loaded by the Nessus engine:

```
if (description)
{
        script_id(90001);
        script_name(english:"Simple FTP banner grabber");
        script_description(english:"
This script establishes a connection to the remote host on port 21 and extracts
the FTP banner of the remote host");

        script_summary(english:"retrieves the remote FTP banner");
        script_category(ACT_GATHER_INFO);
        script_family(english:"Nessus Book");
        script_copyright(english:"(C) 2004 Renaud Deraison");
        exit(0);
}

soc = open_sock_tcp(21);
if (! soc) exit(0);
banner = recv_line(socket:soc, length:4096);
security_note(port:21, data:"The remote FTP banner is : " + banner, proto:"tcp");
```

After you have saved this plugin to disk, you can verify the syntax of the code using the *nasl* interpreter. As of version 3.0.5, the option to compile the plug-in and test its syntax has been changed from −p to −L, although the −p options still seems to work, as does the manual page −W option. Several tests of the −L, -W, and −p option yielded the same results, so we can safely assume that they all do roughly the same thing. The -L option will tell *nasl* to only parse the plug-in with extra warnings, it will not actually execute the NASL script. If the command `nasl -L yourscript.nasl` results in no output, then the syntax of the plugin is correct.

To add your plugin to the Nessus installation, copy it to the Nessus plugins directory, delete the cached database files, and send the main "nessusd" process a "HUP" signal. You may also need to delete the nessus plugin cache database located in `/opt/nessus/var/nessus/plugins-code.db` and `/opt/nessus/var/nessus/plugins-desc.db`. On early 3.x.x versions of Nessus, it was necessary to delete these files and rebuild them when you add a plug-in.

More recent releases (3.0.5 and later), do **not** need the deletion of the files. The engine checks the plug-in index against the plug-in directory and only recompiles the NASL scripts which need to be updated. The location of the plugin directory will depend on your system; it can usually be found in /opt/nessus/lib/nessus/plugins, and in older nessus versions in /usr/local/lib/nessus/plugins or /usr/lib/nessus/plugins. You will need root privileges to add your plugin to this directory and restart the server:

```
# cp test_script.nasl /opt/nessus/lib/nessus/plugins/
# rm /opt/nesuss/var/nessus/plugins-code.db
# rm /opt/nessus/var/nessus/plugins-desc.db
# killall -HUP nessusd
```

After restarting the server (with the "HUP" signal), open the Nessus client and connect to the server. After authenticating, verify that your new plugin shows up in the family "Nessus Book" shown in Figure 11.1.

Figure 11.1 Nessus Book

Now, disable every plugin except this one, and run a test scan against the FTP server of your choice. You should obtain the report shown in Figure 11.2.

Figure 11.2 Nessus "NG" Report

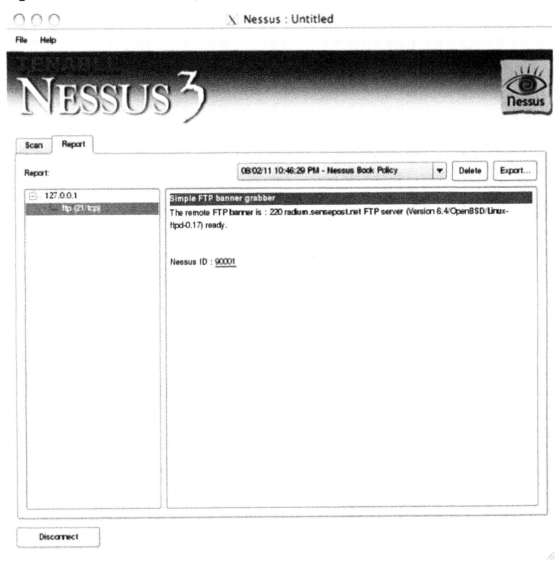

If the results look like Figure 11.2, it worked! However, this plugin is still not 100-percent Nessus compliant:

- It assumes that FTP servers are bound to listen on port 21.

- It establishes a connection to port 21 without first making sure that the port is actually open.

- It does not respect the FTP protocol entirely.

These issues might seem minor, but can cause serious problems in the overall performance and accuracy of a Nessus scan. Fixing these issues will prevent unnecessary network connections, potential false positives when other services are using port 21, and false negatives when the FTP server is running on a nonstandard port. Recent versions of Nessus include thousands of unique plugins; small problems across the entire plugin tree can have a noticeable impact on the scan results. Even a single misbehaved plugin can result a measurable drop in scan performance and cause havoc across the target network.

So, let's fix each issue to make this plugin more "Nessus friendly."

Assuming that the FTP Server Is Listening on Port 21

During the scan, Nessus builds what we call a Knowledge Base (KB). Basically, every script can write down facts about the remote host—the ports that are open, the banner of various services, the version of installed software and patches, and so on. By using the KB efficiently, you can speed up your test and make it "smarter"—the trick is to know which plugins provide the KB data your plugin needs.

For example, instead of assuming the FTP server is always on port 21, you can ask the KB to tell you the port number of any FTP discovered by the service detection plugin.

```
port = get_kb_item("Services/ftp");
if (! port) port = 21;
soc = open_sock_tcp(port);
```

This code means:

- I want to know the port of an FTP service on the tested system.

- If no FTP service was identified, fall back to using port 21.

- Connect to the remote FTP service.

Every identified service is located under the "Services/xxx" hierarchy in the KB, where "xxx" is the name of the detected service. If the remote host happens to run two FTP servers—one on port 21 and another on port 2121—Nessus will detect this condition and will execute your script twice; once with a port value of 21, and once with a value of 2121. Internally, this actually results in the plugin spawning off a cloned copy of itself for each value stored in that KB key. If the service has not been recognized, we fall back to port 21—useful in situations where the service detection plugin encounters a problem. When running this plugin from the command line, the KB does not exist, so providing a default value is the only way we could test this script from outside the Nessus engine.

Establishing a Connection to the Port Directly

Since the Nessus engine usually performs a portscan, there's no need to connect to a port that has already been detected as closed. It wastes bandwidth and time—especially if the target system is behind a firewall. The NASL function `get_port_state(<port>)` will tell you if a port is closed. It returns 0 if the port is known to be closed, and 1 if the state is unknown (not in the portscan range) or open. We will modify our plugin to check the state of the port before trying to establish a connection to it:

```
port = get_kb_item("Services/ftp");
If (! port) port = 21;
If (! get_port_state(port)) exit(0);
soc = open_sock_tcp(port);
```

Respecting the FTP Protocol

One last assumption has been made so far: the FTP banner is sent as one line. In reality, FTP banners might split up across multiple lines. This is common practice with many large FTP servers (such as ftp.lip5.fr), which provide the terms of use in the banner itself. Our plugin would fail because it only reads the first line.

The FTP protocol defines that all lines starting with the string "220-" are followed by another line, while lines starting with the string "220-" signify the last line of the banner. Our plugin will need to be modified to take this into account:

```
port = get_kb_item("Services/ftp");
if (! port) port = 21;
if (! get_port_state(port)) exit(0);
soc = open_sock_tcp(port);
banner = line = recv_line(socket:soc, length:4096);
while (line = ~ "^220-")
{
        line = recv_line(socket:soc, length:4096);
        banner += line;
}
security_note(port:port, data:"The remote FTP banner is : " + banner,
proto:"tcp");
```

This modification will cause the script to read the first line of the banner from the server and then continue to read data as long as the new line starts with "220-." As each new line is received, the data is added to the variable "banner."

In this particular case, this functionality has already been implemented as the `get_ftp_banner()` function in the "ftp_funcs.inc" script library. We will now modify our plugin to use this library:

```
include("ftp_func.inc");
  port = get_kb_item("Services/ftp");
  if (! port) port = 21;
  banner = get_ftp_banner(port:port);
  security_note(port:port, data:"The remote FTP banner is : " + banner,
proto:"tcp");
```

There are many advantages to using library functions, such as `get_ftp_banner()`, instead of writing the code ourselves. If a new type of FTP server becomes popular, one that provides the banner in a slightly different way, only a single library function would need to be modified to support it. Additionally, many of the library functions will use smart caching techniques to reduce the number of connections made to the server. The first time the `get_ftp_banner()` function is called, it will store the FTP banner in the KB. Each successive call to this function will first check the KB for the banner and return it if one is found, removing the need for each plugin to connect to the FTP server on its own. Considering that in any given scan, there might be dozens of plugins that all need to analyze the FTP banner, this is a huge improvement in terms of efficiency and bandwidth usage.

Wrapping It Up

Now that our plugin is "smarter," we need to modify the description section to indicate that this script must be run after the find_service.nes service detection plugin. The find_service.nes plugin is responsible for determining what type of application is running on each port found during the portscan phase. Almost every plugin in the Nessus distribution depends on this plugin or its slightly more advanced sibling, find_service2.nasl. We use the `script_dependencie()` function to tell the Nessus engine that our plugin must always be launched after find_service.nes.

```
if (description)
{
        [...]
        script_copyright(english:"(C) 2004 Renaud Deraison");
        script_dependencie("find_service.nes");
        exit(0);
}
```

Once this is done, we copy the plugin over our old one in the Nessus plugins directory, restart the Nessus engine, and launch a test scan. Since the new plugin is able to identify FTP servers on any port, you will need to enable one of the portscan plugins to find FTP services on ports other than 21.

More Advanced Scripting

You now know the basics of writing a NASL plugin, how to access the Knowledge Base, and how to report a vulnerability. Let's explore some of the interesting built-in functions and libraries of the NASL language.

String Manipulation

NASL is quite flexible when it comes to working with strings. String operations include addition, subtraction, search, replace, and support for regular expressions. NASL also allows you to use escape characters ("\n", and so forth) using the `string()` function.

How Strings Are Defined in NASL

Strings can be defined using single quotes or double quotes. When using double quotes, a string is taken "as is"—no interpretation is made on its content—while strings defined with single quotes interpret escape characters. For example:

```
A = "foo\n";
B = 'foo\n';
```

In this example, the variable "A" is five characters long and is equal to "foo\n", while variable "B" is four characters long and equal to "foo", followed by a carriage return. This is the opposite of how strings are handled in languages such as C and Perl, and can be confusing to new plugin developers.

We call an interpreted string (defined with single quotes) a "pure" string. It is possible to convert a regular string to a pure string using the `string()` function. In the following example, the variable "B" is now four characters long and is equal to "foo", followed by a carriage return.

```
A = "foo\n";
B = string(A);
```

If you are familiar with C, you might be used to the fact that the zero byte (or NULL byte) marks the end of a string. There's no such concept in NASL—the interpreter keep tracks of the length of each string internally and does not care about the content. Therefore, the string "\0\0\0" is equivalent to three NULL byte characters, and is considered to be three bytes long by the `strlen()` function.

You may build strings containing binary data using the `raw_string()` function. This function will accept an unlimited number of arguments, where each argument is the ASCII code of the character you want to use. In the following example, the variable "A" is equal to the string "XXX" (ASCII code 88 and 0x58 in hexadecimal).

```
A = raw_string(88, 0x58, 88);
```

String Addition and Subtraction

NASL supports string manipulation through the addition (+) and subtraction (−) operators. This is an interesting feature of the NASL language that can save quite a bit of time during plugin development.

The addition operator will concatenate any two strings. The following example sets the variable "A" to the value "foobar", and then variable "B" to the value "foobarfoobarfoobar".

```
A = "foo" + "bar";
B = A + A + A;
```

The subtraction operator allows you to remove one string from another. In many cases, this is preferable to a search-and-replace or search-and-extract operation. The following example will result in the variable "A" being set to the value "1, 2, 3".

```
A = "test1, test2, test3";
A = A - "test"; # A is now equal to "1, test2, test3"
A = A - "test"; # A is now equal to "1, 2, test3"
A = A - "test"; # A is now equal to "1, 2, 3"
```

String Search and Replace

NASL allows you to easily search for one string and replace it with another, without having to resort to regular expressions. The following example will result in the variable "A" being set to the value "foo1, foo2, foo2".

```
A = "test1, test2, test3";
A = str_replace(find:"test", replace:"foo", string:A);
```

Regular Expressions in NASL

NASL supports `egrep(1)`-style operations through the `ereg()`, `egrep()`, `ereg_replace()` functions. These functions use POSIX Extended regular expression syntax. If you are familiar with Perl's regular expression support, please keep in mind that there are significant differences between how NASL and Perl will handle the same regular expression. The *Wikipedia* (http://en.wikipedia.org/wiki/Regular_expression) has a great description of regular expressions in general and the differences between each type.

The `ereg()` function returns TRUE if a string matches a given pattern. The string must be a one-line string (in other words, it should not contain any carriage return character). In the following example, the string "Matched!" will be printed to the console.

```
if (ereg(string:"My dog is brown", pattern:"dog"))
{
        display("Matched\n");
}
```

The `egrep()` function works like `ereg()`, except that it accepts multiline strings. This function will return the actual string that matched the pattern or FALSE if no match was found. In the following example, the variable "text" contains the content of a UNIX "passwd" file. We will use `egrep()` to only return the lines that correspond to users whose ID value (the third field) is lower than 50.

```
text = "
root:*:0:0:System Administrator:/var/root:/bin/tcsh
daemon:*:1:1:System Services:/var/root:/dev/null
unknown:*:99:99:Unknown User:/dev/null:/dev/null
smmsp:*:25:25:Sendmail User:/private/etc/mail:/dev/null
www:*:70:70:World Wide Web Server:/Library/WebServer:/dev/null
mysql:*:74:74:MySQL Server:/dev/null:/dev/null
sshd:*:75:75:sshd Privilege separation:/var/empty:/dev/null
renaud:*:501:20:Renaud Deraison,,,:/Users/renaud:/bin/bash";

lower_than_50 = egrep(pattern:"[^:]*:[^:]:([0-9]|[0-5][0-9]):.*", string:text);
display(lower_than_50);
```

Running this script in command-line mode results in the following output:

```
$ nasl egrep.nasl
root:*:0:0:System Administrator:/var/root:/bin/tcsh
daemon:*:1:1:System Services:/var/root:/dev/null
smmsp:*:25:25:Sendmail User:/private/etc/mail:/dev/null
$
ereg_replace(pattern:<pattern>, replace:<replace>, string:<string>);
```

The `ereg_replace()` function can be used to replace a pattern in a string with another string. This function supports regular expression back references, which can replace the original string with parts of the matched pattern. The following example uses this function to extract the Server: banner from an HTTP server response.

```
include("http_func.inc");
include("http_keepalive.inc");
reply = http_keepalive_send_recv(data:http_get(item:"/", port:80), port:80);
if (! reply) exit(0);

# Isolate the Server: string from the HTTP reply
server = egrep(pattern:"^Server:", string:reply);
if (! server) exit(0);
server = ereg_replace(pattern:"^Server: (.*)$",
        replace:"The remote server is \1",
        string:server);
display(server, "\n");
```

Running this script in command-line mode results in the following output:

```
$ nasl -t 127.0.0.1 ereg_replace.nasl
The remote server is Apache/1.3.29 (Darwin)
$
```

The NASL Protocol APIs

The Nessus installation includes quite a few function libraries written in the NASL language. These libraries are located in the plugin directory and use the ".inc" filename suffix. Almost every plugin in the Nessus distribution uses these libraries in one form or another. They provide you with high-level access to protocols that would be both time consuming and error prone to implement on a per-plugin basis. Once your plugin starts using the NASL function libraries, any improvements to those libraries will be passed to your plugin as well. This section presents some of the most widely used protocol libraries and the functions they provide.

HTTP

To use the HTTP APIs, your script should include() the http_func.inc and http_keepalive. inc libraries. These libraries work together to provide simple, efficient access to the HTTP protocol. If you write a script that uses this API, you should set "http_version.nasl" as a dependency of your plugin. The http_version.nasl plugin in turn depends on a large number of fingerprinting and web server analysis scripts. These scripts are responsible for initializing various sections of the Knowledge Base that are used by the HTTP function libraries.

These two libraries contain the following functions:

- **`get_http_port(default:<port>)`** Returns the port number on which a web server is listening. If no web server has been identified on this system, the specified port parameter will be returned. This function uses a call to `get_kb_item()`; one instance of this plugin will for spawned for each active web server. Additionally, this function will verify that the web server is actually active and responsive before returning it to the calling plugin. This last step is required to work around a few broken web server implementations, which can slow the scan.

- **`get_http_banner(port:<port>)`** Returns the banner of the remote web server listening on the specified port. This banner will be stored in the KB and subsequent calls to this function will result in the cached banner being returned.

- **`http_get(item:<file>, port:port)`** Returns a HTTP GET request that is automatically configured to use the correct version of the HTTP protocol for that host and port.

- **`http_keepalive_send_recv(port:<port>, data:<req>)`** Sends an HTTP request to the remote host and returns the results. If the remote host supports persistent HTTP connections, then the connection state is maintained for the lifetime of the plugin. Any subsequent calls to this function will reuse this connection, reducing the latency and overhead associated with creating a new connection.

- **cgi_dirs()** Returns an array containing all the directories that contain CGI executables or dynamic pages (by default, this function returns "/cgi-bin", "/scripts", and "/"). The webmirror.nasl and DDI_Directory_Scanner.nasl plugins will populate this list through web crawling and directory guessing techniques, respectively.

- **can_host_php(port:<port>)** Returns FALSE if the remote web server is known to not be able to host PHP dynamic pages; it returns TRUE otherwise. Many plugins that test for flaws in PHP web applications will use this function to save bandwidth and reduce scan time.

- **can_host_asp(port:<port>)** Returns FALSE if the remote web server is known to not be able to host ASP dynamic pages. Many plugins that test for flaws in ASP web applications will use this function to save bandwidth and reduce scan time.

In the following example, let's imagine that the PHP page "foo.php" is vulnerable to a directory traversal attack—requesting foo.php?file=/etc/passwd will return the content of file "/etc/passwd". To check for this flaw, we will use cgi_dirs() to get a list of directories that might contain dynamic pages. For the sake of brevity, we have not included the description section of this plugin, but make sure that any HTTP plugins you write have a call to the script_dependencie() function for "http_version.nasl".

```
# Determine on which port the remote web server is listening
port = get_http_port(default:80);
# If there is no port or if the port is known to be closed, quit
if (! port || ! get_port_state(port)) exit(0);
# Loop through all the CGI directories and request foo.php?file=/etc/passwd
foreach dir (cgi_dirs())
{
  # Make an HTTP GET request
  req = http_get(item: dir + "/foo.php?file=/etc/passwd", port:port);
  res = http_keepalive_send_recv(port:port, data:req);
  # If there is no reply, it means the remote server is dead - quit
  if ( res == NULL ) exit(0);
  # Alert if we see the contents of /etc/passwd in the reply
  if (egrep(pattern:"root:.*:.*:0:[01]:.*", string:res))
  {
    security_hole(port);
    exit(0);
  }
}
```

FTP

To use the FTP APIs, your script should `include()` the ftp_func.inc library. You do not need to set any dependencies to use this API.

This library contains the following functions:

- **get_ftp_banner(port:<port>)** Returns the banner of the FTP service that is listening on the specified port. Just like the `get_http_banner()` function call, it will store the banner in the KB and return a cached copy if possible.

- **ftp_authenticate(socket:<socket>, user:<user>, pass:<password>)** Authenticates to the remote FTP server using the supplied username and password, returning a nonzero value if the server accepts the login request. The socket parameter must have been initialized with `open_sock_tcp()` prior to this function being called.

- **ftp_recv_line(socket:<socket>, retry:<retry>)** Reads a reply from the remote FTP server. If the reply is a multiline message (such as a long banner), it will return all associated lines. If retry is set, then it will reattempt the connection should it fail.

- **ftp_pasv(socket:<socket>)** Sends a *PASV* command to the remote host, parses the response, and returns the decoded port number to use for data transfers. The socket parameter should be associated with an active TCP connection that is already authenticated to the FTP service.

- **ftp_recv_data(socket:<socket>, line:<line>)** Reads the data sent by the FTP service after a RETR (download) request. The socket parameter should be associated with an active TCP connection to the port number returned by the `ftp_get_pasv_port()` function. The line parameter should be the reply from a previous *RETR* command (see the plugin ftp_rhosts.nasl for an example).

- **ftp_recv_listing(socket:<socket>)** Reads the data sent by the FTP server after an NLST or LIST (directory listing) request. The socket parameter should be associated with an active TCP connection that is already authenticated to the FTP service.

- **ftp_send_cmd(socket:<socket>, command:<cmd>)** Sends a raw FTP protocol command to the remote FTP server. The socket parameter should be associated with an active TCP connection that is already authenticated to the FTP service.

NFS

To use the Network File System (NFS) APIs, your script should `include()` the misc_func.inc and nfs_func.inc libraries.

Nessus contains a nearly complete NFS client API. It allows you to mount and unmount NFS partitions, and read the content of a directory or a file. Of course, these functions are dependent on the target system being configured to allow access to the NFS exports in the first place.

Since all the NFS functions are written in NASL, they are independent from the underlying operating system. This means that even if your system does not support the NFS protocol, Nessus will still be able to interact with remote NFS services.

When dealing with the NFS protocol, you will to need to use two privileged (port 1024 or less) UDP sockets; one to communicate with the actual nfsd daemon (RPC 100003) and another to access the mountd daemon (RPC 100005). The following example obtains the port numbers for the nfsd and mountd RPC services, and then associates a privileged UDP with each.

```
nfsd_port = get_rpc_port(program:100003, proto:IPPROTO_UDP);
if (! nfsd_port) exit(0);
nfsd_socket = open_priv_sock_udp(dport:nfsd_port);

mountd_port = get_rpc_port(program:100005, proto:IPPROTO_UDP);
if (! mountd_port) exit(0);
mountd_socket = open_priv_sock_udp(dport:mountd_port);
```

After using this example code to configure the sockets, the following NFS functions are available:

- **mount(socket:<mountd_socket>, share:<sharename>)** Attempts to mount the specified remote share. It returns NULL on failure, or a file handle (fid) on success.

- **readdir(socket:<nfsd_socket>, fid:<fid>)** Returns the contents of a directory pointed to by the specified file handle. It returns NULL on failure, or a list of entries on success.

- **cwd(socket:<nfsd_socket>, fid:<fid>, dir:<dir>)** Changes the current working directory to one specified in the "dir" parameter. The "fid" parameter must point to the current working directory. This function returns NULL on failure, and a file handle pointing to the new directory on success.

- **open(socket:<nfsd_socket>, fid:<fid>, file:<filename>)** Opens the specified filename inside the directory associated with the "fid" parameter. It returns a file handle pointing to the opened file on success, and NULL on failure.

- **read(socket:<nfsd_socket>, fid:<fid>, length:<length>, off:<off>)** Reads data from the specified file handle (created by open() function), limited to the number of bytes specified by the "length" parameter, and starting at the offset specified by the "offset" parameter.

The following example attempts to mount the root file system ("/") of the remote server, over the NFS protocol, and then read the first 4096 bytes of the "passwd" file.

```
include("misc_func.inc");

include("nfs_func.inc");

nfsd_port = get_rpc_port(program:100003, proto:IPPROTO_UDP);

if (! nfsd_port) exit(0);

nfsd_socket = open_priv_sock_udp(dport:nfsd_port);

mountd_port = get_rpc_port(program:100005, proto:IPPROTO_UDP);

if (! mountd_port) exit(0);

mountd_socket = open_priv_sock_udp(dport:mountd_port);

root = fid = mount (socket:mountd_socket, share:"/");

if (! fid) exit(0); # Could not mount / - exit

# Go to /etc

fid = cwd(socket:nfsd_socket, fid:fid, dir:"etc");

if (! fid) exit(0);

# Open the file "passwd" in /etc

fid = open(socket:nfsd_socket, fid:fid, file:"passwd");

if (! fid) exit(0);

# Read the first 4096 bytes of the file, starting at offset 0

content = read(socket:nfsd_socket, fid:fid, length:4096, off:0);

if (! content) exit(0);

umount(fid:root, socket:mountd_socket);

close(nfsd_socket);

close (mountd_socket);

display("The remote password file contains :\n", content);
```

To use the Network File System (NFS) APIs, your script should `include()` the misc_func.inc and nfs_func.inc libraries.

Other Protocol API Libraries

Nessus contains protocol libraries for several other protocols not fully detailed here. Each library contains the functions needed to access resources over the network. Table 11.1 shows a brief listing of the function libraries and their intended purpose.

Table 11.1 Function Libraries

Library Name	Protocol	Description
aix.inc	N/A	Functions for local scanning of AIX hosts. This library mainly to pull patch levels from the AIX system.
backport.inc	N/A	Functions to check for the back-porting of patches into newer operating system revisions.
byte_func.inc	N/A	Byte level functions for switching and manipulating byte order.
charset_func.inc	N/A	EBCDIC to ASCII/ASCII to EBCDIC conversion functions
cisco_func.inc	Cisco Devices	Extracts version information from Cisco Devices
crypto_func.inc	N/A	Cryptographic functions. Including MD5, MD4, NTLM hash creation, DES cipher, RC4, xor, and others.
dns_func.inc	DNS	Functions for constructing Domain Name Service queries.
ftp_func.inc	FTP	Functions for dealing with the FTP protocol. Detailed above.
hostlevel_funcs.inc	R-Protocols	Functions for accessing R-Protocols like RSH, RLOGIN, REXEC and others of this family.
hpux.inc	N/A	Functions for local scanning of HPUX hosts. This library mainly to pull patch levels from the HPUX system.
http_func.inc	HTTP	Functions to deal with the HTTP protocol. Detailed above.
imap_func.inc	IMAP	Functions to deal with the IMAP protocol.
ip.inc/ip6.inc	IPv4 and IPv6	Functions to deal with packet assembly of IPv4 and IPv6 packets.
kerberos_func.inc	KRB	Functions to deal with Kerberos inter-actions. This library also contains the functions needed to work with Active Directory Kerberos implementations.
ldap.inc	LDAP	Functions to deal with LDAP queries.

Continued

Table 11.1 Continued. Function Libraries

Library Name	Protocol	Description
macosx_func.inc	N/A	Functions for local scanning of Mac OS X. This library mainly extracts bundle information and carbon library information.
misc_func.inc	N/A	Contains Knowledge Base functions for dealing with storing and versioning of KB items.
mysql_func.inc	MYSQL	Functions dealing with the "mysql" database.
network_func.inc	N/A	Old friends from C are kept here. For example ntohl() ntohs(), and other useful things like ip_checksum(). Useful for raw packet construction.
nfs_func.inc	NFS	Functions for dealing with the NFS protocol. Detailed above.
nntp_func.inc	NNTP	Functions for dealing with the Network News Transport Protocol.
pop3_func.inc	POP3	Functions for dealing with the POP3 (Post Office Protocol version 3).
raw.inc	IPv4/IPv6	Functions for creating raw IPv4 and IPv6 packets
smb_activex_func.inc	SMB	Functions for checking which versions of Active X controls are installed on a target.
smb_file_funcs.inc	SMB	Function for getting files from a remote SMB server.
smb_func.inc	SMB	This is the meta-include for all smb related functionality. It includes many other files to compose a complete SMB API.
smtp_func.inc	SMTP	Functions to deal with Simple Mail Transport Protocol.
snmp_func.inc	SNMP	Functions to deal with Simple Network Management Protocol.
solaris.inc	N/A	Functions for local scanning of Solaris hosts. This library mainly to pull patch levels from the Solaris system.

Continued

Table 11.1 Continued. Function Libraries

Library Name	Protocol	Description
ssh_func.inc	SSH	Functions to deal with Secure Shell Protocol.
ssl_funcs.inc	SSL	Functions to deal with Secure Sockets Layer protocol. It is important to note that this also covers any services which use SSL not just HTTPS protocol.
sunrpc_func.inc	RPC	Functions to query Sun Remote Procedure Call services.
tcp.inc	TCP	Functions to assemble TCP packets (for IPv4 or IPv6).
telnet2_func.inc	TELNET	Functions for dealing with extended telnet protocol options.
telnet_func.inc	TELNET	Cursory Functions for dealing with telnet (banner grabbing, option negotiation, etc.).
tftp.inc	TFTP	Functions to handle TFTP protocol transactions.
uddi.inc	UDDI/HTTP	Functions for making UDDI requests over HTTP. (XML packaging methods.)
udp.inc	UDP	Functions to assemble UDP packets (for IPv4 or IPv6).
url_func.inc	Various	This contains functions to encode and decode URLs in escaped format per RFC 2396/RFC 2732.
debian_package.inc freebsd_package.inc qpkg.inc rpm.inc slackware.inc ubuntu.inc	N/A	These collected functions deal with the extraction of package information from their respective types of host. They mostly deal with version number extraction from the package databases of the Unix/Linux/BSD derivatives in their file name, with the exception of qpkg, which deals with Gentoo Linux.

The Nessus Knowledge Base

As mentioned earlier in this chapter, plugins have the capability to store and retrieve data that can be accessed by other scripts. This system is called the Knowledge Base, or simply KB, and is covered extensively in Chapter 9. The Knowledge Base stores one or more values for a given name. This name is a simple descriptive identifier for the data that it references. During the course of a Nessus scan, each target system is provided with its own individual KB. As each plugin obtains more information about the system, it will slowly populate the KB with data. Other plugins can access this data to information about a service, retrieve a password successfully guessed by another plugin, or set a flag stating that a certain patch has been applied.

The NASL API provides three functions for manipulating the Knowledge Base:

- **`set_kb_item(name:<name>, value:<value>)`** Creates the Knowledge Base entry specified by the "name" parameter, with the data specified in the "value" parameter. The value can be an integer, a string, or simple Boolean flag such as TRUE or FALSE. If a KB entry already exists for the specified name, both the old and new values are kept. Any given KB entry can have an indefinite number of values associated with it.

- **`get_kb_item(<name>)`** Retrieves the value of the KB entry specified by the "name" parameter. If the specified entry does not exist, this function will return NULL. If the specified entry has multiple values, the calling script will be executed multiple times, each time with a different return value for `get_kb_item()`.

- **`get_kb_list(<name>)`** Similar to `get_kb_item()`, except that instead of retuning a single value, it will return a list of matching values. Unlike `get_kb_item()`, this function will never result in the calling script being executed multiple times. The `get_kb_list()` function supports wildcards when specifying the entry name. For example, calling `get_kb_list("Services/*")` will return all the ports for which a service has been identified.

Summary

In this chapter, we discussed the beginnings of the NASL language, the original design requirements, and how the language has evolved to meet the challenges of modern vulnerability assessments. We then analyzed the structure of a NASL script and walked through the process of creating a new Nessus plugin from scratch. After reviewing many of the advanced features of the NASL language, we introduced the protocol libraries and how they can be used to develop robust Nessus plugins. Finally, we concluded the chapter with a brief review of the Knowledge Base and the NASL functions that are used to access it.

Solutions Fast Track

Why NASL?

- ☑ No existing scripting language met the requirements for Nessus plugins.
- ☑ Plugins written in C or Perl were unwieldy and could be a security risk.
- ☑ The NASL language was designed specifically for security testing.
- ☑ NASL scripts are self-contained and easy to update.
- ☑ The NASL interpreter code is clean and easy to extend.

Structure of a NASL Script

- ☑ NASL scripts are composed of two sections: the script description and the script body.
- ☑ The script description contains information about the script itself.
- ☑ The script body contains the NASL code that performs the vulnerability test.
- ☑ The Nessus engine uses the script description to manage the plugin set.

An Introduction to the NASL Language

- ☑ If you already know C, Perl, or PHP, learning NASL is straightforward.
- ☑ Complex network tests can be accomplished in only a few lines of code.
- ☑ NASL provides a wide range of string-matching and manipulation techniques.
- ☑ The NASL libraries encompass a wide range of complex network protocols.

The Nessus Knowledge Base

☑ Plugins communicate with each other by setting variables in the Knowledge Base.

☑ The Knowledge Base is only available when a script is launched by the Nessus engine.

☑ During a Nessus scan, each system has its own Knowledge Base.

Frequently Asked Questions

Q: What were the main reasons behind the development of the NASL language?

A: When the need for NASL was first realized, none of the current scripting languages met the requirements for virtual machine security, resource usage, and cross-platform support.

Q: You mention that the Nessus engine is not technically a vulnerability scanner; has anyone developed another use for the Nessus engine and NASL language?

A: Not at this time, but don't let this stop you if you want to be the first. Recent versions of Nessus now include the capability to access remote machines over the SSH protocol. This feature could be easily extended to allow remote patch deployment, network monitoring, and almost any other administration task, simply by creating a custom set of plugins. The NASL protocol libraries already have full access to the SMB protocol, allowing remote administration of Windows systems as well.

Q: At one point, the concept of "trusted" scripts was introduced. What are "trusted" NASL scripts?

A: In an effort to completely remove the old "C" plugins from Nessus, the development team has created a system that allows specific scripts to perform "dangerous" functions, such as system command execution. These scripts have a cryptographic signature placed at the very top of the file; if this signature is not verified against the official Nessus certificate, the plugin will not be allowed to access these dangerous functions. Trusted scripts will become much more common starting with Nessus 2.2. As of version 3.0.5 of Nessus, most of the core library plugins shipped are signed and considered trusted. They can be differentiated from a normal plugin by a large comment block at the top of the file starting with "#TRUSTED <long hex string>".

Q: The NASL protocol API section does not seem to be complete. Where can I obtain more information about the functions in the NASL libraries?

A: Please refer to the NASL reference in Appendix A of this book. The latest version of the NASL reference can be online, linked from the www.nesssus.org web site. A brief synopsis is included in the chapter, but an entire book could be written on just the APIs available in Nessus.

## Chapter 12

The Nessus User Community

Solutions in this chapter:

- **The Nessus Mailing Lists**

- **The Online Plug-In Database**

- **Reporting Bugs via Bugzilla**

- **Submitting Patches and Plug-Ins**

- **Where to Get More Information and Help**

☑ **Summary**

☑ **Solutions Fast Track**

☑ **Frequently Asked Questions**

Introduction

Nessus enjoys widespread support in the field of computer security today due in no small part to the work of its principal authors. However, design and coding excellence will only take a product only so far. What sets Nessus apart from other network vulnerability assessment tools is its openness and its user community.

With the transition to the 3.0 version series of Nessus, the Engine itself has been made a closed-source product, but the plugins are still readable. This allows the freedom for new plugins to be written or adapted by the user base. There has been some controversy with this move, but as of the writing of this book, this is the path that Nessus will take for the present.

Thanks to the continued openness of the plug-in library, anyone can browse the plug-ins source to learn how they work. Moreover, with the knowledge gained, anyone can contribute to the Nessus Project by adding features to and fixing problems in the existing plug-in base, deriving new plug-ins from existing ones, and developing third-party tools and resources.

Thanks to its user community, such contributions are indeed being made. For the older series (pre 3.0), in terms of software, you can currently find a Nessus client for Windows, several Web-based interfaces for configuring and managing scans, various tools for displaying and managing results, programming interfaces such as the Net::Nessus::ScanLite and Parse:: Nessus::NBE Perl modules, and a continuous stream of plug-ins; all authored by dozens of individuals and businesses not explicitly part of the Nessus Project. In terms of resources, The Nessus FAQ (available at http://www.nessus.org/plugins/index.php?view=faq) and Edgeos' Nessus Knowledge Base (available at http://www.edgeos.com/nessuskb/) have a wealth of knowledge to help users understand Nessus. The user community even contributes by simply submitting signatures for previously unidentified services in response to instructions in reports from the various fingerprinting plug-ins. This form of contribution alone has proven extremely valuable, for it has enabled Nessus to leapfrog its competition in the area of service fingerprinting.

The newer 3.0 series also have a full range of clients supported as of the writing of this book. They include Linux, FreeBSD, Solaris, Windows, and Mac OS X. It is important to note that a License to use Nessus is only required if the user required a current plugin feed. If a seven day delay is acceptable, then no plug-in feed license is needed. If you need to purchase a commercial plugin feed for Nessus, it can be obtained by contacting Tenable Network Security at http://www.tenablesecurity.com. The commercial Nessus license is recommended if you're conducting security scans for an organization, such as a company or non-profit, because the additional support and functionality can boost your internal security efforts tremendously.

In his paper entitled "Shoulders of Giants" (available at www.cyber.com.au/users/conz/ shoulders.html), Con Zymaris argues that open-source software will dominate competing paradigms. Essentially, open source allows a project to get a head start by avoiding the need to reinvent the wheel and to gather momentum more quickly through the free exchange of ideas.

Further, as a project grows to dominate its field, whatever paradigm it might follow, it tends to draw interest away from its competitors in a snowball effect.

Although the core engine for Nessus has become proprietary, the Plug-in base follows the more open source approach and retains the properties deemed so desirable by Con Zymaris' paper.

The Nessus Mailing Lists

The Nessus mailing lists are the primary means by which the user community interacts. There are four lists currently, as shown in Table 12.1. The signal-to-noise ratio for the three discussion lists is generally quite high. Their tone is professional and academic, not as collegial as, say, Snort users with its drinking game, but not full of flame wars either.

Table 12.1 Description of the Nessus Mailing Lists

List	Description
nessus	Discussions about all things Nessus.
nessus-announce	Announcements of new releases. Moderated.
nessus-devel	Discussions about software enhancements and fixes.
plugins-writers	Discussions about writing plug-ins and the NASL language.

Of the discussion lists, *nessus* is the most active, broadest in scope, and probably most useful to the average reader. Much of the traffic consists of questions and answers rather than actual discussions, and topics include Nessus and Nessus client front ends, the plug-ins, vulnerabilities themselves, third-party add-ons, and so forth. *Nessus-devel* tends to be much more discussion oriented, with the focus on revisions to Nessus and the NASL language. For example, past threads have focused on overhauling plug-in families and adding 64-bit support to Nessus. *plugins-writers* leans more toward questions and answers, generally how to accomplish something in NASL or whether plug-ins are properly testing for vulnerabilities. None of these lists has an actual charter, though, and in practice there's a fair amount of overlap among them, so don't worry too much about which list is the most appropriate. If you're still hesitant, browse the archives to get a better feel for each list's suitability.

All of the lists are operated using Mailman, a powerful and popular open-source mailing list management package. If you subscribe to other mailing lists on the Internet, chances are that you're already familiar with Mailman; if not, don't worry, since Mailman is tightly integrated with the Web. That is, you can subscribe to any of the mailing lists or access their archives by visiting http://list.nessus.org/ or http://mail.nessus.org - both of witch take you to the same place (see Figure 12.1).

Figure 12.1 Web Interface to the Nessus Mailing Lists

There are four mailing lists dedicated to Nessus :

> *nessus* : is a general discussion list about Nessus   [Subscribe] [Archives]
>
> *nessus-devel* : talks about the developement of the upcoming versions   [Subscribe] [Archives]
>
> *nessus-announce* : is a low traffic, moderated list, which is dedicated to the
> announce of the availability of new releases.   [Subscribe] [Archives]
>
> *plugins-writers* : is a list dedicated to the writing of new Nessus plugins. If you
> want to write your own checks, you should subscribe to it   [Subscribe] [Archives]

Done

Subscribing to a Mailing List

Mailman gives you the option of subscribing to one of the Nessus mailing lists either through a Web-based interface or via e-mail. Regardless of which method you choose, subscribing is a two-step process: First, you submit a request to subscribe, and then you confirm that request. After that, you should be added to a list automatically and receive a welcome message with general instructions for using the list and a list password that you will need to configure your list settings.

If you want to join the *nessus* mailing list, here's what you have to do:

> **NOTE**
>
> In the following examples, replace the final instance of *nessus* in the URLs and the leading instance in e-mail addresses with the name of the desired mailing list. Note that all of the Nessus mailing lists use lowercase names.

- If using the Web-based interface, point your Web browser to http://mail.nessus.org/mailman/listinfo/nessus. In the middle of the page is a form for subscribing. Enter your e-mail address, fill in the other fields as desired, and click Subscribe.

- If using e-mail, send a message to nessus-request@list.nessus.org, with the command *subscribe* as either the subject or the only line in the message body.

- In a short time you should receive an e-mail from Mailman asking you to confirm your request. Visit the link included in the e-mail or reply to it to do so.

Notes from the Underground...

Identifying Messages from the Nessus Mailing Lists

When delivering messages sent to any of the Nessus mailing lists, Mailman uses a special value for the SMTP envelope sender to facilitate bounce processing. Specifically, it appends the string *–bounces* to the address of the mailing list; for example, for *nessus* it's *nessus-bounces@list.nessus.org*. Further, mail transfer agents such as sendmail and postfix place the envelope sender in the Return-Path message header and use it in the UNIX From line.

You can take advantage of these two facts to white list messages sent to the Nessus mailing lists, have them bypass spam filters, or automatically filter them into separate folders. For example, the following procmail recipe will automatically file messages from any of the Nessus mailing lists into a folder named Nessus:

```
:0:
* ^Return-Path: .*-bounces\@list\.nessus\.org
Nessus
```

If you're using Outlook 2000/2002, you can achieve the same functionality by adding rules to filter on this header for each mailing list to which you've subscribed:

Continued

If the folder Nessus doesn't yet exist, select **File | New | Folder** to create it under your mailbox and click **OK** when finished.

1. Select Tools | Rules Wizard.
2. Click **New**.
3. If using Outlook 2002, make sure **Start from a blank rule** is selected.
4. Select **Check messages when they arrive** if it isn't already selected, and then click **Next**.
5. Check **with specific words in the message headers** (you might have to scroll down to see this option) and click on **specific words** under **Rule description** at the bottom.
6. Enter **Return-Path: nessus-bounces@list.nessus.org** in the textbox and click **OK**.
7. Click **Next**.
8. Check **move it to the specified folder** if necessary and click on **specified** in **Rule description** at the bottom.
9. Select the folder **Nessus**, and click **OK**.
10. Click **Finish**.
11. Click **OK**.

Mailman supports a number of options for message delivery. For example, you can choose to receive messages bundled as a single digest once a day, not receive your own postings, or disable delivery in the event you're away on vacation or are just too busy. Go to the Member Options page at http://mail.nessus.org/mailman/options/nessus, enter your list password, and click **Log in** to review or change these options. If you don't know your list password, click the **Remind** button to have Mailman send you your password. You can also use that link to unsubscribe from the mailing list. As before, you will need to confirm your request.

NOTE

Exercise care if you decide to change your list password: Mailman sends passwords out in the clear both in response to clicking the **Remind** button on the Member Options page and as part of a monthly reminder.

Sending a Message to a Mailing List

To send a message to one of the discussion lists, simply address it to the list name at list. nessus.org; for example, nessus@list.nessus.org. Shortly after Mailman receives it, the message will be redistributed to the list's subscribers based on their user settings. Currently, you do not need to subscribe in order to post a message to one of the Nessus mailing lists; however, messages from non-subscribers are held for review, which can result in significant delays.

Before you actually send your first message, review these general guidelines:

- If you're asking a question, check the Nessus FAQ (http://www.nessus.org/ plugins/index.php?view=faq) and search the list archives first. You might find the answer without having to wait for an answer or even subscribe to a list!

- Give your message an appropriate subject header. For example, a message with the subject "False positives with Printers and plugin 12345" has a better chance of attracting attention than a message entitled simply "Help."

- Start a new thread rather than posting a new question to an existing thread. People might have decided not to follow a particular thread, and this ensures that they don't miss your message.

- Use Bugzilla rather than the mailing lists to report bugs. It's okay, though, to post a message to a list to point people to your bug report to alert them to the problem if you think the problem is serious.

- Trim quoted text when replying to a message.

- Consider directing replies to the mailing list unless otherwise requested so that everyone has the option to participate in the thread and so that they'll appear in the archives. In addition, unless otherwise requested, do not CC posters too, since the lion's share on the Nessus mailing lists are themselves subscribers.

- If you are trying to manage your subscriptions using e-mail, append **–request** to the list's address (for example, for *nessus* it's nessus-request@list.nessus.org) and send your messages to that address.

- Don't send test messages to the list. If you need to send a message, just do so. Otherwise, if you haven't received messages for a while and are curious, check the list's archives. If people are indeed sending messages and you're not receiving them, visit the list's Member Options page (for example, http://mail.nessus.org/mailman/ options/nessus) and log in with your e-mail address and list password. You will see a notice at the top of the page that follows if Mailman has suspended your subscription for excessive bounces. If it has, follow the instructions Mailman provides to re-enable mail delivery after you've corrected any problems. Regardless, sending test messages will only aggravate other subscribers.

NOTE

By default, Mailman archives messages sent to the Nessus mailing lists, munging e-mail addresses of senders somewhat in an effort to foil spammers. Including a special header line in your messages—either **X- Archive: no** or **X- No-Archive: yes**—instructs Mailman to not archive your messages. Realize, though, that doing so reduces the value of the list's archives.

Accessing a List's Archives

Archives of every Nessus mailing list are currently available on the Web through mail. nessus.org. Access to the archives is open, even to various search engine robots and Web crawlers.

For example, to browse, the archives for *nessus*, point your Web browser to http://mail. nessus.org/pipermail/nessus/. For each month for which archives are available, you can view messages by date, subject, author, or thread, or retrieve the entire collection as a UNIX mbox file (see Figure 12.2).

Figure 12.2 Web Interface to the Nessus Mailing List Archives

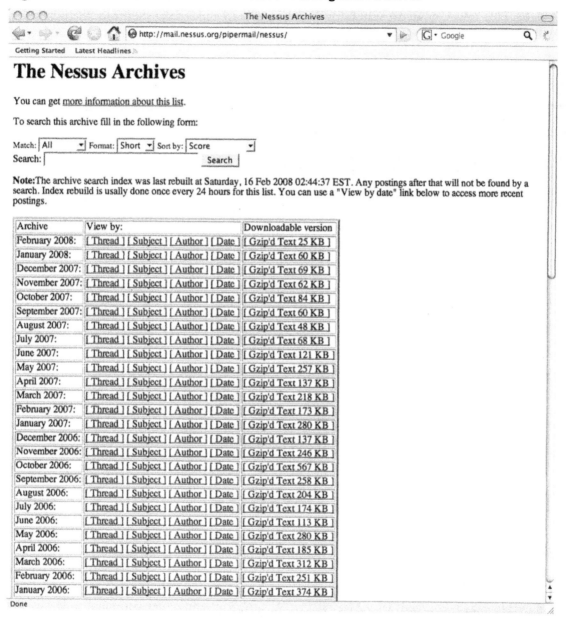

The mailing list archives on mail.nessus.org currently has a built-in search capability. While it searches the mailing list archives well enough, using Google to search the list archives can have the added benefit of Google's advanced page ranking system to locate commonly asked questions.

Searching Google with the inurl query modifier is a good way to limit queries to the mailing list site. For example, you could locate the announcement of version 2.0.10's release with the following query: `inurl:mail.nessus.org inurl:nessus-announce` `2.0.10`. This tells Google to search for the string *2.0.10* and restrict results to documents with both *mail.nessus.org* and *nessus-announce* in the URL.

Notes from the Underground...

Alternative Archives

Several other sites also archive one or more of the Nessus mailing lists; you can find them using a straightforward Web search. Two such sites deserve special recognition. Refer to them if the archives on nessus.org are temporarily unavailable or don't meet your needs.

- 10 East's Mailing list ARChives (MARC) service maintains archives of *nessus*, *nessus-announce*, and *nessus-devel* extending back nearly to the birth of Nessus and provides a view by thread within date as well as a search capability. Visit marc.theaimsgroup.com/?l=nessus (replace *nessus* with another list name if desired) to see the archives for the mailing list *nessus*.

- Gmane gateways several of the mailing lists both from and to Usenet newsgroups and offers access to them via NNTP and the Web. If you prefer to keep your mailbox uncluttered, refer to nntp://news.gmane.org/: gmane. comp.security.nessus.general is for *nessus*, gmane.comp.security.nessus. announce is for *nessus-announce*, and gmane.comp.security.nessus.devel is for *nessus-devel*.

The Online Plug-In Database

One of Nessus' strengths is its extensive and continually updated collection of plug-ins, over 20,548 as of February 2008. This sheer number, though, can lead to problems. For example, sometimes Nessus determines that a vulnerability exists, and you need to better understand how it arrived at that determination, perhaps because the system administrator of a supposedly vulnerable system contends it's a false positive. In addition, sometimes you need to learn which plug-in tests for a particular vulnerability, perhaps to help management assess the risks of the latest worm du jour.

The Online Plugin Database, available at cgi.nessus.org/plugins/, can help resolve such problems. It supports several means of access: view by plug-in family, view by popularity (determined by accesses to the Online Plugin Database and covering only plug-ins with a CVE ID, Bugtraq ID, or some other type of cross-reference), list recent additions, and search plug-ins by keyword.

Clicking on a plug-in's name or ID from any of these pages leads to an overview of that plug-in, including its family and description, cross-references if available, and even notes contributed by users. It also contains links to the plug-in's source (only if written in NASL), a list of plug-ins in the same family, and cross-references. See Figure 12.3 for an example.

Figure 12.3 Overview of a Plug-In

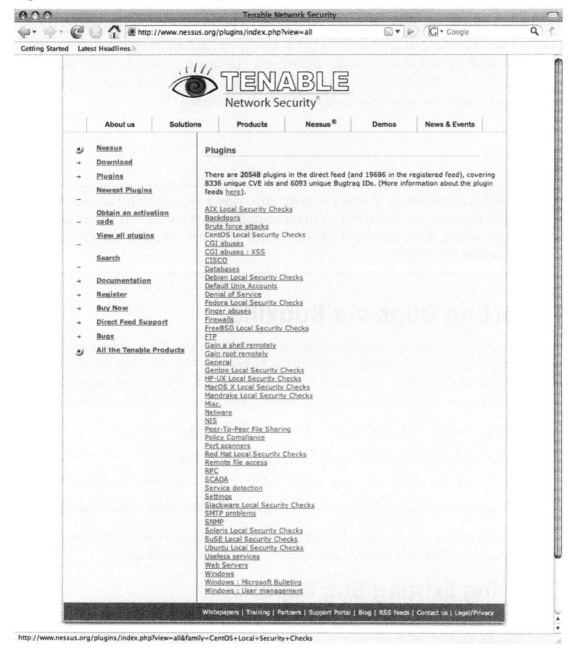

User-contributed notes are a relatively new feature, introduced in 2003. They are particularly interesting, as they can help users understand precisely how a plug-in operates, the vulnerabilities for which it tests, or steps to address those vulnerabilities. If you have a question or want to alert others about a particular plug-in, feel free to add a note.

Staying Abreast of New Plug-Ins

The Online Plugin Database offers two ways to learn about new Nessus plug-ins: a Web page at www.nessus.org/plugins/index.php?view=newest, and, for those who use a news aggregator, an RSS feed at www.nessus.org/rss.php. The first lets you select the most recent 10, 20, 40, or 80 additions, and the second shows only the most recent 20 plug-ins. In either case, you'll get a list of plug-ins and their descriptions.

NOTE

These resources list only new plug-ins; they don't say anything about changes in existing plug-ins. Thus, if you need to maintain a consistent set of plug-ins for your scans, don't blindly trust the output of either resource before running *nessus-update-plugins*.

Reporting Bugs via Bugzilla

The Nessus Project's Bug Tracker, located at bugs.nessus.org/, uses the popular Bugzilla software to track bugs (and enhancement requests) in Nessus, its associated plug-ins, the Nessus installer, NessusWX, and Web sites in the nessus.org domain. It offers several advantages compared to posting a message to one of the mailing lists or e-mailing someone directly:

- It ensures that your bug report will not be overlooked.
- It keeps you abreast of efforts to fix the problem through a series of e-mail alerts.
- It helps project developers coordinate and prioritize their efforts to address bugs.
- It reduces duplication of effort by serving as a reference for the user community.

So, if you think you've uncovered a bug in Nessus or a related product, first check with Bugzilla to see whether it's a known issue and, if not, report it using Bugzilla.

Querying Existing Bug Reports

Bugzilla provides two methods for searching bug reports: a simple *QuickSearch* and a general query. You can access both from the project's Bug Tracker homepage.

In a QuickSearch, Bugzilla treats search terms as case-insensitive substrings; for example, *nasl* matches reports containing the strings *NASL* and *libnasl*, as well as *nasl* itself. By default, a QuickSearch covers only unresolved bugs, although you can extend the search to all bugs by prefixing the query with the word *ALL* (must be uppercase). Finally, if you enter a bug number as the only search term, Bugzilla will return the corresponding bug report in its entirety. To perform a QuickSearch, enter a search term or two in the form at the lower left of the page, and then click **Show**. For example, Figure 12.4 illustrates how you might perform a QuickSearch for unresolved bug reports of Nessus bugs containing the term "bug".

Figure 12.4 A QuickSearch

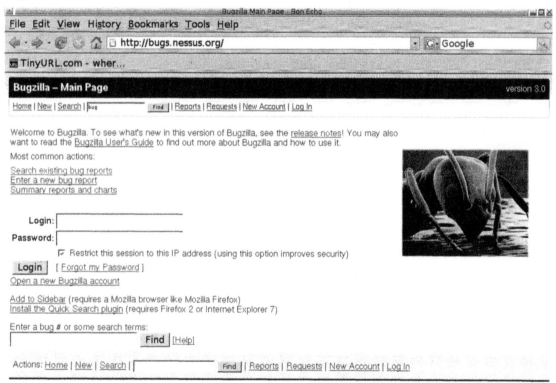

In a general query, you have a large degree of control over the search: you can select from a wide variety of search methods (for example: substrings, whole words, regular expressions, and case-sensitive), limit the fields in which the terms occur, and even restrict results by date. To perform a general query, click the link labeled **Search existing bug reports** and fill out the form that follows as desired. For example, Figure 12.5 illustrates how you might fill out the form to perform a general query similar to the earlier QuickSearch but limited to only those bugs affecting the UNIX-based nessus client.

If you find this form daunting, you can generally obtain good results by just entering your search terms in the **Summary** field and clicking **Search**.

Figure 12.5 A General Query

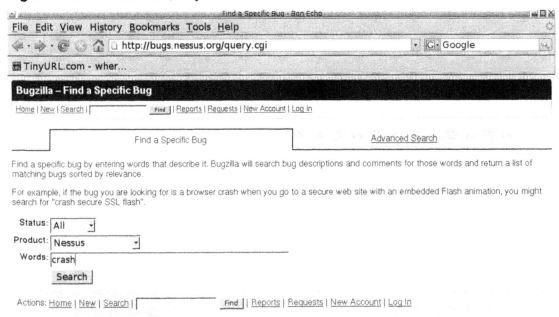

If any entries match your query, you will see a list, as in Figure 12.6. Click on the bug **ID** to view the report in detail.

Figure 12.6 Query Results (trimmed image)

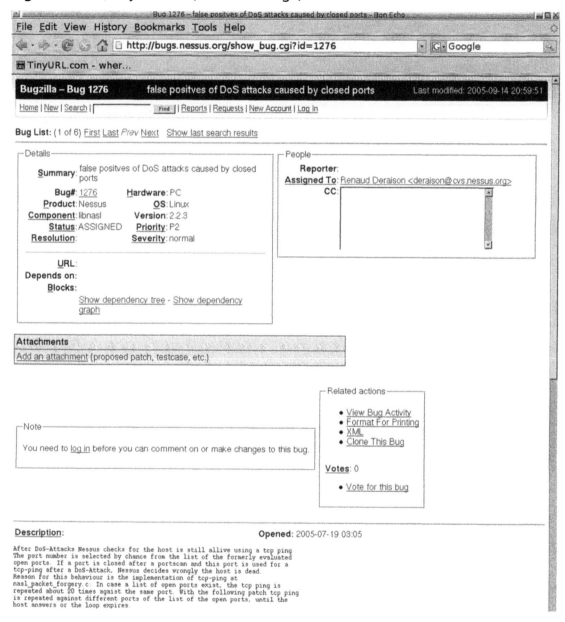

Creating and Logging In to a Bugzilla Account

While you can query Bugzilla anonymously, you must log in to a Bugzilla account to report a new bug or update an existing one. To create an account, visit bugs.nessus.org/createaccount.cgi and enter your e-mail address (see Figure 12.7).

Figure 12.7 Bugzilla Account Creation

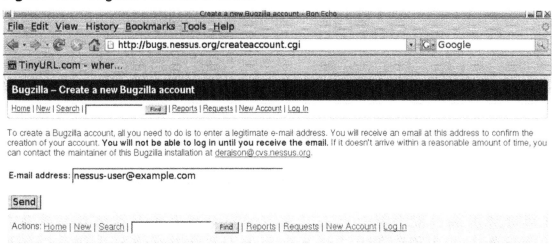

Bugzilla will create the account and send you an e-mail with your login name (typically your e-mail address) and a randomly generated password. After this, you can change your account password or preferences using the form at http://bugs.nessus.org/userprefs.cgi.

NOTE

As currently configured, bugs.nessus.org does not accept Web traffic encrypted with SSL. Exercise care if you decide to change your Bugzilla account password.

To log in to your Bugzilla account, visit bugs.nessus.org/query.cgi?GoAheadAndLogIn=1 or click on the **Log In** action at the bottom of any of Bug Tracker's pages. Bugzilla uses cookies for authentication, so make sure your browser is configured to accept them, at least from bugs.nessus.org. Enter your e-mail address (or account name, if different) and password, and then click **Login**. (If you have forgotten your password, you can fill out a form in the middle of the page to submit a Change Password Request.) Once you've authenticated, Bugzilla will display the general query page.

Tools & Traps...

Cookies

By default, the cookies that Bugzilla uses for authentication last, for all practical purposes, indefinitely; even across machine reboots. This can be a problem when accessing Bugzilla from a shared machine. To have a browser forget those cookies, visit bugs.nessus.org/relogin.cgi or click on the **Log out** action at the base of any of Bug Tracker's pages. This link appears only if you're actually logged in.

Submitting a Bug Report

Let's suppose you uncover a bug and search Bugzilla only to determine that you're the first to come across the issue. You understand that the best approach is to report the bug through Bugzilla—but how do you do it?

Before you submit a bug report, first verify that the bug is reproducible and then try to narrow it down. For example, if nessusd appears to hang during a scan, examine the process list to see if there is a common set of plug-ins running and look at the *nessusd* message log to see which targets are in the process of being scanned. Now, rerun the scan. If it completes successfully, take note of the problem but don't submit a bug report; just chalk up the earlier hang to sunspots, user error, or the like. If it hangs a second time, check again which plug-ins and targets are active. If they are the same, examine the plug-ins or targets themselves for issues you might not have been aware of earlier. Perhaps you had selected a UDP scan with a large port list (such scans can take up to 24 hours per host). Perhaps the targets aren't real, but merely part of a LaBrea tarpit (enable plug-in #10796, *scan for LaBrea tarpitted hosts*, to detect such hosts and flag them as dead). Even if you are unable to solve the problem yourself, your efforts will mean a higher quality bug report. Now you're ready to use Bugzilla:

1. Log in to your Bugzilla account as just described.

2. Click **Enter new bug report** at the base of the Query page or go to **bugs.nessus.org/enter_bug.cgi**.

3. Select which product the bug affects. The choices are:

   ■ **Nessus** nessusd, the UNIX-based nessus client, plug-ins, and the like.

   ■ **NessusClient** the nessus client, for any platform.

- **nessus–installer** The stand-alone installation script for Nessus.

- **NessusWX** A Nessus client for Windows.

- **www.nessus.org** Web sites in the nessus.org domain.

4. Enter information about the bug in the form that follows; see Figures 12.8a and 12.8b. Choose the appropriate values from the list boxes, especially the Component field, and enter a helpful summary and description. (Note that Bugzilla automatically fills in the Platform and OS fields based on your browser. You might have to change them; for example, if you're using a desktop PC running Windows to report a problem with nessusd.)

5. Click the **Commit** button at the bottom of the form to file the bug report. If everything goes okay, Bugzilla will show you a copy of your bug report.

6. Add an attachment (for example, process trace, log segments, patches, and so forth) while viewing the bug report, if appropriate.

If you also want to announce your discovery (for example, if it involves unexpected and dangerous behavior), send a message to one of the mailing lists and be sure to point people to your bug report.

Figure 12.8a A New Bug Report

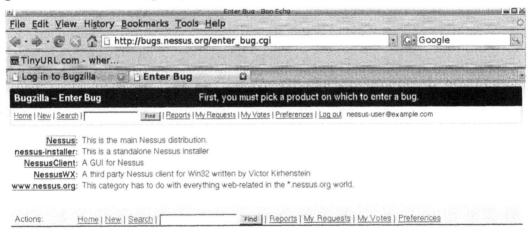

Figure 12.8b A New Bug Report (Continued)

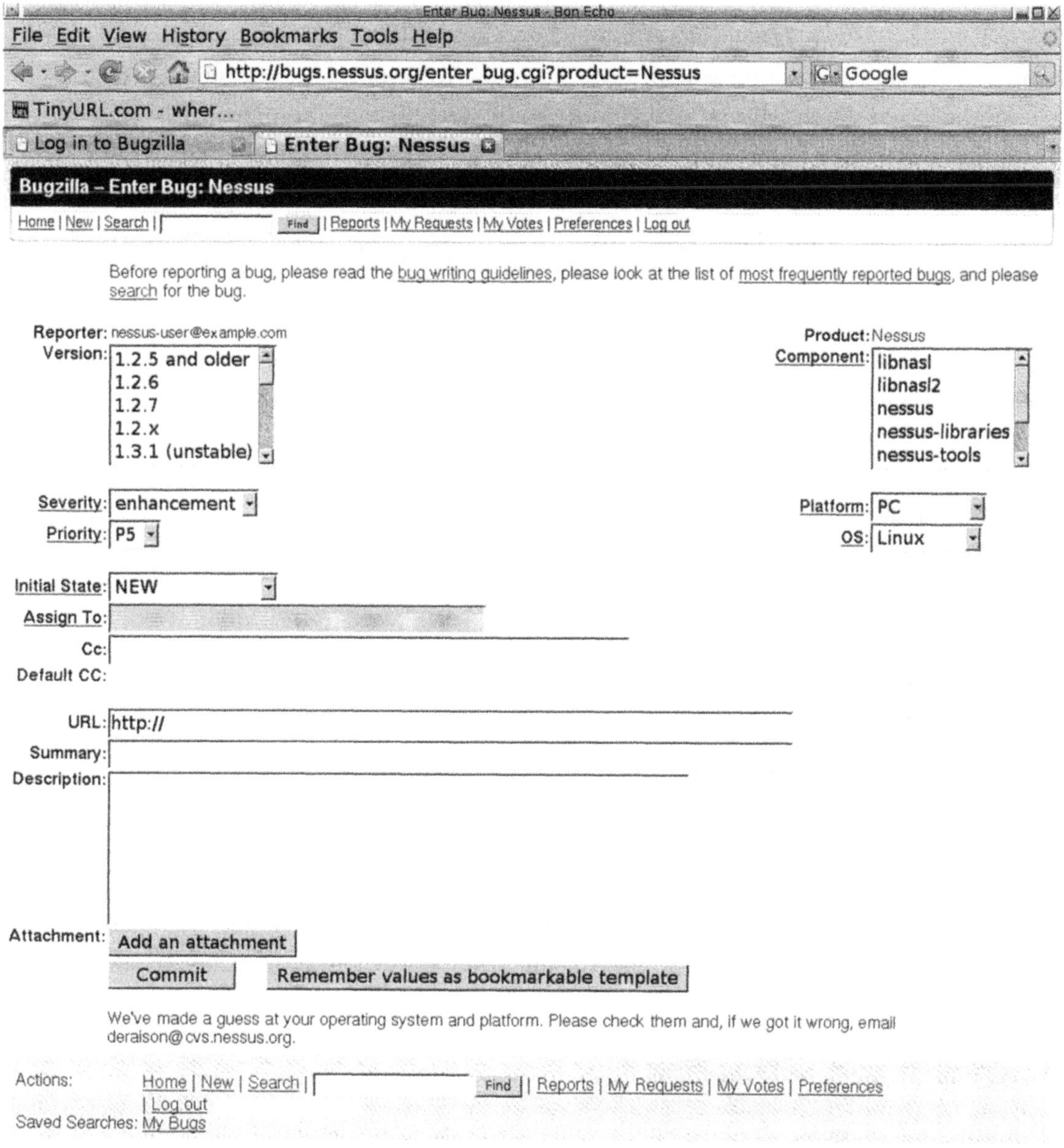

It's important that you include as many details in your report as you think are appropriate and be as specific as possible. It's also important that you limit your report to relevant details. Put yourself in the shoes of the person who will be addressing your report. What exactly does he or she need in order to replicate the problem? Is there anything special about your installation? If you need help, refer to the general Bug Writing Guidelines, available at bugs. nessus.org/bugwritinghelp.html.

Bugzilla will notify you by e-mail once it has filed your initial bug report and every time the report is changed, until it is eventually closed. Occasionally, the person handling your report will add a comment to your report requesting additional information, which will result in another e-mail from Bugzilla. To respond, log in to your Bugzilla account and add comments or attach files while viewing the bug report. You can also do this if you simply learn something new about a bug, or even if you weren't the one to file it.

Submitting Patches and Plug-Ins

Throughout the project's history, many individuals and companies have written enhancements and plug-ins for their own purposes and then contributed them to the project. Renaud Deraison, the project leader, estimates that third parties have been responsible for around 30 percent of the plug-ins written during the past two years.

You don't have to be a programming whiz to contribute in this fashion, though; even simple editorial patches will improve the quality of Nessus. For example, if you notice while browsing a plug-in that one of the CVE IDs is wrong, you could submit a patch that corrects it. In addition, if you feel the documentation is lacking in some fashion, you could rewrite it and submit that as an enhancement request.

Contributing is what matters, however your skill level, interests, and time allow.

Submitting Patches

As of the 3.0.5 version of Nessus, the engine does not have public source code. The plug-ins and clients, do still have publicly available source. As such, you can, and should, use Bugzilla to point out issues with Nessus; for example, bugs or shortcomings, the documentation, any of the plug-ins, or even in the project's Web sites. Renaud and others on the project team will address them as resources allow. You can help the process by including patches to the existing code in your bug report or enhancement request whenever possible. Be sure to use unified diff format (diff -u …) against the most current release.

Submitting Plug-Ins

With the large number of vulnerabilities uncovered on a daily basis, it should come as no surprise that plug-ins do not exist for every vulnerability. If you need a certain plug-in but one doesn't exist, we encourage you to write your own (see Chapter 11) and contribute it to the user community.

When writing your plug-in, you might find it convenient to use an existing plug-in as a template. This is indeed a common practice—Renaud estimates that 90 percent of plug-ins currently are derived in some fashion from others. Post a message to plugins-writers if you need help or want to see if someone else is working on a similar plug-in.

Once you've written and tested your plug-in, e-mail it directly to Renaud at deraison@ nessus.org. Use a value such as **99999** for the script ID to avoid confusion. Renaud will review your contribution and add it to the plug-in database, at which point, others will get it when they next run *nessus-update-plugins*.

Where to Get More Information and Help

The Nessus Web site is a good starting point for more information on Nessus. Two sections are of particular interest: Documentation (www.nessus.org/documentation/) and Plug-Ins (http:// www.nessus.org/plugins/index.php?view=newest). Be sure visit the mailing list archives, under Documentation as they contain a wealth of knowledge. And the section entitled Plug-Ins offers a great deal of information on the actual work horse components of Nessus.

The Nessus FAQ, available at www.nessus.org/plugins/index.php?view=faq, is another excellent source of information. Thanks to a facelift in late 2006, the Nessus FAQ offers a collection of questions and answers and a form to comment on existing answers.

If you're interested in information about configuration settings in the Nessus client or server components, visit The Nessus Knowledge Base at www.edgeos.com/nessuskb/. There you will find information about every option and configuration variable in both the Nessus client and server. Note that the configuration files sections do not cover the 3.0.5 and later ~/.nessus-client/Policies.xml configuration files, but many of the options use the same keywords, but are kept in an XML format.

In some cases, the user-contributed notes in the Online Plugin Database (cgi.nessus.org/ plugins/) offer valuable insight into plug-ins and their corresponding vulnerabilities.

Finally, if all else fails, post a question to the *nessus* mailing list. Many bright and helpful people on the list would be happy to help you.

Summary

The user community forms an active and important part of the Nessus Project. By submitting bug reports, enhancement requests, and new plug-ins, and developing third-party tools, the user community improves the quality of the project. In addition, through resources such as the mailing lists, user-contributed comments in the Online Plugin Database, and the Nessus FAQ, the user community serves as an educator, enriching and expanding the user community. We hope that through this chapter, and indeed this entire book, we have provided you with the knowledge you need so that you too can join the community if you're not already a part of it and help make Nessus even better than it is today.

Solutions Fast Track

The Nessus Mailing Lists

☑ Five mailing lists: *nessus* (general discussion about Nessus), *nessus-announce* (announcements of new releases), *nessus-devel* (discussions about upcoming versions of Nessus), and *plugins-writers* (discussions about writing plug-ins).

☑ Subscribe or view archives at http://list.nessus.org/.

☑ Include **X-Archive: No** header to prevent message archival.

The Online Plug-In Database

☑ Access the database at http://cgi.nessus.org/plugins/.

☑ There are several methods for viewing plug-ins: by family, recent releases, or popularity. You can also search for strings in names, descriptions, summaries, references, and the like.

☑ The RSS feed at www.nessus.org/rss.php lets you track plug-in additions.

☑ Follow links in the plug-in overview to read references to associated CVE entries, Bugtraq IDs, and the like.

☑ User-contributed notes might accompany plug-in overviews to improve understanding of a plug-in or the vulnerabilities for which it tests.

Reporting Bugs via Bugzilla

☑ Bugzilla is available via the Web at http://bugs.nessus.org/.

☑ Bugzilla handles both bug reports and enhancement requests.

☑ Entries cover Nessus and its plug-ins, the Nessus installer, NessusWX, and nessus.org.

☑ Search terms in a QuickSearch are case-insensitive substrings.

☑ You must create an account to enter a new bug report or to update existing ones.

☑ E-mail messages track activity.

Submitting Patches and Plug-Ins

☑ Contribute in whatever way you can; code and editorial changes are both of value.

☑ Submit patches as part of a Bugzilla bug report or enhancement request.

☑ Use existing plugins as templates when writing new ones.

☑ Email plugins directly to Renaud Deraison: deraison@nessus.org.

Where to Get More Information and Help

☑ For guidance on configuring and running scans, see the Documentation section of the Nessus Web site at www.nessus.org/documentation.html.

☑ For general queries, consult the *nessus* mailing list and its archives along with the Nessus FAQ at http://www.nessus.org/plugins/index.php?view=faq.

☑ For configurable settings in the Nessus client and server, browse The Nessus Knowledge Base at www.edgeos.com/nessuskb/.

☑ For insight into plug-ins and their corresponding vulnerabilities, view the user-contributed notes in the Online Plugin Database at http://cgi.nessus.org/plugins/.

Frequently Asked Questions

Q: Where can I find a list of tools that work with Nessus?

A: Unfortunately, there is no definitive list of such tools. The Nessus FAQ (http://www.nessus.org/plugins/index.php?view=faq) is a good place to start, post a query to one of the mailing lists, or use your favorite Web search engine.

Q: I posted a question to one of the mailing lists, but no one responded. Should I resend it?

A: First, visit the list's archives to verify whether the message actually made it to the mailing list. Understand that mail is a batch process, and delays up to several days are possible. In addition, realize that mail from non-subscribers is moderated, a process that might take several days. If your message has yet to appear, wait a week before resending. If it is available in the archives, give readers plenty of time to respond. History shows that few questions on the mailing lists go unanswered completely, but some responses come after a week or more. Posting your question repeatedly in a short period of time does little to convince readers of your message's importance—and much to aggravate them.

Q: I stopped receiving messages from one of the mailing lists. What happened?

A: Use your e-mail address and list password to log in to the list's Member Options page (for example, http://mail.nessus.org/mailman/options/nessus). If your subscription is disabled, you will see a notice at the top of the page along with an explanation as to why. One likely cause is that Mailman received a number of consecutive bounces after sending messages to you; once a preset limit (typically seven) is reached, Mailman disables your subscription and sends you a note. These bounces generally indicate a problem with your mail server (you might have exceeded your mail quota, for example), so investigate the problem on that end first.

Q: How can I learn more about composing queries in Bug Tracker?

A: Visit www.mozilla.org/bugs/text-searching.html.

Q: I tried searching Bugzilla for a bug that I know exists, but I can't find it. Why?

A: Searches by default cover only unresolved bugs. If you can't find an entry you know exists, make sure you're searching all bugs. If doing a QuickSearch, prefix your query with the word *ALL*; in a general query, you must select all the values in the Status field.

Q: Why hasn't a bug I reported two weeks ago been fixed?

A: Before you complain too loudly, first make sure that the problem is not on your end. Check the bug report in Bugzilla to make sure someone has not requested additional information. While Bugzilla would have sent you an e-mail of such a request, understand that mail is sometimes lost, and that ultimately the responsibility to respond lies with you. If there aren't any requests and the bug is serious, you might send the person to whom it was assigned a gentle reminder by e-mail; otherwise, be patient, and use your time to pinpoint the problem and develop a fix for it.

## Chapter 13

Compliance Monitoring with Nessus 3

Solutions in this chapter:

- **What is Compliance?**
- **The Nessus 3 Compliance Engine**
- **Using Nessus 3 Compliance**
- **Nessus 3 Reporting**

☑ **Summary**

☑ **Solutions Fast Track**

☑ **Frequently Asked Questions**

Introduction

Over the span of the last 5 to 6 years, compliance with security regulations has become more of a hot button issue to organizations that operate on the Internet. Initially, the various legislation and regulations provided more guidance than steadfast requirements. But as the area of compliance has evolved and become more mature, organizations are slowly being pressed into understanding and complying with these regulations. This chapter will lead the reader through a discussion about some of these security standards and show how the reader can use Nessus 3 to help monitor and ensure compliance within their own organization.

Understanding Compliance

So, what are we talking about when we refer to compliance? When the Internet began to be used for legitimate business in the 1990's, there wasn't as much concern about the security of servers or transactions. In fact, looking back now, it's a bit frightening to consider how many servers were possibly compromised during those emerging years.

Somewhere around the year 2000, however, people started to realize just how dangerous it would be to lose all that information that was being stored and transmitted across the Internet. These "visionaries", as it were, sat down and created the first documents recommending a variety of security policies, processes, and configurations.

However, a quick look through the news archives since the year 2000 will show that a good number of organizations failed to embrace the importance of these recommendations, resulting in loss of sensitive or private information from customers, employees, or the company itself. This is where compliance comes into the picture. The governing organizations realized the need to create enforceable regulations in a variety of industries. This was the birth of a number of regulations, such as HIPAA, FERPA, GLBA, NERC, PCI and ISO 17799. But even with all of these great strides towards compliance, only recently have we seen progress towards actually enforcing these regulations and follow through with punitive action for those organizations that fail to comply.

Table 13.1 shows examples of the regulations and legislation in a variety of industries. It should not, however, be considered an exhaustive list. The detailed discussion of every available regulation is beyond the scope of this chapter.

Table 13.1 Example Security Guidelines and Regulations

Industry	Compliance Documents	Web Page
Healthcare Industry	HIPAA	http://www.hhs.gov/ocr/hipaa/
Financial	PCI Compliance	https://www.pcisecuritystandards.org/
Education	FERPA	http://www.ed.gov/policy/gen/guid/fpco/ferpa/index.html
Utility/Public Service	NERC	http://www.nerc.com/
International	ISO27002:2005	http://www.iso.org/iso/home.htm
Federal Government	NIST 800 Series, FIPS documents	http://csrc.nist.gov/

HIPAA

The Health Insurance Portability and Accountability Act (HIPAA) was released in August of 1996 by Congress to improve the efficiency and effectiveness of the health care system in the United States. As part of HIPAA, privacy and security rules were included, providing guidance for the protection of private and sensitive patient information. HIPAA provides only the most general of guidance and does not include technical details concerning the implementation of hardware and software.

Payment Card Industry (PCI)

The payment card industry, or PCI, is the term used to describe organizations that process all types of payment cards, including credit cards, debit cards, ATM cards, and pre-paid cards. On September 7th, 2006, the PCI Security Standards Council was created by American Express, Visa, MasterCard, Discover, and the Japan Credit Bureau in order to manage and maintain the PCI Data Security Standard (DSS). The DSS provides requirements to organizations that process payment cards for providing secure transmission and storage of customer information before, during, and after a transaction occurs.

FERPA

The Family Educational Rights and Privacy Act is not actually a recent developed, as it was turned into law in 1974. The real goal of FERPA was to protect student information from unauthorized disclosure or use. But over time, as technology as evolved, security pendants have started using it as a basis for technological security requirements wherever student information is stored or transmitted.

NERC

The North American Electric Reliability Corporation (NERC) was created as a non-profit organization in 1968 to provide guidance on how to ensure the reliability of all interconnected power systems in the United States, as well as parts of Canada and Mexico. NERC standards include penalties to power organizations that fail to comply, including the security of those systems.

ISO/IEC 27002:2005

ISO/IEC 27002:2005 was originally released by the International Standards Organization as ISO17799 and subsequently renumbered in July of 2007. This document provides guidance at an International level about the security requirements of information systems. 27002:2005 is thought to be the best International guide on best practices for risk assessment, security policy, access control, and more.

NIST 800 Series

The National Institute of Standards and Technology (NIST) provides guidance to the Federal Government on a number of subjects, including information security. The publication series we're most interested in is the 800 series, which address information security, specifically. This series was established in 1990, but the latest document to be released at the time of this publication is the DRAFT version of 800-115, which addresses Information Security Testing.

WARNING

It should be noted that these documents are constantly being updated, and eventually retired, over time. Professionals in the field of information security should continue monitoring their evolution to ensure they're addressing every possible requirement.

The Nessus Compliance Engine

If you've been working in the information security arena for any time at all, you've probably already heard of Nessus. For years, Nessus has been one of the foremost vulnerability scanners available to professionals. The best part about the software was that it was free. But, as good as the tool has been over the years, it received a well deserved makeover and re-writes several years ago when its author teamed up with Tenable Network Security to improve performance and functionality. Part of that evolution includes the implementation of a compliance engine that allows users to verify that their systems meet the requirements set in place by their governing bodies, regardless of the industry.

Compliance with Nessus

When we discuss compliance in its most general sense, we're talking about how a system meets certain requirements on how that system should be configured. As we read previously in this chapter, the exact configuration requirements can vary from regulation to regulation. Tenable has created a mechanism within the Nessus software that allows you to test against any compliance requirements you need. This works regardless of the operating system in question.

To best serve the needs of its users, Tenable created a text-based functionality that allows users to create their own configuration check files. In addition, Tenable provides users of its Direct Feed service with access to a variety of these files that correspond to the regulations and requirements from a variety of industries. Regardless of whether the user chooses to create their own configuration check file, or use one provided by Tenable or another source, the basic format is in a .audit file.

Types of audits

Nessus compliance audits come in two basic flavors, configuration checks and content checks. The configuration checks are what most people think of when considering a host audit. For example, if you work in a government agency and fall under the NIST security requirements, then you want to ensure your servers meet the configuration guidelines set forth in the NIST 800 series of requirements. Content checks perform a search on the target host looking for specific types of content, per your requirements. As an example of this type of audit, consider the healthcare industry, which is required by law to protect private patient information. We could easily perform a content audit of the target host to search for any files that contain a social security number, or other personally identifiable information.

TIP

Bear in mind that you are not limited to only one type of audit. You can quite easily perform both configuration and content checks on the same targets at the same time using Nessus 3, easing the audit process by allowing you to utilize a single tool for vulnerability scans, configuration checks, and content searches.

Tenable Security currently offers a wide variety of content audit policies that can be utilized with your Nessus 3 software. Before you go and create your own, check with their support portal to see if you can save some valuable time by using an already existing file. Some of the content audit policies available in the support portal at the time of publication include:

- Adult Media

- Corporate Confidential Information

- Employee Identification Number

- Employee Salary List

- Financial Statements

- Source Code Leakage

- Credit Card Numbers, and

- Social Security Numbers

.audit Files

.audit files within Nessus are completely flexible and can contain and many or as few configuration checks as a user finds necessary. In addition, the .audit file should be operating system specific, depending on the platform being tested. You can use the provided .audit files from Tenable Security (plugins-customers.nessus.org/support-center/), or you can create your own.

Once you learn the format of the .audit files, you can easily create your own checks. Use the examples from the Tenable Security Support Portal for an idea on how to create them yourself. Tenable also provides several tools to create .audit files. The Configuration-to-Audit tool, or c2a, parses a text configuration file and creates a Nessus 3 compliant .audit file. The c2a tool is useful for UNIX systems.

The second tool is the Windows Nessus Policy Creator, or WNPC. The WNPC can be run on an already configured Windows system to create an .audit file based on that configuration. If you've already gone through the trouble of configuring a Windows server to meet specific configuration requirements, you can use this tool to create .audit file and save yourself some work on your remaining Windows systems. Both of these tools are available from the Tenable Security support portal to subscribers of the Direct Feed and Security Center services.

Figure 13.1 Tenable Security Support Portal

Customer Support

Main Menu	**Currently Not Logged In**
🏠 Home	A feature on this page may require that you log in to the Support Center. To log in, please enter your login details in the box to the left.
Login	Please note the following dates and hours for Tenable Customer Support.
E-mail: [ ]	<u>Monday through Friday, 9:00 AM to 5:00 PM EST</u>
Password: [ ]	Tenable will be closed during the following observed holidays for 2007 and the beginning of 2008:
[Log in]	**Monday - September 3**
<u>Forgot Password /</u> <u>Activate Account?</u>	**Monday - October 8** **Thursday - November 22** **Friday - November 23** **Monday - December 24** **Tuesday - December 25** **Monday - December 31** **Tuesday - January 1**
Knowledgebase	
Search by keywords: [ ]	If you are not a Tenable customer but are looking for Support for Nessus, please see the following URL's for assistance:
[Find]	<u>Nessus Mailing List</u> <u>Other Nessus Mail Lists</u> <u>Nessus Documentation</u> <u>Security Center, LCE, PVS & Nessus Training</u>

An image of the Tenable Security Support Portal is shown is Figure 13.1. At the time of publication, Tenable offers a variety of .audit files. For example, audit files are available for Linux, UNIX, and Windows, as well as files for NIST regulations, DISA requirements, Center for Internet Security (CIS) guidelines, SANS checks, and PCI audits.

Tools & Traps...

Custom or Off-The-Shelf

If you're the security administrator for a large organization, you're probably trying to decide whether it's best to use the .audit files provided by Tenable Security or whether you should just create your own. Unless you have very specific needs that vary dramatically

Continued

from the majority of standards and regulations already supported by Nessus, you're probably better off using the ones they've already provided to you. At the very least, if you review the files they have available and you find discrepancies, you can always just add what you need to their files. This could very well save you time and headaches since they've already done most of the work for you. If, however, you're one of those few organizations that has very specific requirements (the military is a good example of this), then you may have no choice than to create a custom .audit file.

How .audit Files Work

.audit files are created using plaintext and contain a formatted command structure reminiscent of XML or HTML. At the top of the file, we tell the Nessus 3 audit engine what type of checks we've included in the .audit file. This is done via the *check_type* statement. Here are two examples of this statement:

```
<check_type: "Unix">
<check_type: "Windows">
<check_type: "WindowsFiles">
```

The commands and directives for a Windows .audit file are very different than those in a UNIX .audit file. By using the *check_type* statement, we're telling Nessus 3 which set of directives will be used within the .audit file. The *UNIX* and *Windows* statements tell Nessus 3 that we're checking compliance on that particular operating system. However, the format of the .audit files for compliance checks and content checks are very similar, and the designation *WindowsFiles* tells Nessus 3 that we're going to check for content within the files on the hard drive.

Examples

Let's look at some examples of .audit files and dissect their actual format. Please keep in mind that there are literally hundreds of potential compliance checks for each operating system. The examples shown here are not intended to provide a comprehensive list, but instead to show you what's possible.

First, let's look at an example of a Windows oriented .audit file (Figure 13.2).

Figure 13.2 Example Windows .audit Format

```
# Copyright 2007 Tenable Network Security Inc.
# Version 1.0
<check_type : "Windows">
<group_policy: "CIS Domain Controller Enterprise">
# 2.1.1 Minimum Password Length: 8 Characters
<custom_item>
```

```
type: PASSWORD_POLICY
description: "2.1.1 Minimum Password Length: 8 Characters"
value_type: POLICY_DWORD
value_data: 8
password_policy: MINIMUM_PASSWORD_LENGTH
</item>

# 2.1.2 Maximum Password Age: 90 Days
<custom_item>
type: PASSWORD_POLICY
description: "2.1.2 Maximum Password Age: 90 Days"
value_type: TIME_DAY
value_data: 90
password_policy: MAXIMUM_PASSWORD_AGE
</item>

# 2.2.1.1 Audit Account Logon Events Success and Failure
<custom_item>
type: AUDIT_POLICY
description: "2.2.1.1 Audit Account Logon Events: Success and Failure"
value_type: AUDIT_SET
value_data: "Success, Failure"
audit_policy: AUDIT_ACCOUNT_LOGON
</item>

# 2.2.1.2 Audit Account Management: Success and Failure
<custom_item>
type: AUDIT_POLICY
description: "2.2.1.2 Audit Account Management: Success and Failure"
value_type: AUDIT_SET
value_data: "Success, Failure"
audit_policy: AUDIT_ACCOUNT_MANAGER
</item>

# 2.2.1.4 Audit Logon Events: Success and Failure
<custom_item>
type: AUDIT_POLICY
description: "2.2.1.4 Audit Logon Events: Success and Failure"
value_type: AUDIT_SET
value_data: "Success, Failure"
audit_policy: AUDIT_LOGON
</item>
```

Now let's look at an example for Red Hat Linux. Again, these examples were provided by Tenable Network Security. If possible, we highly recommend that you subscribe to their Security Center or Direct Feed products since they'll provide you with most of the .audit files you could possibly require. Figure 13.3 provides a Linux example.

Figure 13.3 Linux .audit Example

```
# (C) 2007 Tenable Network Security
# Last Modified: 08/16/07
# Version: 1.0.1
<check_type:"Unix">
<custom_item>
        #System         : "Linux"
        type            : FILE_CONTENT_CHECK_NOT
        description     : "1.2 Validate Your System Before Making Changes, should
                          pass /var/log/* do not contain any files with error,
                          warning or critical messages."
        file            : "/var/log/*"
        regex           : "(error|warning|critical|alert)"
        expect          : "(error|warning|critical|alert)"
</custom_item>

# 1.3 Configure SSH
<custom_item>
        #System         : "Linux"
        type            : FILE_CONTENT_CHECK
        description     : "1.3 Configure SSH - Check if Protocol is set to 2 and
                          not commented for client"
        file            : "/etc/ssh/ssh_config"
        regex           : ".*Protocol*"
        expect          : "^[^#]* *Protocol 2"
</custom_item>

<custom_item>
        #System         : "Linux"
        type            : FILE_CONTENT_CHECK
        description     : "1.3 Configure SSH - Check if X11Forwarding is set to
                          yes and not commented for server"
        file            : "/etc/ssh/sshd_config"
        regex           : ".*X11Forwarding*"
        expect          : "^[^#]* *X11Forwarding yes"
</custom_item>
```

```
<custom_item>
        #System          : "Linux"
        type             : FILE_CONTENT_CHECK
        description      : "1.3 Configure SSH - Check if IgnoreRhosts is set to yes
                           and not commented for server"
        file             : "/etc/ssh/sshd_config"
        regex            : ".*IgnoreRhosts*"
        expect           : "^[^#]* *IgnoreRhosts yes"
</custom_item>
<custom_item>
        #System          : "Linux"
        type             : FILE_CONTENT_CHECK
        description      : "1.3 Configure SSH - Check if RhostsAuthentication is
                           set to no and not commented for server"
        file             : "/etc/ssh/sshd_config"
        regex            : ".*RhostsAuthentication*"
        expect           : "^[^#]* *RhostsAuthentication no"
</custom_item>
```

Up until now, we've concentrated primarily on the actual configuration settings within the operating systems. But earlier we mentioned that there are actually two slightly different types of compliance checks we can perform with Nessus 3. The second type of check is based on content. The example provided in Figure 13.4 shows how we can scan the files on a system for content related to salary information of the employees of the organization.

Figure 13.4 Compliance Content Check: Salary Information

```
# Copyright 2007 Tenable Network Security Inc.
# This policy looks for Excell and Adobe files that are likely to
# contain spread sheets holding employee salary figures.
# Updated : March 28, 2007
<check_type : "WindowsFiles">

<item>
      type: FILE_CONTENT_CHECK
      description: "Determine if server is hosting a financial statement"
      file_extension: "xls" | "pdf"
      expect: "[Ss]alary" | "SALARY" | "DOH" | "HIRE DATE" | "Hire Date" |
      "START DATE" | "REVIEW" | "[Bb]onus" | "[Oo]ptions"
```

```
        file_name : "employee" | "salar"
        max_size : "5K"
</item>
</check_type>
```

Using Nessus 3 Auditing

The compliance auditing function is as easy to use as the vulnerability scanning function you may already be familiar with at this point. In fact, if you can perform a vulnerability scan with Nessus 3, you'll have no issue checking for compliance using the tool. For this section, we'll go through the actual steps you'll perform to run audit checks on a system. At this point in the discussion, we're assuming you already have the appropriate .audit files you want to use for the scan.

Updating Nessus 3 Plugins

Updating the Nessus Plugins is a different process with the new version of Nessus. In the following examples, we'll use the Windows version of the software. We use this version because, as of the publication of this book, Tenable only provides the Compliance Auditing function as part of the Windows package of the software.

As opposed to previous versions of the Nessus software on this platform, the update plugins interface is a completely separate executable. You can find this option from your Start Menu, as shown in Figure 13.5.

Figure 13.5 The Nessus Menu with Plugin Update Option

When you start the Nessus *Update* Plugins Interface, it should look similar to Figure 13.6. It's simple and to the point. There is an **Update** button in the top right hand corner of the window, and a check box at the bottom left of the window. The checkbox allows the user to purge the existing plugin database prior to installing the latest plugins. This is generally considered to be the best option, assuming you have the time, since it ensures your software always has the latest versions of all available plugins.

Figure 13.6 Update Plugins Start Screen

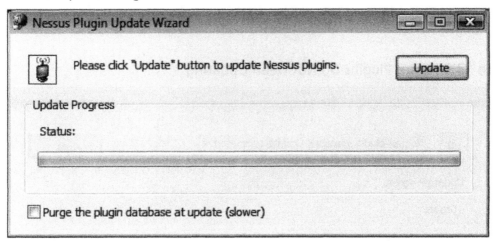

Tenable designed the interface to be both intuitive and easy to use. The first thing we want to do after starting the Nessus 3 software is to update the plugins. Updating the plugins means that we have the most up-to-date signatures for the software, resulting is less chance of missing vital security flaws in our target. It really is as simple as pressing the **Update** button on the interface.

Once the plugins start the update process, you'll see a number of progress messages appear in the window, along with a progress bar. These messages give you the status of the three phases of the plugin update process, Downloading, Extracting, and Installing the plugins. Once the updates are complete, a *Finished* button will appear. Simply click on this button to close the pop up window. Figure 13.7 shows this window.

Figure 13.7 The Updating Plugins Window

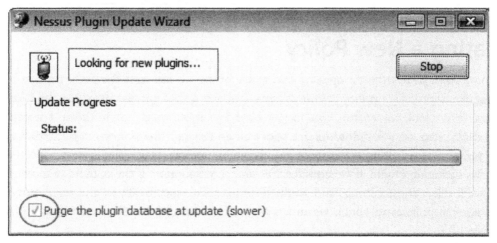

In the event your plugins are already completely up-to-date, the dialogue box will inform you of this and present you with an **Exit** button. An example of this is given in Figure 13.8.

Figure 13.8 Nessus Plugins Do Not Need Updating

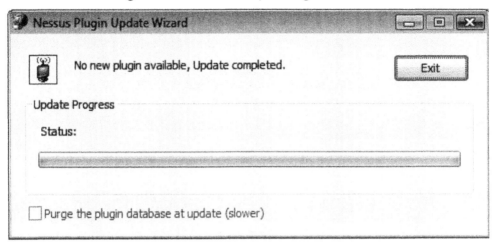

> **NOTE**
>
> In order to avoid confusion, it is best to remind the user that only subscribers to the Tenable Security Center or Direct Feed products are eligible for the audit functionality of the Nessus 3 software. In addition, non-subscribers will only receive plugin updates which are 7 days or older, whereas subscribers have access to the plugins immediately upon release by Tenable.

Creating a New Policy

Once you have your software updated and ready to go, we can start the audit process by creating the appropriate policy within Nessus. Policies define specifically what the Nessus 3 software will check for within your target host. For instance, if you're doing a normal vulnerability scan on a Windows target, you will go through the policy configuration and create policy that tells Nessus to check for the vulnerabilities that relate specifically to a Windows operating system. If we consider this same configuration is the context of a compliance audit, we'll select those settings and .audit files that relate specifically to the regulations or organizational policies to which we must adhere. The main Nessus 3 client window is shown in Figure 13.9.

Figure 13.9 The Nessus 3 Client Window

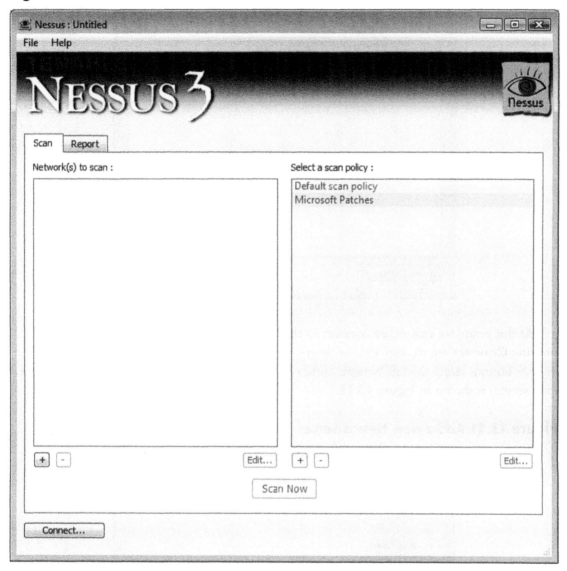

With the Nessus 3 client interface open, we'll first need to login to the server. Pressing the **Connect** button at the bottom left of the interface will bring up another dialogue, shown in Figure 13.10. In our case, we have the Nessus server loaded on the local computer, so the Nessus Client automatically provides the localhost option in the *Select a Nessus Server* window.

Figure 13.10 Select a Nessus Server

At this point, we can either connect to the localhost by highlighting that option and pressing **Connect**, or, we can add (or delete) another server to the list by pressing either the + or − buttons along the left bottom corner of the dialogue. An example of the + dialogue (add server) is shown in Figure 13.11.

Figure 13.11 Add a New Nessus Server

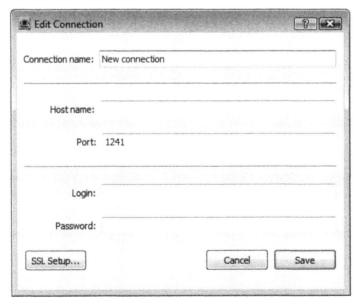

As seen in Figure 13.12, we can tell that our connection is complete to the server by the **Disconnect** button on the bottom left of the window. Pressing this button does the obvious; it disconnects us from the server once our session is complete.

Figure 13.12 Nessus 3 Manage Policies Window

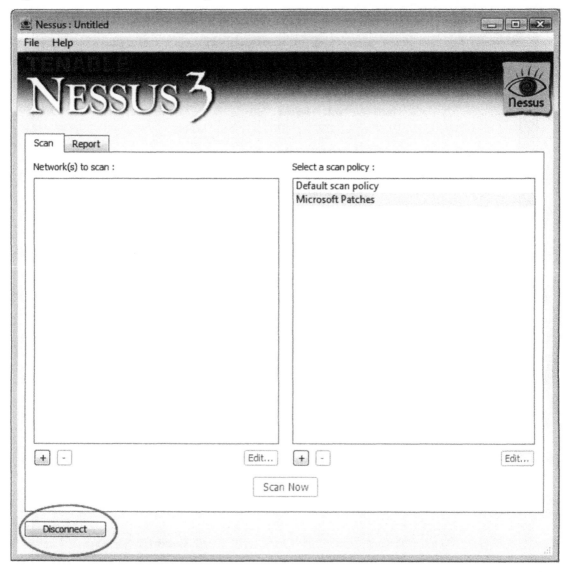

Also seen in Figure 13.12 are two subwindows. The window on the left hand side of the dialogue allows us to define the hosts or networks we'll we scanning. The right hand side allows us to define the policies we'll use during the scan. For our purposes, we're going to start by first defining our policy. Pressing the + button on the bottom left side of the *Select a scan policy:* window will allow us to add a new policy. Once pressed, a new window will appear, as seen in Figure 13.13. The interface should look familiar to users of previous versions of Nessus. It uses a standard tabbed function along the top.

Figure 13.13 Edit Policy Window

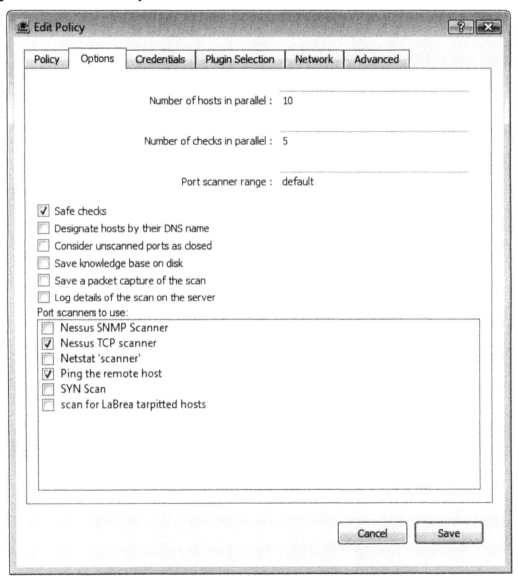

Initially, we'll want to click on the *Policy* tab, which the far left of our tabbed options. This allows us to define the new policy's name, provide comments about the nature of this policy, and whether or not we want to share this policy across multiple sessions. When you come back to the Nessus 3 software later, you want to be absolutely clear about the configuration of each policy listed, so it's a good idea to always include relative comments. For this example, we'll call our new policy Windows XP Audit, and then click the **Save** button, as shown in Figure 13.14.

Figure 13.14 Name the New Policy

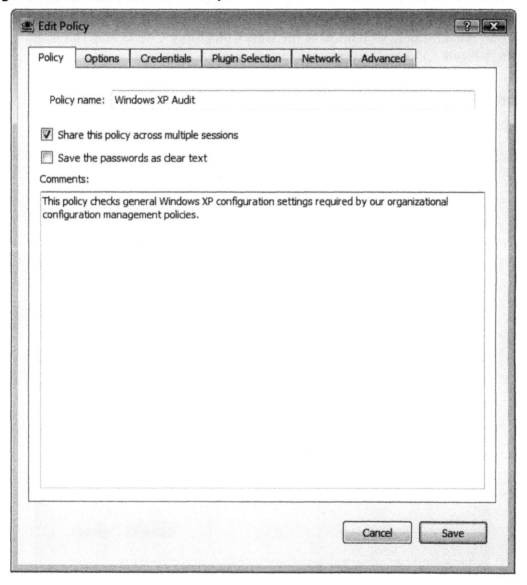

Now we'll move on *Plugin Selection* tab. If you scroll through these settings, you should see that every plugin is enabled by default. This is most useful if we will be running a vulnerability scan along with a full compliance audit. But for our purposes, we'll click on the **Disable all** button at the bottom right hand corner of the window, allowing us to completely customize this policy to our needs.

We want to begin by enabling the *Policy Compliance* plugin. This plugin is listed about halfway down the list of plugins, as seen in Figure 13.15. Once we do this, the window will show three new checkboxes, listed as Unix Compliance Checks, Windows Compliance Checks, and Windows File Contents Compliance Checks. All three of these sub-plugins are enabled once we enable the *Policy Compliance* plugin. But since this is going to be an audit policy for Windows only, we'll uncheck the Unix Compliance Checks box. This is also shown in Figure 13.15.

Figure 13.15 Select Policy Compliance Plugins

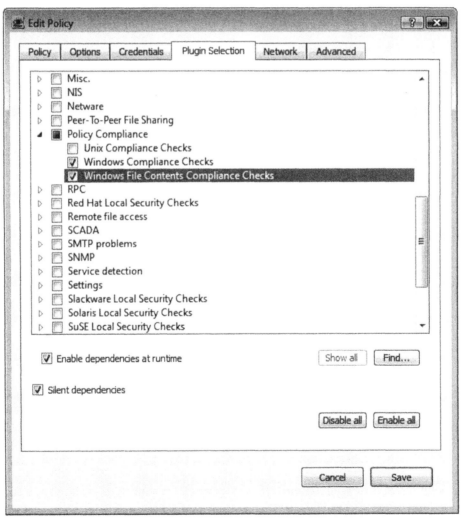

At this point, we've told the policy that we want to use strictly compliance auditing functionality in this policy. We have not enabled any vulnerability scanning functionality, although that is certainly a viable option. Due to the nature of compliance auditing, Administrator or root access is required to access the target system. Without this access, the software can not complete a full and comprehensive audit of the operating system. Now we want to define the actual .audit file we'll use for our compliance scans. .audit files are specially formatted files that tell Nessus what settings to look for, and which ones are pass or fail. Tenable provides a good many of these files for subscribers, but you're also able to create your own, based on organizational needs.

Clicking on the Advanced tab, at the top right of our tabbed options will bring us to a new window. This window has a drop down menu and 2 checkboxes. As we select different options from the drop down menu, the options and checkboxes below the menu will change accordingly. Since we've told Nessus that we'll be performing solely compliance checks in this policy, we'll scroll down to the *Windows Compliance Checks* option from the menu and select it. See Figure 13.16 for an example.

Figure 13.16 Getting ready to edit policy settings

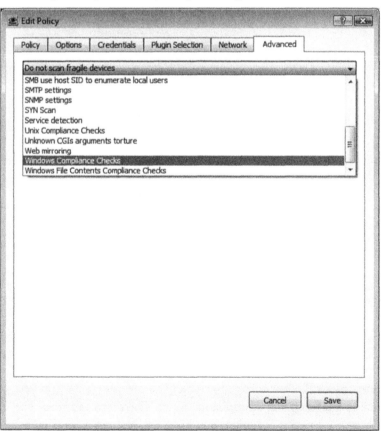

Our new dialogue box looks like that shown in Figure 13.17. As you can see from the example, we've already pressed the Browse button and selected a .audit file from our filesystem. Within that particular .audit file are all the settings we'll check for in our compliance audit.

As a side note we can also use the drop down menu to select the *Windows File Contents Compliance Checks*. Once that's done, we browse through our file system for the .audit file containing the checks we want to run against file contents on the system. The process works the same and you *are* able to run both file content checks and host compliance checks at the same time in this manner. For this example, we're going to use the *PCI_Windows.audit* file from Tenable. This file will allow Nessus 3 to audit the host to ensure compliance with the mandated PCI configuration requirements.

Figure 13.17 Selecting a .audit File

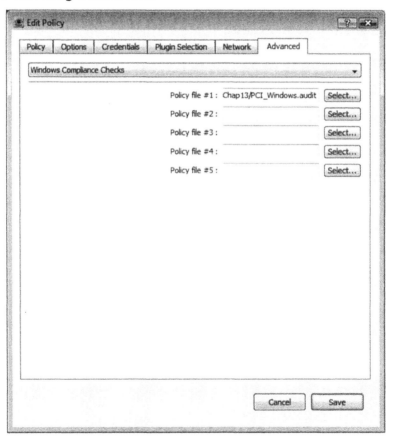

The final settings we'll alter relate specifically to the user accounts and passwords Nessus will need to perform our compliance audit. The third tab from the left, across the top of the window is labeled *Credentials*. Clicking on that tab brings us to the window shown in Figure 13.18. As you can see, the structure of the configuration windows is similar across the board, containing a drop menu (where required) and a number of options relating specifically to that configuration option.

By default, Nessus brings up the **Windows Credentials** option, which is just what we need for our scan. At this point, we'll enter a user name, along with the appropriate password, in order to perform the audit. Remember as you do this that the account must have adequate privileges within the target system to access sensitive areas and registry settings. You can also use domain accounts to perform these scans, assuming the account also has the requisite privileges to the system. Now, we'll save our changes by clicking on the **Save** button in the bottom right hand corner of the screen.

Figure 13.18 Adding Credentials

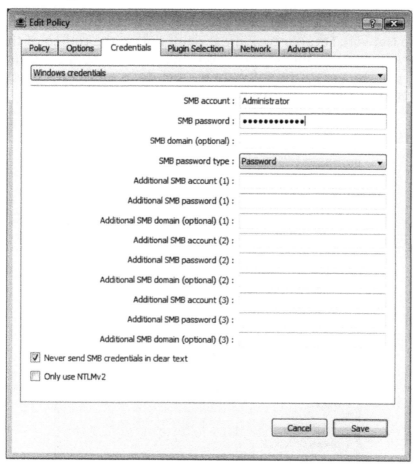

In the Credentials tab you can also add the root password the SSH password box if you're using Linux or UNIX. Alternatively, you can also use an SSH public/private key pair, which provide much better security when authenticating to the target system. If you're auditing a Windows target on a Domain, ensure you enter the name of the domain as well.

Starting Your Audit

Now we have a policy that applies specifically to the system you want to audit. Now we just need to run the audit itself. On the left hand side of the Nessus 3 window we see the *Network(s) to scan:* dialogue. Click on + at the bottom left of that part of the window to add a new host or network to scan. For our example, we're going to select the **Single Host** option and enter *localhost* as the Host name. But as you can see in Figure 13.19, you can add a network range, an individual subnet, a single host, or a list of hosts from a flat file.

NOTE

Tenable Network Security took great pains during the coding of the Nessus 3 software to ensure minimal impact on your network during a scan. Because of this, you can expect the software to operate as efficiently as possible, with little negative impact for your network and users.

Figure 13.19 Selecting Your Target

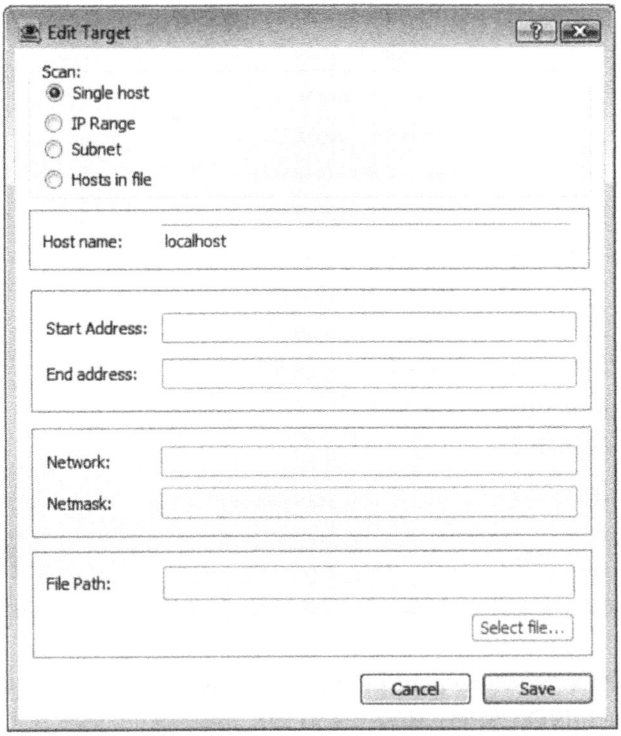

The process from this point on is simpler than in previous versions of Nessus. Simply highlight the host or network you want to scan (in our case we're scanning *localhost*), and highlight the policy you'll use to scan (we're going to use *Windows XP Audit*). Then just press **Scan Now**. An example is shown in Figure 13. 20.

Figure 13.20 Scan in Progress

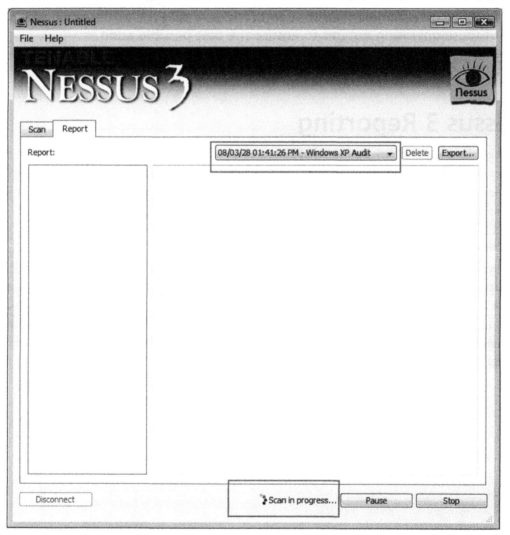

The actual audit time will depend on the number of hosts you've selected, whether or not you added any vulnerability scanning or other options to this job, and the speed of your network at the time of the audit. Since we're only scanning the localhost for our example, it should be a quick audit.

NOTE

The Microsoft Windows XP Home was created without many of the remote management and connection functions available in the Professional version of the operating system. The same can be said for Microsoft Vista. Nessus 3 is unable to function properly with either of these operating systems as the host OS. It's recommended that you consider using the Professional versions of these operating systems to ensure the best possible audit.

Nessus 3 Reporting

Tenable Network Security built a reliable and easy to use reporting functionality into Nessus 3. It doesn't require any special software, instead opting to use freely available web browsers that are likely installed on most computers anyway. Findings are identified as High, Medium, or Low, in relation to actual vulnerabilities, but are referred to as PASSED or FAILED in relation to compliance checks.

Once your scan has completed, the *Report* tab of the Nessus 3 window will pop up with your results. The top of the page will have the Nessus 3 logo and directly below that will be the lists of hosts you've scanned/audited in this run of the software. To the left of each listed host is a small arrow. Click on this arrow will expand the finding areas for that host/network. Areas in red are considered High rated vulnerabilities. When you highlight a host/network in the left hand panel, you'll see a Scan Summary for that host in the right panel. An example is in Figure 13.21.

Figure 13.21 Scan Summary

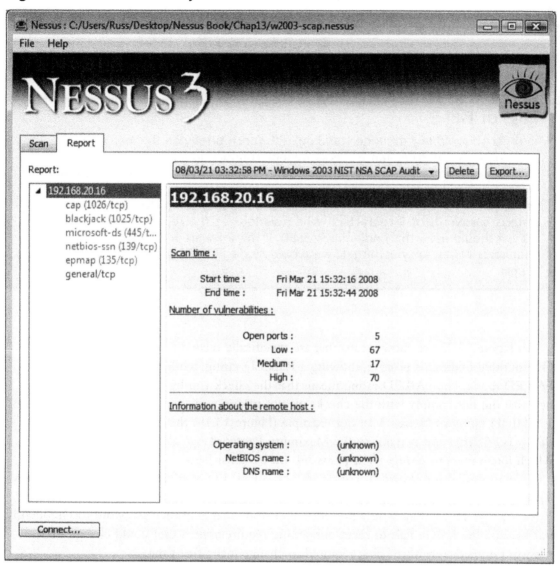

The scan summary provides information on when the scan was started, when it completed, and the number of vulnerabilities found based on High, Medium, and Low severity ratings. Other information about the host, such as operating system type, will also be provided, assuming Nessus 3 was able to determine this information.

Tools & Traps...

Pass or Fail

In order to avoid any misunderstanding, let's touch briefly on the idea of Pass or Fail as it relates to the compliance checks we'll be conducting against our target. Let's say that we're a financial institution with Federal regulations that control the strength of our passwords. Our regulations state that a password length of 8 characters or longer are required for all users. When we conduct our audit, using Nessus 3, the software detects passwords of 8 characters. When we look at the report for this compliance scan, it should show this finding as PASSED. If the software had found passwords of 7 characters or less on our target, we would see a FAILED response in our Nessus 3 report.

In Figure 13.22, we show results that are specifically related to our compliance checks. One of these findings is positive, showing a PASSED rating, while the other shows a FAILED rating. The FAILED rating means that the check run by Nessus 3 found information that did not comply with the checks we put in our .audit file. A FAILED rating counts as a HIGH rating to Nessus 3. In our example (Figure 13.19) the first compliance check shows as PASSED and pertains to the Maximum Password Age allowed on the system, which forces users to change their passwords on a regular basis.

The second check shown in Figure 13.22 has FAILED to meet our .audit requirements. This finding tells us that the target host fails to meet our requirements for Minimum Password Age. This setting would prevent a user from changing their password too frequently, but because the system fails to meet our setting requirement, a user could change their password immediately after being required to change it the first time.

Figure 13.22 Compliance Check Examples

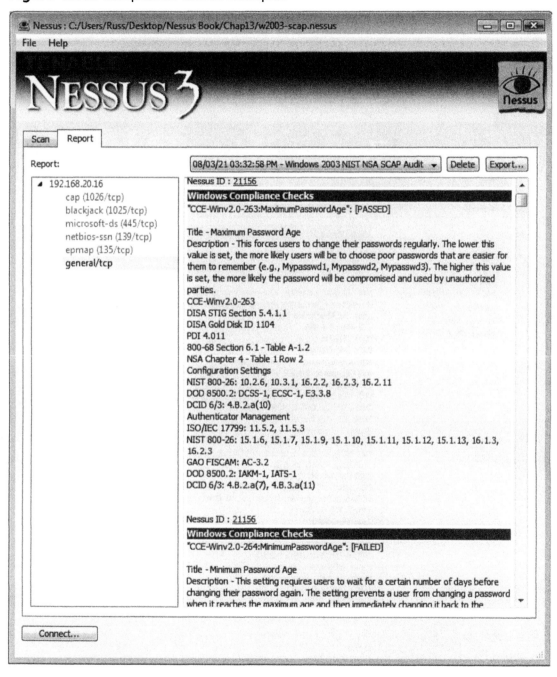

In some instances, a compliance check will fail simply because the value does not exist in the registry. For instance, in Figure 13.23, a check came back as a failure because Nessus 3

could not access the key value that was stated in the .audit file. Those checks will come back as yellow in the report.

Figure 13.23 Another Compliance Failure

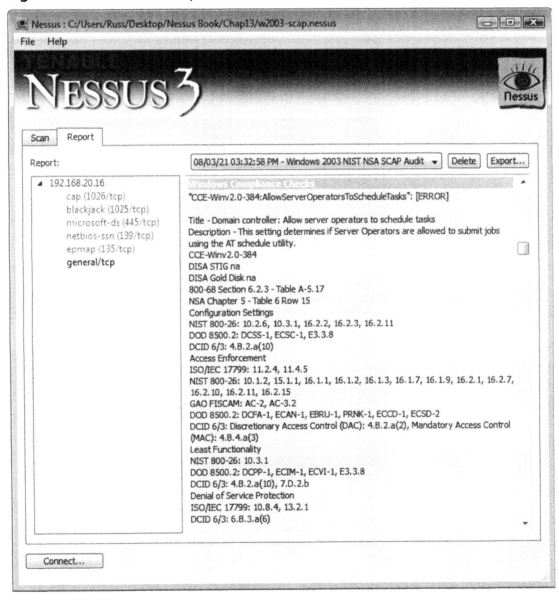

The report interface for Nessus 3 is very easy to use. Once the report comes up, after your audit, you can export the report via the **Export** button on the top right corner of the Nessus 3 report window. We've shown an example of this in Figure 13.24. As you can see from the image, you have three options for exporting your scan report, HTMl, NBE, or NSR formats. The dialog is a standard file dialog, allowing you to save the file to anywhere on the filesystem to which you have access.

Figure 13.24 Exporting the Nessus 3 Audit Report

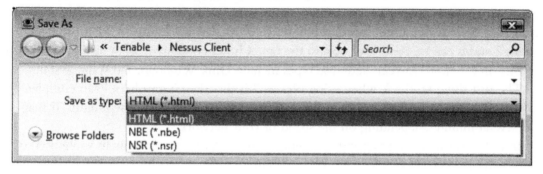

Summary

Nessus 3 is the latest version of the popular Nessus software to be released to the public. It is a complete rewrite of the original code and provides dramatic improvements in the areas of effectiveness, efficiency, and speed. Tenable Network Security has increased the value of the product by including a number of sample configuration files that are available to registered users of their Direct Feed or Security Center products.

Nessus 3 can be used to check compliance against any known regulation or requirements. This includes FERPA, HIPAA, NIST, CIS, Sarbanes-Oxley, and NERC. The compliance checks used within Nessus are completely dependent on the statements you place in the .audit file. .audit files are text based configuration files that tell Nessus 3 what to check for. Nessus 3 audits can be performed against the target host's configuration, or against content in the files on the host. Current .audit file types include Unix, Windows, and WindowsFiles.

The first thing to check when using Nessus 3 is that the plugins have been completely updated. The plugin update process will download, extract, and install the plugins. It may take several minutes, depending on the speed of your network.

In order to run an audit against a system, we must define the credentials to be used on that system. In order to be effective, these credentials must be for the root or Administrator user on the target, depending on the operating system. We'll also need to select or define a policy to use on this audit. Because of the new interface, this process is much more intuitive. We select the policy and select the appropriate .audit files to use during the audit. We do this by clicking on the Advanced tab at the top of the window. Drop down to the compliance option you want and browse for the .audit files you want to use in each section. Now we click on **Save Settings**.

To start the scan, we select the Start Scan link from the main Nessus 3 window. When the audit has completed, the Nessus 3 report will pop up immediately. Findings are divided into High, Medium, and Low categories. Audit findings are classified as either PASSED or FAILED. The designation of PASSED means that the configuration option Nessus 3 looked at was correct, according to our .audit file. A designation of FAILED means the configuration for that option was not correct, or was not located. The report can be exported from Nessus by clicking on the **Export** button.

Solutions Fast Track

What is Compliance?

- ☑ Compliance has become more and more important over the last few years.
- ☑ The term compliance indicates a requirement to meet certain configuration guidelines to protect information.

☑ There are a number of important compliance options, depending on your industry. They include FERPA, HIPAA, NIST, DoD, CIS, PCI, NERC, and Sarbanes-Oxley.

☑ Most compliance obligations do not contain a tremendous amount of technical detail.

The Nessus 3 Compliance Engine

☑ Nessus 3 conducts audits against a predefined .audit files.

☑ .audit files can contain checks on the configuration of a target, or against the content of files on the target system.

☑ Auditing can be conducted against UNIX/Linux, Windows, or WindowsFiles.

☑ The audit capability of Nessus 3 is only available to subscribers to the Tenable Security Center or Direct Feed products.

☑ Tenable Network Security provides .audit files for use by subscribers of one of these services.

Using Nessus 3 Compliance

☑ The Nessus 3 interface is easy-to-use and easy-to-understand.

☑ Nessus 3 audits are started by defining the policy you want to use, including appropriate credentials and .audit files to use.

☑ Audits can include vulnerability checks in addition to configuration and content checks.

Nessus 3 Reporting

☑ Reporting within Nessus 3 is done through your web browser.

☑ Reports come up automatically once the scan is completed.

☑ Configuration checks that meet the requirements defined in the policy come back as PASSED in the report.

☑ Configuration checks that do not meet the requirements defined in the policy come back as FAILED.

☑ The report can be saved using the browser's Save As function.

Frequently Asked Questions

Q: Can I create my own .audit files for use with Nessus 3?

A: Yes. Any user can create their own .audit file to meet their needs. But it's important to reiterate that the audit functionality of Nessus 3 is only available to users of the Direct Feed or Security Center.

Q: When you say that Nessus 3 auditing can be performed against UNIX, does that include all flavors of Linux as well?

A: Yes. Nessus 3 will allow you to check the configuration on a wide variety of UNIX/Linux platforms. The only real requirements are SSH access to the target host and a useable root user account and password.

Q: How do I get compliance checks within my Nessus 3 software?

A: If you are a Security Center or Direct Feed subscriber, your Nessus 3 will already have the compliance audits. Simply update your plugins.

Q: Is there a charge for the compliance plugins?

A: The compliance check plugins are a complimentary upgrade for Nessus 3 Direct Feed subscribers.

Q: Is detailed documentation available to help me create my custom audit policy?

A: Once you sign up for Direct Feed, you'll have access to a plethora of detailed documentation and examples at the Tenable Security Support Portal.

Q: Is an agent required on the target host in order the compliance checks to work?

A: No. The compliance scans are run solely through the use of 100% credentialed network scans.

Q: What systems can be audited?

A: Nessus 3 will audit Windows NT 4.0, 2000, XP, and 2003 server. It will also audit Solaris, Linux, BSD, Hp/UX, and Mac OS X.

Q: Where can I find more information about the Nessus 3 compliance scans?

A: http://www.nessus.org/documentation/index.php?doc=compliance

Index

Printed and bound by CPI Group (UK) Ltd, Croydon, CR0 4YY

03/10/2024

01040340-0001